EXEMPLUM

EXEMPLUM

The Rhetoric of Example
in Early Modern France and Italy

JOHN D. LYONS

Princeton University Press
Princeton, New Jersey

Copyright © 1989 by Princeton University Press
Published by Princeton University Press,
41 William Street, Princeton, New Jersey 08540
In the United Kingdom: Princeton University Press, Oxford

Lyons, John D., 1946–
Exemplum: the rhetoric of example in early modern
France and Italy / John D. Lyons.
p. cm.
Bibliography: p.
Includes index.
ISBN 0-691-06782-1
1. Exempla.   2. French literature—16th century—
History and criticism.   3. French literature—17th
century—History and criticism.   4. French lan-
guage—Early modern, 1500–1700—Rhetoric.   5.
Machiavelli, Niccolò, 1469–1527—Technique.   6.
Rhetoric—1500–1800.   I. Title. PQ239.L96 1989
840.9′004—dc20 89-33501

This book has been composed in Linotron Bembo

Clothbound editions of Princeton University Press books are printed
on acid-free paper, and binding materials are chosen for strength and
durability. Paperbacks, although satisfactory for personal collections,
are not usually suitable for library rebinding

Printed in the United States of America
by Princeton University Press,
Princeton, New Jersey

To Patricia and Jennifer

CONTENTS

CONTENTS

The purpose of this book is to demonstrate the crucial importance of an ancient, major, but neglected figure of rhetoric in the literature of sixteenth- and seventeenth-century France and Italy. Example, like metaphor, metonymy, antithesis, and other more commonly discussed figures, is traditionally one of those discursive structures taught as part of rhetoric. Whether rhetoric be defined as the examination of the means of persuasion, as the art of speaking well, or as the study of tropes and figures, it has always included consideration of figural language. This concern with figural language occurs in the context of assumptions about what the users of that language, both speaker/writer and listener/reader, consider to be a representation of reality. Because rhetoricians have not ignored the consequences of language for our view of reality—what Paolo Valesio has called the ontological dimension of rhetoric—this discipline is necessarily a study of the reciprocal relationship between the structure of language and the structure of what a society considers to be real.[1] Metaphor, for instance, can only be recognized if users of metaphor are persuaded that certain things are not "literally" true. "My love's eyes are suns" can only appear figural if the reader perceives some difference in the use of the term *sun* in this statement. The task of rhetoric is to refine endlessly the concept of that difference.

To approach the study of figural language by concentrating on example may appear peculiar in several ways. Example is too obvious and too subtle to fall within the range of most literary scholarship. Unlike metaphor, antithesis, diaphora, and other figures, which depend on the reader's initiative and training to recognize, example is often labeled as such. Texts do not say "here is a metaphor," but they do say "for example . . . " Yet once the text has advertised an example, the complexity, not to say trickiness, of the relationships established is often completely unperceived by the reader. Perhaps this is because example is so central to systems of belief that we occasionally think of it as the direct manifestation of reality when, in fact, example is a way of taking our beliefs about reality and reframing them into something that suits the direction of a text. Example may therefore qualify as the most ideological of figures, in the sense of being the figure that is most intimately bound to a representation of the world and that most serves as a veil for the mechanics of that representation.

There is a kind of muteness or invisibility—almost an unspeakability—of example, as I have found in mentioning to colleagues that I have been studying example. The reaction is quite different from what I have seen when I have said something like "allegory in early seventeenth-century poetry" or "narrative structures"—answers that allow the conversation to continue without missing a beat. When I say "example in Montaigne," for instance, there is inevitably a pause, after which they say "What do you mean by 'example'?" or "Oh, you mean you are studying *exemplum*."

This study, then, has a dual intention. On the one hand, I hope to restore example to its central place in figural rhetoric and thus to participate in what I sense is an imminent rediscovery of that figure. On the other, I want to use the conceptual instrument thus provided to give a new reading to several major texts within my own field of interest, early modern French and Italian literature. These two aims are intertwined and dialectical, for the writers I have studied do not themselves ignore the difficulties and the powers of example. The study of each of the early modern texts considered in the following chapters will indicate different possibilities of exemplary rhetoric and its display or concealment.

Before going any further, I should give a simple working definition. An example is a dependent statement qualifying a more general and independent statement by naming a member of the class established by the general statement. An example cannot exist without (*a*) a general statement and (*b*) an indication of this subordinate status. Moreover, examples are most frequently used to (*c*) provide clarification of the general statement and (*d*) demonstrate the truth of the general statement. The kind of dependent statements used and the relationship between the general statement and the subordinate statement are simply too varied to be specified in any general definition of example, though for the early modern period examples are predominantly chosen to reach common ground of belief in a domain that writers and readers will recognize as reality.

The difficulty of reaching such common ground in the early modern period is what gives the rhetoric of example in that period a particular fascination. This is a period stricken by a crisis of belief so severe that it led to wars, massacres, and executions, yet writers differing in both general principles and the specific ground in reality by which they attempt to clarify and validate those principles nonetheless continue to make use of a basic rhetorical figure, example. This common rhetorical practice in the face of contradictory visions of reality leads to lively and often paradoxical texts, revealing the push and the pull of various currents of thought. The observational scientific current, already powerful in the late Middle Ages, is reinforced by the writings of Telesio, Dee, Bacon, Harvey, and many others. The Protestant call for a return to the reality of the Scriptures and an escape from the delusions of scholasticism and dogma is, in its way, a return to direct experience of belief in a verifiable and commonly available evidence, the word of God, newly restored to its purity by textual scholarship. The Protestant concern with Scripture would seem to inhibit attention to the world of material experience, but economic and social history proves otherwise. The material world, no longer burdened by an allegorical significance, becomes available alongside Scripture for a study of fallen nature. General statements may therefore appeal to one or both of these domains for supporting instance. Concurrent with this growing attention to the material and scriptural world, the increased knowledge of antiquity provides a third major form of apparently objective and shareable reality. For Machiavelli, as for Montaigne, this domain, which is neither Scripture nor physically present, becomes a powerful and credible source for evidence of general laws of conduct. In such a situation, the rhetoric of example cannot remain what it was in a Greek *polis* nor as in the very different rhetoric of the medieval sermon. In a city-state, the familiar and local events would serve as basis for public application of a speaker's statement. In a Catholic sermon, a stock of traditional anecdotes, accumulating over the years, was not in conflict with a sharply renewed sense of secular and biblical history.

The writers of the sixteenth and seventeenth centuries reacted to the changed horizon of belief by attempting to connect general statement with specific and purportedly convincing instances, calling attention to this gesture with frequent use of the term *example*. For many writers the rhetoric of example became less an illustrative technique, through which a general statement would be impressed upon an audience, than a process of discovery, in which the tension between instance and general statement forced modifications in that statement. In some ways examples became more difficult to find. An increased respect for historical and textual accuracy led to demonstrations of concern about accuracy and verisimilitude in the choice of examples or their invention. On the other hand, the raw material available for the formation of examples was proliferating—through textual scholarship, voyages of discovery, scientific observation—in such a way that the increase of data threatened to become an impediment to knowledge if it were not structured by statements that showed pattern and hierarchy. Hence came the need to fit instance to rule, example to statement.

Before going into the detail of early modern practice of example, I will try to give a broad view of the rhetorical doctrine of example and to indicate some of the questions that can now, in the twentieth century, be asked about exemplary texts. A review of two millennia of rhetorical theory reminds us of constants in the concept of example and some of the variations in the terms for this figure. Because it seems important to avoid excessive and arbitrary restrictions on the structure and function of example as seen in this tradition, I consider two recent studies that narrow the concept, taking it into what I call the "pragmatist deviation." The consequence of an exclusively pragmatic definition of example would be to disqualify almost all of the works studied here from the category of exemplary texts. Against this highly selective view, I propose seven characteristics of example derived empirically from a study of the texts of six early modern authors. My principal concern, however, is to allow the play of these texts to manifest the rhetoric of example. I take their examples very seriously and try to read them carefully and as naïvely as possible.

ACKNOWLEDGMENTS

Hugh Davidson and Philip Lewis provided crucial encouragement and support at the very outset of this project. Kevin Brownlee, Robert Cottrell, Joan De Jean, Patrick Henry, Mary McKinley, Stephen G. Nichols, Richard Regosin, David Sices, and Marcel Tétel all read—or listened at length to—substantial portions of my work in progress. Their comments and questions were invaluable.

I thank the trustees of Dartmouth College for sabbatical leave, the National Endowment for the Humanities for fellowship support, and the University of Virginia Center for Advanced Studies for research time and material support. I am grateful to Patricia Carter of the Baker Library and to the librarians of the Ecole Normale Supérieure for their generous help.

The following portions of this study appeared in earlier form as articles: part of chapter 4 as "Subjectivity and Imitation in the *Discours de la méthode*" in *Neophilologus*, part of chapter 2 as "The *Heptameron* and the Foundation of Critical Narrative" in *Yale French Studies*, and a section of chapter 5 as "Narrative, Interpretation and Paradox" in *Romanic Review*. I am grateful to the editors for permission to make use of this material.

EXEMPLUM

Tout exemple cloche   —Montaigne

les exemples sont les roulettes du jugement. Les traducteurs français
disent parfois les 'béquilles' du jugement: ce sont bien des roulettes
(*Gängelwagen*), non pas les planches-à-roulettes (*skateboard*).
                                                       —Derrida

EXEMPLUM, in medieval Latin, meant "a clearing in the woods."[1]
This sense of the term, often forgotten, sheds light on many characteristics of the rhetorical figure, example. Only the clearing gives
form or boundary to the woods. Only the woods permit the existence
of a clearing. Likewise, example depends on the larger mass of history
and experience, yet without the "clearings" provided by example that
mass would be formless and difficult to integrate into any controlling
systematic discourse. Most of all, the clearing, the *exemplum*, posits an
inside and an outside—in fact, the clearing creates an outside by its
existence. This duality, significant for all understanding of example in
language, parallels another that has occasionally appeared in literary
study. A facile and summary opposition is sometimes made between a
rhetorical and a referential (or serious) approach to literary texts.[2] Such
an opposition, though difficult to support theoretically, indicates the
way our culture, even in the most ambitious deconstructive criticism,
uses a dichotomy between an inside and an outside of discourse. The
more frantically critics attempt to preserve the text from foundering
in the seas of referentiality, the more reference returns, leaking in faster
than it can be bailed out with the most sophisticated critical implements. There is good reason for this struggle to be perpetual. In the
wake of De Man, Derrida, and Foucault, it would be difficult to claim
to use language in an innocent, transparent way to refer to a reality
independent of language. Yet the attempt to rid language of its depen-
dence on belief in something else would be equally naïve. Discursive
practices are social practices; our language is always shaping its
shadow, its outside.

It is not surprising that example should emerge at this moment as
an object of scrutiny on the part of numerous literary critics, philosophers, and historians.[3] Example is the figure that most clearly and explicitly attempts to shore up the "inside" of discourse by gesturing

toward its "outside," toward some commonly recognized basis in a reality shared by speaker and listener, reader and writer. In order to appeal to such an outside, example must in some way construct or reconstruct its reference, altering the perception of the world by selecting, framing, and regulating (that is, subordinating to a rule) some entity or event.

The recent interest in example emerges against a background of long indifference to this figure, while certain "master tropes" have been consecrated subjects of literary theory and criticism. The number of books and articles on metaphor, for instance, dwarfs any bibliography of example.[4] Yet metaphor and example are both rhetorical figures that can trace their status in rhetorical theory at least back to Aristotle's *Rhetoric*.[5] Perhaps it would be best to call example metaphor's forgotten sibling, or at least its country cousin.

The oblivion into which example had until recently fallen may indicate that it poses a threat. Literary criticism has a particular stake in textual exemplification as procedure. This is perhaps one of the reasons why example is generally not an *object* of literary-critical study, for it is difficult to study the very tools one is using to carry forth the study. It would be more than tiresome to supply here instances—examples—of critical use of examples in common practice. But the critical text, to the extent that it claims some status as theoretical statement, fabricates examples as part of its own validation. The more literary criticism aspires to exceed paraphrase, the more it generates examples. Paraphrase would tell us simply what the object text says. Criticism attempts to locate the text within various larger descriptive categories, whether these be tropological patterns, literary schools or styles, socio-historical movements, ideologies, generative poetic models, philosophical doctrines, or other categories. When the literary text is studied in view of achieving such broader description, the critical text will subsume the literary text as example.

It is clear also that certain broad movements of intellectual history would be uncomfortable to study example too closely. For a positivist or a realist, the basis of all assertion is shaken when examples of laws and rules are revealed as discursive constructions like any other rhetorical figure. A more sophisticated approach of the deconstructionist type, however, might well be embarrassed by its need to use examples (if only in the form of textual reference) for the kind of appeal for support it requires from an "outside." Every example can be deconstructed, and, in an approach that moves forward by selecting and deconstructing exemplary texts, the whole critical movement could be derailed by an excessive attention to its initial gestures.

Yet, most of all, example may be, like Poe's purloined letter, too obvious to attract attention. Like the letter that hangs out in the open in the minister's office, the example is out in the open. It is not hidden like the metaphor nor does it purport to hide something. Examples are usually labeled neatly, displaying themselves with an *exempli gratia* or a "for example." The example seems to proclaim the speaker's common cause with the audience in looking at the world the way it is. Although fable, which is generally classified as a type of example, does appear to be sufficiently obscure to awaken the decrypting of literary analysis, historical and pseudohistorical examples seem not to be the invention of the speaker but common property about which we can have few suspicions.

One result of overlooking example for so long is that even rhetorically aware students of discourse lack an instrument of considerable power for certain kinds of analysis. They also—and this is particularly poignant in the case of historians—lack a sense of the general and traditional practice in which they are engaged. The following case illustrates the occlusion of example as object even in the very instance when both classical (ancient) rhetoric and ordinary nontechnical language would recognize an example. Hayden White writes of historical narratives,

> as a symbolic structure, the historical narrative does not *reproduce* the events it describes; it tells us in what direction to think about the events and charges our thought about the events with different emotional valences. The historical narrative does not *image* the things it indicates; it *calls to mind* images of the things that it indicates, in the same way that a metaphor does.[6]

It is certainly possible that historical narrative can play a role other than that of example, but to move from the functioning of historical narrative to the metaphor and to create a direct equation in the working of metaphor and historical narrative in regard to their way of "calling to mind" elides the nonmetaphorical figure with which historical narrative is much more closely linked in practice. The particular orienting gesture of telling in what direction to think about events is characteristic, not of metaphor (which, generally speaking, does not present conceptions in the temporal ordering of events) but of exemplification, with its connection of general statement or maxim and local or specific actualization of that maxim. White's failure to take into account example as figure has a certain irony in view of his own use of example.[7] Oddly enough, anyone interested in rhetoric and history could find some worthwhile and refined discussion of the rhetorical structure of historical narrative in a commonly available textbook of the fourth century B.C., Aristotle's *Rhetoric*.

FROM *PARADEIGMA* TO *EXEMPLUM*

The history of example is generally begun with its appearance in Aristotle's *Rhetoric* and *Topics*, where it is described as one of the two means of persuasion. In the second chapter of the first book of the *Rhetoric*, Aristotle identifies the only two means of producing belief as example (*paradeigma*) and enthymeme. He adds:

> The difference between example and enthymeme is evident from the *Topics*, where, in discussing syllogism and induction, it has previously been said that the proof from a number of particular cases that such is the rule, is called in Dialectic induction, in Rhetoric example; but when, certain things being posited, something different results by reason of them, alongside of them, from their being true, either universally or in most cases, such a conclusion in Dialectic is called a syllogism, in Rhetoric an enthymeme. (1.2.1356b)

Example is thus established as one of the two bases of all rhetorical argumentation, as one of the two ways of producing belief in a general public about matters that can be (or must be) treated without hope for absolute logical certainty. In distinguishing Dialectic from Rhetoric, Aristotle is, of course, referring to the fact that the former is a specialized discourse between dialecticians while rhetoric is the more open and less technical form of speech used for more general audiences.

Rhetoric is based, as Aristotle points out, on opinion or shared belief and is aimed at arriving at conclusions on matters about which there is no "necessary" truth but only probabilities. To engage in rhetoric with any effectiveness, therefore, it is necessary to take into account the knowledge and belief of the audience:

> The enthymeme and the example are concerned with things which may, generally speaking, be other than they are, the example being a kind of induction and the enthymeme a kind of syllogism, and deduced from few premises, often from fewer than the regular syllogism; for if any one of these is well known, there is no need to mention it, for the hearer can add it himself. For instance, to prove that Dorieus was the victor in a contest at which the prize was a crown, it is enough to say that he won a victory at the Olympic games; there is no need to add that the

prize at the Olympic games is a crown, for everybody knows it. (*Rhetoric* 1.2.1357a)

Aristotle notes that some orators are fond of enthymemes while others prefer to base their arguments on examples, and he finds that arguments based on examples are just as effective in persuading as those based on enthymemes, even though the latter "meet with more approval" (presumably among theorists of rhetoric). Aristotle divides examples into two kinds, one consisting of telling things that have happened in the past, the other fictions invented to support the argument:

There are two kinds of examples: namely, one which consists in relating things that have happened before, and another in inventing them oneself. The latter are subdivided into comparisons or fables, such as those of Aesop and the Libyan. It would be an instance of the historical kind of example, if one were to say that it is necessary to make preparations against the Great King and not to allow him to subdue Egypt; for Darius did not cross over to Greece until he had obtained possession of Egypt; but as soon as he had done so, he did. Again, Xerxes did not attack us until he had obtained possession of that country, but when he had, he crossed over; consequently, if the present Great King shall do the same, he will cross over, wherefore it must not be allowed. (*Rhetoric* 2.20.1393a–b)

In the second group Aristotle places "comparison" (*parabole*) and "fable" (*logos*). Comparison is illustrated from Socrates:

For instance, if one were to say that magistrates should not be chosen by lot, for this would be the same as choosing as representative athletes not those competent to contend, but those on whom the lot falls; or as choosing any of the sailors as the man who should take the helm, as if it were right that the choice should be decided by lot, not by a man's knowledge. (*Rhetoric* 2.20.1393b)

Fable is illustrated by passages from Stesichorus and Aesop.

The original twofold division is thus in fact threefold, historical example, parable, and fable, and this tripartite scheme reappears in the history of rhetoric when Cicero, in *De inventione*, speaks of the use of narrative in oratory. One use of narrative conveys the facts of the case at hand, a second is a digression merely to amuse the audience, but the third use, as described by Cicero, is "wholly unconnected with public issues, which is recited or written solely for amusement but at the same time provides valuable training."[8] Within this category Cicero locates history (*historia*), "an account of actual occurrences remote from the recollection of our own age;" argument (*argumentum*), "a fictitious narrative which nevertheless could have occurred;" and fable (*fabula*), "the term applied to a narrative in which the events are not true and have no verisimilitude." The three are parallel to Aristotle's categories of example, since the content of the *parabole* or comparison is clearly possible even though it is fictitious, while the fable in both cases is both fictitious and impossible.[9]

Use of example is recommended strongly by all Roman rhetorical texts, but the types of example and the utility of example in different kinds of oratory are topics that receive very different, sometimes even contradictory treatment. Quintilian is more important than any other theorist in the promotion of example, yet he enters into great and often confusing detail, for instance, in attempting to draw the boundaries that separate example (*exemplum*) from simile (*similitudo*). In brief, the degree of similarity between the things compared seems to be, for the author of the *Institutio oratoria*, the determining factor in distinguishing the two figures. Simile is like example when the things compared are completely similar and do not involve a metaphorical "translation" from one thing or situation to another, but simile becomes unlike example when it compares animals and objects to people.[10] Hence, example is the figure of comparison in which the things compared are most similar. On the distinction between historical and fictitious examples, Quintilian notes the further nuance that fictitious examples drawn from ancient sources take on a value different from that of fictions invented for immediate use: "For while the former [historical examples] have the authority of evidence or even of legal decisions, the latter [fictitious examples invented by the great poets] also either have the warrant of antiquity or are regarded as having been invented by great men to serve as lessons to the world."[11]

What holds together the categories of example, historical-factual and poetic-fictitious, is their potential for further occurrence or replicability, which Aristotle emphasizes in the example of the Great King. This is an important, but implicit, part of example's role as one of the three kinds of artificial proofs.[12] This diachronic repetition appears when Quintilian discusses the use of rumor, common opinion, and precedents (*exempla*).[13] References to these previous cases constitute examples and are persuasive to those who believe in the continuity of things through time, even in the contradictions of history.[14]

In passing from ancient rhetoric to medieval and modern rhetoric in the Romance languages, we encounter the problem of relating the word *exemplum* to the word *example*. In fact a further distinction should be made between the Latin word *exemplum* and the vernacular (English, French, Italian, etc.) word *exemplum*, the latter being a technical term of literary criticism. Although the Latin *exemplum* seems merely to be the equivalent and cognate of the English *example*, the vernacular *exemplum*, which dates apparently from the nineteenth century, is used in a variety of denotative and connotative senses different from the word *example*.[15] This creation of a pair of terms *example/exemplum* in some ways serves to continue the already mentioned occlusion of example as rhetorical figure but, on the other hand, does not offer the advantage of a stable, univocal analytic instrument. Frequently invoked in studies of medieval and particularly of Renaissance literary texts, *exemplum* seems to be used with progressively greater assurance of generic consistency as the user of the term describes a period further from Latin and Neo-Latin literature.[16] *Exemplum* in this dominant vernacular usage denotes a "short narrative used to illustrate a moral point."[17] In this sense the word is often said to denote a literary genre or "subgenre," recognizable to all readers of medieval and Renaissance texts.[18] Recently, however, one scholar has broken with this critical consensus to indicate, albeit tentatively, that *exemplum* (in the sense of narrative example) is not a genre but a "device."[19] The distinction between "device" and "genre" may not seem particularly important at first glance, but the consequences for our understanding of texts containing examples are ultimately considerable. These include assumptions of the independent and self-governing character of examples, which would, as genre, obey rules different from those of the larger texts in which they might find themselves.[20] But more important, and more elementary, is the way in which the generic assumption cuts off the wealth of associations that have historically characterized the word *exemplum* itself.

Exemplum is, first of all, etymologically akin to the verb *eximere*, "to take out, to remove, to take away, to free, to make an exception of." Therefore, the example is something cut out and removed from some whole. In this sense example is synonymous with a modern term that appears very different: *detail*. The detail is also removed, cut out (*dé + tailler* in French, *de + tagliare* in Italian). In both its Latin origin in *eximere* and the widespread medieval usage of the "clearing in the woods," *exemplum* concerns a distinction made between a prior whole and a resultant fragment.[21] This etymological characteristic of the Latin and subsequent Romance and English terms makes explicit something that is not indicated in the Greek term, to which *exemplum* has from the earliest times served as equivalent, *paradeigma*.[22] Aristotle defines the latter as a relation established between units of equivalent wholeness, a whole to a whole, a part to a part, not of a part to a whole, and so on. Aristotle's description does not exclude the act of selection or of fragmentation of a mass to obtain, analytically, the parts that will be compared. The term that he uses, however, does not stress such a procedure. Instead *paradeigma* remains associated with a rhetorical function, or act in view of an effect, rather than with the formal features that are emphasized in the term *example*, for *paradeigma* is related to *paradeiknumi* ("to exhibit side by side, to make comparisons, to indicate or point out") and to *deiknumi* ("to bring to light, to show forth"). The Greek term is therefore always associated with light, showing, seeing, and pointing; the Latin term concerns selection, excision, textual combination, and discontinuity. This difference may well account for some of the breadth of the use of the Romance term, particularly in those cases where users of texts roughly categorized as *exempla* are accused by contemporaries of having lost track of the basic purpose of *exemplum*, that is, of having created *exempla* that are not paradigmatic, illustrative, or persuasive.[23] A further, somewhat amusing, consequence of the "cutting out" that is embedded in the word *example*, is that examples are generally studied exemplarily, that is, scholars spend their time gathering examples of examples.

A second important feature of the historical lexicography of the term *exemplum* is that the word came to be associated as much with the Greek *eikon* as with *paradeigma*.[24] This movement, which is entirely consonant with the rhetorical function of example in Aristotle, permits the spread of example from linguistic to non-linguistic forms. At the same time the visual form of example leads to the ontological consequence that examples have the quality of seeming rather than of being, they are associated with *species* and *imago*, and are therefore within the realm of all that is specious and imaginary. Since example or *paradeigma* already had dubious claims of respectability in Aristotle, who repeatedly places example in rhetoric, destined for the nonspecialist audience, rather than in the more learned dialectic, the association of example with the image is a further blow to the ability of example to attain independent representational dignity. The consequences of example's association with things that appear to be are complex and often ironic, as we will see in the work of Montaigne, Marguerite de Navarre, and Pascal. But we must note that in the earliest texts concerning example and its use, example has about it the dangerous quality of falling from the dignity of the broader, more abstract truth, into a specious but moving semitruth or limited truth. In short, the public of examples is persuaded by what the speaker (or painter) holds out for it even though the speaker may know that this appearance is a misrepresentation justified only by the good end intended.

Another characteristic of *exemplum* is that it frequently concerns, or is even equated with, narration (one medieval glossary equates the terms by sticking them together, *exemplare narrare*). Even though this is not the dominant lexicographical meaning, within clerical milieux narration seems to be a major signification of the term.[25] One of the results of the use of the term *exemplum* to indicate narration is that it becomes difficult to draw the line between narration in general and narration with a specific, narrow function, the "exemplary" function in the sense of concrete instance of a general statement. Instead *exemplum* is often used to mean *any* narration in an oratorical (or rather, preaching) situation, regardless of the function of the narration.[26] When *exemplum* reaches the point of identification with the act of narration in general, it loses the Aristotelian sense of *paradeigma*. Yet example remains departure from the direct discourse of the orator. Even if the narrations are intended for pleasure and not as illustrations of a doctrine or proposition of faith, the narration is conceived of as separate from the main body of the sermon, as an intercalated entity. The sense of *exemplum* as *eikon* inlaid in a pavement is closer here than the rhetorician's *paradeigma* or the dialectician's induction.

Finally, the term *exemplum* reveals the importance of the idea of reproducibility in example, for *exemplum* denotes both the model to be copied and the copy or representation of that model, a sense that is maintained in the French noun *exemplaire* as copy (of a book, etc.). This coexistence of apparent opposites is an indication of the way *exemplum* (and example) is not a static, isolatable unit but the relationship created or assumed between things. When Machiavelli, for instance, says of a certain historical act that it has *radi esempli*, he means that this act has rarely been copied, that it has "few copies" or "few imitations." But an *exemplum* or *esemplo* in the sense of copy is only possible if the act or object in question is seen as corresponding to an earlier act or object that is the *same*. In this respect, time is an important dimension of example, which reveals an identity that appears across chronological boundaries. In other words, the concept of example, as embodied in the medieval *exemplum*, does not concern identities that appear in conditions of total simultaneity. Yet the importance accorded the temporal order is paradoxically linked to the way example allows an act or object to reappear at different periods and thus to defeat change. If an *exemplum*/copy can allow the past not only to be alluded to or reflected upon but actually resuscitated, then time itself can be subordinated to a higher, more powerful order.

The breadth of meaning of the term *exemplum* before the sixteenth century prepares us for the realignment that occurs in Renaissance vernacular literatures, in which the cognates of *exemplum* free themselves from narrow association with preaching and from a synonymic identification with narration, yet maintain many resonances of these earlier usages. *Exemple* and *esempio* in French and Italian, and *ejemplo* in Spanish, begin a return to the more classical rhetorical meaning of instance demonstrating a general rule. This is, however, not to say that Renaissance and early modern writers use example as a simple demonstrative tool. The opposite is the case in the authors studied here. Yet the consciousness that an example is not merely *any* narrative but a narrative with a claim to a particular form of truth (the relationship of general class to particular instance) is what allows sixteenth- and seventeenth-century writers to use example in a highly ironic way.

EXAMPLE IN THE RENAISSANCE

Humanist thought throve on example. Example is textual, in keeping with the humanist emphasis on philology. Example is historical and thus suited those who wanted to recover the wisdom of antiquity. Example could be conceived as a tool of practical social change, as a guide to action, in keeping with the strong moral purpose of many early humanists. Finally, example is the product of a system of collection and commentary and thus suited the predilections of a class of professional textual scholars, including that large number who, through the practice of the judiciary professions, were accustomed to the complicated task of sifting records for concise statements of precedent, classified under abstract rubrics.[27]

The compilation of collections of passages from ancient authors and thus of examples and quotations not only was a pedagogical practice recommended by humanists from Erasmus to Vives, but became a staple of publishing. Passages were extracted from authors as examples of style, and the passages were classified—like medieval clerical *exempla*—under topic categories, manifesting the potential for generating the relation of maxim to example. Given the humanist insistence on rhetorical studies and the preference for textual rather than abstract, purely logical, persuasion, example, rather than syllogistic or purely assertive discourse, took on a dominance that merits for the period from the fifteenth through the early seventeenth centuries the appellation "the age of exemplarity."[28] While the use of examples cannot be disputed, the purpose and effect of their use is explained in different ways.

Most poetic theorists who speak about example in the sixteenth century either attribute to it the function of providing specific models of conduct for imitation by the readers or shift the discussion of example from worldly reference to models for writing.[29] The emphasis on proposing models of conduct is a consequence of the general moral outlook of many humanists, summarized recently as "the belief in the importance of the active life and the conviction that we are best persuaded to ethical praxis by the rhetorical practice of literature."[30] Polydore Virgil plainly locates the value of history in its examples:

> Histories, of all other Writings, be most commendable, because it [*sic*] informeth all sorts of people, with notable *examples* of living, and doth excite Noble-men to insue such activity in enterprises, as they read to have been done by their Ancestors; and also discourageth and dehorteth wicked persons from attempting of any heinous deeds or crime, knowing, that such acts shall be registred in perpetual memory, to the praise or reproach of the doers, according to the desert of their endeavours.[31]

History was widely thought of as the source of subject matter or *res* for poetic use, where such moral exemplarity flourished in the dominant Platonic-Horatian poetic theory of the Italian Cinquecento, a current that affected even the reading of Aristotelian poetics to contain all poetics within the boundaries of the moral sciences.[32] Bernard Weinberg summarizes the position of poetics in the sixteenth-century Italian theories as part of moral philosophy:

> Poetics belongs to both [ethics and politics] since it offers *examples* of how happiness is achieved or lost by various kinds of persons in various situations. It must therefore offer these *examples* in such a way that the right moral lessons will be taught and the proper effect produced.[33]

The repetitive justification of literature on the basis of its ability to produce examples of conduct to imitate or to shun is amply documented by Weinberg's study and can just as easily be found in the theoretical treatises and prefaces of other nations in the sixteenth century. The supposition of such a utilitarian poetics is that the audience will tend to imitate the examples proposed. Such examples are therefore neither aesthetic, abstract, nor speculative, but aimed at direct behavioral modification. Throughout this theorization of example, the subject matter is clearly emphasized at the expense of style, that is, in the

13

division between *res* and *verba*, moral purpose is particularly attached to *res*, the domain of example; while pleasure, making the example or other moral lesson more acceptable, is the end of *verba*.[34]

Within the great chorus of theoretical praise for the examples found in literature, certain qualifications appear when more thoughtful writers attempt to adjust and refine example within the moral science of poetics. One broad area of such reflection concerns the relation between example and the reality of everyday life. There appears a possible contradiction between the desire to make use of existing, historically real, cases and the desire to provide models that conform in the highest degree with the ideal rule of conduct being inculcated in the reader or audience. Aristotle, in discussing the usefulness of historical example, held that the future most often resembles the past. Hence, an example from the past will, most probably, contain a pattern that will be pertinent to the situation under deliberation. This argument which grounds example in probability and inferential reasoning is fused with—one might even say confused with, or subjected to—the Platonic-Horatian insistence on the purely ethical function of example. When this happens, probability and inference, indicating what may happen, are subordinated to prescription and normalization, what ought to happen. The sixteenth-century concern with decorum (or verisimilitude) was a manifestation of an attempt to stabilize the relationship between past and future by merging both in a timeless ideal representation. The past per se is not the primary value. Rather the authority of the past becomes the raw material for the corrective genius of the writer in his quest to influence the future conduct of the reader or audience.

Examples, when they are not frankly fictional, must be corrected in order to fit ideological models.[35] This "fit" is produced often by the simplest of example-making procedures, selection or excision of examples from the mass of somewhat similar things (events, persons, or other entities). In this case the purity or unmixed quality of examples may be emphasized. Some theorists feel that the examples provided should be both bad (what the poet "dehorteth," to use Langley's apt Latinism) and good; others hold that the representation of the good is the sole valid exemplarity. Next to the formation of correct example by selection is another technique consisting of *addition* or intensification.[36] Correction by addition or selection is a feature of all literary verisimilitude to the extent that the latter requires adjustment of instance to rule. Commenting on verisimilitude in seventeenth-century French practice, Kibédi-Varga remarks:

Observing [the norm of] verisimilitude is not to compare . . . but it is to render comparable, to locate in each thing, what can be repeated, compared, and generalized. And if a thing resists, it must be corrected (*embellie*). The true which is not verisimilar has no place in literature.[37]

Repetition (or the detection of repetition), comparison, and generalization are the steps on which induction is founded, and induction is the dialectical sibling of example.

In the seventeenth century, dictionary definitions connect example (*exemple*) to the preservation of certain traditions and to teaching. It is not surprising, in a period that is so concerned with its own position in history, that example should serve as a means of covering the present with the cloak of the past. This figure therefore becomes the rhetorical figure that, more than any other, is connected with authority. In the *Dictionnaire de l'Académie* (1694), the definition itself and the examples of use are highly significant:

EXAMPLE . . . That which is worthy of being put forth to be imitated or to be avoided . . . It is also said of a thing which is similar to the matter at hand and which serves to authorize it, to confirm it . . . *You say that that was done in the past, I maintain that it is new, that there are not, that there never have been examples. That is without example. Give me an example of it. I will find you a hundred examples in history. You say that that way of speaking is proper; then give me examples taken from good authors. I am supported by examples.* [EXEMPLE . . . Ce qui est digne d'estre proposé pour l'imiter ou pour le fuir . . . Il se dit aussi, d'Une chose qui est pareille à celle dont il s'agit & qui sert pour l'authoriser, la confirmer . . . *Vous dites que cela s'est fait autrefois, je soustiens qu'il est nouveau, il n'y en a point, il n'y en eut jamais d'exemples. cela est sans exemple. donnez m'en un exemple. je vous en trouveray cent exemples dans l'histoire. vous dites que cette façon de parler est bonne, apportez-m'en donc des exemples tirez des bons autheurs. je suis fondé en exemples.*]

This definition is quite far from the Aristotelian *paradeigma*, which drew its value from the degree to which the interlocutor or public would recognize both factuality and similarity. Example in this ancient sense was inherently neutral and could only be judged, when used, on the basis of effectiveness. The Academy instead gives priority to the "worthiness" of the example (*ce qui est digne*), though the worthiness is linked, not directly to the imitation, but to the gesture of proposing imitation or avoidance. Such an approach suits a rhetoric divorced from the practical problems of convincing—problems that were of more importance in a democratic or even a parliamentary regime—and has become more concerned with the problems of decorum. Examples are meant to fit a stable, ritual order. Just as verisimilitude, in the classical poetics, triumphed over truth, so the exemplary triumphed over the example. The second definition returns to a common ground of example in similarity, but the Academy uses terms suggesting that the interest of similarity is to replicate decisions *already made*—to confirm, to authorize. The citations of usage, in italics in the text, indicate the extent to which example guards the threshold between the old and the new, or rather, the extent to which example is used to guard against newness. The quality of an expression is judged according to its history. Example is the figure that provides foundations.[38]

The piety of this theorizing of example on the part of lexicographers and theoreticians of poetics contrasts with the practice of authors who are neither. The spectacular and subversive potential of example interests authors like Machiavelli and Marguerite de Navarre much more than the simple representation of a model for imitation. One important theorist of composition in the Renaissance does, however, provide a richer view of example, closer to the view of the practicing writers than to the view of the authors of treatises of poetics. Erasmus, in book 2 of his textbook, *De copia*, treats "abundance of subject-matter" and gives ways to find things to say. These "methods" (*rationes*) are eleven in number and include "enrichment of material," "variation," "causes," and so on.[39] The use of examples appears as a section of method 11, "Accumulation of proofs and arguments."

Erasmus's use of the term *exemplum* is quite broad, as are the purposes of using examples:

> A most effective means of making what we are saying convincing and of generating *copia* at the same time is to be found in illustrative examples, for which the Greek word is *paradeigmata*. The content of the examples can be something like, unlike, or in contrast to what we are illustrating, or something greater, smaller, or equivalent. Contrast and dissimilarity reside in features such as type, means, time, place, and most of the other "circumstances" . . . We include under "examples" stories, fable, proverbs, opinions, parallels or comparisons, similitudes, analogies, and anything else of the same sort. (p. 606)

The first distinctively new note in Erasmus's definition of example is his conscientious return to the classical, Aristotelian, doctrine of the *paradeigma*, thus grounding his remarks on example broadly in rhetoric

rather than more narrowly in poetics. This classical grounding is continued in the extreme flexibility Erasmus allows example in its relationship to the main body of the discourse, which the examples illustrate. The list of terms included under the general heading *example*
points to the useful insight that an example is not a self-contained and
inherently definable type of discourse. Instead, *example* is the term
used for the function of a unit of discourse within a whole. This concept runs decidedly against the tendency of some to see example as
being necessarily embodied in a genre like the narrative, for even an
opinion, according to Erasmus, can be an example. While one can give
a historical account to exemplify an opinion, one can also, to develop
the Erasmian line, give a series of opinions to exemplify, for instance,
a typology of some sort.

A second important point in Erasmus's teaching on example is the
reason given for using examples. Like all of the material Erasmus presents in *De copia*, example is meant to expand the quantity of things
one has to say while avoiding a fall into meaninglessness. Example
gives some form to a mass that would otherwise lose its direction and
structure. Persuasion is not, for Erasmus, the sole or even the dominant reason for introducing examples: "not only to make our case look
convincing, but also to dress it up and brighten, expand, and enrich
it" (p.607). He goes on to indicate that example plays a role in any kind
of rhetoric, not only deliberative or forensic, but also epideictic or less
generically defined forms of speech:

> Illustrations play a leading role, whether the speech is the sort that
> debates what action should be taken, or urges to a particular
> course of action, or is intended to console someone in grief, or is
> laudatory or vituperative; in short, whether one is trying to con-
> vince one's audience, move them, or give them pleasure. (p. 607)

Example is limited neither by the verbal form (e.g., narrative versus
statement of opinion) nor by the intended effect on the receiver of the
speech. Nor, as Erasmus goes on to point out, is example drawn from
any single kind of source, for it can be historical or fictive, theological,
biblical, or philosophical. It may be drawn from antiquity, from recent
history, or from contemporary events, even from the experience of the
speaker.

Example is a particularly apposite case of the preoccupation with
accumulation and expenditure or dispersal that Terence Cave has so
forcefully analyzed in Erasmus's thought.[40] In the section entitled
"Method of Gathering Examples" (*Ratio colligendi exempla*) Erasmus
describes the student who "flits like a bee" through the garden of lit-

erature and discovers that there is too much to collect. Therefore, while the writer is often haunted by the dread of not having anything to say—this is the basis for the very title of *De copia*—the opposite problem confronts the reader who will become a writer. This leads Erasmus to locate a feature that will be very significant in our description of example: the need for selection. "Since there is such an abundance of material that one cannot gather everything," he writes, the student "will at least take the most striking and fit this into his scheme of work" (p. 639).[41] The indication that the student is not merely collecting but selecting the "most striking" (*praecipua*) reveals the continued or even revived and intensified presence of the etymological root of example in the gesture of cutting—*eximere*—by which the unit of discourse is fashioned by its excision from a mass of text that is not retained. Machiavelli makes precisely this comment in dedicating *The Prince* when he claims that his book is the *reduction* of all his reading and experience into a small volume (*in uno piccolo volume ridotte*).[42] Machiavelli, like Erasmus, is therefore a partisan and practitioner of the elimination of what is "left over" when the writer has made his preparations.

Erasmus differs from theorists, like Polydore Virgil, who recommend using examples of good and bad conduct to imitate or to avoid. The Erasmian selection is not based on the quality of the conduct contained in the example but on the quality of the textual *res* and *verba* as they—separately or together as the occasion arises—offer themselves as useful to the writer. The distinction is of enormous importance. Despite Erasmus's undeniable emphasis on the moral and religious utility of the act of writing, this emphasis does not provide the key to the selection of material. Instead the "striking" or "outstanding" (*praecipua*), an aesthetic-rhetorical criterion, is for Erasmus the criterion for selection in the gathering of *copia*. An example of good conduct that is not striking would be of no use, for example is not a moral concept but a discursive one. It is not conduct per se but the embodiment of conduct in an unusually noticeable form that lends itself to the needs of the writer or speaker. Having accumulated the necessary material, which one could call the "protoexemplary material" (passages, anecdotes, names, etc., characterized as *striking* and rare), Erasmus's student is in a position to pass to the actual creation of an example by connecting this protoexemplary material with a maxim or subject-heading. The material collected has no permanent or inherent standing as example, for it must be set into a context to reach its exemplary significance:

The death of Socrates can be used to show that death holds no fear for a good man, since he drank the hemlock so cheerfully; but also to show that virtue is prey to ill will and far from safe amidst a swarm of evils; or again that the study of philosophy is useless or even harmful unless you conform to general patterns of behaviour. . . . This same incident can be turned to Socrates' praise or blame. (p. 639)

The last of these comments derives from the humanist custom of practicing alternative arguments from the same case, the arguments *in utramque partem*, on both sides. The general thrust of Erasmus's teaching here, however, is to move beyond the simple binary classification of the protoexemplary material toward a freer conception of the usability of such material. As Erasmus concludes, on the basis of the example from the death of Socrates, "All this makes it quite plain . . . how many purposes the same illustrative example can serve" (p. 641).

Erasmus's work is representative of the explosively inventive use of example by writers who neither classify examples in an ethical dualism of good and bad nor use the term example as mere synonym of narration. Perhaps the very marginality of example, caught between disciplines since the earliest descriptions in which it figures, accounts for the kinship between Erasmus and the writers examined in the chapters that follow. The works of Machiavelli, Marguerite de Navarre, Montaigne, Descartes, Pascal, and Lafayette situate themselves in each case either on the margins of poetic discourse or literature (a relatively uncodified genre such as the novella or the short fiction that was called the *nouvelle historique*) or else frankly reject poetry and eloquence to constitute "new" practical discourses, which escape from the dominance of textual canons.[43] It is now widely recognized that the Renaissance fascination with the collection of discursive units embodying wisdom—proverbs, *sententiae*, examples—does not, in the most original and consequential writers of the period, result in the embellishment and transmission of models of conduct. To the contrary, each of these authors questions the effect of examples when commenting on historical or hypothetical examples.

The rapid review of this historical-theoretical background prevents us from taking a narrow view of the function of example, whether by limiting example to a single illocutionary purpose or by attributing to example alone a power of exhortation that is, potentially, within the bounds of all figural discourse. Before moving to some descriptive guidelines for the study of exemplary texts in the following chapters, it is worth contrasting the broad and complex view of example that obtains in the tradition to recent deductive and restrictive uses of the terms *example* and *exemplary text*.

RECENT STUDY OF EXAMPLE: THE PRAGMATIST DEVIATION

Exemplary texts have recently been studied by scholars interested in the pragmatics of discourse. Unfortunately, both their starting point—consisting of the assumption that all example is *exemplum* in the modern vernacular sense—and their methodological aims—the necessity of concluding that speech acts necessarily and directly modify the behavior of the receiver—result in an unjustified restriction in the category of exemplary discourse. Susan Suleiman has defined the exemplary narrative as being necessarily and essentially "injunctive."[44] In her description of such narratives, Suleiman divides them into three functions or levels—narration, interpretation, and injunction—and argues that implicitly or explicitly all exemplary narrative has a behavioral aim and not merely a cognitive one. Furthermore, there exists, in this view, a hierarchy among the three functions in which the most important function is the injunction or moral imperative and the least important the narration itself. Suleiman points out the interesting paradox that follows from this description: the narrative level is the least important of the three, yet it is indispensable if a text is to be considered exemplary narrative, for without the narration no text is narrative. The more important functions, the interpretation and the injunction, may be implicit but the least important function, the narrative, must be explicit.

This description, elaborated on the basis of biblical parable of the nonallegorical type (most New Testament parables are allegorical) and a fable, has many interesting and useful aspects.[45] But its insistence on the necessity of injunction in the pragmatics of example has the unfortunate consequence of denying exemplary status to any narrative text that is not injunctive. Hence, as Suleiman writes of several fables of La Fontaine, "The function of these fables is absolutely not to communicate values which can serve to construct an ethics (or even a pragmatics) but only to depict, without illusions, 'le monde comme il va.' "[46] If one establishes the explicit category of " 'non-exemplary' fables" (Suleiman, "Le Récit exemplaire," p. 482), one can easily discover "non-exemplary" examples, that is, texts containing the explicit designation *example* but not, implicitly or explicitly, the injunctive function essential, in Suleiman's view, for the existence of a true exemplary narrative.

The excessive emphasis on injunction confuses an essential or defining feature of example with a frequent but not necessary use of example. Part of the problem is the use of the term *exemplum* without a distinction between one traditional or evolutionary sense of the term and its root sense. If it is used as a synonym for "narrative example," there seems no logical reason to suppose that injunction is a necessary component of such narrative. One could easily adduce many "narrative examples" that are not injunctive. Historical narrative and scientific research provide many narratives presented as manifestations of a general rule, which is not an ethical but a cognitive value.

In the case of those fables of La Fontaine mentioned as nonexemplary narratives, it seems perfectly proper to consider them as examples of what Suleiman calls *le monde comme il va*, in other words, as the manifestation of certain supposed constants of social conduct. There is also every reason to suppose that the tradition of the *exemplum*, as narrowly and historically defined, and the example in its broadest theoretical sense are both operative in texts like La Fontaine's *Fables*, since the absence of moral lesson is played against possible expectations of a kind of simplification to a predictable and limited series of "moral" lessons. The reduction of the pragmatics of example to the function of "enjoining" seems, therefore, to be unacceptable on historical and theoretical grounds.

Another study emphasizing the pragmatics of example is Bruno Gélas's description of "manipulative fiction."[47] Gélas moves the discussion from consideration of the individual *paradeigma* or *exemplum* to the act of what he calls "exemplarization." He also removes the limitation, imposed by Suleiman, requiring that all exemplary narratives contain an "injunctive." Moving the emphasis to one of the other three functions earlier used to describe example, Gélas interprets: "what the *exemplum* implies (that which it introduces) is not only or not primarily a rule, but the belief that the *exemplum*'s relationship to the rule is exactly the relationship which joins anecdotal manifestation to a transcendental truth. In this sense, no exemplarisation is possible except on the grounds of an agreement on a *theory of manifestation* which is also the theory of a reading practice."[48] This insight, which seems a proper basis for a general theory of the pragmatics of example, is, however, undercut by Gélas's argument that example is necessarily a more "manipulative" discursive strategy than other forms of argumentation. By assuming the position of narrator, argues Gélas, the speaker removes himself from the discursive exchange in which he was only one of the partners and becomes a monopolizing enunciator, able to demote the others to the status of audience and to keep them from speaking. The "audience," according to Gélas, suffers numerous consequences from this move, for it is denied access to the interlocutive second-person form, is "cut off from all possibility of formulating a judgment of truth," is "made to leave behind the initial situation in order to focus its interpretive performance on the narrative report alone," and is "forced, finally, to admit implicitly the relation of adequacy between that narrative and a rule of action."[49]

Although this purports to be a description of the discursive situation in which the example is used, it seems to neglect any credible discursive situation. For example, there is no particular reason to deny to the interlocutor, become (temporary) audience, the ability to formulate a judgment of truth—though the tactic of the example does impose a series of consequent moves on the audience. As Gélas notes, attention is focused on the narrative, and the listener's response will necessarily involve either an analysis of the story or the formulation of a counter-example. In short, by making the example an absolute rhetorical tool (and it seems to undermine the possibility of any rhetoric to imagine an absolute discursive "weapon"), this description ignores the fact that example is only part of a discursive situation.

There is already a hint of this problem in Gélas's allusion to what he calls the "(infrequent) metanarrative commentary provided by the narrator himself" (Gélas p. 84). The metanarrative commentary, or explicit attachment of the example to a systematic discourse containing the general rule that the narrative manifests, is *not* rare in most discursive situations. The particular reference here is undoubtedly to the parables studied by Suleiman—not the most typical case of exemplification and, in any case, not without metanarrative commentary. Moreover, the assumption that the exchange ends with the acceptance, by the listener, of the example as definitive and adequate proof of a general principle is to deny that example is only one element of discourse, that it is used in combination with others, and that only the study of the context formed around the example can give a proper understanding of its use (and in some cases, permit us to recognize that the narrative in question is an example). At the most, the particular manipulative powers of example described by Gélas may represent the goal of the user of the example, rather than the effects of the use of example. Just as an imperative, for instance, does not necessarily produce the perlocutionary effect of obedience, so an example does not necessarily produce the result of a replicated or imitated act.

The giver of an example, furthermore, may impose the example on the listener, as Gélas suggests, but an example may equally well be invited, even imperatively required, by the listener, as in "Give me an example of that!" The focus on the elements of a narrative example may allow the giver of the example to gain an advantage in the course of the discussion. This, however, is the traditional Aristotelian function of rhetoric, to study the effective ways of persuading in view of operating such a persuasion. The construction of an example is not inherently more manipulative than the construction of an enthymeme, the rhetorical syllogism. When viewed in the context of fictions generally, the example seems less manipulative than many nonexemplary fictions that aim at purely emotive effect (pathos), since example has a distancing function when revealed *as* example.[50]

It is nonetheless useful to recall, from Suleiman's description, the three functions—interpretive, narrative, and injunctive—even though certain modifications should be brought to this description before it can be adopted as a generally valid theory of the pragmatics of example. Specifically, of these three functions only the interpretive is truly necessary for example; narrative and injunctive are optional. Since Suleiman and Gélas both give definitions of narrative example, narrative is a required feature of the texts they describe. In describing example in general only the relation between generalization and specific instance is essential, and this relation is an interpretive one. Unless the reader realizes that the instance is given to represent or support a broader statement, the reader cannot recognize example. Such an interpretive function is present even in cases in which the reader is meant to perceive a disruption in the application of instance to rule (or rule to instance), for without knowing that an exemplification is being attempted—or parodied—the ironic disruption cannot be perceived.

It is wrong to assume (despite the opinion of such critics as Stierle, Suleiman, and Gélas) that exemplary texts are necessarily part of a small group of texts having an explicit doctrinal meaning. "Exemplary texts" thus become identified, for the critic, with didactic texts or with texts having the primary function of manipulating the reader into a position of learner. Such didactic texts do use examples. But many other texts have a doctrinal content, yet do not use examples. A novel neither exemplary nor a *roman à thèse* is not without meaning nor without the conveyance of an ideological position. Consequently, as used in this study, the term *exemplary text* means one that makes use of examples, not one that imposes or enjoins a specific example or a univocal interpretation of example.

In fact, exemplary texts may not have as their primary function the conveying of a "message," for, like most of those texts that have found their way into the recent category of literature (in the sense of *belles lettres*), example can provide a form that is used for providing pleasure for its own sake. To limit example to the conveying of a determined

23

message is akin to insisting that any dramatic work that assumes the form of tragedy must take ritual catharsis as its aim. This reduction of the purpose of example becomes even more suspect when it is seen that the historical ground on which it is based is a limitation of the whole history of example to the putative practice of one period (the *exemplum* of the Middle Ages), whereas the use of example in classical antiquity is much broader.

Examples, as we have noted earlier, are generally not autonomous texts but are elements within texts. To analyze them in entire separation from their contexts limits the validity of the textual description and cannot have any interest in the description of the pragmatics of example, for all pragmatic studies must assume some form of communicative exchange. The interpretive mechanism of example may include an internal interpreter within the exemplary unit itself. But such an interpreter can provide only part of the meaning, for the example is told to some audience, which can decide to accept, reject, or modify the interpretation made by the internal interpreter. We will consider later an extremely interesting use of the internal interpreter in the case of *La Princesse de Clèves*, where there are many layers of "internal" interpretation. The contact of these layers permits interpretation to take place.

Our working definition of example takes into account the pragmatic situation in which this discursive instrument is used by positing that all examples are dependent texts, and that they occur in the context of another text, hierarchically superior, which systematizes multiple examples and relates them to a maxim. By this definition examples are not freestanding texts. Gélas is perfectly correct to note that the study of example should be replaced by the study of exemplarization, for such a term indicates that example occurs within discourse, not outside it.

Although most of the examples treated in this work are narrative, there seems to be no advantage to creating a split between narrative and nonnarrative examples at the outset. Furthermore, the pragmatic characteristics of example include the possiblity of transferring to the reader or listener some of the activity of actualizing or expanding examples that are present only in the most allusive way in texts. Just as intertextual reference can take on the form of very slight indications in the surface of a text, even when the allusion opens the way for an experienced reader to recognize large networks of textual kinship and significance, so too a single proper noun in an exemplary context can permit the reader to complete the development of a textual line of argument. The earlier example from Aristotle concerning the Great

King could be rewritten, "The example of Darius and Xerxes shows that the present Great King will cross over into Greece after his conquest of Egypt." Although this example is not narrative in its textual form, the reader who understands the reference will be capable of expanding this concise indication into "Darius and Xerxes crossed over into Greece after conquering Egypt"—certainly a brief narrative, but an undeniable narrative expansion nonetheless. Similarly, an exemplary "kernel" such as "It is easy to find sedimentary rocks in New England, for example, limestone and sandstone," can be expanded by the unrealized predication "Limestone is a sedimentary rock."

In countering the drive to define example exclusively as narrative (on the formal level) and as moral injunction (on the pragmatic level), I do not dispute the great frequency with which these two features are present in texts that use example. The texts with which the present study will be concerned in detail, however, frequently use nonnarrative and noninjunctive examples even though the writers of these texts are aware of potential connection of their texts to narrative/injunctive exemplarity. Such deliberate disconnections in texts by such writers as Machiavelli and Montaigne become revealing to the extent that contemporary (i.e., medieval and Renaissance) and modern expectations are not fulfilled. When a writer does not use an example as an explicit model for imitation, and when a writer produces an example without giving it narrative form, the result is no less an example on account of the deviation of the text from certain traditions of example. The possibility of such variation on the pragmatic possibilities of example is one source of the interest of literary texts—their ability, in other words, to bracket or fictionalize the content of history and to suspend the apparent speech acts that constitute their situation of enunciation.

Seven Characteristics of Example

A thoughtful reading of late Renaissance texts that use examples leads one to doubt the usefulness of the rough-and-ready dictionary definitions that are current and to reject the solution offered by a reduction of example to a narrow pragmatics.[51] Something both more precise and more capacious seems necessary as a starting point, even at the price of creating ad hoc and naïve categories. I think that the following are useful and productive concepts for exploring sixteenth- and seventeenth-century exemplarity. They may prove to have an application to the examples of other periods and languages.

Iterativity and Multiplicity

Both in the form it takes in texts and in the view of the world that it projects, example depends on repetition. We can recognize example because of our habit of seeing pattern in text and in the historical world. In the example of the Great King, Aristotle gave two specific occurrences of the Persian king's strategy of crossing to Greece after subduing Egypt. A repetition appears in the text and in the historical world. Often, however, the textual repetition is abandoned in favor of a single instance that stands for many similar cases in the historical world. This condensation of many instances into a smaller number of verbal references to history fits the category that Genette has called the "iterative" form of narrative.[52] Whether the surface textual form of an example is that of a sentence, a longer narrative sequence, or a noun, matters much less than its formal and semantic iterativity, the way in which one stated instance alludes to a whole network of such instances. The term *iterative* describes the way a condensed textual statement stands for an extensive historical repetition of similar events.

Aristotle's example of the Great King actually takes a different approach to narrative example. He repeats the instances rather than allowing Darius's crossing to stand also for Xerxes'. This "repetitive narrative," in Genette's terms, is not as common as the more concise iterative type. What Aristotle is doing here, however, illustrates the *multiplicity* of example: many historical events mentioned together invite the reader to relate them to a general rule. The example of the Great King does not itself contain the word *example* or any synonym thereof. Most examples do begin with an expression like "for example," *exempli gratia, per esempio, par exemple,* and "for instance." These are *explicit examples.* Yet even in an *implicit example* a competent reader or listener, such as Aristotle supposes, can recognize exemplification. The combination of a general rule (generally given in the present tense) with a specific historical event (generally given in a past tense) is one of the conventions for recognizing an example in a text. A second, and more revealing convention, is the clustering of examples within the text itself, a clustering described by the term *multiplicity.* This characteristic is set out by Aristotle:

> If we have no enthymemes, we must employ examples as demonstrative proofs, for conviction is produced by these; but if we have them, examples must be used as evidence and as a kind of epilogue to the enthymemes. For if they stand first, they resemble induction, and induction is not suitable to rhetorical speeches except in very few cases; if they stand last they resemble evidence, and a

witness is in every case likely to induce belief. Wherefore also it is necessary to quote a number of examples if they are put first, but one alone is sufficient if they are put last; for even a single trust-worthy witness is of use. (*Rhetoric* 2.20.1394a)

Aristotle describes here the effect of several examples given in a row, from which one can draw in conclusion the general rule that one wishes to assert. The difference in effect between examples given before the rule and examples given afterward is that the repeated examples will themselves lead the audience to seek the thread linking the different instances. The listener will thus do a good deal of the work, by following, so to speak, the scraps of bait leading to the orator's trap and, through a process of induction-reduction, participating in the puzzle to which the orator will finally announce the answer—which by then the public will be only too glad to accept. The other use of example, the single example given after the enthymemic (or deductive) demonstration, is meant to bring down to the concrete a concept that has already been granted in the abstract. But even the single example appearing in the textual surface is used on the supposition that others can be generated by the reader. The rule that forms one instance into an example serves as the generative kernel around which other events can gather in an exemplary pattern. What may seem at first a stylistic or technical observation is thus the trace of a whole ideology of pattern and repetition.

Multiplicity is the term that stresses the redundancy of example within a single moment (that is, the way speakers or writers give several at once as if to support a point), while iterativity stresses the way an example that explicitly points to an event that happened once actually stands for many similar events occurring through time. Example supposes that it is possible to construct a *class* of events or entities such that mentioning one or more of the entities will allow one to perceive the general description and, conversely, that mention of the general description will permit recognition of one or more of the subsumed entities. Perelman and Tyteca describe this operation succinctly: "It is by their relation to a given rule that phenomena become interchangeable, and, on the other hand, it is by their enumeration that the point of view from which they have been compared to one another emerges."[53] Therefore it is impossible to consider as example the manifestation of a class of one.

When used in an example, an entity loses its autonomy and unicity. The two following sentences, which at first glance seem synonymous, have a very different rhetorical function. One may say "The black

27

spruce is an example of a coniferous tree," or "The black spruce is a coniferous tree." However wordy and awkward the first sentence is, in an argument about the types of trees such a sentence would subordinate the ontological statement about the black spruce to the statement about the category to which the spruce belongs. This subordination occurs even in implicit examples, where the sentence "The black spruce is a coniferous tree" is juxtaposed with the sentence "There are many coniferous trees in our region."[54] Subordination differs from simple replacement. Occurrences and events in examples not only can be but must be both themselves *and* representative of something else—of the subordinating concept—and must be replaceable in that function with other events or entities.[55]

Example is therefore based on the view that the apparently infinite number of possible events can be contained within a limited structure or repertory of rules. The occurrences or manifestations of a general rule will therefore be limitless, but the underlying rules will be finite. The practice of rhetoric is based, says Antonius in Cicero's *De oratore*, on the idea that "all the possible subjects of debate are not founded on a countless host of human beings or an endless diversity of occasions, but on typical cases and characters, and that the types are not merely limited in number but positively few."[56] It therefore seems that viewed as example no narrative utterance can be truly singulative nor even repetitive, but is necessarily iterative.

Exteriority

Example is a way of gesturing outside the pure discourse of the speaker/writer toward support in a commonly accepted textual or referential world. As external to discourse, or as a unit of discourse separated from the unqualified enunciation of the speaker alone, example can be conceived as something that speaker and audience, writer and reader look toward as possible common ground. In this case example would be outside the "inside" constituted by the discourse of direct assertion and would itself be a closed entity, which would present itself to be beheld by the public. Example is part of argumentation as a kind of *evidence* in the full Latin sense of *evidentia*, something capable of being seen, radiating its visibility outward (*ex + videre*). Although example is often associated with authority, it differs from simple authoritarian assertion by appealing to something that diverts the audience from a direct affirmation and says "see for yourself."[57]

To point outward at this thing, this evidence, is also to make example exterior to the truth being argued.[58] As Warminski says of the example or *Beispiel* in Hegel, "*Beispiel* refers to that side of the knower/

known, subject/object, relation which is taken to be inessential, accidental, that which is not the truth of knowing."[59] Learning about appearances is only a means, not an end. New appearances can be invented to lead toward the same fundamental knowledge. This approach encourages the fall into pure fiction, the fabrication of appearances without any substructure or concreteness. But this distinction between knowledge and perception in rhetorical exchange nonetheless is possible only in light of the knowledge that is posited as the goal of example. Example is, in other words, only the "outside" of knowledge and discourse when an "inside" is created rhetorically.

The most emphatic exteriority reached by example occurs when example is contrived as spectacle, as a significant appearance enacted outside or at the very frontier of language. The ancient and medieval association of *exemplum* with painting, inlaid pavement, and rhetorical *imago* is amply confirmed by Renaissance practice. Machiavelli, in his recurrent interest in exemplary punishment, and Marguerite de Navarre, in her fictions of self-discovery through a kind of disjointed imaging, make suggestive use of spectacles created intentionally or inadvertently for an audience.

Another figure that is revealingly close to example in its display of an "outside" to discourse is quotation. Quotation has in common with example that it interrupts the speech or writing of a discourse and imports material from "elsewhere." In quotation this importation or foreignness is most evident, particularly since the Renaissance, when quotation marks and italics began to be used to set off the phrase that the writer disowned or attributed to another.[60] Even before the graphic marking of quotations, the reader could perceive, by such lexical clues as *inquam*, *dixit*, *ait*, and so forth, that the speaker had changed, and that the quoted material was enunciated by someone other than the general author of the text. When the quotation was in Latin and the rest of the text in the vernacular, as happened ever more frequently throughout the sixteenth century, the distancing of text and quotation increased. The writer of the text was able to display the utter foreignness of the very words of the quotation, words that come from elsewhere.

Although example is generally not displayed graphically as separate from the text in general, both quotation and example, in some gesture toward an "elsewhere," seek to provide a support for the assertion of the writer. They both imply a statement such as "If you doubt what I say, you have only to look at *this* (quotation, example) to see that my assertion is true independent of my making it." This gesture toward an *outside* of the writer's discourse has a peculiar and even contradictory directionality. As Compagnon has argued, the quotation attempts to include the outside within the present text, while the allegation—designating a specific instance without quoting—is an explicit gesture away from the present text toward an outside world, textual or nontextual.[61] It would complicate matters immensely to try to trace the fine semantic line that exists historically between allegation and exemplification—a relationship rendered even more problematical by the fact that the contemporary usage, especially in American English, inverts the etymologically dominant meaning of allegation as reference to proof.[62] Example seems to be intermediate between quotation and allegation by being present in the text, as having some weight of its own without extratextual existence (e.g., fictitious examples), yet as not having the closed self-sufficiency of a quotation.

Quotation requires a shift in enunciation. When the speaker stops speaking, the quotation begins. Thus quotation is a form of "silence" on the part of the speaker, who stands back, joins the audience or readership, and makes it clear: "I am not saying it! [*Ce n'est pas moi qui le dis!*] But I have heard it said or can imagine it being said." The speaker reports something and does not even assume what he is reporting into his own words. The quotation is hearsay evidence, but unlike most hearsay evidence the quotation has a specific weight derived from the very form of the utterance reported. Unlike a paraphrase, a quotation must not be altered in its form (or form of expression, in Hjelmslev's terms), and in this way the form is emphasized. The dominance of the form gives the quotation a curious semantic flexibility, for the use of a consecrated expression, refrain, *bon mot*, and the like may very well occur in a situation that completely changes not only the reference but even the meaning of the quoted utterance. Because of the shift in enunciation, the quotation is a kind of common property, since neither the speaker nor the audience is "saying" it but is only repeating it. Even self-quotation refers to something the speaker said, not to something he might now say. The quotation can be used by either side to buttress different arguments. By appropriating what comes from elsewhere, the quotation can produce effects that have little to do with argumentation at all. Mutual recognition of a quotation known to speaker and listener can have a phatic effect, testing and confirming the channel of communication, waking up the audience. The deliberate alteration of meaning or reference that can occur when such a recognized utterance is reused can produce many further aesthetic effects based on the tension between maintained form and altered semantics.

Example neither emphasizes the form nor requires a shift in speaker. Despite its reference outside the immediate speech situation to objects, persons, or events not present, the example is conveyed most often in the words and voice of the speaker. The use of quotation in graphically marked form, that is, in the form known since the sixteenth century, is a way of distancing the speaker even from words of his own, as I might now speak of "quotation," suggesting some doubt on my part as to the appropriateness of the term. Example requires the speaker to do the opposite—to appropriate, even at the risk of a certain contamination, an experience that is not present and may never have been that of the speaker. In other words, quotation allows the speaker/writer to distance what he is saying whereas example requires the speaker/writer to adopt or bring closer something that may come from far away.

Discontinuity

The discontinuity of example is related to this exteriority, but while exteriority concerns the position of the example in relation to the speech situation of the persons (speaker, listener) involved—their perception of the gesture toward an evidence—discontinuity concerns the status of example as fragment of another whole, a separation within the domain of what the ancients conceived as *res* or matter. This discontinuity is implicit in the very concept of *eximere*, "to cut out." All examples are chosen, isolated from a context and placed into a new context within which they are visible precisely because this discontinuity fits into the rhetorical/discursive exteriority. For this reason critical description of example constantly relies on terms like *intercalated* and *interspersed*. Or, with a slight change of perspective to emphasize the example material rather than the direct discourse, the term *frame* is used for the same purpose of locating the border between the excised and refitted material and the surrounding isotopy. This structure, a veritable mosaic of transferred material, gives the speaker/writer the chance to emphasize the discontinuity to varying degrees, to produce, for instance, the "rift" that Brownlee has described in the work of Juan Ruiz.[63]

If there were no discontinuity in exemplification, there could be no detection of the resemblances and repetition, since this detection depends on the differentiation of qualities or acts that are—temporarily—given a particular status and emphasis. In the example of the Great King, no attempt is made to compare the whole of the life of different kings. Instead a single sequence of acts is selected from the biographies of the various kings to be set forth in an example cluster. Discontinuity also applies to the textual surface of an exemplary text, since a shifting back and forth must be recognized between discourse and history for

31

the supportive (or occasionally ironic and contrapuntal) effect of example to be felt.

Rarity

Rarity is the term I will use to describe a complex system of values and expectations based on both extratextual and textual ideas about frequency of occurrence or normal behavior. One face of this concept is the notion that certain individuals act in a way far above or far below average achievement. The "hero" is someone who is stronger, smarter, or more devoted than most people. The legendary criminal or sinner is much worse than most people, and so on. The choice of an example—for instance, an example of a saint—requires the bringing forth of one member of a class of which the others are left behind, unmentioned. The rarity of example, in this use of the term (as social rarity), supposes that before such an act by the speaker/writer the community already perceived a scale of norms and excesses among entities laying claim to a certain quality. For example, there are ordinary princes and there are exceptional princes. A person who displays "exemplary virtue" is therefore likely to be a person who displays unusual, atypical virtue. Examples and the category or paradigm from which they are selected (Cesare Borgia, for instance, and the category of "princes") can therefore be considered in terms of abundance and lack, or of frequency and infrequency of occurrence.

On the other hand, rarity can be conceived in terms of its textual status. An example may be rare because it is not often mentioned in texts, even though it may be something quite common in everyday life. To invoke the concept of rarity does not mean, therefore, adopting an ideology proclaiming an objective difference between the values of persons or acts. Although many examples are based on such an ideology of heroic idealism, other examples use rarity as a means of demonstrating the failure of language to include objective reality. The "rare" example is therefore something that is rarely spoken about, something that may be deliberately suppressed. The dialectic between text and life (mentioned above by Polydore Virgil) is such that a competition for inclusion in texts is noticeable in classical texts—certain kinds of deeds are understood to "merit" or buy inclusion in the textual tradition because of their infrequency. On the other hand, something quite common in everyday reality can become rare textually simply by being overlooked, so that it can be used in a text where it stands out by its unusual quality. This "economics" of example, by singling out the rare and the unusual, can lead to a brilliant critique and deflation of example. Montaigne's *Essais*, in particular, make a very explicit description of the accumulation, distribution, and valuation of examples—on the level of the writing of the *Essais*—and strip the veil off the posturing that occurs among the exemplary figures or characters in an apparently conscious effort to attain the status of "rare example."

Artificiality

The artificiality of example is its quality as a semiotic act. To say that examples are artificial means simply to recognize that no example exists independently of the formulation of generalities and specific instances. Any critique of rarity must emphasize the artificial nature of example, the fact that an example is made by "inventing" significance out of the continuum of experience or of prior statement. In this invention, which confers many qualities, including (on occasion) rarity, on the instance chosen, an act, entity, or event is transformed from "itself" into an "example *of.*" The exemplary quality of such act, entity, or event does not inhere in itself but in this gesture of subordination to a broader category. Examples, in short, do not happen; they are made. This making appears in texts on the level of the writer and on the level of the character as manipulator of appearances (Montaigne uses the example of Epicurus).

Undecidability

Undecidability, or open-endedness, characterizes example as it does most inductive reasoning. The serial nature of example has been mentioned as a textual feature of the figure, and this seriality may derive from the always insufficient quality of example as complete proof. Of course, in the Aristotelian tradition, example is not meant to offer certainty but only probability. In attempting to close the holes of an argument from example, numbers of examples are introduced to create a preponderance in favor of a certain pattern; yet the possibility of a single counterexample destroying the pattern always lurks, threatening the exemplary system.

As a guide to future conduct or expectation, example raises the specter of anomaly. Just as a general rule is derived by neglecting the individuality of cases, so also the use of past examples to predict the future supposes that similarity will prevail over difference. This supposition is questioned most pointedly by Lafayette, whose two principal novels explore the gap between predictions and occurrences, and point toward the always-looming exception to any pattern. In Lafayette's work as well, the connection between exemplary rarity and exemplary open-endedness is accentuated. Since examples often are chosen from among the exceptions rather than from among the most common, ba-

nal occurrences, then example finds itself in the paradoxical position
of arguing in favor of a norm while displaying the fascinating exceptions to the norm.

Excess

Excess is the last of the important characteristics of example appearing
in this practical description of early modern texts. Example is excessive
because any element of historical reality and even any fiction adduced
to support a generalization will have characteristics that exceed what
can be covered by the generalization. A brief story told about Nero to
illustrate his cruelty will include details about Nero or about Roman
life that are incidental to Nero's cruelty. To account in general terms
for these other details, we could add other generalities or rules that
apply to Nero (his hypocrisy), to emperors (their authority), or to Romans (their submission or periodic revolts). To make an example of an
object is to account for only one limited aspect of that object. To say
that the Parthenon is an example of the Doric order is to neglect the
fact that the Parthenon could also be an example of a building damaged
by twentieth-century pollution. In such a brief and limited case we can
recall that the example is a dependent statement drawing its meaning
from the controlling generality. As the dependent statements grow
into complex narratives, however, the number of other concepts that
can be illustrated by the narrative begins to threaten the control of the
generality. The dependent statement may bring details that cast an entirely new light on the apparently simple generality being illustrated,
or both writer and reader may be carried away by the richness of the
concrete instance to the neglect of the concept to be illustrated.

With these generalities in mind, it seems impossible to go much further without some *real* examples from the texts of the sixteenth and
seventeenth centuries. To begin, there is no author more appropriate
than Machiavelli, who was fascinated by problems of beginnings and
foundations. For him example had a crucial link with beginning and
with example's position at a threshold between fidelity to the origin of
example and fidelity to the controlling discourse that attempts to use
and subordinate what the past had left. The characteristics of example
summarized in this introduction are visibly at work in *The Prince* and
the *Discourses on the First Decade of Livy*.

Machiavelli: Example and Origin

Omnia mala exempla bonis initiis orta sunt.   —Julius Caesar

Examples for Machiavelli, as for Aristotle, are occurrences that reveal a general pattern across time. They link the past to the future, and thus allow us to make decisions in the present. A major problem, however, is that classical history, the source of most of Machiavelli's examples, is surrounded by an aura not compatible with a level and dispassionate view of recurrent cause and effect. Machiavelli alludes several times to the way his contemporaries, influenced by the humanist enthusiasm for antiquity, divide time into a legendary, heroic past of exemplary, almost godlike individuals, and a fallen, ordinary present filled with limited men. To be sure, princes are still praised, but present-day humanity is always competing against a gilded view of the past. To show his reader a more satisfying and useful way of looking at history, Machiavelli must insist on a break with the respectful preservation of the past. Claiming to write a text on a new science, Machiavelli attempts to fragment the continuum of history into a new, discontinuous collection of illustrative instances.

At each step of the way, however, he must take into account the almost magical effect of certain events that classical texts themselves portray as endowed with a kind of transcendent, supernatural quality. Livy, as the principal source of examples, moves in a direction largely opposed to Machiavelli, for Livy exalts origins, the virtues of olden days, and respect for events that reveal the intervention of inexplicable forces. Machiavelli cannot ignore the powerful attraction, for both the ancient Romans and humanist moderns, of these consecrated examples, designated explicitly by the term *exempla* in Livy's text. Yet Machiavelli perceives that both he, as writer, and the political leader have the power to make examples, to disrupt and recast society's memory of the past.[1]

Two initial discoveries permit the inquiries of *The Prince* and the *Discourses*. First, Machiavelli recognizes the mobility and availability (*disponibilité*) of the historical fact. Many readings of Machiavelli stress that his choice of examples follows the needs of the argument. He by no means subordinates his reasoning to the "facts" of history.[2] On the contrary, the deductive or rationalistic thrust of these texts bends brief historical narrative or allusion to the needs of a specific argumentative moment.[3] As Felix Gilbert observed, "Machiavelli used the material which experience offered in an almost arbitrary manner, and he transformed and stylized facts and events with freedom and ease."[4] Michael McCanles similarly recognizes the noninductive and even nonreferential character of Machiavelli's writing.[5] Second, Machiavelli accepts that others have already discovered that history can be manipulated and shaped into meaningful units or *exempla*. By accepting this, Machiavelli is prepared to enfold within his own rationalistic view of history the irrational itself, basis of much of historical exemplification.[6]

This chapter will attempt to deal with the complex and overlapping issues raised by Machiavelli by organizing them into three basic problems, affecting three categories of persons: authors, historical characters, and modern political leaders. The first problem is the relationship between Machiavelli's own writing and the historical texts he uses as his basis. This problem of authorship and origins involves a curious parallel between Machiavelli, as founder of a new science, and the political leader, as founder of a new regime. These parallel acts of creation involve both the use of the past and its partial obliteration. A second issue is Machiavelli's return to examples used by actual historical *characters*. Some famous figures like Cesare Borgia made examples in their political acts. Such acts are often staged as impressive spectacles. Under this category of spectacle, we consider Machiavelli's truly remarkable analysis of the phenomenon of "exemplary punishment." Finally, we confront Machiavelli's somewhat despairing avowal that while example is a powerful implement in the hands of the statesman, example may in fact not be able to alter the conduct of leaders themselves. In other words, example may be condemned to be a figure always turned irremediably toward the past, as justification for what has been done, and never toward the future, as effective guide to action. Therefore, contemplation of example in history may have a purely theoretical or even aesthetic value.

ORIGINS AND AUTHORSHIP

It is sometimes remembered that Machiavelli's *The Prince* is not a complete political theory but rather a treatise that emphasizes the challenges facing a *new* prince. It is less often recalled that a basic challenge to Machiavelli is that of establishing his own *new* writings on the practice of princely power.[7] The contrast between new and old is fundamental to the prince's situation as it is evoked in the first chapter of *The Prince*: "Princedoms are either hereditary, in which case their lord's ancestors have been the ruling princes for a long time, or they are new. The latter are either totally new, as was Milan for Francesco Sforza, or they are like appendages to the hereditary state of the prince who acquires them, as is the Kingdom of Naples for the King of Spain" (*P*, 7/97). From this point on *The Prince* is concerned with the difficulties and opportunities of the prince's newness. Machiavelli also faced the problem of newness in his role as author:

> Although the envious nature of men, so prompt to blame and so slow to praise, makes the discovery and introduction of any new principles and systems as dangerous almost as the exploration of unknown seas and continents, yet, animated by that desire which impels me to do what may prove for the common benefit of all, I have resolved to open a new route, which has not yet been followed by any one.[8]

This affirmation concerns both the newness of his doctrine—the content—and Machiavelli's role as speaker. Machiavelli expects that this new route (*una via, la quale, non essendo suta ancora da alcuno trita*) will bring him considerable difficulties by the reaction that it will provoke among the readership. His authority, like that of the new prince, runs against the habits that make old doctrines and old principalities easy to maintain.

Both Machiavelli and the new prince must deal with that strong force identified by Machiavelli as memory, which favors historically established princes or republics. The Romans had to face this problem in Gaul, Spain, and elsewhere in places where there had been earlier princes, "as long as people continued to remember those princedoms, the Romans were always uncertain of their hold on those states; once that memory was eradicated, with the power and permanence of the empire, their hold became secure" (*P*, 15/133). The memory of the old among the people of a new principality is so powerful that there are really

> no sure methods to keep possession of such states except devastation. Whoever becomes master of, but does not destroy, a city used to living as a free community may expect to be destroyed by it, because during an insurrection the city can always take refuge in invoking the name of freedom and its traditional institutions [*gli ordini antichi suoi*], which are never forgotten, whatever the course of time or whatever favors be accorded. (*P*, 16/139)

The prince can deal with memory in numerous ways, by toleration or by brutal extinction of the nation's cultural past. Things are not so simple, however, for Machiavelli as writer. He draws his lesson from memory itself, and the extinction of memory poses special problems. In the dedicatory letter to Lorenzo de' Medici at the beginning of *The Prince*, Machiavelli notes that his prize possession for offering to this ruler is "my knowledge of the deeds of great men, learned from wide experience of recent events and a constant reading of classical authors [una lunga esperienza delle cose moderne e una continua lezione delle antique]" (*P*, 5/93). The prince and the writer of political doctrine are therefore, it seems, opposed in their use of the past. One must attempt to eradicate the memory of the past while the other must constantly refer to it and examine it.

This opposition is more apparent than real, for both prince and writer must to some extent obliterate the past. The obvious princely destruction of the signs of the past draws our attention away from the subtle destruction that the writer must perform in his struggle for authority. In *The Prince* and the *Discourses*, one of the fundamental strategies for gaining authority is deliberate rupture and isolation at the moment of founding. Authority derives from the term *author* (Latin *auctor*) as originator or founder—Machiavelli uses the Italian word *autore* for those who found states and religions as well as for authoritative writers. The new prince is an originator by virtue of his newness but must overcome the people's sense of their own disrupted cultural origins. The very founding of a reign creates an apparently irresolvable tension with the other, earlier founding as transmitted to the present by cultural myth or memory. Yet a prince's problem of bringing discontinuity into a society that is committed to continuity, to its *costumi antichi*, is only a small part of Machiavelli's broad and almost obsessive concern for the originators of society and for the regeneration of society by a reenactment of that founding gesture. Because Rome is acknowledged both as the source or foundation of Florentine history and as the greatest example of a properly conducted republic, Romulus as founder of Rome occupies a special position in Machiavelli's work.[9] Romulus, like Moses, is not only remarkable for things he does deliberately and consciously, but for things that have isolated him as foundling and thus created the conditions for a proper founding. Romulus and Moses, the founding foundlings, are the purest examples of authorial separation from the past, of starting anew.[10]

The disconnection of Romulus and Moses from their own origins is a precondition of their ability to disrupt and begin states: "It was essential for Romulus not to remain in Alba, and for him to be exposed to die when he was born, so that he might become the king and founder of Rome" (*P*, 17/147). While in *The Prince* Machiavelli speaks of this necessary isolation of the founder in a context of the struggle for survival that creates *virtù*, the *Discourses* broaden the consideration of this solitude. Romulus is seen as separated not only from his paternal origin but from all others. He constituted a unique *autore* whose concentrated authority was unmixed, undivided, and not transmitted to heirs:

> Many will perhaps consider it an evil example [*di cattivo esemplo*] that the founder of a civil society, as Romulus was, should first have killed his brother, and then have consented to the death of Titus Tatius, who had been elected to share the royal authority with him. . . . But we must assume, as a general rule, that it never or rarely happens that a republic or monarchy is well constituted . . . unless it is done by only one individual; it is even necessary that he whose mind has conceived such a constitution should be alone in carrying it into effect. (*D*, 94/138)

Solitude at the moment of action is joined to a rupture between the founder and his successors, for Machiavelli specifies that "The lawgiver should . . . be sufficiently wise and virtuous not to leave this authority which he has assumed either to his heirs or to any one else . . . " (*D*, 95/139).[11] Machiavelli's idealized description of the founder of a nation thus indicates that such an *autore* must be deprived—at least provisionally—of a connection with the past, especially with his own family past, that he must ruthlessly isolate himself in the present, and that he must assure for the future that he has no heirs.

This invigorating isolation also appears in Machiavelli's description of early Rome's separation in space, a separation that is—like Romulus's fratricide—a cutting away. Rome destroyed the neighboring cities, says Machiavelli, to make the city of Rome itself grow larger. In this, "The Romans acted like a good husbandman who . . . cuts off the first shoots a tree puts out, so that by retaining the sap and vigor in the trunk the tree may afterwards put forth more abundant branches and fruit" (D, 189/289). The simile of the good husbandman (*buono cultivatore*) unites a number of the negative or destructive concepts typical of Machiavelli with the positive concept of production and growth. It is probably not by chance that this husbandman does not merely prune the plant but prunes specifically the first shoots (*primi rami*), thus accentuating the connection of destruction to newness. Pruning, cutting away, snuffing out, killing—these are all the necessary actions of a founder of states, of gardens, and even of religions. In the *Discourses* the creation or imposition of a religion is linked to the "extinguishing of memory" (*queste memorie de' tempi per diverse cagioni si spengono*). Christianity wiped out the ancient rituals and theology (*ogni memoria di quella antica teologia*), but the Church failed in its attempt at total innovation by maintaining the Latin language, through which antiquity transmitted the deeds of the excellent men of that religion (*D*, 192/296).

The vast network of Machiavelli's comments on founders and on the importance of origins may seem at first to have little to do with Machiavelli's self-presentation as author, but a closer look shows an essential similarity. Machiavelli's work, after all, draws on historical example, and the *Discourses* are an explicit commentary or gloss upon the preeminent historian of Roman origins, Livy, author of *Ab urbe condita*.[12] Yet Machiavelli, in *The Prince* and the *Discourses*, is not acting as historian. He is a commentator or metahistorian fascinated by the power of memory and by the struggle of founders to destroy that memory or, at least, to attenuate and control it. In announcing the newness of his own work, Machiavelli wrestles with the distinction between his text and that of others. The decisive difference is that Machiavelli is a pruner, cutting back the lush growth of history.

The introduction to the second book of the *Discourses* presents Machiavelli's major criticism of the effect of historiography and of the historical vision:

> Men ever praise the olden time, and find fault with the present, though often without reason. They are such partisans of the past that they extol not only the times which they know only by the accounts left of them by historians, but, having grown old, they also laud all they remember to have seen in their youth. . . . we never know the whole truth about the past, and very frequently writers conceal such events as would reflect disgrace upon their century, whilst they magnify and amplify those that lend lustre to it. (*D*, 177/271)

The problem of the past is that we do not know *all* about it, and what we do know is probably falsified to some extent. The problem of the present is that we do know *all* about it, but even then the facts are falsified by our personal prejudices and emotions:

> It is very different with the affairs of the present, in which we ourselves are either actors or spectators, and of which we have a complete knowledge, nothing being concealed from us; and knowing the good together with many other things that are displeasing to us, we are forced to conclude that the present is inferior to the past, though in reality it may be much more worthy of glory and fame. (*D*, 177/271–72)

What is not hidden, what is totally known (*le quali per la intera cognizione di esse non ti essendo in alcuna parte nascoste*) is just as misleading as what is only partially known. We are here back at the situation of any founder, any *autore*, confronted with the necessity of cutting away, of destroying something in order to provide for growth. Romulus, we recall, had not only to be separated from his past but to isolate himself in the present. Similarly the new prince must extinguish the memory of the past while also killing off all those living persons—notably the aristocracy—who approach him in rank and power.[13]

Machiavelli's situation as author, as founder of a new discourse, does not require annihilation of other contemporary writers, but it does require sacrifice of a mass of knowledge and of feeling that has blinded humanity to truths associated with history. If complete knowledge of the present prevents us from seeing the truth of the present, then Machiavelli must reduce the present to an abstraction by excising the pertinent features and leaving the remainder behind, by "alienating" those features from our experience through a kind of *Verfremdungseffekt*. Such a strategy is undoubtedly behind the glorification, in *The Prince*, of Cesare Borgia as the perfect prince, forcing the reader of that work (particularly the contemporary Florentine reader) to distinguish between subjective loathing and objective recognition of skill.[14] In regard to the past, which we know incompletely, Machiavelli must fight our tendency to believe what has been written by demystifying the ancient writers so that we do not believe ourselves essentially inferior. This too requires a cutting away or sacrifice so that Machiavelli, like Romulus, can begin without a past, fresh, and unswerving, even if he later (like Romulus rediscovering his grandfather) selectively readmits portions of the past.[15]

In presenting his own work as new, Machiavelli declares a resolute isolation from the influences around him and describes himself as desiring "to perform without respect those things which I believe bring a common good to each person" (*D*, 73/103). This is an allusion to the corruption of historians who have allowed political pressure to distort the accounts they leave posterity. Declaring authorial independence is a way of establishing an authority different from that of the prince and beyond the feelings of the present. This isolation of the author unites the sacrifice metaphors to the simile of perspective in the dedicatory letter of *The Prince*, where distance from the object of knowledge is presented as indispensable:

> I trust that it will not be deemed presumptuous if a man of low
> and inferior condition ventures to treat of, and establish rules for,

a prince's administration. People who draw landscapes proceed to a low point on a plain in order to study the nature of mountains and higher elevations: they proceed to mountaintops in order to study the nature of the lowlands. Just so, to understand the nature of the people fully, one must be a prince; to understand the nature of princes fully, one must be of the people.

[Né voglio sia reputata presunzione se uno uomo di basso ed infimo stato ardisce discorrere e regolare e governi de'principi; perché, così come coloro che disegnano e paesi si pongono bassi nel piano a considerare la natura de'monti e de'luoghi alti e, per considerare quella de'bassi, si pongono alti sopra e monti; similmente, a conoscere bene la natura de'populi, bisogna essere principe, e a conoscere bene quella de'principi, bisogna essere populare.] (P, 5/95)

All true understanding is, therefore, understanding from the outside. Yet, while Machiavelli is extremely "modern" in espousing an epistemology of exteriority, he is also engaged in a rivalry of sorts with the prince in regard to sources of authority. Machiavelli's perspective simile indicates that learning entails a certain lacuna or a blindspot, which limits both speakers and publics. What we say and what we write contain the trace of our own distance from what we speak of, just as the drawing that is made of the lowlands records its viewpoint, and therefore its separation, by omitting the mountaintop.

Our relation to past and present involves problems of perspective, varying between excessive distance and excessive closeness. The only exception consists—oddly—in those "matters pertaining to the arts, which shine by their intrinsic merits, which time can neither add to nor diminish" (D, 177/272). In this unusual assertion of the transcendence of the artistic object, which does not depend on the attitude or circumstances of the viewer, Machiavelli ascribes to the work of art an immanent clarity (tanta chiarezza in sé) requiring no further labor to disengage or distance the work from human passion. In dealing with historical factuality, on the other hand, we suffer from the writer's excessive proximity to a particular viewpoint. Art is already distant, whereas the Machiavellian text, dealing with things that might touch us closely, must make itself distant from both political power and the passions of everyday experience.

In the letter to Lorenzo, the near/far dichotomy of the perspective metaphor is matched by the opposition between contraction and expansion. Condensation, selection, and elimination are the processes by which the text came into being. The precious gift that Machiavelli

presents is based, we recall, on a continual study or reading (*lezione*)
of ancient history: "I have extensively and diligently scrutinized and
thought through these matters; I have now reduced them into a little
volume which I send to Your Magnificence" (*P*, 5/93). The concept of
reduction that appears here for the first time in *The Prince* is actually
part of a semantic paradox in Machiavelli's Italian. *Ridurre* means "to
reduce," as it is translated here, but it also can mean "to bring back, to
recall." In the latter sense, *ridurre* is frequently used by Machiavelli to
introduce examples, as when he begins an account of the experiences
of Pope Alexander VI in governing the ecclesiastical territories by saying, "la qual cosa, ancora che sia nota, non mi pare superfluo ridurla in
buona parte alla memoria" (*P*, 31/213). If we did not translate but
transliterate this expression into English, we would have something
like "reduce to memory," and, although this (dimininishing or reducing) is not literally what Machiavelli is doing when he provides an example, the etymological kinship that the Italian maintains from the
Latin *reducere* is worth remembering. Every time an example appears
in a text, we know that history is being subordinated to some form of
argument and is being contained in a manifest ideological framework.[16] Therefore, both the condensation described in the terms *in uno
piccolo volume ridotte* and the insertion explicit in the expression *ridurre
a memoria* belong to the same evocation of Machiavelli's compositional
process, which he represents as a form of extraction and refinement.

Extraction of what is significant in history contrasts with the prevalent bad use of history. In the proemium to the first book, Machiavelli
attributes the lack of science in governance to a failure to follow the
examples of antiquity. This failure derives from "the lack of real
knowledge of history, the true sense of which is not known, or the
spirit of which they [men] do not comprehend. Thus the majority of
those who read it take pleasure only in the variety of the events which
history relates, without ever thinking of imitating the noble actions
. . . " (*D*, 74/104). The pleasure in variety (*varietà degli accidenti*) conveys mankind's inability to reduce history to what is significant. Variety is a form of the massive excess of history, which Machiavelli must
pare away, keeping only what is useful. It is hardly surprising that the
perspective metaphor of the letter yields here to a simile from sculpture: "how often . . . a great price is paid for some fragments of an
antique statue, which we are anxious to possess to ornament our
houses with, or to give to artists who strive to imitate them in their
own works . . . " (*D*, 73/104). Machiavelli chooses to speak of fragments rather than of a statue in its integrity, for the fragment has a
greater mobility—commercial, physical, and aesthetic—than a whole

statue. The commercial value of the fragment may derive from its rarity and suggestive incompleteness. But the really important aspect of this object is in the use we can make of it. Its unity as a work lost, the ancient statue now consists of smaller pieces, which can be integrated into new contexts. Representation is no longer the dominant purpose. When given to the artist to imitate, the fragment can be assimilated into a new artistic vernacular.[17] No longer as works but as pieces, the art of antiquity can form a series of paradigms or storehouses for the modern artistic vernacular.

Machiavelli's avowed purpose is to gain for the historical *exemplum* the dignity and utility of the statuary fragment. This simile is complemented by the reference to the judicial rules, which are more useful than history because they have undergone the process of reduction, of fragmentation and redistribution. Laws are "reduced to a system" (*ridutte in ordine*, D, 74/104—an expression that can, depending on context, be read as reduced to an order or brought back in an order). As useful parts that are within our power of manipulation but do not produce the effect of paralysis induced by the variety of history as a whole, example, like judicial precedent and the pieces of a statue, can only result from a discontinuity imposed on a previous wholeness.

Choosing to set forth a *new* way to understand politics through a limited reading, Machiavelli is aware of the difficulty of having to depend upon the past while blocking access to it, throwing his own text as a filter between us and Livy. It is much easier to create a theory out of nothing, asserts Machiavelli in the celebrated passage in which he speaks of the *verità effetuale della cosa* (P, 40/255), the actual truth of things or "the truth of the matter as facts."[18] Many have described imaginary states that "have never in fact been seen or known to exist." The danger of such writing is that the distance between how one lives and how one *should* live is so great that a prince who leaves behind what is done for what should be done learns how to ruin himself. This facile distinction between the real and the ideal—intended to distinguish Machiavelli's text from those of many precedent theoreticians all the way back to Plato, while advertising his importance to the prince—temporarily sets aside the more important distinction that occurs elsewhere in Machiavelli between one real occurrence and another, between different fragments of history and their respective values. The difficulty of this enterprise of dealing with the materials—it is tempting to say, the detritus—of history appears if we associate another statue simile to the one given above. The founder of a new republic must also wrestle with the effects of memory, though it is easier to govern people who are without memory:

And doubtless, if any one wanted to establish a republic at the present time, he would find it much easier with the simple mountaineers, who are almost without any civilization, than with such as are accustomed to live in cities, where civilization is already corrupt; as a sculptor finds it easier to make a fine statue out of a crude block of marble than out of a statue badly begun by another. (*D*, 100/148)

Sculpture reappears as model of political foundation, but in this latter simile Machiavelli indulges in the nostalgia for a fresh start, *without* fragments, a start comparable to that of the imaginers of states that have never existed. The problem is the problem of beginning, and the badly started statue (a marble *male abbozzato da altrui*) constrains the would-be founder. If one begins with a crude block of marble, one must destroy all that stands in the way of the final design. The statue badly begun is worse than a fragment, which can give a suggestion but can never itself be a beginning, only something from before the beginning. Machiavelli's approach to history exorcises the mass by extracting the significant detail but must still deal with much that is *male abbozzato*.

Machiavelli's vision of history does, however, contain a place for this absence of example—this purely ideal state started from a true origin—in the history of Rome. Referring to Rome's fashion of associating conquered states rather than making them subjects, Machiavelli asserts that "the plan adopted by the Romans . . . is the more to be admired as they had no previous example to guide them [non c'era innanzi a Roma esemplo]" (*D*, 191/295). Pointing to recent mistakes of the Venetians, Machiavelli declares, "they deserve the more blame, as they had less excuse, having before their eyes the method practised by the Romans, which they might have followed, whilst the Romans, having no precedents to guide them, had to develop the system exclusively by their own sagacity [i Romani sanza alcuno esemplo] (*D*, 223/348). By casting the Romans into the role of a people beyond time and without the need to fragment history, to reduce it in order to imitate it, Machiavelli justifies his own use of the Livian text as an originary and absolute block on which to exercise his extractive force. If the Romans are a people without precedents yet not imaginary, then Machiavelli can deal with the *verità effetuale* while at the same time dealing with the kind of absolute that appeals to writers of abstract political theory. In effect, the gap between the ideal (*come si dovrebbe vivere*) and the real (*come si vive*) is closed by the Romans since even what seems to have been bad about Rome turns out to be an effective good if the proper distance from the details is assumed.

Machiavelli makes a telling remark on the possible effect of Livy on a reader who does not adopt the Machiavellian attitude. In seeing all the struggles between plebes and patricians, one might conclude that Roman society was full of disorder and therefore not a proper guide for a constitutional organization. Machiavelli insists that the larger picture of this "disorder" reveals the best possible republican order:

> I maintain that those who blame the quarrels of the Senate and the people of Rome condemn that which was the very origin of liberty, and that they were probably more impressed by the cries and noise which these disturbances occasioned in the public places, than by the good effect which they produced. . . . Nor can we regard a republic as disorderly where so many virtues were seen to shine [*dove siano tanti esempli di virtù*]. For good examples [*li buoni esempli*] are the result of good education, and good education is due to good laws; and good laws in their turn spring from those very agitations which have been so inconsiderately condemned by many. . . . all these things can alarm only those who read of them. (*D*, 83/119–20)

Reading Livy can be misleading without the Machiavellian filter, which silences for us the cries of the senate and of the people. The disorder of Rome can be seen as a disorder in the apprehension of the history of Rome in which the signs, the *buoni esempli*, are obscured by the *grida*, the inarticulate noise of the mass. Once again in this passage example is the figure that spans the distance between Machiavelli's "new" way of understanding and the daily experience of mankind, in other words, the gulf between theoretical discourse and historical reality. Machiavelli speaks of the production of examples as internal to the historical process itself and not external to it, not only what the writer does to history. The order of example rises by progressive refinement from agitation to laws, from laws to education, from education to good examples, which are *tanti esempli di virtù*. What Machiavelli seems to do here is to establish his text as the ultimate instrument of historical progression (a progression perhaps not so much chronological as conceptual), for he extracts from the Livian account the most significant examples from among those formed in the inexorable workings of historical struggle. In doing this he protects his reader from the excessive information of the Livian texts.

This curious duplicity between Machiavelli and the historical process that he uncovers is, in certain important passages, connected with the conscious production of example by political leaders. This conscious exemplification, as opposed to the unconscious and purely mechanical or abstract process of events (from agitation to laws, etc.) is a reminder of the parallel that repeatedly occurs between Machiavelli and the political-historical *autori* or founders. Both are concerned with the control of the people's memory, *la memoria delle cose antiche*, and with the total or selective destruction thereof.

THE SPECTACLE OF HISTORY

Political leaders have historically been active in providing examples and making use of them. Many of Machiavelli's examples are examples in the second degree: accounts of princes or republics furnishing or using examples. In practice this activity of historical figures is based on the creation of spectacle, exemplary appearances in which some doctrine or general principle shines forth. Machiavelli's choice of historical incidents worthy of the name example stresses visibility and invisiblity. All example serves rhetorically as the tangible instance of an intangible general law. Occasionally the goal of political leaders is to prevent their subjects or citizens from seeing certain things. When the leader fails, the glimpsed truth becomes the example of a deeper and dangerous continuity. On the other hand, leaders sometimes need to break the routine with a spectacle that conveys a set of laws or challenges the public to believe that there *is* a higher law, however mysterious.

Machiavelli describes these *esempli* in many major passages of the *Discourses* and *The Prince*, passages in which his attempt at dispassionate analysis does not always eliminate the mystical quality that is a component of the example's effect on the people. Machiavelli does not always view these historical creations of example as a voluntary or conscious project of the political class; he is concerned with the content and the effect of example, once recuperated by those in power. The control of appearances has, as a subcategory, concealment, the basis of the deceit so often ascribed to the Machiavellian leader. But deceit should be understood in the larger context of the production and interpretation of appearance. For one thing, many, probably most, of the appearances created *in* the historical world (as opposed to those appearances shaped explicitly by the historiographer) cannot be classified as either true or false. Indeed certain *esempli*, designated as such, are appearances in search of the necessary generality or law they must have, for every example is an example *of* something. In other instances the political class has specifically created laws that generate examples.

Maintaining appearances, the political leader alternately keeps the lid on the hidden continuity of human nature and provides outlets or vents for the pressure of this universal force. Machiavelli supposes that such pressure is not punctual but continuous and that it is still there even when it is not perceptible. Through this belief in the existence of that which is not seen, Machiavelli creates a parallel between human nature and a broader epistemological conception of the continuity of forces, which human intellect can seize only in the ventings or out-croppings we call examples. The two notions are linked early in the *Discourses*:

> All those who have written upon civil institutions demonstate (and history is full of examples to support them) that whoever desires to found a state and give it laws, must start with assuming that all men are bad and ever ready to display their vicious nature, whenever they may find occasion for it. If their evil disposition remains concealed for a time, it must be attributed to some un-known reason; and we must assume that it lacked occasion to show itself; but time, which has been said to be the father of all truth, does not fail to bring it to light.
> [Come dimostrano tutti coloro che ragionano del vivere civile, e come ne è piena di esempli ogni istoria, è necessario a chi dispone una republica ed ordina leggi in quella, presupporre tutti gli uo-mini rei, e che li abbiano sempre a usare la malignità dello animo loro, qualunque volta ne abbiano libera occasione; e quando al-cuna malignità sta occulta un tempo, procede da una occulta ca-gione, che, per non si essere veduta esperienza del contrario, non si conosce: ma la fa poi scoprire il tempo, il quale dicono essere padre d'ogni verità.] (*D*, 81–82/117)[19]

The writers who describe human society are concerned with a clarifi-cation of mechanisms for which our terminology is frequently visual. Machiavelli writes of demonstration (*dimostrano*, from the Latin *mon-strare*), and although this choice of a visual term is not entirely free, since Western languages generally force us to use the catachresis of sight for comprehension or persuasive proof, Machiavelli continues the emphasis in plainly deliberate ways as the passage continues. What is shown by the examples of history is that men show their evil nature whenever they have an opportunity to take it out of its concealment (where it *sta occulta*). Why this nature remains hidden most of the time is a matter that we do not know (or cannot see, because this reason is also *una occulta cagione*). Eventually though, in time, what is hidden (and perhaps the reason for the hiding) will come forth.[20]

There is a certain nervousness and insecurity in Machiavelli's tone as he introduces the study of appearances and concealment, a nervousness that has left stylistic evidence in his use of what I elsewhere call the hyperbolic-litotic example ("history is *full* of examples").[21] Machiavelli's insecurity derives in part from the realization that all appearances (and with them all examples) are to some extent fabrications. The normal appearance of men is a fiction that serves the purposes of the individuals concerned and also the purposes of society to the extent that laws are meant to keep the evil on the inside, where it does less social harm than when it has a chance to manifest itself. The revelation of the evil within men is also a fabrication of the view of action constructed within the temporal perspective that history affords.

The appearances of normal good are treated by Machiavelli quite explicitly as *examples* produced by the strictures of the foresighted legislator. Such examples have already been mentioned in conjunction with the creation of good examples through good laws: "good examples are the result of good education, and good education is due to good laws and good laws . . . spring from those . . . agitations" (*D*, 83/119–20). The equation between example and fabricated appearance could not be clearer. Good examples are produced by a social organization to perpetuate certain behavior.

In saying that good laws lead to good examples, Machiavelli leaves open the exact use of the term *example*, though the context makes it seem that examples are not purely demonstrative—that is, not merely the manifestation of law—but injunctive or imitative, meant to perpetuate certain behavior. For the theorist, good examples are useful in constructing or reconstructing the laws manifested in them. For the social man, examples are useful in enforcing laws that should be known but that slip into a form of political unconscious if they are not reinforced or reaffirmed by example.

In view of what Machiavelli says about the origins of society and especially about the example of Romulus the founder, it is not surprising that example often connotes violence. As appearance, example must be vivid, memorable, and persuasive, and must also be in a situation of contrast with some background in which the exemplified quality or act is lacking or invisible. Many of Machiavelli's examples concern precisely the tension between concealment and revelation. In these cases neither what appears on the surface nor what is under the surface is exemplary. Instead the contrast between the two and the putative expenditure of energy or force constitute the exemplary phenomenon. One class of appearances that preoccupies Machiavelli concerns the cloaking of innovation in ancient forms. Such concealment illustrates *a contrario* the priority of example over law in governing people, and it demonstrates as well the malleability of example, its capacity for attachment to different systems of law. If appearance and essence are ever concomitant and equivalent, it is in the moment of the founding example of those like Romulus. Other leaders, if they cannot be full *autori* and annihilate the past in a new beginning, must use the appearances of the past while emptying them:

> He who desires or attempts to reform the government of a state, and wishes to have it accepted and capable of maintaining itself to the satisfaction of everybody, must at least retain the semblance of the old forms; so that it may seem to the people that there has been no change in the institutions, even though in fact they are entirely different from the old ones. For the great majority of mankind are satisfied with appearances, as though they were realities, and are often even more influenced by the things that seem than by those that are [lo universale degli uomini si pascono così di quel che pare come di quello che è: anzi molte volte si muovono più per le cose che paiono che per quelle che sono]. (*D*, 122/182)

Appearance is both necessary and sufficient to reassure the people, because the people are moved by such *signs* or authority, appearances that link the present with the past. The people are thus seeking a kind of continuity, which often requires the breaking apart of law and its outward trappings, between forms and orders. It is important that the readers of the *Discourses*, like the political leader, be aware of the rupture of being and appearance, but it is necessary that the people be unaware of such a contrast. What strikes the people particularly is the sudden appearance of change, by which the discrepancy between appearance and being is revealed. Such a sudden manifestation occurs in the example of Appius Claudius, who changed "too suddenly from one quality to the extreme opposite" (*D*, 148/225). Appius's slip, which revealed by an *atypical* display his deeper character, links the spectacle of example to its rarity: the exhibition of his evil disposition would have been less striking and not exemplary if he had always behaved that way. But rarity characterizes examples of an entirely different order when an occurrence is not merely unusual on the scale of individual persons but on that of a whole nation. Exceptional occurrences, witnessed by many people, become the basis of social cohesion by suggesting the existence of a superior regularity or norm. The exceptional display—particularly when it is violent and bloody—reorders all values and establishes a new hierarchy.

Machiavelli's texts refer frequently to scenes of death and dismemberment, scenes not only embodied in the text in examples but described as a principal source of useful social exemplification. This use of appearance as spectacle is governed by an economy of rarity that links it with example in general. Machiavelli accentuates the seemingly gratuitous and irrational character of such displays. In a chapter entitled "How much the soldiers of our time differ from the ancient orders," Machiavelli begins by declaring:

> The most important battle ever fought by the Romans in any war was that with the Latins during the consulate of Torquatus and Decius. As by the loss of this battle the Latins, as a matter of course, became slaves to the Romans, so would the latter have become slaves to the Latins if these had been victorious. Titus Livius is also of the same opinion; and represents the two armies to have been in all respects equal as regards numbers, discipline, bravery, and obstinacy, the only difference having been in the commanders, those of the Roman army having displayed more skill and heroism than those of the Latins. We also observe, in the course of this battle, two unprecedented occurrences and of which there are since then few examples; for to sustain the courage of their soldiers, and render them obedient to command and more determined in action, one of the two Consuls killed himself, and the other slew his son.
>
> [La più importante giornata che fu mai fatta in alcuna guerra con alcuna nazione dal Popolo romano, fu questa che ei fece con i popoli latini nel consolato di Torquato e di Decio. Perché ogni ragione vuole che così sarebbero stati servi i Romani, quando non l'avessino vinta. E di questa opinione é Tito Livio: perché in ogni parte fa gli eserciti pari di ordine, di virtù, d'ostinazione e di numero; solo vi fa differenza che i capi dello esercito romano furono più virtuosi che quelli dello esercito latino. Vedesi ancora come nel maneggio di questa giornata nacquono due accidenti non prima nati, e che dipoi hanno radi esempli: che di due Consoli, per tenere fermi gli animi de' soldati ed ubbidienti a' comandamenti loro e diliberati al combattere, l'uno ammazzò se stesso e l'altro il figliuolo.] (*D*, 209–10/326)

Machiavelli emphasizes, as central to his version of the event, that the two deaths are unprecedented and that there are few examples (*radi esempli*) of subsequent similar acts. The rarity of these acts is heightened by their occurrence in the (perhaps hyperbolically described) most important battle in all of Roman history, a battle chosen ostensibly to illustrate Machiavelli's belief that the ancient organization of infantry is superior to the medieval one. Curiously, however, such an illustration is based on a case in which the organization of the infantry was not the deciding factor in victory, for both armies were organized in the same fashion and were equal in every other respect. The Roman leaders, though, had more *virtù*—and after saying this Machiavelli passes abruptly with few words to the one manifestation of this force that seems to have tipped the balance in favor of the Romans: two unprecedented incidents. After the passage quoted, Machiavelli repetitiously returns to the similarity of the two combatant armies, which have the same language, discipline, arms, and titles. Before passing on to a review of the three battle lines used by the Romans, Machiavelli declares that the equality of the two forces was such that it was necessary that "something extraordinary should occur" for one side to win, and identifies that factor by saying "partly chance and partly the heroism of the Consuls gave occasion to Torquatus to sacrifice his son, and Decius to kill himself."

Here out of a background of exceptional—and exceptionally emphasized—equality arises a nation that is different. This encounter is not only the battle in which one nation arises out of two, but the battle in which difference arises out of sameness.[22] Only retrospectively can the kernel of that emerging difference be perceived, since before the battle it was invisible—the difference between the leaders of the two nations. This difference is invisible because it was caused by what followed the confrontation; it is a difference in the historiography of this event. The Roman leaders differ, thereafter and in history, not only from the Latin leaders but from all previous leaders. They emerge, as the Roman nation itself does so often, as acting without example and therefore as examples of the *absolute difference*. Once again Machiavelli confirms the structure of example as being the irruption of extreme difference from a context characterized as lacking difference, as bland and normal.

Machiavelli offers no clues why suicide and filicide should give courage to the Roman soldiers, and the context, through its absence of detail, leads one to believe that only the extreme and extraordinary nature of such violence matters.[23] In Livy's account, the death of Decius the consul is a sacrifice to all the supernal and infernal gods. Decius recited prescribed prayers and charged into the Latin ranks bringing terror to the enemy as if he were a supernatural being, and bringing assurance to the Roman army that all the anger of the gods would be concentrated on him. Livy's account includes comments on the failure of more recent Romans to observe similar pious rules of sacrifice and gives to Decius a much less original and unprecedented role than he has in Machiavelli's version. Machiavelli has altered the Livian description of this incident by transforming Decius from an observer of a traditional, patriotic, and sacrificial mode to an originator of a new and memorable form of semiotic violence. This rearrangement is in keeping with Machiavelli's quest for both originary examples and the exceptional. As Barberi-Squarotti observes, "Machiavelli is not interested in the reality, the modalities, nor even the phenomenology of events, but only in their mythic and exemplary form."[24]

We touch here at a part of Machiavelli's thought that cannot be contained entirely within the perfectly rational conception that many entertain of the writer of the *Discourses*. The sacrifice of Decius can be rationalized in many ways, especially as an example of the importance of religious forms in giving courage to troops on the eve of battle. Machiavelli performs such a reduction elegantly in the example of the Pollarius (which we will consider shortly). But in Decius's case Machiavelli does not surround the mention of this extraordinary event with any explanation that would fit the death into a maxim of military governance, nor does he give, as Livy does, a balanced account of the relative effect of Decius's self-sacrifice compared with Manlius's clever use of his reserve forces—although organization of infantry is the explicit subject of the chapter. Instead Machiavelli surrounds Decius's death with mystery, conveying it as entirely self-inflicted (*l'uno ammazzò se stesso*) and beyond the bounds of precedent.[25] Far from using Livy here as the raw material for a refinement into rational system, Machiavelli produces a far more bizarre and gratuitously macabre effect.

A more rational and manipulative intent appears in Machiavelli's thoughts on the spectacle of sacrifice later in the *Discourses*. In the introduction to book 3, he elaborates a doctrine of exemplary sacrifice that uses such appearances as a means of reminding people of their origins.[26] Two important themes of Machiavelli's thought are connected in such deaths: the importance of appearances that can manifest the hidden or forgotten laws and the link between example and origin.

Machiavelli begins the third book, devoted to the example of individual men who made Rome great, with the chapter entitled "To assure a long life to a sect or a republic it is necessary to bring it back often to its origin." Machiavelli points out that the greatest danger to any body is progressive disorganization or entropy. The form of the body must be refreshed or renewed, or as Machiavelli says, bodies must be led back to their beginnings (*riducano verso i principii loro*). This return can be caused by an external event, like a war, or by an internal factor, either a law or a leader. In fact these two causes turn out to be only one, since the law, says Machiavelli, requires a virtuous citizen to give it vigor. At the same time, men act only in terms of institutions, either by creating or recreating them. No individual is of importance to Machiavelli except in this perspective.[27] The simple affirmation that states need capable leaders, however, is not particularly original or profound. Machiavelli goes on to profess a more striking belief in spectacular public executions:

> The most striking instances of such execution of the laws, anterior to the capture of Rome by the Gauls, were the death of the sons of Brutus, that of the Decemvirs, and that of the corn-dealer, Spurius Maelius; and after the taking of Rome by the Gauls, the death of Manlius Capitolinus, that of the son of Manlius Torquatus, the punishment inflicted by Papirius Cursor upon his master of cavalry, Fabius, and the accusations of the Scipios. As these were excessive and remarkable cases they caused on each occasion a return of the citizens to the original principles of the republic; and when they began to be more rare, it also began to afford men more latitude in becoming corrupt. [Le quali cose, perché erano eccessive e notabili, qualunque volta ne nasceva una, facevano gli uomini ritirare verso il segno: e quando le cominciarono ad essere più rare, cominciarono anche a dare più spazio agli uomini di corrompersi.] (D, 254/399)

Like the sacrifice of Decius most of these executions involve the spectacle of punishment, and the concept of punishment serves to justify the spectacle of death. Exemplary punishment produces fear in potential evildoers, so the usual argument runs, and leads them to reason, "If I act in the way this criminal acted, then the same punishment will be inflicted on me." Michel Foucault has called this approach the "rule of lateral effects," by which punishment becomes more important for the public than for the criminal.[28] This conception seems almost adequate for a small number of the public executions mentioned with relish by Machiavelli, but most of the spectacular executions escape this simple explanation. Instead, I think, the exemplary punishment model is a weak and purely intellectual way of describing those useful social sacrifices that punctuate Machiavelli's text and seem to have the same effect whether or not the person executed is guilty of a crime. Whereas the usual notion of exemplary punishment is based on simple logic of imitation (if A behaves like B, A's punishment will follow the pattern of B's punishment), in Machiavelli the most effective punishments are explicitly detached from ordinary imitation. Machiavelli is here close to a phenomenology of example that provides the basis for even the "ordinary" notion of exemplary punishment, but which everyday rationalism finds difficult to accept. A punishment is exemplary to the extent that it *exceeds* the requirements of the crime being sanctioned. This excess distinguishes "exemplary punishment" from "punishment," for the latter is addressed to a defined case while the former is addressed beyond both criminal and crime to a wider audience, reducing the immediate instance to the status of pretext.

All of the cases cited here by Machiavelli can be seen as a form of exemplary punishment, punishment that ranges far beyond the ordinary and is "excessive and remarkable." Machiavelli's doctrine here approaches the conception of the *felix culpa*, the "fortunate sin" of Christian theology, by which Adam gave God the chance to show His love for mankind by sacrificing His Son (compare the legal dictum, *Ex malis moribus bonae leges natae sunt*).[29] The "crimes" of these individuals provided the occasion for an unusual and fearful spectacle, which reinvigorated not only the observation of particular laws transgressed by those executed, but all the institutions of Roman society. Once again the idea of rarity shapes the example. To be effective, the punishments must be exceptional and impress the people. An exceptional punishment is only warranted by an exceptional crime. The rarefaction of such crime would diminish the occasions for such execution. Hence criminals can strengthen the social order by serving as pretexts for ritual executions, yet too many criminals and executions would render punishments ordinary and thus lacking in the quality of remarkableness that Machiavelli considers necessary.

A way out of this circle is afforded by an approach placing priority on the execution. In some ways a remarkable execution is what makes the crime itself remarkable, and a look at some of the expiatory victims enumerated by Machiavelli justifies this description. When Manlius Torquatus killed his son for having fought the Gauls victoriously, the punishment had a tragic, paradoxical, disproportionate quality. When Quintus Fabius was destined to be killed by order of Lucius Papirius Cursor after an overwhelming victory by Fabius's troops against the Samnites, the outcry of soldiers, tribunes, and people on behalf of the victorious general prevented his execution on charges of disobedience to the orders of the dictator Papirius.[30] These are two cases of excessive and even inverted institutional reaction to the act of a citizen. In both cases a victor is punished for the action that led to his victory. The punishment is merited, in the contrary view, by the paramount importance of preserving the chain of military command. Without the victory the punishment would be of no importance and would not generate an example. Many sanctions meted out for disobedience to orders are ordinary and therefore do not serve the purpose of returning to the founding principles. Furthermore, without victory the offense might not have merited capital punishment since the crime would not have generated a dangerous example. The exemplary nature of the crime permits and requires the exemplary punishment, which is, in some ways, seen as the punishment of the innocent and the sacrifice of a hero.[31] The punishment, we have said, makes the crime itself remarkable, or even "creates" the crime to the extent that punishment when unexpected defines retroactively what was permissible. Something that otherwise would not have appeared as a crime is thus constituted as such by the sanction. There may have been—indeed, there almost certainly were—occasions for the conversion of individual initiative into public punishment, but no leader seized the occasion to perform this dialectical act (dialectical in the sense that an individual's virtue heightens the effect of his punishment while the punishment accentuates both the virtue and the crime).

One of the most unusual things about Machiavelli's description of the use of punishments in returning to origins is his specific schedule. There should be at least one such execution every ten years:

> It would be desirable . . . that not more than ten years should elapse between such executions, for in the long course of time men begin to change their customs, and to transgress the laws; and unless some case occurs that recalls the punishment to their memory and revives the fear in their hearts, the delinquents will soon become so numerous that they cannot be punished without danger. (*D*, 254/400)

Such a schedule strengthens the view that punishment makes the exceptional crime, since the need for a spectacular execution has an independent regularity, measured by time elapsed rather than on a case by case basis. Instead of the victim, Machiavelli has in mind the needs of the potential criminals, the people in general, who require that law be recalled (*si riduca loro a memoria*) by an example.

This striking nonpenal conception of punishment, directed at the people through the vehicle of the criminal, becomes more unusual when linked to the purely sacrificial gesture of the good man. Oddly enough, the appearance of a good man and the execution of a bad man are equivalent and interchangeable events and have the same effect of bringing back the memory of origins. Although Machiavelli says that such a good man can have an effect without a law that leads him to inflict a spectacular punishment, the gesture that impresses the people is generally so much like a punishment that no law is necessary—one may even doubt that the law is more than an excuse or rationalization for the basic act of sacrifice:

> Such a return to first principles in a republic is sometimes caused by the simple virtues of one man, without depending upon any law that incites him to the infliction of extreme punishments; and yet his good example has such an influence that the good men strive to imitate him, and the wicked are ashamed to lead a life so contrary to his example. Those particularly, who in Rome effected such beneficial results were Horatius Cocles, Scaevola, Fabricius, the two Decii, Regulus Attilius, and some others, who by their rare and virtuous example [*i loro esempli rari e virtuosi*] produced the same effect upon the Romans as laws and institutions would have done. And certainly if at least some such signal punishments as described above, or noble examples, had occurred in Rome every ten years, that city never would have become so corrupt. (*D*, 255/400–1)

Horatius Cocles (Horatius the One-Eyed) and Fabricius could pass as simple heros of positive achievement and moral principle. Regulus Attilius, Scaevola, and most of all the Decii, whom we have already met, are victims of extreme and largely self-inflicted physical suffering and mutilation. Regulus fulfilled an oath by returning to Carthage to be tortured and killed. Scaevola burned off his right hand by plunging it into fiery coals and holding it there while Lars Porsenna, leader of an attack on Rome, watched with admiration. The Decii are the two consuls, father and son, who offered themselves sacrificially in two different battles, or, as Machiavelli says of the father, "he killed himself." The effect of these examples seems to be the same as that of the punishments, and while the good examples give something to imitate, the equivalence between the spectacular suffering of good and bad makes the passage seem as if Machiavelli is talking about something besides simple imitation. The exceptional punishment has an effect on the observance of all laws and institutions and not just on the observance of the law for which the punishment was inflicted. So, with the exemplary action of the "suicide," Decius produces something more than a series of other sacrificial suicides (in fact, Machiavelli has already claimed that Decius did not have many direct imitators). Both groups of exemplary victims serve a common symbolic function of returning society to its beginning, its initial rigor and even terror.

Machiavelli's reference to the Medici in this context is enlightening. He says they felt it necessary to "retake the government" (*ripigliare lo stato*) every five years. By this expression, "they meant to strike the people with the same fear and terror as they did when they first assumed the government" (D, 255/400). But the phenomenon of the people's dimming memory (*la memoria si spegne*) requires a renewal of the terror.

Decius's sacrifice and Scaevola's self-mutilation can be interpreted as sources of stark terror even more than as specific indications of acts that citizens should perform. Like the exemplary punishment, which exceeds its immediate or apparent cause, the good men who are of "so much example" *(tanto esemplo)* exceed by their representation of self-sacrifice the purposes of being models for similar action. When we recall that Roman society is based on the example of Romulus the founder (D, 94/138) whose parricide was a justifiable terror, we can see the relationship between the sacrificial examples that form a chain of memory linking present society to its origins. Examples and exemplars are not proposed here as generally imitable acts or persons but as periodic calls for similar public events, breaking through the complacency of everyday life to recall the source of all law. This perspective raises a question about the final relationship between law and example, one for which we will not attempt to impose an answer on Machiavelli's enigmatic text. Machiavelli says several times that good laws cause good examples. But are not the examples of these exceptional men, arising "without depending on any law that incites him to the infliction of extreme punishments," manifestations of a force that precedes laws, a force by which and upon which laws are founded? If so, example can be understood in Machiavelli's text as a kind of epiphany, an appearance revealing the originary force itself rather than the entirely derivative force of laws.[32]

Machiavelli's comments in the introduction to the third book of the *Discourses* on the role of example in religion or sects reinforce the extralegal view of example. Connecting Christ, Saint Domenic, and Saint Francis, Machiavelli opposes these figures to the hierarchy of the established church, casting the two saints as revolutionaries who follow the "example of the life of Christ" and found "powerful new orders" (in the early sense of rules rather than in the edulcorated modern sense of religious associations, *si potenti gli ordini loro nuovi*). In such cases more than in the Roman examples, the accent is on an imitability of the exemplar up to a certain point (adoption of poverty, renunciation of revenge, etc.), although the exemplars themselves are practitioners of an excess in regard to these virtues. But the memorial function justifies Machiavelli's linking of religious and secular examples.[33]

One powerful form of persuasion by example is the deliberate and tendentious use of precedent for partisan ends. Machiavelli found in

Livy cases in which the Roman respect for the past took on religious overtones and made available a powerful means for political leaders to intimidate the people by reference to a sacred past, which held the key to future safety. Four examples from Livy (*alcuno exemplo*) in two chapters of the Roman's text (1.13–14) provide an increasingly detailed view of the mechanism by which an authoritative interpreter uses the traditional religion to move the people.[34] The abuse of interpretive power, however, can lead to spectacular sacrifice.

The culminating example in this series taken from Livy unites the conception of example as message from the past with the conception of example as cyclical eruption of permanent forces. When the tension becomes sufficiently great between the example and the statement that example is proposed to support, bad faith may appear as a byproduct of the interpretive process. Under such circumstances the audience requires a release of that tension and a diversion from the gap between example and statement. We sometimes describe forced interpretations as doing violence to the text. Machiavelli sees in Roman history a channel for that violence in the sacrificial destruction of the interpreter. Hence the chapter on the exemplary punishment of the interpreter of auspices, the "Chicken Officer."

During the third Samnite war, Lucius Papirius, Consul, had completed almost all preparations for a battle against the Samnites. To order an attack he had first to consult the Pollarius, or chicken officer, who was in charge of the sacred fowls: "if the fowls ate freely, then it was deemed a favorable augury, and the soldiers fought confidently, but if the fowls refused to eat, then they abstained from battle" (*D*, 106/156). In Machiavelli's view this belief offers great opportunities for a skillful leader, since the belief in authority is here, as in the previous examples, on the side of the people, while authoritative practice is conceived as empty or purely exterior by those who possess authority. For them the power of religious belief never stands in the way of reason: "when they saw a good reason why certain things should be done, they did them anyhow, whether the auspices were favorable or not; but then they turned and interpreted the auguries so artfully, and in such manner, that seemingly no disrespect was shown to their religious belief" (*D*, 106/156). When Papirius ordered the auspices, the Pollarius could see that the army and the consul wanted to fight and "being unwilling to deprive the army of this success" he reported to the consul that the chickens were eating, even though, in fact, they refused to eat. The Pollarius here is carrying out, in a sense, his duty, which concerns predicting the outcome of the battle. He knows that its chances are as good as those fought while the chickens were eating.

59

But his confident judgment of the future based on observations in the present is cloaked in an appeal to an authority from a tradition, which bypasses observation of the present to reach the future from the distant beliefs of the past. The Pollarius's "interpretation" is the most radical told by Machiavelli, and properly appears in climactic position, for the Pollarius simply converts the negative sign into a positive one, completely inverting the message.

If the example stopped here, we would learn how misinterpretation allowed Papirius to win the battle, "which forever enfeebled and broke the power" of the Samnites. But the example is more complex, for it contains a second level of interpretation—in effect, an example within an example or an example of how to make an example. One of the other Pollarii reveals that the chickens were not eating. The pious nephew of Lucius Papirius reports this to his uncle who replies

> that he expected him to do his duty well, and that, as regarded himself and the army, the auspices were favorable, and if the Pollarius had told a lie, it would come back upon him to his prejudice. . . . And so that the result might correspond with the prognostication, he commanded his lieutenants to place the Pollarii in the front ranks of the battle; and thus it happened that, in marching upon the enemy, the chief of the Pollarii was accidentally killed by an arrow from the bow of a Roman soldier. When the Consul heard this, he said that all went well and with the favor of the gods, for by the death of this liar the army had been purged of all guilt. (*D*, 106/157)[35]

A complex network of synecdochic and metaphoric relationships emerges in this example. Just as the Pollarius is placed in parallel with the corn (as the thing consumed in the revelation of the divine), so the consul takes the place of the Pollarius. The latter's report about the chickens (*riferì al consolo*) is in parallel with the consul's report about the death of the Pollarius (*il consolo disse*), and both report the same thing: all is going well and the gods are favorable (*gli auspicii procedevono bene/ogni cosa precedeva bene*). One level of the system is used up or reduced, since the consul intervenes directly in religious matters to replace the discredited former interpreter. In another sense, of course, the Pollarius replaces the consul. Somebody must be lying, and the consul's refusal to take seriously the allegation brought forth by his nephew indicates, even without the context of Machiavelli's commentary on the "adaptation" of religious rules, a potentially culpable desire not to know the truth. By arranging the sacrifice of the Pollarius, Lucius Papirius is able to reflect to his soldiers the desire to be free of the anger of the gods. He behaves as did the Pollarius in telling the soldiers what they want to hear. This second circle, however, does not have the flaw of the first since it is not falsifiable. The fact of the chickens' eating or not eating could be disputed, whereas the interpretation of the Pollarius's death is not disputable. The Pollarius, in dying, is like any sacrifice, a synecdoche for the group whose sin he expiates: a part dies in place of the whole. Yet the Pollarius is also a metaphor for the consul, whose place he takes as the "liar."

In standing in punishment before the multitude, and in justifying by his death the good judgment of the consul, the Pollarius assumes the role of an "example" in the sense of a spectacular and exceptional victim of the kind we have earlier seen in Machiavelli's accounts of ritual death. As in the case of Remirro de Orco's death at the orders of Cesare Borgia and the exhibition of Remirro's body on the piazza at Cesena, as described in *The Prince*, the Pollarius both takes the place of his superior—and thus, as appearance, blocks access to his master—and represents a quality existing in the master who arranges the sacrifice (an example of justice or an example of wisdom). As sacrifices examples also reflect the qualities of the multitude who watch (Remirro, we recall, was cruel and bloodthirsty just as the people are at Remirro's execution). The Pollarius who dies is an example of and for the soldiers who kill him and see him killed. He confirms that tampering with the sacred traditions leads to death (an example of a general rule), and he is a monitory example, showing specifically what will happen to any soldiers who try to violate the law. By manifesting the power of the gods to distinguish between true and false versions of their messages, the death of the Pollarius strengthens the whole system of auguries by a metadiscursive (or meta-augural) message. Yet probably the most important thing about the Pollarius's death is that it confirms the rhetorical process by which the skilled leader (and rhetorician) permits the people's desire and opinion to be reflected back to them.

Machiavelli's commentary on this example constitutes still another level since Machiavelli views Lucius Papirius as being an example of skill in the exploitation of religious belief. Just as the Pollarius says what the soldiers want to hear (fictionalizing the past by misstating what the chickens had started to do) and just as the consul tells the soldiers what they want to hear (fictionalizing the future, to some extent, so that things turn out as they wanted in the death of the Pollarius), so Machiavelli finds in Livy a passage that supports his argument.

It would be difficult to advance the example of the Pollarius as a model for all interpretation in Machiavelli, but the approval shown for

Lucius Papirius's handling of the discrepancy between belief and desire to believe supports the concept that authoritative utterance should be based on a rational misinterpretation of traditions (or on a tradition of misinterpretations) to produce an appearance that coincides with public opinion. The sequence of examples concludes with the very brief counterexample of Appius Pulcher, who wanted to attack the Carthaginians despite a negative response from the chickens. Seizing the chickens who refused to eat, he tossed them into the sea, saying "Let us see whether they will drink." After his defeat he was punished whereas Papirius was rewarded, "not so much," says Machiavelli, "because the one had been beaten and the other was victorious, but because the one had contravened the auspices with prudence, and the other with temerity" (D, 106–7/158). Prudence, which could be defined here as recognition of the requirements of circumstance, dictates attention to opinion, which, in Machiavelli's view, is the basic concern of the whole augural system. The Pollarii were not there to find out what the gods wanted but "to inspire the soldiers on the eve of battle with that confidence which is the surest guaranty of victory." Because the soldiers expect victory, victory comes. Hence the mirroring that structures the example of the Pollarius is confirmed on still another level, for the future does indeed reflect the desire of the soldiers, their undampened ardor. The leader's role is to reconstruct the messages of the past—or messages transmitted with the guarantee of the past—so that the signs of the eve of battle resemble the desired future. The augural system, or broadly speaking the whole Roman religious system, becomes in Machiavelli's text a clearly rhetorical one. In saying this we do not reduce rhetoric to the level of convincingly stated untruth (though Machiavelli abounds in advice that does rely on deception) but the the skillful use of signs. In the case of Lucius Papirius there was, in a sense, no actual untruth told by the consul (however much he seems to have participated in the concealment of a truth), since Papirius did not believe, any more than Appius Pulcher did, that the chickens' refusal to eat actually signified a Roman defeat was imminent. The auspices have no meaning in themselves but only offer the elements of a semiotic of prediction and exhortation. Auspices thus cannot be judged as true or false but only as convenient or inconvenient, and the inconvenient auspices offer greater scope for a leader's demonstration of rhetorical skill.

Despite Machiavelli's apparent ability to speak in a technical and nonmoralizing tone about this series of interpretations of religious signs from omen to oath, the culmination of the example sequence with two examples of punishment (those of the Pollarius and of Appius Pulcher) can be described as a means of representing *en abîme* within the text a certain fear of dealing in such matters. This does not mean that Machiavelli felt any guilt about religious matters whether conscious or unconscious, but the two punishments, of which at least one is an exemplary punishment, guarantee (in some sense even generate) the codes derived ultimately from the violence of the Romulan parricide. When the tradition is invoked to suit present opinion, Machiavelli seems to say, the tension arising between the desire to believe and the perception that much must be sacrificed to make that belief correspond with appearances demands a vent. The Pollarius therefore serves as the specific expiatory victim of the Papirian strategy and as a reminder of the violence that underlies Machiavelli's hermeneutics and his whole rhetoric.[36]

IMITATION

Example is often conceived in terms of imitation and reproducibility. The idea that an example should provide a directly reproducible series of acts is so central to example that one scholar has even claimed that no narrative should be qualified as exemplary if it does not contain an implicit or explicit imperative saying, in effect, "do likewise!"[37]

Machiavelli states clearly and often that his work is useful as a guide to political action, and he is careful to evaluate historical examples with respect to their imitability. In the proemium to book 2 of the *Discourses*, Machiavelli says he will discuss the comparative merits of antiquity and the present "so as to excite in the minds of the young men who may read my writings the desire to avoid the evils of the latter, and to prepare themselves to imitate the virtues of the former, whenever fortune presents them the occasion" (*D*, 179/274). Elsewhere Machiavelli speaks of the desirability of imitating different models to achieve various goals, such as to create a princedom or maintain a republic.[38] Machiavelli casts doubt on the imitability of examples, however, by demonstrating that different approaches can produce the same results, while apparently similar approaches can lead to disastrously different results. Because example has been lifted out of situation to become an example, we are frequently incapable of determining exactly how our circumstances and those represented in the example are related. Machiavelli points out that mankind is generally incapable of recognizing useful examples until it is too late to profit from them. Only retrospectively do similarity and difference appear. Finally, even if we could fully understand the knowledge contained in historical examples, we could not apply it because we behave according to our inherent nature and not according to a willed adherence to intellectual judgment.

Like Montaigne, Machiavelli points to cases in which the same results were obtained by opposite means. Machiavelli does not recognize reassuringly that there are a variety of approaches to a single problem, but plunges the political leader into a kind of desperate wager. Since we know that Machiavelli repeatedly rejects moderation and the middle way, there is no hope of achieving an effective approach by a process of averaging or otherwise reconciling extremes.[39] Instead Machiavelli forces the political leader into practical extremism, a position in which one risks all. The equal success of opposite approaches aggravates the difficulty of the leader by making it apparently impossible to distinguish in advance between the extremes. The most important Machiavellian text on this problem is the chapter of the *Discourses* entitled "Why Hannibal by a different course of conduct from that of Scipio achieved the same effects in Italy as the latter did in Spain [Donde nacque che Annibale con diverso modo di procedere da Scipione fece quelli medesimi effetti in Italia che quello in Ispagna]" (*D*, 300–1/473–76). This chapter follows another on an act of humanity by the Roman general Camillus, in which Machiavelli sets forth the great value of mercy in influencing potential subjects. "This example shows," says Machiavelli, "that an act of humanity and benevolence will sometimes have more influence over the minds of men than violence and ferocity" (*D*, 299/472). Yet the one lesson of the chapter on Hannibal and Scipio is that "he who makes himself beloved will have as much influence as he who makes himself feared, although generally he who makes himself feared will be more readily followed and obeyed than he who makes himself beloved." The affirmatives seem to balance one another, for what sometimes happens (*qualche volta*), as in the example of Camillus, is the opposite of what generally happens (*il più delle volte*). The presentation of Hannibal's method after Camillus's and Scipio's approach seems deliberately to unsettle a growing persuasion that humaneness is a generally appropriate tactic. It turns out that despite the success of the two Romans, they are rather the exceptions than the rule, and Hannibal, who appears as a counterexample, manifests the rule.

If we look at the beginning of Machiavelli's chapter on contrary means, we see he represents the reader's astonishment at this turn in his remarks:

> I think that some people may be astonished to see that some generals achieve by the very opposite course of conduct the same re-

sults that have been attained by those who have conformed to the
rules we have recommended above. This would make it seem that
victories do not depend upon one or the other course of conduct,
and that the virtues which we have extolled in the preceding chapter do not render you more happy nor more powerful, inasmuch
as both glory and reputation are often acquired by the very opposite means. (*D*, 300/473)

Machiavelli continues by describing the two leaders' conduct in
terms that make the difference as extreme as possible. On one hand
there is affection, respect, humanity, benevolence. On the other, violence, cruelty, rapine, and "every kind of perfidy." But the result is the
same (*il medesimo effetto*). Here Machiavelli deliberately sets himself,
with the reader, on the outside of the occurrence, looking on in astonishment and stressing every source of wonder, including the crescendo
of difference that abruptly turns to sameness. Machiavelli then shifts
his own stance to an explanatory one, giving two reasons for these
similar effects. It seems as if Machiavelli is trying to show why the
astonishment produced by the outward appearances is not warranted,
that the apparent opposition hides a common mechanism, so that similar means yield similar effects. But Machiavelli only ends up speaking
in terms so general as to be almost useless (all novelty succeeds) and in
reproducing the opposition between humanity and cruelty in their
subjective mirror image—love and fear—here described as internal
properties of the conquered population. Therefore, in shifting the focus of the passage from that of the amazed observer of historical effect
to that of the analyst who deals in causes, Machiavelli has hardly advanced at all, because the inside view is merely the outside view turned
over, but without any new information. Since Machiavelli knows this,
he reaches a stasis in his description of the advantages of the two approaches by declaring, "It matters little . . . by which of these two
systems he proceeds, provided he be a man of sufficient courage and
ability [*pure che sia uomo virtuoso*] to have made a great reputation for
himself." Nothing succeeds like success! The lesson to be drawn from
the examples of Scipio and Hannibal therefore does not provide much
useful information to someone seeking a method to reproduce their
success, since this achievement is inherent in their *virtù* and makes the
contrary tactics work.

Having reached a peak in the description of their success, Machiavelli starts to describe the danger of the two contrary approaches. One
could at least hope to learn which of the two approaches is the more
risky and to be avoided by a person of lesser *virtù*, but Machiavelli

pursues the difference in means and identity in effect on the downward slope:

> Either of these extremes may be productive of great evils, that will be apt to prove ruinous to a prince; for he who carries too far the desire to make himself beloved will soon become contemned, if he deviates in the slightest degree from the true path; and the other, who aims at making himself feared, will make himself hated, if he goes in the least degree too far; and our nature does not permit us to keep the middle course. (D, 300/474)

The utility of these examples is just about nil, since either approach will work for a man of *virtù* and either will bring failure to a man lacking in *virtù*, and *virtù* inheres in persons, not in acts or methods.

The aporia that seems to mark this chapter is characteristic of Machiavelli but not always so openly displayed. This aporia appears as such only from the point of view of a historical agent. To the observer standing outside the event causality can be dealt with by neat textual mechanisms like what has been called Machiavelli's "pseudo-causal 'because.' "[40] There is a value to the study of examples, but not the directly imitative or reproducible value that a rapid overview combined with a moralistic tradition might lead us to suppose. Instead, examples from history demonstrate that imitative conduct cannot succeed because only a perfect adaptation of individual skill and circumstance produces a desired effect. This doctrine makes the analytic study of history interesting only for a general retrospective understanding. The knowledge gained is always separated from the present, constructed out of fragments of the past. The actions of men in the present, on the other hand, cannot be based on such fragments because only an immediate relationship between the innate character of the political leader and the needs of the moment will bring results, not a mediate relationship to the present through the past.

A phrase borrowed from Livy indicates well the relative scope of human understanding and historical event: "Fortune blinds the spirits of men when she does not wish them to oppose her designs" (D, 244/381). Yet sometimes Machiavelli begins a section of his work sounding as if he could put an end to this blindness by sifting out good examples from the bad. He begins one chapter:

> The false opinions, founded upon bad examples [*fondate in su i mali esempli*], that have been introduced amongst us in this corrupt century, prevent men from liberating themselves from the force of their accustomed habits. Would it have been possible thirty years

ago to have persuaded an Italian that ten thousand infantry could have attacked, in an open plain, ten thousand cavalry and as many infantry? and not only to have fought, but actually to have defeated them, as we have seen that the Swiss did at the battle of Novara, already referred to [*per lo esemplo da noi più volte allegato*]? And although history is full of such examples, yet they would not have believed it; and if they had, they would have said that nowadays the troops are better armed, and that a squadron of mounted men would be able to charge a solid wall of rock, and therefore could not be resisted by mere infantry. (*D*, 221/344)

Machiavelli reveals here the unraveling of all exemplary knowledge.[41] There is an apparently unshakeable determinism about what people will believe and will refuse to believe. The best that Machiavelli can do is to write a hypothetical history of Italy. This historical rewriting, with its intense note of pathos, accumulates conditional verbs:

thus republics and princes would have committed fewer errors, and would have been stronger in resisting the assaults of any enemy that might unawares have come upon them. They would not have put their hope in flight, and those who had the direction of the government of state would have been better able to point out the means of aggrandizement, or the means of preservation. They would have believed that to increase the number of their citizens, to gain allies instead of subjects, to establish colonies to guard the conquered territories . . . (etc., *D*, 221/344)

It is as if Machiavelli were a helpless shorebound observer, watching the stream of history but with no rope to throw to his compatriots as they drift past. Machiavelli's gesture here, however, is more than discouragement or annoyance with his contemporaries. His affirmation flies in the face of the supposed utility of all exemplary knowledge. The examples that fill history are not hidden, they are ignored or they are considered inappropriate for application to the present circumstances.[42] Since Machiavelli frequently argues the difference of circumstance in explaining why the same tactic produces different results (and vice versa), he cannot criticize this view in a general way. All he can do is argue, after the fact, that the comparative judgment of specific instances was wrong, that people either ignored the examples of history entirely or did not ignore them but chose the wrong ones.

The very least that republics should have learned from the examples of the ancients was that, failing to adopt the methods listed by Machiavelli, "they would have put a curb upon all ambition . . . prohibiting

67

all conquests and confining themselves merely to providing for their security and defence; as is done by the republics of Germany, who live in that manner, and have thus enjoyed their liberty for a long time." But this last in Machiavelli's string of hypotheses concerning the profitability of example is revealed, suddenly thereafter, as a *complete impossibility*. Even if a republic tries to enjoy freedom within its own borders and not to molest others, others will come to attack the peaceful republic. The example of Germany is exemplary of the inimitable: "The fact that the free cities of Germany have been able to exist in this fashion for a length of time, is owing to certain conditions prevailing in that country, such as are not found elsewhere, and without which they could not have maintained their institutions and existence [nasce da certe condizioni che sono in quel paese, le quali non sono altrove, sanza le quali non potrebbero tenere simile modo di vivere]." The first part of the chapter reduces what the Italians might have learned from example to the very minimum and then concludes with an example of this minimal wisdom, an example that then appears to be unusable.

The German example is outside the experience and the capacity of Italians. This exteriority is the source of example's appeal and danger at the same time. We look *at* an example or *hear about* an example from the position of a spectator, listener, or reader. The separation between us and the example may be temporal or spatial, it may simply be a difference of person, but example is outside us. The exteriority of example constitutes its usefulness in making a science, as Charles Singleton has brilliantly observed.[43] But being outside of us, example does not reveal all. First, it is as much a screen as a sign; second, historical example has a hidden face. Writing of Hannibal, Machiavelli says:

> No one will pretend to say that Hannibal was not a master in the art of war; and if, when he was opposed to Scipio in Africa, he had found it to his advantage to prolong the war, he certainly would have done so. And perhaps, being a good general, and having a good army, he might have done as Fabius did in Italy; but as he did not do so we must suppose that he was influenced by important considerations [*si debbe credere che qualche cagione importante lo movessi*]. (D, 283/447)

This *qualche cagione importante*, which caused Hannibal to behave in a way different from what Machiavelli would expect, opens a rift in exemplary material generally, for there are important considerations in all historical incident that can only be conjectured and on the basis of biased texts.[44] This is one of Machiavelli's more candid admissions of our blindness to the subjective side of historical action.

We are ignorant of our own situation, precisely because we know it only from the inside. Limits are only discovered too late: "Men commit the error of not knowing when to limit their hopes, and by trusting to these rather than to a just measure of their resources, they are generally lost" (*D*, 241/378). The impossibility of measuring oneself (*misurarsi*) is a constant of Machiavelli's thought. Its clearest expression appears in the dedicatory letter to Lorenzo in *The Prince*. We earlier considered perspective as manifestation of the space between painter and landscape, observer and observed. The serious consequences of that separation are now clearer. No prince can know princes, no commoner can know the common people. An optimistic construction would hold that this conception forces prince and people to be interdependent, but the *reductio ad absurdum* of this view is fairly easy. Macropolitics and international relations would fall to the commoner, who would maneuver the prince as a blind figurehead through those realms, while the prince would dispossess the people of all control over their daily lives. Or, to push the simile further, as soon as the commoner took control of the prince, the commoner would lose the distance that previously gave him the advantage in the first place. Moreover, as Machiavelli's pessimism in *Discourses* 2.19 indicates, people only believe what they are ready to believe. Hence, the commoner's view of the prince's situation and the prince's view of the commoner's situation may be exact, but nowhere does Machiavelli say that such views can be communicated to the party about whom they are held.

The landscape painting is an apt simile for Machiavelli's view of human nature and the impossibility of doing more than representing it accurately. "All the actions of men resemble those of nature" (*D*, 187/290). Therefore, while effects and causes unfold in a coherent way in time ("time, father of all truth"), men cannot perceive the effects in advance nor can they understand the relationship of ancient example to their own situation. The historical exteriority works like the exteriority imposed by space (for the painter) or class, but the historical exteriority—the ability to see coherent pattern in tidily arranged histories from the past—is more general. Men can understand the reasons for the failure (or success) of others but cannot get a perspective on their own situation, until, of course, it changes. Hence the failure of exemplary teaching:

> The ambition of men is such that, to gratify a present desire, they think not of the evils which will in a short time result from it. Nor will they be influenced by the examples of antiquity, which I have cited upon this and other points. (*D*, 225/351)[45]

Two major sections of *The Prince* and the *Discourses* concern the most damning observation about the profitability of exemplary, or any other, learning. Machiavelli entitles one chapter of the *Discourses*, "How it is necessary to change with the time if you want always to have good fortune," but he devotes the chapter to expounding men's inability to change their natures. There are two necessary conditions to success. The first is to follow the promptings of one's own nature and not to try to adopt the characteristic approach of another person, which one could never master. The second condition is to live in a period that specifically requires such a nature. The example of Fabius shows that he had a single approach to fighting Hannibal, which did not change when circumstances changed. Fortunately for Rome, Fabius was not allowed to remain in control when the need for someone of his character had passed. A leader's success is not due to greater wisdom, but to a kind of Darwinian natural selection, eliminating leaders whose behavior (and hence, nature) is not suited to the times. All a man can do is struggle vigorously and blindly, as he knows how, until fortune either exalts him or strikes him down:

> That we cannot thus change at will is due to two causes; the one is the impossibility of resisting the natural bent of our characters; and the other is the difficulty of persuading ourselves, after having been accustomed to success by a certain mode of proceeding, that any other can succeed as well. It is this that causes the varying success of a man; for the times change, but he does not change his mode of proceeding [*perché ella varia i tempi ed elli non varia i modi*] (*D*, 281/442–3)[46]

A similar assessment of the value of learning about political conduct appears in the example of Giuliano della Rovere, Pope Julius II, in *The Prince*. This example shows the unprofitability of examples by demonstrating that individuals succeed blindly by doing what their nature compels them to do. As a group, men succeed by varying their tactics because as a group men have different natures. But individually they are not able to profit from this variability:

> We discover that men use varying tactics with regard to the means of fulfilling the goals they have before them, namely, glory and wealth. One acts with circumspection, another with impetuosity; one with force, another with craft; one with patience, another with precipitousness: yet each man succeeds with these different methods. We also discover that of two circumspect men, one succeeds in his project and another does not; by the same token, two

men of different propensities may thrive equally well, one by being circumspect, the other by being impetuous. (*P*, 64/365)

Machiavelli illustrates this principle with the successes of Giuliano,
whose nature led him to treat everything impetuously. Machiavelli has
doubts about Giuliano's sagacity, but Giuliano always succeeded
thanks to the good fortune of being in situations that required that
approach:

> Pope Julius II used impetuous tactics in every one of his exploits.
> He found the times and circumstances so harmonious [*e tempi e le
> cose conforme*] with his tactical methods that he always pre-
> vailed. . . . Therefore Julius, with his impetuous move, achieved
> what no pope, even possessing the utmost human prudence,
> could ever have done. . . . I prefer to pass over his other exploits:
> all were similar, all succeeded perfectly. His short life allowed him
> no experience to the contrary. If there had come a time when he
> needed to use his tactics circumspectly, it would have led to his
> downfall; he would have never deviated from those methods to-
> ward which nature predisposed him. (*P*, 64–65/369)

Since he could not alter his way of behaving, he could not imitate examples of other leaders. Like so many other exemplary figures in
Machiavelli—including the Roman nation as a whole—Giuliano succeeds by not following examples. He only provides them for Machiavelli's collection.[47]

In short, Giuliano represents the futility of a discourse based on a
rhetoric of example, a futility that is combined with a longing for the
absence of example and the paradoxical exaltation of the Roman nation
as the exemplary achievement of those who were able to start without
examples. In thus mythologizing Roman origins, Machiavelli may appear to betray the very science that he uses as the foundation of his
own discourse, the study of history. The relationship thus established—through the example—with historical sources of authority
manifests, at one level, the schism that runs throughout Machiavelli's
thought and appears, on another level, as the paradox of tactical politics. Michael McCanles has defined the latter as the requirement for
"total self-dependence, an achievement that *Il Principe* exhibits as at
once necessary and impossible."[48] Yet, at the same time, Machiavelli is
establishing writing as an inevitable and fecund violation of the past as
system in favor of the past as fragment, as point, as discontinuous and
unstable repertory of rhetorical implements.

The *Heptameron* and Unlearning from Example

Ne nous resjouissons de nos vertuz, mais en ce que nous sommes
escriptz au livre en Vie, duquel ne nous peult effacer Mort, Enfert
ne Peché.

Io porto le corna, ciascun lo vede;
ma tal le porta, che no lo crede.   —Marguerite de Navarre

IT HAS LONG BEEN a commonplace that the series of *exempla* used by
medieval preachers are the basis of the medieval and Renaissance
genre of the novella collection.[1] Marguerite de Navarre's novellas,
published as the *Heptameron* (1559), rise beyond this generic association of storytelling with example to mount a sustained, complex, and
witty attack on the usefulness and even the possibility of creating examples. Even the simplest reading of the *Heptameron* must see the narratives as attempts, by the fictive character-storytellers, to give examples, for the term *exemple* recurs in their dialogue to designate the
individual novellas. But as a reader combines references to medieval
preaching and to rhetoric in general with indications of religious doctrine, it seems that Marguerite is raising questions of a magnitude appropriate for a period that witnessed the decline of the novella collection and the rise of the novel in its place. The novella is the genre that
attempts or pretends to show the world through examples, while the
novel in the seventeenth century centers on the vain quest for examples. Thus the *Heptameron* appears increasingly as a turning-point in
the history of European narrative, caught in the trap of a distinction
between the true and the real.

Machiavelli was concerned with the distinction between the writer
and the political leader. Marguerite, basing herself in the same problem
of representation as Machiavelli, pushes further into the simpler but
more general division between the person speaking, an "I," and everyone else ("you," "they"). This emphasis on the "I" has both religious and rhetorical importance. Grace penetrates unseen into the individual soul, and this internal difference distinguishes one person
from another in a way that can be experienced only subjectively. But
the "I" has another property that appears where examples are con-

cerned. Whenever writers or speakers use examples, they appeal outside their own subjective affirmation toward an objective or shared perception of reality. Like Machiavelli, Marguerite points to the blindspot of representation as conveyed in the perspective metaphor from *The Prince*. One must be a commoner to know a prince, just as one must stand on the plain to see the mountain. Marguerite takes this further to stress the blindness of each individual to himself or herself. Examples take on greater importance because only through an external representation can I know myself. But how can I recognize an example of conduct pertinent to myself if I cannot see myself except in the great mass of apparently contradictory narratives? Moreover, in attempting to persuade others of a truth in which I believe, how can I overcome the gap between subjective and objective statement, between what I affirm and what other people see of me alongside that affirmation?

Despite the collective framework of the *Heptameron*, a group of men and women exchanging stories and commenting on them together, Marguerite's thematic emphasis is on the predicament of isolated individuals whose statements and beliefs conflict with convention. In the four sections of this chapter the prologue, tales, and frame-discussions will be shown to correspond to a doctrinal critique of the rhetoric of exemplary narrative. First, primarily in the prologue, Marguerite places her novellas in the dual traditions of the Boccaccian novella collection and ecclesiastical oratory. As she does this she establishes key terms such as *true history*, introduces stock characters such as the monks, and uses the setting to reverse the roles between the laity and the clergy. Second, in a section on the concept of the witness, a reading of the first story of the *Heptameron* will demonstrate Marguerite's view of the difficulty of seeing oneself as compared to the ease with which we witness the deeds of others. The story of a judicial inquiry into a murder helps us understand the problems of providing true history, Marguerite's goal of going beyond rhetoric. A third section of this chapter describes two interlocking tales that deal with the direct conflict between an individual's word and institutions that, in preventing direct expression, generate third-person exemplary narratives. The effect of one of these narratives, the story of Rolandine's aunt, on other characters makes it seem that examples in the *Heptameron* do not support or demonstrate anything. As a way out of this impasse, the concluding section proposes a return to generic considerations in the light of religious doctrines presented within the text. Examples seem discredited as a means of providing any positive model. Discourse itself seems suspect, but in the light of grace, sin and ugliness convey a humiliating and negative exemplarity.

TALES AND TRUE HISTORY

A scatological and salacious book by a religious author, the *Heptameron* is pulled in two directions, toward a pure and abstract lesson and toward a depiction of crude and lawless existence. One movement is toward a *livre de Vie*, the divine law, and the other toward the merely human, a *livre de vie*. Between the two lies the risk of a book that seems without order or pattern—a potential *livre dévié*. The tension between this aspiration to an expression of doctrinal purity and the semblance of a recognizable image of social life is increasingly recognized as an inescapable characteristic of Marguerite de Navarre's work. It is now often described as the "ambiguity" of the *Heptameron*, an ambiguity that appears most forcefully when two levels of discourse meet and clash at the border between the internal tales or novellas themselves and the discussions or commentary on the tales given by the frame-characters, the storytellers (*devisants*).[2] The conflict between an intemporal or transtemporal representation of conduct (the paradigmatic axis) and the actualized or temporally anchored representation of conduct (the syntagmatic axis) is latent in almost all novella collections. Such conflict is certainly characteristic of those collections following the Boccaccian model in which the frame-narrative sets forth judgments of value on the conduct of the novella characters and in which the "examples" of conduct appear as an explicit form of rivalry or correction of previous examples.

The prologue of the *Heptameron* establishes the frame-narrative within which a group of ten aristocratic storytellers gather far from the everyday world to tell stories that, as they insist, faithfully portray the everyday life they have left behind. Like the Boccaccian frame-narrators of the *Decameron*, who flee plague-infested Florence by taking refuge in the pleasant hills nearby, the narrators of Marguerite de Navarre's story collection are escaping disastrous flooding by taking refuge in the monastery of Notre Dame de Serrance in the Pyrenees. The reference to Boccaccio is made even clearer in the description of a collaborative writing project at the court of Francis I. The frame-character Parlamente, often identified with Marguerite de Navarre, proposes the *Decameron* as model for their gathering:

> I don't think there's one of us who hasn't read the hundred tales by Boccaccio, which have recently been translated from Italian into French, and which are so highly thought of by King Francis I, by Monseigneur the Dauphin, Madame the Dauphine and Marguerite. . . . I have heard that the two ladies I've mentioned, along with other people at the court, made up their minds to do the

same as Boccaccio, except in one thing: they should not write any story that was not a true history [*véritable histoire*].[3]

The plans Parlamente reports called for a gathering of ten persons, each of whom, including the two ladies and the Dauphin, would tell ten stories. From these storytellers would be excluded all those who had studied and were men of letters, for fear that the stories would be corrupted by art ("de paour que la beaulté de la rethoricque feit tort en quelque partye à la vérité de l'histoire" [9/69]). This gathering of lay persons, without admixture of scholars or rhetoricians, is clearly a direct claim to descend from and to rival Boccaccio. The group in Serrance to whom Parlamente announces this project is, within the fiction of the frame narrative, not the courtly group that originally undertook the neo-Boccaccian novella collection, for events had forced the family of Francis I to abandon their pastime, says Parlamente (9/69). Despite this distancing of historical figures and fictive narrators, to which we will return later, the generic claims of the *Heptameron* appear both in the attributes of the frame and in this direct allusion to the *Decameron*.[4]

The second tradition to which Marguerite de Navarre attaches her book is that of the example or *exemplum*, though this claim is made not within a single direct announcement but through repeated uses of the term *example* (*exemple*) at the juncture between story and discussion. This term recurs with extraordinary frequency in the *Heptameron*, in contexts that support its interpretation, first, as narrative intended to teach a moral lesson and to enjoin a specific conduct and, second, as a reference to some reality external to the speaker's discourse for the purpose of increasing the persuasive effect of such discourse. The first of these meanings appears in statements by the frame-narrators, as when Longarine says of one tale, "I don't think it's an example that young girls should follow. I suspect there are some you'd like to persuade to do so. . . [si n'est-ce pas une (*sic*) exemple que les filles doyvent ensuivre. Je croy bien qu'il y en a à qui vous vouldriez le faire trouver bon . . .]" (42/106). Longarine implies that the purpose of the narrative is to provide a pattern of conduct and to make that pattern attractive. Even clearer is the frame-narrator's declared intention about his own narrative. Saffredent says of novella 3: "There, my ladies, is a story that I give you as an example. When your husbands give you little roe-deer horns, make sure that you give them great big stag's antlers! [Voylà, mes dames, une histoire que voluntiers je vous monstre ici pour exemple, à fin que . . .]" (27/880).

Equally present in the *Heptameron* are uses of the term *exemple* in the second sense, that is, without any injunctive, ethical force, but with a cognitive function. When example is used in this way it appears paired with a term for discourse or *parole*. Parlamente, disagreeing with a position taken by another frame-character, says "What you say carries so little weight that it requires reinforcing by means of an example. So if you have one in mind, I invite you to take my place and to tell it to us. That doesn't mean that we're obliged to believe you on the strength of just one story [vostre propos est de si petite auctorité, qu'il a besoing d'estre fortifié d'exemple . . .]" (356/460). In the dichotomistic rivalry between the genders, example is sometimes invoked to strengthen the purely verbal contention of superiority by a gesture outside of the world of discourse. Hence, Oisille challenges the male storytellers by saying, "let the men, who are so fond of representing us women as lacking in constancy, produce an example of a husband who was as good, as faithful and as constant as the woman in this story [viennent . . . et me monstrent l'exemple d'un aussy bon mari . . .]" (174/253). Here, of course, "example" is not a physical, nondiscursive entity—a real, flesh-and-blood husband—but a verbal representation of a husband. Therefore, although the challenge seems to be, as Parlamente says above, to fortify the word with something other than the word, Oisille's exhortation clearly demonstrates that *exemple* is a kind of narrative, responding to another narrative, rather than a true movement outside of language.

The frame-narrators are making a distinction between word (or doctrine) and example, but both of these conceptions are internal to the world of language. This is probably a more difficult conception for twentieth-century readers to grasp than for the contemporaries of Marguerite de Navarre, for the world of the *Heptameron* is still a highly idealistic one, fully confident in the omnipresence of the Logos. To use the metaphor so powerfully implemented by Terence Cave, the movement between the discussion and the narrative in the *Heptameron*, and therefore between "word" and "example," is all within the folds of language, part of the rhetorical alternation between *verba* and *res*.[5]

There is nonetheless a tension between the concept of example as narrative and the example as movement "outside," into the world of action. In the proliferating series of narratives and counternarratives, "examples" are contrasted with "words." One character is described as "the doctrine and example for the others" (*la doctrine et l'exemple*, 138/214). In another tale a male character, desirous of impressing on a woman that he has truly changed conduct, tells her that "she had been the cause of a complete change in his life through her holy words and virtuous example" (*par ses sainctes paroles et bon exemple*, 99/169). *Exemple*, used to mean a sequence of actions or the retelling of that sequence, comes very close to being identified with the particular use of *exemplum* as narrative illustrating the application of moral rules.[6]

Such a use of example can be understood as an allusion to the didactic oratory of the church and takes on a special resonance given the setting of the narrative frame in the monastery of Notre Dame de Serrance. The Franciscans' preaching plays a major, and apparently harmful, role in many of the novellas, as we will soon see. *Exemplum* as part of this preaching links the frame narrative setting with the tales as secularized *exempla*. Marguerite de Navarre sets forth in this way the double literary-historical tradition within which she intends the *Heptameron* to be read, and in so doing pushes the conflicting claims of the two currents to an extreme. The characters of the frame-narrative escape the lowly world of the plains by being both physically elevated and situated in an ecclesiastical habitat. Yet the depiction of monks is so negative that the *Heptameron* is set in the center of the world of evil rather than above the plague as is Boccaccio's book. The monks of Serrance are no exception to the general reputation of such orders, for the abbot who welcomes them is "not a particularly nice character [assez mauvais homme]." Because he conforms to the falseness of the monks, as described later in the *Heptameron*, he welcomes them appropriately: "he, who was a true hypocrite, put on the best possible appearance . . . [luy, qui estoit vray hypocrithe, leur feit le meilleur visaige qu'il estoit possible . . .]" (6/65).[7]

The paradox in the expression "true hypocrite" will become a major interpretive key to the novellas. Truly a hypocrite, the abbot is also *vray* in the sense of being an accomplished, entirely "false" hypocrite, one who performs his role with aplomb and therefore does exactly what his guests want him to do, though for the wrong reasons. If he had been a less successful hypocrite and had allowed his evil interior to appear in all its unpleasantness, he would have been less useful to the arriving aristocratic storytellers. Yet if he had allowed his evil to appear, he would have been less evil, since he would not have added falseness to the many other sins that are implied here. The abbot is an *example* of the hypocrite. He is typical of a whole series of individuals like him—the monks in general—for whom he stands in the prologue. In his duplicity, the abbot constitutes an intertextual gesture toward the kind of discourse associated with monks since Jean de Meun's Faux Semblant in the *Roman de la Rose*.[8] In mentioning the abbot in her prologue narrative, Marguerite de Navarre is playing with the relationship between two senses of the term *example*, since the abbot is not an "exemplary narrative" but an example in the more basic sense of representative instance. Yet this particular representative instance is also, given the historical association of monks with sermons based on *exemplum*, a metonym for the *exemplum* as rhetorical form.

The *Heptameron* plays not only on different meanings of the word *example* but with exemplary exteriority and the related concept of closure. If examples are the "other" of discourse, whatever it is that fortifies the *propos* or the doctrine, texts using examples have to create some distance between general statement and example. There has to be a standpoint for viewing the example. If examples are closed units, which are in turn enclosed within the predominant discourse, then their closure is necessary to the orderly functioning of the overall argument. Variations on the theme of closure are certainly prominent in the prologue and the frame of the *Heptameron*. The terminology we use to describe novella collections emphasizes the tradition that such closure is a defining feature of the genre, for otherwise we could not use terms like *frame-narrative* and *internal stories*. Marguerite de Navarre makes this characteristic more evident by choosing a monastery for the *locus* of her—dare one say?—frame-narrative, for the storytellers are more truly enclosed than in Boccaccio. While Boccaccio and Marguerite de Navarre both contrast the place where the novellas are set and the place where they are told, the *Heptameron* locates a frame (the dialogue and narratives of the storytellers) within a frame (the monastery and its conventions). Secular narrators and their examples of the goodness and evil of men and women are surrounded by monks, with their tradition of sermons with *exempla*. The normal relation between clergy and laity, speaker and listeners, is reversed; at the conclusion of days two and three of the *Heptameron*, the monks are found hidden in a ditch behind a hedge listening to the tales. Since those two days of narration contain seven tales in which monks play a major part, the monks are both the topic and the audience of the novellas. The "inside" of the tales therefore mirrors the "outside" of the represented audience of the novellas. Yet one of the things about monks is that when they are out in the open you cannot see what they have inside them—as demonstrated by the abbot. It is therefore appropriate that the monks be concealed while they listen, because concealment is their nature.

These closures and enclosures indicate that we are not dealing with a realist narrative convention, despite the apparent humility or ugliness (and hence "realism") of the events and concrete specifications of the novellas. Instead, a largely fixed and allegorical or symbolic meaning is assigned to such features as the monks. The containment of the narrators and narration within the monastery is also a containment of the narratives within a tradition of exemplary narratives from which the lay narrators do not seem able to locate an exit. Can a narrative example lead to something other than a narrative example? What does happen when a narrator tries to move from discourse (*propos, parole*) to something that can support that discourse?

Incorporating into her work the tension between claims to objective representation of history and claims to derive ethical norms from this representation, Marguerite brilliantly outlines issues that lead not only to a change in literary fashion but to a crisis in philosophy in the sixteenth and seventeenth centuries. At stake in the *Heptameron* is the role of literature in an era increasingly confronted by a withdrawal of the divine order from the observable world. In attempting to establish order without abandoning the divine, narrative can only displace the transcendent function onto some human agency.[9] Marguerite uses the novella collection's alternation between story and commentary to probe the way the disorder of everyday actions are related to a higher order of rule and pattern. The *Heptameron* does not choose the easy path of smoothing out contradictions between the two levels, but pushes them to an extreme.[10]

She does this first in the celebrated claim of the prologue that the court of François I was elaborating a set of novellas similar to those of Boccaccio in all respects except the veracity of the stories ("different from Boccaccio in one respect: to write no novella that is not true history"). Marguerite has established a criterion limiting what can be told, exposed the problem of learning something from actual event, and divided the text into two fields of language, which differ not only in enunciating form (objective narrative versus discussion) but also cognitively (actuality versus potentiality).[11] In this context history does not seem to mean a handing down of the past, a reconstruction of it, a bridge between generations of persons or books. Veritable history means a narrative of actual events, not the linking of events through time. Things read in books are not worthy of inclusion because books are the domain of those who have studied and will allow what they have read to replace what they have seen. The letter has been set against the word, and the word wins, at least within the fiction of the frame-narrative. The *Heptameron* is a book modeled on another book but in which writers are banished. This paradox, which is part of a larger paradox in the *Heptameron*, is supposed to lead to the elimination of any tale not relatively recent, most often within the lifetime of the frame-characters. The triumph of synchrony is complete. But in fact synchrony is only a mask for achrony, for a time-free vision; the narrators both assure us of the actual occurrence of events in a knowable time and place and then, on several occasions, withhold the references that permit us to anchor the stories in any historical locus.

For instance, there is the story of a Franciscan, "whose name for the sake of his order I shall not reveal" (187/267). There is Parlamente's story, which she presents by saying, "It's such a true, such a lovely story, that I'm anxious for you to hear it without more ado. I was not an eye-witness to the facts, but they were recounted to me by a very close friend of mine, a man who was devoted to the hero of the story and wished to sing his praises. He made me swear, however, that if I should ever tell the story to anyone else, I would alter the names of the people involved. So everything that I shall tell you is true to life, *except the names of the people and the places*" (54/120). Like a sociological study of Middletown or the psychiatric case of Mr. N, both studies exalt empirical truth while denying importance to the notion of historical specificity. The tales in the *Heptameron* do not need names and places, even when they are given, for the events neither grow out of one another nor necessarily occur only in one place. The story of one Franciscan fornicating in one nameless monastery might be understood to refer to another Franciscan fornicating in another monastery. The notion of historical truth is therefore stripped of its referential content; truth in stories somehow affects the status of the acts recounted but does not localize such stories. The presence of a court figure like Marguerite de Navarre in some of the stories guarantees the actualization of certain conduct but does not signify a properly historical unicity, but only a stamp certifying that a conceivable act (from a paradigm of acts) has found its way into the domain of the actual (in a syntagmatic combination). The historical aspect of events is thus either hovering outside the center of the story (as in the arrival of the Queen of Navarre after Sister Marie Heroet has withstood the brutal advances of her confessor in story 22) or stripped from the recognizable event (as in the telling of the Lorenzaccio story in tale 12).

Second, accentuating these contrasts, Marguerite has further expanded the frame-narrative in such a way that apparent inconsistencies or contradictions between the stories and the discussions can no longer be taken lightly. Third, Marguerite has stressed the latent problems of the novella collection by harkening to its traditional origin in the *exemplum*.

The claim to present "veritable history" may be a pose, as has been suggested, but the question remains: what does Marguerite force us to do to cope with this "pose"?[12] How can the couple history/example be guiding lines toward understanding the creation of the ambiguity of the *Heptameron* and of its place in the culmination of the novella tradition in France?

The beginning of an answer may lie in the complex of cognitive and discursive concepts that cluster around the term *history*. Cognitively, history, as fact or recognized event, differs from fiction, as plausible but nonrealized event. This contrast between history and fiction is, however, complicated because both must appear in language and in so appearing are subject to discursive classifications that do not break into the same neat pair. Discursively, history (*récit d'histoire*) finds itself in contrast not with fiction but with discourse (*discours*) according to the indications of who is speaking. Certain statements are marked with indications of who is speaking and in what concrete, usually dialogic, situation. Other statements appear without trace of this situation and to be transcendent, timeless, and "objective." Yet a text bearing the marks of this "objective" history (*récit d'histoire*) may be either fiction or history in the cognitive sense.[13] Discourse can, on the other hand, be narrative, but it does not pretend to objectivity. Instead it is the vehicle for a personal, subjective expression of belief, experience, and judgment. Discourse is the mode in which ethical judgments are made and alternative action is described. The *Heptameron*, like many novella collections, is divided into a domain enunciated objectively as actual event (the novellas) and a domain enunciated subjectively, dialogically, as judgment and statement of alternative or potential event (the discussions within the frame-narrative). The *Heptameron* claims that *all* of the internal narratives that are enunciated "objectively" are history in the cognitive as well as discursive sense.

There is a tendency in *Heptameron* criticism to concentrate on the frame-narrative, but there is no reason to suppose that the discussions of the frame-narrative are favored vehicles of truth. Only an understanding of the relationship between history and discourse in both novellas and discussion can help us understand the way in which the *Heptameron* challenges the didactic possibilities of both modes of enunciation.[14] Moreover, the history/discourse opposition, as a structural feature of the novella collection, reappears in the theme of struggle between objective truth as it is taught in history and subjective truth as it wells up in the discursive behavior of individuals.

TESTIMONY

In its claim to be true history, the *Heptameron* raises the question of the role of the witness, the *témoin*. Avoiding the distortions of the *gens de lettres* and their written rhetoric, the creators of the projected collection that would rival the *Decameron* place upon the internal narrators of the novellas the burden of a special function—relating what they know to be true on the basis of a nonwritten experience. In the first tale Simontault repeatedly uses the words *témoin* and *témoignage*, "witness" and "testimony." This novella itself, proclaimed as "pure truth," gives witness against women. The characters of the novella are explicitly and extensively located within the institutional structure of magistracies, tribunals, and important ecclesiastical and feudal hierarchies—the two male villains are the bishop of Séez and a public prosecutor of the city of Alençon. Therefore, when witnesses and testimony are mentioned, such terms take on a technical resonance, emphasized still more by comments on the relative credibility of different witnesses: "the servants of the dead man ought not to be believed as witnesses" (*creuz en tesmoignage*), the old woman servant who "was the most reliable witness" (*le plus seur tesmoing*), the younger servant who was suborned, taken to Paris, and prostituted "so no one would take her seriously as a witness" (13/75).

Before looking more closely at the first tale, it is worth reflecting on what a witness is and does. A witness is someone who speaks in the first person, who can give evidence of what he or she has seen. The importance society confers on the *spoken* word reaches its peak in witnessing. Even written forms such as the *affidavit* only record a spoken event. Moreover, the speech of the witness is an attempt at a pure discourse, with emphasis on the fact that the speaker (subject of enunciation) is the same as the viewer (subject of a predicate of perception): "*I* know because *I* saw with my own eyes that . . . " Anything else is hearsay. The herdsman's replies to Oedipus in *Oedipus the King* are evidence of the power of the joining of two presences in the witness: presence at the time of the event or crime and presence at the time of the judgment. The witness is thus temporally dual, but represents the possibility or the illusion of a transcendence of this duality of event and judgment, of past and present. Oddly, although the witness has no value unless physically present before the tribunal and actually speaking at the moment of the trial or deliberation, the witness speaks of the past and generally also in the past tense.

The witness is an important part of the forensic process, and may even be the absolutely necessary element to establishment of proof, yet the witness is never the center of the adjudication. In fact the witness has an *excentric* place in all rhetoric. A position on the side of argument is what guarantees the truth of what the witness says. The witness is not himself in question, not the accused party, in a trial. If he were, the selfish interest of his assertion would undermine its credibility.[15] Therefore, although he speaks in the first person at a trial, this first person "I" is an "I" that is somehow stripped of interested motives and cast in the role of a subject beyond litigiousness and outside of human interest, a purefied voice. On the periphery of the forensic opposition in the present, the witness *was* also on the periphery of the event that is now being reconstructed for the tribunal. The testimony becomes more and more credible as the witness's involvement in the event is limited, for perjury might be feared of a witness who was in fact an actor in the incident in question. The witness is on the sidelines in both past and present: in one case an "eye" who sees and in the other an "I" who speaks.

Through the witness, in other words, the visual is transformed into the verbal, the silent into something that can be heard. A beholder during the incident in question, the witness is the passive subject before the event. As speaker during the inquiry, the witness is the subject of discourse but never the subject of the narrative: for example, "While *I* watched, *he* did something." The grammatical first person is often considered the center of discourse, occupying the dominant linguistic position and casting the third person, the person *of whom* one speaks, into the role of the "non-person."[16] In effect, the accused is a kind of "non-person" in the judicial procedure because he is deprived of credible access to speech.[17] All around him people are attempting to represent him in words, but his own words in the present instance are discounted, according to the ancient legal maxim, *Testis nemo in sua causa esse potest*, "No one can be a witness on his or her own behalf."[18] He cannot speak of himself. His image can only be reliably created by the speech of others. In this circumstance the witness occupies the apparently impossible situation of being both the apogee of "personhood" in the power of speech—only his word can be direct affirmation and not secondary reconstruction—and completely on the periphery of past and present events, the act of judgment and the past act that is being judged.

There is a strange similarity between the accused, who cannot speak *for* himself, and the witness, who does not speak *of* himself. They are almost mirror images, or symmetrical halves of an ideal person. The specular relation is an apposite simile, but only a simile, since it reveals the invisibility of one to oneself except through the other, the mirrored self. On the other hand, the quasi-specular quality of the witness involves not only a spatial distancing but a temporal one as well. The witness reveals the self as it was, always dislocated into the time of telling and the time of the told.[19]

These reflections on the status of the witness bear on a central and recurrent structure of the *Heptameron* in which people are shown as incapable of representing their own experience to themselves except through the mediation of narration. Or rather, experience itself is

shown to be a fictitious category since experience supposes a consciousness of the succession of events through which one has passed—
either actively or passively—and the *Heptameron* repeatedly challenges
the claim of characters to possess their own experience. We will shortly
consider the problem of Rolandine and her aunt, who exercise a
greater power after their transmutation into narrative characters about
whom claims are made than when they speak on their own behalf.
Their incarceration, which reduces them to roles of passivity and deprives them of the right to speak, seems to strengthen their position
against the institutional forces that silence them. Displaced from first
person to third person, Rolandine and her aunt provide grounds for a
claim to be restored to a dominant position. Their cases will allow us
to pursue further the relation between first and third persons in the
presenting evidence and will show how "examples" circulate within
the *Heptameron*. Before studying these important novellas, it is worth
looking at the way Marguerite de Navarre sets up the complex of
watching and testifying on one's own and on another's behalf.

The first novella of the first day has special importance in the collection because it establishes the model that other tales may imitate or
reject. Into this founding position, Marguerite de Navarre has set a
complex tale, the first in a series that ostensibly shows "the bad tricks
that women have played on men and men on women." Simontault tells
of the wife of a public prosecutor or procurator who "deceives" her
husband by having a sexual relationship with a bishop (for mercenary
reasons and apparently at the behest of the husband: "son mary la sol-
licitoit de l'entretenir") and then deceives both her husband and the
bishop by having a more erotically motivated relationship with a
young man. The young man, learning that the woman's relationship
with the bishop was more intimate than he had been led to believe,
breaks with the woman, who leaves Alençon for Argentan on the
grounds that the young man, named du Mesnil, is pursuing her against
her will. After moving to Argentan, the woman   .

> sent word to du Mesnil that in her opinion he was the most des-
> picable man alive, that she knew all about the way he had ma-
> ligned the Bishop and herself in public, and that she would see to
> it that he came to regret it. (13/73)

The young man, fearful of the bishop, goes to Argentan, where he tells
her, in a church, that he has not spoken to anyone except herself about
her conduct. Inviting the young man to her house for him to assure
her husband that he is not spreading rumors and does not believe that
the woman has any illicit relationship with the bishop, she sets in mo-

tion an arrangement in which the husband has the young man ambushed and killed. The homicide marks the end of the first half of the tale (in the François edition the narrative up to the murder takes 3½ pages, the rest takes 3 pages, and the discussion takes a half page), and the rest of the novella concerns the attempts by the husband and wife to deal with the legal, political, and financial consequences of the murder. Their first concern is for the witnesses, whom they try to eliminate in various ways. Failing to suppress testimony against them, the husband and wife flee to England. Judged in absentia, they are sentenced to death, and their property is ordered confiscated. Through the political intervention of the king of England, they obtain a pardon and return to France. Back in France, the husband hires a magician (an *invocateur*) with whom he attempts to obtain the favor of the king and the chancellor, and the death of the queen, the victim's father, and his wife. The wife, overhearing this plot, denounces her husband to an official of the duke of Alençon, who sets in motion the legal process leading to her husband's condemnation to the galleys.

This tale would certainly not strike most readers as having an immediate coherence as amatory intrigue. Although there is one act identifiable as the crisis—the death of the young lover—the multiplicity of deceptions, of characters, of administrative and legal officials, and of tactics is overwhelming. The emphasis quickly passes, despite Simontault's claim to give a typical tale of female deception, to various forms of witnessing and of hearsay information or "tales" (*comptes*). The first of these gestures of bearing information occurs when the wife's deception of du Mesnil is told indirectly by the narrator, "she swore to du Mesnil that if she bestowed favors on the Bishop, it was only so that they themselves would have more freedom to indulge in their pleasures" (12/71). Next the young man arrives at the woman's country house when the bishop is already there. Du Mesnil is told by the old servant, "Go somewhere else, friend; your place is already taken." The young man, not satisfied by this claim ("he still could not believe it at all"), stays to watch through the night until three in the morning when he sees the bishop come out of the house. When the woman next comes to see him, he tells her that "she was too holy, having touched holy things, to speak to a sinner like himself" (13/72).

Similar accumulations of claims of knowledge about what has happened occur later, but already we have an interesting collection of three types of claim. The first is the woman's own assertion concerning herself. She not merely declares but swears that her account of the relationship with the bishop is true. The bishop, she says, has only the word (*la parolle*) whereas du Mesnil is the only man who will have something other than the word ("il povoit estre asseuré que jamais homme que luy n'en auroit autre chose"). This devaluation of the word, of her word (her discourse or *parolle*, as it is used in expressions like "word of honor"), occurs on two levels. The young man is receiving her word that the bishop has only her word. The word given to the young lover is thus transmitted as if it were a superior word, a metadiscourse of some sort, capable of containing the debased word it glosses, the untrue word given to the bishop. The young man seems to accept the argument, taking as possible this kind of discursive difference by which one person's speech can split into critical truth and functional falsehood. The woman gives him sexual favors that du Mesnil might consider physical evidence corroborating the word. In fact, things really work the other way around. The physical evidence is mute—not evidence at all but the object of the dispute, not the sign but the "thing." The issue in dispute is whether the woman has an equally physical intimacy with the two men, and only her word attempts to distinguish and limit the physical gestures that bind her to du Mesnil. In fact these gestures are not even named in a direct way but only as "anything else" (*autre chose*). At this point of exhaustion of the evidentiary functions of both word and thing, discourse and reference, it is easy to see why du Mesnil believes the woman: he wants to believe her. The reason for his belief is not in anything she says, for neither her words or gestures, which circle back toward herself, can establish an objective truth. There is simply no object, only a speaking subject.

In a second type of claim about reality, we advance toward firm terrain in the servant's statement to du Mesnil. Here is, at least partially, direct discourse of an eyewitness, not the testimony of an interested party or reported discourse. As a form of "witnessing" or testimony, this discourse comes from outside the center of action, for the servant does not speak of herself.[20] The servant's intermediate place between the woman and the lover distinguishes what she says from the completely untrustworthy, self-serving, and self-referential discourse of her mistress. Although the servant is a delegate of her mistress, she distances herself from the motives and emotions of her employer. In response to the young man's question whether the husband had come, "The poor woman, who pitied him, seeing a youth so handsome, young, and courteous so much in love and so little loved in return, told him about her mistress's wantonness, thinking that, when he heard how things were, he would know better than to love her" (12/72). This oblique view of the woman's actions gives an objective account of the mistress's actions and a judgment of those actions seen from without.[21]

The servant's view compares du Mesnil and the woman and sees a didactic value in the situation ("cela le chastieroit d'aymer"). Objective reality and moral truth, example and general rule, thus coincide in a happy causal relationship, in the servant's testimony.

Du Mesnil's statement of what he has seen is a third claim about reality. The servant's account is only a step in his enlightenment, for du Mesnil stays to see for himself, completing the textual movement from the point of view of the woman to the point of view of the young man. Du Mesnil, "who still could not at all believe it," stayed until three hours after midnight to see for himself the bishop coming out of the house. On next seeing the woman, he gives direct but ironic testimony to her duplicity by telling her that "she was too holy, having touched sacred things, to speak to a sinner like himself." This is a description from a witness separated from the woman. Significantly the internal narrator renders du Mesnil's words as an ironic, and thus split or doubled, statement. Du Mesnil, by referring to the "sacred things," signals his awareness that she has had sexual relations with the bishop, an objective piece of information, but he also parodies her own rhetoric of separation between word and thing, in which the purity of her word is self-guaranteeing because it is solitary and disconnected from "autre chose que la parole." The irony here is that her word, her *parole*, is thrown back at her as truly disconnected from the world of things.[22] Since the bishop has had something "other than the word," the "other" thing, the flesh, which was elided in what she told her young lover, is reconnected in du Mesnil's remark about touching holy things. Du Mesnil, by speaking ironically, pretends to adopt the woman's and bishop's values, casting himself in the role of the outsider, the sinner. The woman's earlier promises so devalued first-person affirmation that du Mesnil's indirect approach may be a way of avoiding the fall into a contrary, but no more valid, first-person counterassertion of his own. Du Mesnil works to make her see herself from the outside by presenting himself as being on the outside, as "sinner."

These three types of claim or affirmation (first-person, third-person, and a hybrid ironic-person, which assimilates aspects of all three persons)[23] all call into question the validity of first-person claims and of subjective appreciation of one's own situation. This first series is only the beginning of a proliferation of statements by some characters about what other characters have done. The woman first misrepresents du Mesnil's actions to her husband, as a means of persuading him to move with her to Argentan, and then draws du Mesnil to Argentan on the grounds that she had heard he was speaking badly of her and the bishop (i.e., bearing false witness). Arriving in Argentan, du Mesnil finds the woman in a church and promptly testifies on his own behalf, "Madame, I come here to swear to you before God that I never spoke of your honor to anyone in the world but yourself . . . " (13/73). The woman cannot dispose of the former lover in the church not only because he has two stout servants with him, but because "there were many people in the church" and thus too many potential witnesses. Claiming to believe what du Mesnil says, she asks him to say it in person in front of her husband. When du Mesnil has been murdered in her house, the question of witnesses becomes even more explicit, as we have seen above.

Although the maidservant forced into prostitution is discredited and the victim's servants are not impartial, there are two usable sources of evidence: the testimony of the older maidservant who escapes by fleeing to the church of the Dominicans and the physical evidence of the bones, which had been burned, mixed with mortar, and built into the house of the procurator. Du Mesnil, who had ironically represented himself as a sinner, in opposition to the "holy things" of the bishop's body, has become a kind of parodic relic, the bones built into a house (as relics are built into altars). Saint-Aignan and his wife are judged in absentia (*par contumace*), on the basis of the witness, the third-person account, with reference to the mute thing that the young lover has become. At this point the story seems to have deviated significantly from Simontault's announced purpose of telling about the bad tricks played by women on men. Instead, the process of determining what other people have done and of evaluating their acts is emphasized with reference to the institutions and the technicalities of legal procedure. For instance, when Saint-Aignan obtains the intervention of the king of England, the king of France sends the detail of the case; moreover, he points out that only the duke of Alençon can grant pardon in a case originating in that duchy.

This shift to the process and mechanisms of the law shows how the novella collection itself frames life as a series of *cases*—the word *cas* appears frequently throughout the *Heptameron* and especially in this novella.[24] Each case is a two-stage judgment, first on the facts of the occurrence and second on the moral or legal values corresponding to these facts. These stages, based on an ideology of objectivity, can also be described in gradations in the syntax of person (from first person to third person) or, metaphorically, in terms of point of view. The judicial system, in its use of witnesses, makes use of such gradations, as the novella points out. The opposed parties have their own interests to defend. Servants, unless particular circumstances intervene, are considered projections of their masters, and thus not trustworthy, objective witnesses. Gradually it becomes clear that both the objective truth of facts and the moral truth derived from and applied to those facts increase as the case in question is distanced, reduced to the third person—the "non-person"—and reified by the institutional frame.

In the *Heptameron*, therefore, self-representation and self-knowledge or knowledge of one's situation are closely linked and, paradoxically, incompatible. Access to the recognized, institutionally sanctioned values of truth and fact is controlled by a collective process of assessment in which third-person, or historical, narrative dominates. If a person can learn about himself or herself, such learning has to pass through a representation from the outside. In this first novella of the *Heptameron*, there is a startling confirmation of this supposition in the final act of witnessing, one of the most startling in a book full of strange forms of self-discovery through representations in, by, and of other characters. From early in the novella the procurator's wife is active in getting rid of witnesses. When she cannot control what people believe by using words alone, she eliminates witnesses, those who connect words with things and who translate the visual into the verbal. People who see things are her greatest danger; in their words she discovers herself (or finds that she has been discovered objectively, as a case: "elle entendit que son cas estoit descouvert").

This final witnessing occurs during the husband's plot with a magician (an *invocateur*) to cause the death of his wife and others. Making wax statues (images, *ymaiges*) is part of this magic, and the wife discovers the whole plan:

> When his wife, who saw everything through the keyhole, heard that he was putting her among the dead, she decided that she would see to it that he died first. And, pretending to go to borrow some money from an uncle of hers named Neaufle, *maître de requêtes* of the Duke of Alençon, she told him everything that she had seen and heard her husband do. (17/77)

Not only discovering what her husband is doing, the wife discovers herself in the form of an image, a statue. This statue is not representational in any realistic way. The collection of statues the magician uses as prototypes for his spells is not made to look like the individuals concerned. Instead each model is simply named to stand for an individual. The husband goes through the wooden statues and names each, "This one will be for the King . . . and this one for my lord the chancellor of Alençon Brinon . . . " and so on. Nonetheless, the statue does represent the wife as token within the magician's convention. In fact, the lack of likeness, the arbitrary and even brutal designation of a statue as herself ("the second woman with arms lowered was his wife, who was the cause of all his troubles"), accentuates the way in which her control over the representation of herself is torn away from her. Confronting, through the keyhole, her image in an object she cannot recognize as herself, the wife reaches the extreme point of her attempt to maintain herself in the first person within a discursive construction of her own. Her response to this outrage, this semiological nightmare, is to play the role of witness within the institutional framework of both kingdom and novella. Finding an administrator, she puts what she has seen into words ("compter ce qu'elle avoit veu et oy de son mary"), thus setting in motion the widening diffusion of this "case" in the judicial-political network:

> The aforesaid Neaufle, as a loyal old servant, went to the chancellor of Alençon and told him the whole story. And, because the duke and duchess were not at court that day, the chancellor went to tell this strange case to the Regent, mother of the King and of the duchess of Alençon, who immediately sent for the provost of Paris, La Barre. (17/77)

The wife's image is the kernel around which this whole case is built, and the wife herself occupies the witness's position, off to one side. The magic makes her see herself as another, so that she can speak of her depiction in the third person and as one of a series.

Serving as the link between her image and the institutional structure, which echoes with the story she tells, the wife confirms the importance of the concept of "veritable history" through a contiguous or metonymic validation.[25] The novellas claim a guarantee to truth through a *nearby* witness, someone who is historically linked to the house of Valois and the court of Francis I or Marguerite de Navarre. In this first novella the judicial-political network, which judges, punishes, and pardons the characters, is the *same* group linked in the prologue with the intended production of a novella collection like the *Heptameron* itself. The concentric circles of telling and retelling—Neaufle tells the chancellor, who tells the Regent, and so on—that begin here culminate in the shadow court of the storytellers. The repeated references to the French court emphasize the claim that narration and tale belong to the same reality. The "case" within this first novella is put together in a way much like the "examples" (*exemples*) within the *Heptameron* as a whole.

The first novella is told as an example of how bad women are to men, and it is like the image of the procurator's wife. The tale is an image of women, for women, but made by a male character-narrator.

Simontault presents the actions of the procurator's wife to the women storytellers: "See, my ladies, what harm comes from a bad woman and how many crimes were committed on account of the sin of this woman [Je vous suplie, mes dames, regardez quel mal il vient d'une meschante femme et combien de maulx se feirent pour le peché de ceste cy]," (18/ 78) as a potential image of themselves. Within the novella, the magic image is the work of two men collaborating in the designation of a general prototype as the statue of a specific woman.[26]

Schematizing the process of representation that will be used in the *Heptameron*, the tale of the procurator's wife sets up the alternation between first- and third-person statement and gives a sample of how a person can see herself in an image. With this emphasis on vision from without, an objective or objectifying view, the *Heptameron* takes as a central assumption the existence of a blind spot, the invisibility of self to self. The wife's self-presentation was inevitably fallacious, but she gives an exact account of how she saw herself in an image, and she recognized her acts in du Mesnil's ironic statement of them. Yet the real value of seeing such representations is not their likeness but their unlikeness, the shock of discovering a gap between our ideas and what corresponds to those ideas in the outside world. The magic image of the novella is not a "likeness" of Saint-Aignan's wife even though it stands for her.[27] What she sees, therefore, is not a mirroring of herself, but her husband's attempt to represent her in the magic system that condemns her to death. The situation forces her to understand this deformed representation (because if she did not admit that the statue stood for her, she would never have been able to undo its magic) even though she does not really "see herself" in the image. Likewise, Simontault's whole story, which is supposed to support a general belief that women do bad things to men, is either excessive or defective, since it says so many other things while not providing conclusive evidence for his evaluation of women. We can see a woman committing some crimes, but this simple plot is overwhelmed by the framework of methods of representing, proving, and disproving.

One reason for this drift is that Simontault, like all the narrators of the *Heptameron*, is representing himself in this story of someone else. The statement with which he makes the transition from story to discussion in the frame-narrative renders this quite explicit:

> You will find that since Eve made Adam sin all women have had the task of tormenting, killing, and damning men. As for me, I have experienced the cruelty of women so much that I think I will never die except through the despair in which one of them has

> cast me. And I am still so foolish that I must confess that hell
> is more pleasant, coming from her hand, than paradise from the
> hand of another. (18/78)

Because the "veritable history" is biased by the narrator's attempt to
represent his own situation, he gives a distorted account in all that concerns men. Just as the judicial process discounts witnesses who have a
stake in the outcome of the trial, so the novella process, which is so
inextricably interwined with that of the judiciary, must discount the
affirmations of an interested narrator. But all narrators, in the conflict
between men and women, are necessarily biased; they all have something at stake. Moreover, they are all struck by the blindness of their
self-representation. The tales are ways in which each storyteller at
Serrance attempts to support the positions expressed in discussion
(first-person discourse) by creating a separate, distanced, and allegedly
more trustworthy "historical" example. The conflict at the discursive
level (I/you) is thus transmuted into a conflict at the historical or story
level (he/she; they/they). The result is that the opponent-partners of
the frame-narrative can discover images of themselves in narrative representation. This discovery is made up of both recognition and revul-
sion; it is truly a discovery through and of alienation.

By displaying the concept of the witness so copiously in this opening novella, Marguerite de Navarre provides a key to the relationship
between the frame-narrative and the content of the novellas. The witness is the link between judgment and event, while excentric or mar-
ginal to both. The example is the link between "truth" and "reality,"
neither pure conceptual language nor pure and naïve vision of the
world. The witness can often say more than he or she means to say,
just as an example can. Both are subject to interrogation by the oppo-
nent, to cross-examination. Witnesses also perform a role in the insertion of example into the act of judgment, for all examples must be
certified by someone other than the speaker who proposes the example. The whole public may be called on to witness to the truth of an
example—this is the most classical practice according to Aristotle and
Quintilian. But in the *Heptameron* examples enter as new, as news (*nouvelles*), on the duplicitous word of the speaker. In this way the figure
of the witness becomes a bridge between narrative process and exemplary discovery, for the speaker, in representing his or her truth, bears
witness against himself or herself just as the characters in the novellas
bear witness against themselves. In this particular form of testimony,
testimony involving a vision of oneself, the *Heptameron* reaches the
most profound union of rhetoric and ideology. The wife who wit-

nesses her unlike representation and goes to testify about this magic representation, is a figure of the exemplary exteriority by which the characters of the novellas reveal themselves despite, or because of, their attempts to control and limit how others perceive them. It is assuredly not accidental that example has been described as the rhetorical figure that most exalts the teacher over the learner, for the process of making examples designates the speaker/teacher as having a power to give to the listeners—perhaps to return to the listeners—a vision of their own life to which they cannot accede directly.[28]

ROLANDINE AND HER AUNT

Example occurs when speakers stop giving their own unsupported opinion, when they move out of discourse and into history. Marguerite has given two interlocking novellas that demonstrate the creation of an exemplary story out of the silencing of a speaker. That the silence is involuntary only illustrates more forcefully that example requires a movement from first to third person and from the uniqueness of the "I" to the multiple and serial nature of the "he" or "she." Like the first novella, the story pair of Rolandine and her aunt concerns men who try to prevent women from speaking and thus turn them into characters who are spoken about. The way in which these novellas interlock (the character in one novella has already heard what happened to the character in the other) raises the question of what can be learned, if anything, from such examples.

The celebrated novellas concerning "Rolandine" and her aunt are among the tales that have been most confidently described as fully historical. These novellas, the first story of the third day and the last story of the fourth day (numbers 21 and 40), both narrated by Parlamente, are apparently based on the lives of Anne de Rohan and Catherine de Rohan, daughter and sister respectively of Jean II, vicomte de Rohan.[29] The narratives are linked in a way unique in the *Heptameron*, for they have a character in common, Jossebelin, Rolandine's father (in novella 21) and her aunt's brother (in novella 40). In the first story Parlamente announces the later one, and in the second story she recalls the first. The heroines' sufferings are in many ways parallel—both are forbidden to marry, both contract a secret marriage that is destroyed, and both are imprisoned in the same castle. The two novellas raise the problem of a repetition in history manifested by a repetition in storytelling. But more important, both stories concern the creation of history and the suppression of discourse.

Rolandine's story is worth recalling in some detail. She is presented as a kinswoman of the queen, at whose court she serves. Her father's neglect and the queen's antipathy cause her to pass her youth without marrying. Resigning herself to this state, she spends her time praying and living in an honest and saintly way. Finally she meets another unfortunate whose state has prevented him from marrying, a bastard.[30] The two of them see one another, first openly, then, after the queen forbids it, secretly, and even contract a clandestine marriage. The many incidents of Rolandine's story form an account of royal attempts to regulate discourse: by silencing Rolandine, blocking every channel of communication with her husband, and extracting words from those who want to remain silent. "If you are willing to speak the truth, you will be saved," the soldiers cry to an accomplice of the lovers before throwing him bound into the water. Only the king's confessor, cleverly reassembling the fragments of a letter, is able to bring the proof of the marriage.

When the queen confronts Rolandine, the heroine erupts in an open challenge to royal and parental authority. Her marriage, which threatens the royal control over history through the succession of family power, also threatens the discursive control of the court. Rolandine defends her action, setting forth individual right and sentiment against the constraint of institutions (her husband would be of the same rank as she "if the love of two persons were valued as much as the ring" [168/246]), and claims that she will remain married: "I am decided to sustain this purpose [*propos*]."

Rolandine's crime is a crime of speech. The *propos* is not merely a "plan" or "intention" but, closer both to the Latin and the modern usage, something *set forth* (*proponere*) or exposed. The disclosure, the revelation of a fissure in the royal control, is clearly the primordial crime:

> Seeing that Rolandine was resolute and that she meant every word she said, the Queen was quite incapable of making a reasonable reply. She burst into tears and went on raging at Rolandine, making accusations and hurling insults at her. "Miserable wretch that you are! Instead of being humble and sorry for the serious offence you have committed, you dare to speak in this outrageous fashion with never a tear in your eye! . . . But if the King and your father heed my words, they'll put you where you'll be obliged to sing another tune [*parler autre langage*]!" (169–70/247–48)

Rolandine's speech in response to the queen's attempt to control and limit her subject is not so much a defense of her marriage as it is of the right to speak the truth:

Since I have none to speak for me, except truth itself, which I alone know, I must declare that truth fearlessly, hoping that, if it is known to you, you will not believe me to be such as you have called me. I have no fear of any mortal hearing how I have behaved. (169–70/248)

What Rolandine says may be intolerable, but that she says it herself, without advocate or intermediary, is even more outrageous. As witness to her own marriage, only Rolandine and her bastard husband could establish its occurrence. Moreover, she establishes a difference between her knowledge of the truth and the possible recognition of that truth by others. Rolandine is setting herself up as an elected vessel of truth. No advocate could speak for her in the same way, so that even though she proposes herself as a substitute for her advocate (who would be a substitute for herself), no substitution is possible. The truth is established by Rolandine's speaking. Though one may argue that the narrator shows sympathy for Rolandine's position, within the world of the novella itself Rolandine speaks alone in defense of the individual word. Essentially she argues for an individualist subjective transcendence of the social authority as incarnate in the queen, king, and father, the historically dominant authorities. On her side, Rolandine alleges a divine Father who is not here but who is the exact inverse of the earthly, real (historical) father: "But I have a Father in heaven, who, I am sure, will give me much patience in proportion to the evils you inflict, and in Him alone I have perfect confidence" (170/249). The "I" is the safeguard of law and divine right. In speaking the truth, Rolandine does not fear God and need not fear any human person. The symmetry is clear. Rolandine is the substitute of her substitute (the advocate); the Father in heaven is the substitute of the father on earth. The earthly father should have spoken out to permit her marriage (he had, on the contrary, given a "cold response" to proposals); she should not have had to marry herself. In a certain way Rolandine is therefore the substitute for her father, but, more radically, she is also the substitute for her Father. God may be on Rolandine's side, but He cannot speak for her; she must speak for Him. God is within her word, not external to it. He was the witness to her marriage ("they kissed in the church before God, whom they took as witness to their promise," 162/240). But she alone in the novella gives witness to Him. God is not one of her listeners but the very truth that she is speaking, a truth known to her: "I know that God and my honor are in no way offended. And that this is what makes me speak without fear, being sure that He who sees my heart is with me . . . " (170/248). This defense of the word (Word) itself runs head-on into the institutional refusal and deprecation of the word, as expressed in the struggle between Rolandine and the churchmen and lawyers over the status of her marriage. These spokesmen,

> arguing with her, *since her marriage existed only in words*, it could be easily set aside, and that they leave one another, according to the King's wish that she do so in order to preserve the honor of her family [*maison*]. She replied that in all things she was ready to obey the King, unless it were a thing against her conscience. But what God has put together, men cannot separate. She asked them not to tempt her with such an unreasonable request, for if love and good will founded on the fear of God are the true bonds of matrimony, she was so firmly bound that neither iron, nor fire, nor water, could break her bonds. (171/250)

Here the identification of Rolandine's discourse with the divine reaches its apogee, for Rolandine has by her pledge not only bound herself but, in a sense, God as well. She could have married another, but once she has given her word, that act is fully guaranteed by God.[31]

The punishment that Rolandine suffers—being shut up in a castle in a forest—is a last attempt to prevent her from speaking, an attempt therefore to exclude her from the world of discourse and to reject her into the world of history (the castle itself comes from the world of history, from the history of her aunt). By shutting her out of the city, out of the court, beyond any human society, the forces against Rolandine prevent her from being a subject of discourse and convert her into the "non-person," as Benveniste defines the third person of grammar.[32] Within the world of the novella, people will hear *about* Rolandine, but they will not hear Rolandine:

> Although she [had done] wrong, the punishment was so harsh and her constancy so great, that it made her offence seem a virtue. Her father, when he heard the pitiful news [*nouvelle*], refused to see her, and sent her to a castle in a forest—a castle which he had built in previous years for a purpose which is worthy of being recounted. (172/250)

Already Rolandine is, within the novella, the subject of third-person narrative. Her story is told by her father as a *nouvelle*, with the full ambiguity of that term: not only a piece of news but, in a collection of stories that cites its model in "Boccaccio's novellas," also a novella, within which Rolandine is a character. While Rolandine's words were and remain dangerous—so dangerous that her father's refusal to see her may not only be a punishment for her but also a defense for himself—her *nouvelle*, her history, turns out to be equally dangerous and achieves the opposite result from that intended by her enemies. Now, not Rolandine's speech but the reports about her, her story, change the perception of what she did. This transformation, by which *fault* becomes *virtue*, is not due to a voluntary gesture by Rolandine but to the action of her enemies ("the punishment was so great") and is therefore one of Rolandine's characteristics as *persona* within a story.

From this moment on, Rolandine disappears from the novella as speaker and appears only as character.[33] We are fully within the story—and indeed within the *histoire* of Rolandine, whose discourse is now redeemed and guaranteed, as she said it would be, by the story of what God does next. For instance, the husband is unfaithful: "Thus it was that the divine Goodness, who is perfect charity and true love, had pity on her sorrow and looked upon her long-suffering, for not many days later the bastard in full pursuit of another woman met his end" (173/252). So this loving and deadly God acts to rid Rolandine of her troublesome brother: "But God provided for them. For one day this brother who wanted to keep everything for himself died unexpectedly, leaving behind him both his own inheritance and the inheritance that rightly belonged to his sister" (174/253).

To recapitulate quickly the relationship between history and discourse in the story of Rolandine (story 21), we can identify three allied concepts that are all grouped under the term history: the historical narrative (*récit d'histoire*), the actual occurrence, and those institutions traditionally the subjects of historical narrative and that frequently attempt to control that narrative (kings and aristocratic houses). In another contrast to these historical instances, Rolandine represents the concept of discourse—as the speech of a subject of enunciation (a speaking "I")—chiefly as an act opposed to the silence mandated by the historical institutions. Moreover, the subject of this discourse, once silenced, becomes the subject of history.

Rolandine's aunt ended up in the same castle. In the act of narrating, the castle serves therefore as the first-mentioned and principal link between the two stories and the two women. Within the world of both narratives the castle serves the same function, keeping the woman from talking, and represents the authority of the same person in two roles (as brother and as father). The castle is a concrete form of the institution of the *maison* or family. Rolandine's marrying a bastard without her father's consent was a threat to his *maison* (171/250), and the castle is that form of a *maison* that can prevent further injury to its name. The figure of the castle thus unites historical institution with historical narrative, because it marks the moment in novella 21 when the heroine stops speaking and becomes a historical character. The castle also marks the conjunction between two historical narratives. Moreover, the castle serves as the figure for historical occurrence, for what has preceded something in time, since the castle is what remains from a previous event, the incarceration of a nameless woman.

This nameless woman, the sister of the comte de Jossebelin in story 40, is beautiful and loved by her brother so much that "he preferred her to his wife and children." From a combination of love and avarice, Jossebelin keeps her from accepting any of the worthy proposals of marriage made to her. When her youth has passed, she and a young gentleman who lives as a servant in Jossebelin's household fall in love. Having heard her brother say that there is no one he would prefer as brother-in-law, she and her lover marry, before a priest and witnesses, and pass several years of clandestine wedlock before Jossebelin discovers the arrangement. Thereupon he has the husband killed before the wife's eyes and then has a castle constructed in a forest for the specific purpose of keeping his sister from talking: "being afraid that his sister would seek revenge or would appeal to the law, he had a castle built in the middle of a forest in which he shut her up, forbidding anyone to speak with her" (277/370). The castle does not stop people from talking about the brother's crime, and there is no indication of steps taken to prevent reports of his action. But the castle does prevent his sister from executing a specific discursive act with judicial effect, the act of accusal. Jossebelin forbids people to talk to her, not about her. The consequence of this silencing is remarkably similar to what happened in Rolandine's case. The aunt's prison makes her a saint. Refusing to consider another marriage proposed to her by her brother, she finishes her life in her prison in patience and austerity so that after her death "people from far and wide visited her remains as if she had been a saint [comme à une saincte]" (277/370). The culmination of her fame occurs when she will never speak again.

The historical institution of the family or *maison* in both instances functions to repress the heroine's dangerous speech, but by doing so causes her to reappear as a dangerous character within a story. In the long run the heroine—who is thus both heroine of the novella and heroine of a certain fabulation occurring within the novella—triumphs over the authorities who have persecuted her. But it would be difficult to say that one instance of language wins out over the other. The heroine of the word does win, but not through the word itself. Rolandine is right. God did strike her enemies. But this is evident only within the novella as narrative, as *histoire*, for her discourse alone did not prevail.

Having seen the struggle between history and discourse in the primary diegetic level of the *Heptameron* in novellas 21 and 40, we are able to consider the discussions themselves in a new light. One might even go so far as to say that in a certain way the stories comment on the discussions. The discussions are, like Rolandine's angry statement to the queen in story 21, discourse that represents the values and judgments of individuals. These opinions do not grow out of the stories that are told; instead, the opinion precedes and motivates the story. Each storyteller chooses to counter the position of an interlocutor in the discussion by an appeal to history as example. But no example from history can ever exhaust history. There may always be a counter-example. This explosive potential of the novella is clearly recognized as both an opportunity for formal perfection and as a threat, for novella collections are often described or titled in ways that accentuate an arithmetic constraint (*Decameron, Heptameron, Pentameron, Cent Nou-velles nouvelles, Les Quinze Joies de mariage*), which sets a limit to the potentially endless material.

Marguerite has chosen to set a second condition to limit the prolif-eration of her narratives, the requirement of historical actuality. But even this, without the arithmetic limit, would be endlessly productive. The first words of the first day of the *Heptameron* are Simontault's:

> Ladies, I have been so ill rewarded for my long and devoted ser-vice, that, in order to avenge myself on Love and on the woman who is so cruel to me, I shall do my utmost to collect together all the accounts of foul deeds perpetrated by women on us poor men. And every single one will be the unadulterated truth. (11/70)

This desire to be exhaustive and to make a complete enumeration, *ung recueil*, is the great weakness of the story as didactic tool. Remaining in the pure realm of historical narrative, it cannot rise into the realm of judgment and value because all affirmation is undermined by the end-less process of new experience and counteraffirmation.

Such judgment, the ethical side of a novella collection, must come from outside of the event itself, from the discursive commentary ap-plied to the narrative. If this seems circular, that is because it is circular and, once more, risks running on forever. The discussion elicits stories to back up positions in the discussion, which then produces more sto-ries to back up contrary positions. Another way to put this is to say that the discussions are not really interpretative but polemical, and the goal of the examples is not to extract truth from them but to use them to establish one's authority within a discursive situation.

The discussion following the story of Rolandine is brief and oriented strictly along the lines of Rolandine's fidelity and her lover/husband's infidelity. All the rest—the antagonism and persecution inflicted on Rolandine (and to a lesser extent her lover), their stratagems to overcome the obstacles created by the queen, the loyalty and cleverness of their intermediaries, Rolandine's eloquent and courageous defense of her rights—all this is simply not mentioned.[34] In designating the story as an example, the frame-narrator, Parlamente, says of Rolandine, "Well, Ladies, let the men, who are so fond of representing us women as lacking in constancy, produce an *example* of a husband who was as good, as faithful and as constant as the woman in this story" (174/253).[35] One could, in fact, easily read the comments of the discussants as praising only Rolandine's fidelity after her arrest, thus setting aside more than half of a long and extremely detailed story in this brief discussion.

In the case of the nameless aunt (in story 40), Parlamente points the discussion in a direction exactly opposed to the action of the tale's heroine:

> Ladies, I pray God that you will take note of this example, and that none of you will wish to marry merely for your own pleasure, without the consent of those to whom you owe obedience. For marriage is an estate of long duration, and one which should not be entered into lightly or without the approval of our closest friends and relatives. Even then, however wisely one marries, one is bound to find at least as much pain as pleasure. (277/370)

The irony of this "interpretive" statement is hard to ignore if one considers that the heroine's "closest kin" is precisely the person who destroys her every hope of marriage out of motives that the narrative itself indicates are based on his own good and not his sister's; that the marriage was not long-lasting because of the action of the kinsman whose function should be (in Parlamente's reasoning) to increase its duration; and that the only pain associated with this particular marriage is its termination, not its internal strivings.[36] Parlamente's comment would apply as well, if not better, to Rolandine's story, for the aunt was guided in her choice of a husband by her brother's opinion and did not openly defy authority, whereas Rolandine disobeyed her father, the queen, and the king. Rolandine, moreover, married without a priest or human witness. It seems almost as if the "lessons" of the two stories had been scrambled. One could easily imagine assigning to Rolandine's aunt praise for fidelity to a husband. After all, she married only once, and after her husband's death she refused to marry again, preferring to live out her days in saintly widowhood. Conversely, the blame that the aunt receives for having married without permission could easily be given to Rolandine. The cross-reference of the two stories is such that the commentary on one is bound to affect our reading of the other.

The comments in the discussion of story 21 are largely in agreement in praise of Rolandine. The second discussion is much more specifically addressed to the events of the narrative and shows much less agreement. In other words, the first story precedes a discussion that either trivializes the narrative by ignoring most of it or swerves away from the narrative altogether, while the second story produces considerable disagreement about the behavior of the characters. This is an extremely interesting outcome in view of the second comment on the second story, Oisille's affirmation of the efficacy of the example of the aunt: "In all truth, said Oisille, even if there were neither God nor law to teach girls to be good, this example is sufficient to give them more reverence for their parents than to think of marrying according to their own wishes" (277/371). Oisille, the most scripturally oriented of the frame-characters, is the least likely to argue a position in the hypothetical absence of God or law. Yet here she declares that this utterly secular history would be sufficient to teach women their "place."

Oisille strongly affirms not only the correctness of a certain conduct but the convincing didacticism of the "history as example." In other words, we have a test-case for the rhetorical efficacy of example at least insofar as the extreme claim to effect change in the conduct of the audience or receiver is concerned, the claim to constitute a new "secular scripture" that could function outside the older Scripture. Perhaps we should take Oisille's claim as hyperbole; at least she is saying the example works. But it doesn't. The story of the aunt was the second of the two only in the order of narration, but the story of the aunt took place before the story of Rolandine. If anyone knew the aunt's story, that person must have been Rolandine. Yet her conduct was not affected by it in any apparent way, unless one assumes that the accumulation of injustices can be considered as explaining *a contrario* the niece's refusal to submit. Thus the insistence on behaving *like* the aunt would be implicitly a manifestation of Rolandine's determination not to accept the story as manifestation of a rule of the folly of disobedience. Not only does the effect of the aunt's example on Rolandine run against the interpretation given by Parlamente and Oisille, but the second story runs into a strong rebuttal from several of the other frame-characters.

Nomerfide most strongly attacks the center of Oisille's contention that the outcome of history, the evolution and conclusion of actual event, can itself teach a value.[37] Even the misery of this widow is not decisive, in Nomerfide's view, for history as source of meaning can only be actualized by a subjective decision, one that appears in language as discourse. Nomerfide's demonstration of this principle involves a combination of personal commentary and a restatement of the story of the aunt in concise historical terms:

> She who has a good day in the year is not unhappy for her whole life. She had the pleasure of seeing and speaking for a long time with the man she loved more than herself; and then she had marital pleasure with him without any pangs of conscience. I consider this happiness so great that it seems to me to surpass the ill that she suffered. (277/371)

What Nomerfide says here seems perfectly to agree with the values of Rolandine and her aunt, yet this statement has vaster implications than a simple criticism of a given interpretation of an example. Nomerfide is showing that any story, any historical account, can be simultaneously respected in its detail and called to support widely varying subjective values.[38] Thus she underscores the malleableness of history, which awaits the imposition of meaning through the discursive statement of either an external commentator—a frame-character of the *Heptameron*—or an internal commentator like Rolandine herself. We might even say that history (as the actual) and histories (as the linguistic statement of the actual) await the discourse of a subject who alone can select values and a pattern of conduct from among the paradigms offered.

In the frame-narrative, Parlamente, the narrator, and Oisille, the most enthusiastic exponent of the total efficacy of historical example, are not only on the side of those (the queen and father) who limit the freedom of the heroine, but also on the side of the *process* of historical narrative. Yet in the case of these two frame-characters as well, that process escapes their control: Oisille is wrong in her assertion that even without God or law one must accept the lesson of submission taught by the history of Rolandine's aunt.

Rolandine, within the novella, and Nomerfide, outside of it, speak on the side of a subjective right, which is within that very discourse. Rolandine speaks in the name of the eternal truth of God, whose invisible presence compensates for the actual deficiencies of queen and father. This God is not part of her experience, but precisely absent from that experience, outside of time and present only to faith. He is the Word within Rolandine's word. In taking the side of the aunt, Nomerfide underlines the way in which moments can be measured in subjective terms having nothing to do with the way a third party would see the passage of time. To exalt "one good day a year" is to refuse both the teleology of history (always oriented towards consequences) and the tendency of exemplary narrative to deny individual, internal values in favor of external, institutional ones (apparent in the actions of the makers of history—the queen, the brother, the narrator). Yet Nomerfide accepts history as occurrence and uses it to authorize her own discursive statement of value.

It would be difficult to draw any clear conclusions from the *Heptameron* about the relationship between history and the truth of discourse except to say that the relationship is problematic and in a state of flux. Truth is not merely "extracted" from history as content from a container, nor does discourse necessarily follow history to interpret and validate it. Oisille says that history should teach something, but she is wrong about what it taught (at least as far as what it teaches Rolandine, Nomerfide, Geburon, and Simontault). Rolandine's triumph in novella 21, in which she survives the death of faithless husband, avaricious father, and cruel brother to marry again and live happily, is a way in which history seems to give *a posteriori* support of her discourse to the queen. We are confronted here with neither an allegorical history within which truth can be read as preexistent message nor an empirical history systematically used to validate or invalidate hypotheses. Instead, the *Heptameron* marks the grave crisis of history—in all senses of the term—which strikes the sixteenth and seventeenth centuries.

It is easy to think of Marguerite de Navarre's use of example as leading toward an *aporia*. Claims and counterclaims (the "truth" of a discursive "I"), examples and counterexamples (the "truth" of a historical "she," "he," or "they") succeed one another without apparently providing a firm basis for a stable, useful knowledge. Is the *Heptameron* simply a literary pastime after all, without further claim to impart knowledge?

There are reasons for believing that the *Heptameron* is not an aporetic text but a paradoxical one. The clues to the distinction between aporia and paradox are laid out as early as the prologue, with its emphasis on both theological and generic codes. To arrive at an understanding of this paradoxically exemplary book—or book about paradoxical examples—we must take into account both the doctrinal religious context of Marguerite de Navarre's work and her use of the thematics and structure of the Boccaccian secular tradition in literature. If we do this, we can achieve a sense, first, of how example can reveal truth without providing models of proper conduct and, second, of how the first person, the "I," can yield exemplary knowledge in narrative situations that are profoundly alienating and alienated.

INVOLUNTARY EXAMPLES

If Rolandine was both correct and completely powerless in her first-person assertions, her example—the story about her—may still contain a useful truth. But how can we find it? Marguerite de Navarre shows repeatedly that the only key to knowledge is based on a theology of grace and emphasizes that we are likely to find the truth not in our discourse but in example. Exemplary narratives of Rolandine and her aunt are produced when other characters silence the discourse of these two heroines. There is another novella, story 62, where the switch between discourse and history is more striking, for a narrator makes an involuntary example out of herself. This story, which could be called the "tale of the sheet," demonstrates how an example can derive its power from the narrator's loss of control.

In the "tale of the sheet" a young married woman tells a visiting noblewoman an amusing story (*ung beau compte*) to pass the time, assuring her that the story is true (*le compte est très veritable*). The story concerns a young woman married to an older man. A neighbor tried for several years to seduce her, but not succeeding, went into her bedroom one day when she was alone and raped her. Then, when the servant women were returning, he hastily got up and, not noticing that one of his spurs was caught on a sheet, walked away, taking the sheet with him. And, in conclusion, the narrator declares, "No woman has ever been as embarrassed as I was, when I found myself completely naked!" (378/486). The noblewoman hearing the story and up to then not particularly amused burst out laughing at this revelation, entirely unintended, that the narrator and the character in the story were one and the same woman. The narrator was, as a consequence, entirely and irreparably disgraced: "The poor woman did her best to try to retrieve her honour—but too late, the bird had flown and there was no calling it back!" (378/486).

There are many similarities between this novella and the first novella of the *Heptameron*, the one about the procurator's wife. In both cases women discover a representation that is out of their control. For the procurator's wife this representation is the statue made by the magician. She has no control over it, but it may have a magical control over her. The fear that some harm can come to her from such a "third-person" representation forces her to choose the side of just authority against her husband. In the tale of the sheet the woman telling the tale had no intention of representing *herself* in the story, but when she realizes that she has made a spectacle out of herself and let her story, attached to herself, slip into general circulation, she is profoundly humiliated. This humiliation itself is the principal value of example in the *Heptameron*.

Tale 62 with its involuntary confession shows how effectively Marguerite uses "veritable history" as source of enlightenment to the speaker, the teller of the tale. Narratives may tell an objective truth independent of the will of the narrator. First, the internal narrator, the young woman, insists on cautioning her listeners that they must not repeat the story, thereby heightening the sense of hiding or covering something. Second, the woman within the story, as victim, is told that if she speaks out, her assailant will "tell everyone that she had sent for him" (378/486). Third, the sheet pulled off the bed literally uncovers the victim while serving also, in the telling of the story, to uncover the identity and the shame of the narrator. In addition, the lapsus, thoroughly disgracing the woman, is a result of her attempt not to disgrace herself, first by hiding the event itself in response to her attacker's threat and second by hiding her identity. What is really emphasized is not the thing hidden, the rape, but the act of concealment and the subsequent more damaging revelation. The resultant humiliation is the goal of the story, for, as Oisille says, "when we recount the evil doings of the men and women in our stories, we are not doing it in order to bring shame upon individuals, but in order to remove the esteem [and] trust placed in the mere creatures of God, by means of displaying the miseries to which those creatures are subject, to the end that our hope may come to rest upon Him who alone is perfect and without whom all men are but imperfection" (317/416).

In one of the epigraphs to this chapter, the Italian verses attributed to the stag's head (or antlers, *teste de cerf*) on the wall of a great room (*Io porto le corna, ciascun lo vede; / Ma tal le porta, che no lo crede*), there is a phenomenon similar to what happens in the story of the woman who publicly and unwittingly speaks of the violence to which she was subjected. The stag's head appears in the third story of the *Heptameron*, a story about the adulterous king of Naples and how his wife justifiably cuckolded him with a gentleman of the king's retinue. The king's love affair with the gentleman's wife is quite well known, and the husband is publicly disgraced. On the other hand, the gentleman who has a reciprocal adulterous relation to the queen is quite discreet, so that the king does not know that he too is the victim of his wife's infidelity. Seeing the stag's head on the wall in the gentleman's house one day, the king could not keep himself from laughingly proclaiming that these horns were very appropriately displayed in that house. Thereafter the husband has the inscription written on the stag's head. Although the king realizes that there is some mystery to this inscription, he cannot quite figure it out, even when the gentleman gives him a sibylline interpretation.[39] The interplay between what one knows of oneself and what others know and what one knows others know of oneself is here even more complex than in the tale of the sheet. The king, unlike the woman of the other story, does not know of his disgrace; he is blind to it whereas she was aware of it. She realizes what she revealed after the fact, while the king's disgrace is declared without his knowledge (and to an extremely small group). This blindness to one's own state is the ultimate degradation, and the king is aware that the gentleman knows something that he, the king, does not. The writer of the inscription has a refined superiority over the king, despite the crude satisfaction the king has of his more public amorous victory. The stag's head takes on, therefore, a truly emblematic quality, in proclaiming the biblical precept that we can always see the mote in our neighbor's eye but not the beam in our own. Like the magical statue that is made of the prosecutor's wife in the first story, the stag's head is an image of the king. But the woman was able to recognize the statue as a representation of herself even though it did not look like her, while the king is incapable of seeing the stag's head as a representation of himself as cuckold.[40] The stag's head is generalizable as emblem of exemplarity, for tale after tale shows how the discovery of resemblance is only possible from the *outside*. The insistence on cuckoldry as the quintessential male disgrace is ancient and banal in the novella tradition. Marguerite has seized upon it as archetypal form of all disgrace (that is, all existence without grace). The cuckold is not a man whose wife is unfaithful to him; he is, instead, a man treated by society as being fallen, as having lost control of what is "his." To be a cuckold is to be regarded, looked upon, in a certain way—to have invisible horns. The cuckold can only see the horns of cuckoldry in the eyes of those around him. The best one can learn from example is to recognize in others the "horns" we all wear, the flaws we all have, the failure of control over whatever construction we have put upon ourselves. In other terms, the exemplary is the triumph of the Symbolic over the Imaginary because it represents the victory of the socially imposed, interchangeable version of truth over the delusional individual Imaginary. It is therefore not surprising that the stag's head be a kind of mirror for the king, who lacks the ability to recognize himself in "mirrors." The woman who told the tale of the sheet, however, did recognize herself in the character of her story.

Her story and other such narratives are exemplary, though not in a positive sense. They present a complex lesson of humility. Marguerite de Navarre contrasts her use of example in such tales with the tradition of preaching *exempla*. We have seen that monks play a large role in the *Heptameron*, where they are not only a reference to a contemporary social reality but, even more, a connotative gesture toward a familiar kind of rhetoric. The great expansion in the use of narrative examples or *exempla* in preaching in the thirteenth century is solidly linked to the influence of the preaching orders, the Dominicans and the Franciscans.[41] Monks of these orders made particular use of a rhetoric of *exemplum* and also figured as characters in such narratives.[42] Moreover, the use of example in rhetorical situations—whether example be understood in the narrow sense of *paradeigma* or the broad sense of intercalated narrative or *exemplum*—has since antiquity been associated with speaking to an audience of untrained persons, persons who are not able to grasp doctrines in a more abstract or arid form (we recall Jacques de Vitry's recommendations of *vulgaria exempla ad laicorum excitationem et recreationem . . . interserenda*). Hence, *exemplum* connotes the relationship between a subjected and ignorant laity and a dominant and informed class of preachers.

By putting her storytellers in a monastery, where the laity speaks while the monks listen from behind the hedges, Marguerite de Navarre reverses the traditional relationship. Most pointedly the *Heptameron* narrators choose to give "examples," and within these examples the monks play an important but unenviable role. One-quarter of the *Heptameron* stories are about priests and monks, almost invariably shown in the worst light. By maintaining the reference to the tradition of preaching while altering the roles of clergy and laity, Marguerite de Navarre focuses attention on the institutional claims of teaching with examples (*exempla*) and on the role of the teachers themselves as both givers of examples and exemplary figures—whether for good or evil— in their own conduct.[43]

The lay "invasion" of the monastery inverts the movement typical of novella collections in general—and of the stories of the *Heptameron* itself—where monks, in the fictive "ordinary life," invade the houses of the laity. Such a standard novella situation, reminiscent of Boccaccio, occurs in story 23. A husband is so impressed by the Franciscans that he has a bedroom constructed for them in his house. He consults with them on his most intimate domestic problems, including the morality of sleeping with his wife within a certain time since her giving birth. Another man, in story 31, gives charge of his household to a Franciscan. In both cases the monk rapes the wife. In story 56 an older Franciscan, as confessor, tricks a mother and daughter into allowing a younger Franciscan, in disguise, to marry the daughter.

Monks are parasites. They use up the goods of laity without giving anything in return. They copulate with lay women, thereby becoming the principal makers of cuckolds. This is not, however, the joyous cuckoldry that one occasionally finds in other novellas. The young monk does not replace the stupid old husband to the delight of the willing wife. Fairly typical is the Franciscan who fools a young woman on her wedding night by creeping into her bed in an inn while her husband is still downstairs dancing. He and his companion, upon discovery, are beaten and left in a field with their arms and legs amputated (story 48). Typical again is the Franciscan who kills four servants and carries a married woman off to a monastery to join a group of women held captive in the monastery. The husband discovers the kidnapping, and after the rescue of the captives, the monastery is burned with all the monks in it (story 31). To be a cuckold, to have horns, is not an exclusively male status, as one of the earlier quotations from the *Heptameron* indicates. One might say that the young woman who is fooled into marrying a Franciscan is "cuckolded," since her husband, being a priest, cannot fully play the role of husband and is thus, in a sense, unfaithful to her.

The monks are explicitly described as being the worst of men: "They're good in church and when they preach sermons, but when they get inside a house they are Antichrists" (258/349), says one storyteller. Another, "I'll tell you, as far as I'm concerned, there's no one on this earth tells lies like they do" (347/450). Another, "The mere sight of a monk fills me with horror—I couldn't even bring myself to make my confession to one" (185/265). Not only is their conduct bad, but their spiritual advice, even when not specifically directed toward some interested deceit, is dangerous. In particular, the monks preach a doctrine that leads to overconfidence in oneself or in them. This is apparent in the discussion of the story of the woman who copulates with her son and has a daughter by him. This rewriting of the Jocasta story concerns a woman who tries to discourage her son's natural sexual interest in her maid by taking the maid's place during the night. She cannot, however, resist the pleasure offered by the occasion. Afterwards the son believes he has slept with the maid, and his mother does not tell him what has happened. When he goes off to war, she gives birth to a daughter of whom she eventually loses track and who ends up marrying her father/brother. The construction put on this story by several of the frame-characters is that this woman was overconfident of her own powers, and "the first step man takes trusting in himself alone is a step away from trust in God" (233/321). One storyteller claims that this mother "was one of those foolish, vainglorious women who had had her head filled with nonsense by the Franciscans [*sa res-*

verie des Cordeliers] . . . and thought she was so saintly that she was incapable of sin, as some of them would persuade us to believe that through our own efforts we actually can be . . . " (234/322). Another woman, having been raped by a Franciscan, falls into despair and has no force to support her anguish and shame because, precisely, she believes the doctrines of good works and penitence preached by the Franciscans:

> She had learnt from the Franciscans nothing but confidence in good words, satisfaction for sins through austerity of life, fasting and chastisement. She had remained ignorant of the grace given by our good God through the merit of His Son, ignorant of the remission of sins by His blood, ignorant of the reconciliation of the Father with us by His death and ignorant of the life given to sinners through His goodness and mercy. So deeply was she disturbed . . . that it seemed better by far to die than to live such a life. (191/271)

If Franciscans, and priests in general, are so bad and their doctrines so misleading, why should we read about them and why should the storytellers return so gleefully to monk tales? Is this simply a way of reducing the *Heptameron* to a reformist religious tract intended to alienate the faithful from the church or at least from the church structure? If this is the case, why situate the whole event of the narration in a monastery? Something more complicated is going on, and I believe that Marguerite is using one of the particular characteristics of novella logic as it appears notably in the *Decameron*. The Boccaccian novella is the genre *par excellence* of trickery, not only of the tricks people play on other people but of the tricks people play on themselves, and of the peculiar detours and contortions it takes to avoid being deceived by what you see and what people tell you. In the *Decameron*, one of the outstanding examples of inverted interpretation reaching the proper conclusion (apparently) on the basis of appearances that would seem to lead in an entirely different direction is the story of Abraham, an honest Jewish merchant from Paris who is considering becoming a Christian (day 1, novella 2). Insisting on seeing the capital of Christianity for himself, he makes a trip to Rome, despite the urgings of a Christian friend, who is aware of what a cesspool of vice Rome is, to stay home. To his Christian friend's surprise, Abraham returns determined to become a Christian according to the following logic. Since the pope and cardinals are lechers, sodomites, gluttons, and drunkards, they would seem to be trying to destroy the church by very forceful means. But because the church does not fade away but instead grows and becomes more illustrious, it must be founded on the religion of a true God who saves it from the churchmen.

Marguerite de Navarre has seized upon this form of novella logic, which does not proceed on the mere basis that appearances are deceiving and should therefore be ignored or discounted, but that appearances are extremely valuable if you have the power to decipher them. Marguerite takes this novella twist and combines it with a form of that celebrated theological concept known as the *felix culpa*, by which bad becomes the servant of good and the fall of man becomes the occasion of his redemption. *Felix culpa*, united with novella trickster logic, is systematized in the *Heptameron* into an all-embracing structure that works in the novellas themselves and in the frame-discussions, recuperating everything for the good cause and turning even the monks into an instrument of salvation, perhaps even into the supreme instrument of that form of knowledge peculiar to true Christians.

To understand how this is so, we must recall the emphasis that the *Heptameron* places on salvation by grace. As Oisille, the oldest and most scripturally oriented of the storytellers, observes in the prologue, "a person who knows God will find all things beautiful in Him, and without Him all things will seem ugly" (8/67). Perception, like salvation, does not depend on some external quality but on something that is within the individual mysteriously chosen by God. Many of the preceding quotations have shown the devaluation of good works, as preached by the monks. Another storyteller, Parlamente, applies the concept of grace—or rather, the lack of grace—to sin: "All external sins are the fruit of an inner unhappiness [*infélicité*], which is all the more dangerous and difficult to root out the more it is covered with virtue and miracles" (254/344). Sin itself is a *good* and valuable thing because it reduces our perception of human value to proper proportions. Longarine points out that if we are not fortunate enough to understand our situation by a direct understanding of the Word of God, then sin can play the role of that Word: "if the Word of God does not by faith show us the leprosy of faithlessness hidden within our hearts, God's grace is great indeed when we stumble and commit some visible fault which makes us see clearly the plague hidden within us. And blessed are they whom faith has so humbled that they have no need of external effects to have their sinful nature demonstrated to them" (254/344). By this supreme paradox, sin becomes an instrument of salvation—not only the sin of Adam and Eve, who created the need for Christ to become visible in order to die on the cross, but each sin committed in everyday life that permits us to see, negatively, the *need* for that incarnation and that divine sacrifice. Conversely, the worst possible thing, the most misleading signpost on the way to perdition, is the appearance of a good and holy life achieved by human sacrifice and will: "Those who believe that they surpass others in honor, prudence, and human intelligence, by which they set such store, that they don't render to God the glory that belongs to him" (332/432). While such an attitude toward sin may conflict with modern beliefs, it is not out of place in the evangelical milieu by which Marguerite de Navarre was so much influenced. In describing the beliefs of the Spiritual Libertines, Henry Heller writes, "In contrast to Calvin and, indeed, the Fabrists, the critical moment in the regeneration of man appears to come not at the instant of awakening faith but through the assumption of a state of complete innocence."[44]

If innocence is understood as the relaxation of one's own sense of individual righteousness, then salvation can be seen as coming at the moment of surrender to God's direction of our life. The story of the incestuous mother mentioned earlier illustrates perfectly this doctrine. The mother had been in her maid's bed to prevent her son from committing an entirely natural sin. The son, in fact, has been under the tutelage of a very holy man since the age of seven years—a situation similar to that in the introduction to the fourth day of the *Decameron*[45]—and he had studied nothing but holiness and devotion, but when he was between fourteen and fifteen years of age, "Nature, who is a very secret school master, finding him well nourished and idle, taught him a lesson quite different from that of his tutor" (230/317). The mother wanted to correct this "natural" failing but caused her son to fall into an "unnatural" sin. The second phase of her misguided attempt to do good was to hide the sin from her son and others and as a result to lose sight of her daughter. The third mistake, still done with the intention of avoiding and hiding sin, was to force her son to marry so that she and he could avoid falling into the same sin as before (*craignant de retomber en tel mal dont elle venoit*, 232/320). As a result, her son is twice incestuous through no fault of his own and only by her own attempt to do good and to avoid the sins of a sexual desire that the narrator describes as natural. It would, it seems, have been better, right from the start, to do nothing and to accept the movements of nature, however fallen it may be.

There is thus an alliance between the highest good and sin. The woman in story 30 at every step tries to do good, receives the sacraments, fasts, and ingeniously arranges to make herself and her son better than their human nature can be. As the narrator of the story says, "Instead of humbling herself and recognizing the incapacity of our flesh, which, without the aid of God can only commit sin, she tried by herself and with her tears to atone for the past and with her prudence to avoid future evils, always attributing her sin to circumstance and not to a malicious nature [*non à la malice*], for which there is no remedy except the grace of God" (231/319).[46]

The novella, always the vehicle for a less-than-noble (often called realistic) vision of human conduct, is thus recuperated by Marguerite as a theoretically justified revelation of human evil. The trickster tricked, the *trompeur trompé*, so much a part of the novella tradition, takes on a richer significance to convey the structure of our misguided efforts to save ourselves by clever maneuvering. The best novellas are therefore the ones that most forcefully expose the evil of our conduct. As one of the storytellers, Hircan, says, "When you have taken a good look in this mirror, instead of having confidence in your own strength, you will learn to return to Him in whose hand lies your honor" (260/351).

With the figure of the mirror we return to the *Heptameron*'s resounding claim to convey true history, *véritable histoire*, but with a further understanding of what Marguerite means by history. History is not the linking of events that have succeeded one another in time. There is no continuity to the *Heptameron*'s vision of events, as in epic, romance, or even chronicle. Even though important political authorities or families are mentioned, there is no sense of causality or duration. History means simply that what is in the stories has happened; these events are "actual fact" witnessed by the narrators or transmitted by reliable oral testimony. This emphasis on supposedly recent events is a way of declaring a liberation from the distortions of written history and its rhetoric. But also, like Machiavelli, Marguerite de Navarre wants to avoid an idealization of the people of the past. Synchrony—or rather, a form of achrony—triumphs over diachrony in a timeless representation of the sameness of human weakness. This is a tendency of novella collections in general. They do not provide a linear, temporal succession, but a collage of narrative in which not time but the polemics or thematics of the frame-narrative is the driving force behind the choice of tales. In the *Heptameron* the disbelief in the fruit of human action justifies the achronic vision. The lesson of history, of what happens, is always the same lesson—namely, that substantially nothing changes.

By emphasizing the contemporary, Marguerite ostensibly avoids events that have been transformed by the embellishment of the written form. Veritable history seems to be whatever is not the result of the human imagination or artifice, distorting nature and hiding what is inside us. Paradoxically, the *Heptameron*, though it is written, denigrates writing as a learned perversion. Although the *Heptameron* is fictively portrayed as a series of oral narratives with oral discussions, human discourse in general always is claimed (within that discourse) to be less meaningful than those things that we learn by watching or those things that we say without meaning to.

The actions of the Franciscans speak with more truth than their words, against their intentions, just like the young woman's *lapsus*, but the tension between their words and their actions is what gives particular importance to this revelation. This is because of the importance of the *hidden*, in the *Heptameron*'s view of the world. The monks may not commit slips of the tongue, some embarrassing discrepancy within language, but they illustrate the discrepancy that arises between language and action, a discrepancy all the more revealing because of the monk's role as preacher of a doctrine that blinds people to the reality around them. In story 62 the words slip and let us see the silent slipping of the sheet. In all allusions to the preaching of the Franciscans, the words point to a doctrine of salvation by good works and austerity, thereby exposing the specific weakness of the monks, whose conduct is notoriously bad. The monks, and other priests, are good talkers whose spoken lessons do evil by encouraging confidence in them and in our own actions, but when they are not in church, the monks are bad men whose evil does us good by reminding us of the weakness and presumption caused by their sermons. As one of the storytellers says to another (who exclaims, "My God, . . . won't we ever get through the stories about these troublesome Franciscans?"), "If ladies, princes, and gentlemen aren't spared, it seems to me that the Franciscans are given a great honor by our condescending to speak of them, for they are so useless that, if they didn't do some evil worthy of being remembered, one would never talk about them" (317/415). Franciscans, in other words, are useless except when they do something evil enough to provide material for this negative genre that is the novella.[47] The young wife and the monks are both attempting to cover up some disgrace that they know about. But we all have weaknesses and sins of which we are unaware. What is valuable about narratives in which characters forget their artifice of concealment is that it provides a model and a reminder of abandoning prideful control of appearance.

Of course the *Heptameron* does not recommend *deliberate* sinning as a means of reaching salvation. Instead, as in the tale of the sheet, the *knowledge* of our sinful nature is the goal of exemplary discourse. Forgetting to conceal is a variant of the paradoxical forgetfulness (*oubliance*) recommended by Marguerite de Navarre's spiritual adviser Briçonnet:

> In forgetfulness one acquires all knowledge, of which we remain
> ignorant, and as knowledge grows, so does ignorance. Knowl-
> edge is blindness, so ignorance is, yet ignorance is light when
> compared to knowledge . . . the more one believes one knows,
> the more one becomes ignorant and blind.[48]

Hiding our evil causes sickness and the more unnatural sins, and discovering what is hidden is the primary function of each novella. Marguerite de Navarre thus prefers characters like monks and priests who
continually hide things. The particular accomplishment of such people
is to use language to obscure material reality, to blind us to what we
see.[49] The clergy are instruments of salvation in proportion to their
danger, and the stripping away is all the more worthwhile in view of
the ignorance that they entertain in others. Despite the possible contamination of their doctrine, one should not necessarily flee from
them. Some of the discussions conclude with statements like "the less
you see of them, the less you know them, and the less you know about
them, the higher your opinion of them is. You soon find out what
they're like if you have much to do with them" (185/265). Some such
reasoning may lie behind Saffredent's enigmatic comment, "You
would do better to honor them than to blame them . . . and to flatter
them than to insult them, for they are the ones who have the power to
burn and dishonor others; therefore, *sinite eos*."

The claim to tell a veritable history without the deformations of the
manipulators of the word is based on a doctrine of passive acceptance
of our natural fallen state. This is not only the content of the novellas
(the story of what happens to the characters) and of the discussions but
also the description that the frame-characters give of their enterprise.
The deterministic or passive conception of human action is integral to
the self-presentation of the *Heptameron* and explains the early refusal of
human artifice or rhetoric in Prince Henry's project for a novella collection. If the narrators of the frame-story are not permitted to invent
stories, their initiative is limited to reporting what has happened by the
will of God. The humility topos, frequently associated with a scribal
subservience to earlier texts or authors, is here linked to the direct and
"artless" representation of the world. In this way, certain dangerous
truths can be expressed as if they sprang from beyond the will of the
narrator, who, Cassandra-like, is subjected to speaking truth. In concluding the tale of the Franciscans who rape women and hold them
prisoners in their monasteries, Geburon apologizes:

> I am sorry, Ladies, that the truth does not bring us as many stories
> to the Franciscans' advantage as to their disadvantage, for I am

very fond of the order and it would give me great pleasure to hear some tale that would give me occasion to praise them. But we've sworn so firmly to tell the truth that having heard the accounts of reliable people, I am obliged not to conceal it. (241/329)

The irony of this claim to love the Franciscans is characteristic of an irony that pervades the whole of the *Heptameron*, where truth is dissembled by being exposed where we least expect it. Marguerite's whole tactic is to pit irony against hypocrisy, two forms of dissimulation that are antagonistic, in a form of textual and spiritual homeopathy. Who would expect Franciscans to be the best source of useful Christian instruction? Who would expect that a devout woman's every effort to prevent her son from falling into the sins of the flesh would be her own undoing? If you look where truth seems to be exposed, in the sermons of the learned or the skillful, you find only illusion, but if you look at the sins committed by those learned and apparently ascetic clergy and lay people, you find in their sin the truth of human weakness.

This system casts light on the plots of the novellas, on the narrative process, and on the process of interpretation invited by the *Heptameron* as a whole. *All* of the usual hierarchies are challenged by Marguerite's vision. Just as, within the novellas, spiritual love is almost invariably more dangerous for the characters involved than plain, natural, and sinful lust—"vicious love disintegrates of its own accord, and is unable to survive in a heart that is pure. But 'virtuous' love has such subtle bonds that one gets caught before one notices them" (260/352)—so also in the frame-narrative the apparent hierarchy of spiritual teaching cannot be stably located.

For this reason it is out of keeping with the construction of the *Heptameron* as a whole to seek, as many commentators do, an authorial mouthpiece among the ten storytellers or to assume that Oisille, the oldest and the most conventionally religious of the group, is necessarily the most important source of truth about religion. Instead, a non-hierarchical, polyphonic process of revelation occurs in the frame as it does in the novellas, a process by which truth is just as likely—indeed, more likely—to come forth from the libidinous pleasantry of Hircan or Saffredent. Simontault's wish that all women be as depraved as possible (96/165) does not stand in the way of his producing a vision of humanity thoroughly in keeping with the scriptural lessons of Oisille herself. Simontault's general assessment of humanity boils down to the notion that "to praise man and woman truthfully, one can only say that the best of them isn't worth anything" (307/404).

Drawing lessons from the frame-discussions as keys to interpret the novellas seems a perfectly legitimate procedure, provided that one also draws from the novellas concepts that can allow us to interpret and weigh the affirmations of the characters of the frame. In this view, the turpitude or even the stupidity of a character will not preclude his or her uttering profound truths. Oisille's frequently pompous and often completely misguided interpretations of the stories make her just as much a clown figure as a figure of authority, but her clownishness does not guarantee the fallacy of anything she says any more than her scriptural readings guarantee her truthfulness.[50]

This ironic procedure, by which the author exposes truth where we are not likely to look for it, also implies the adoption of a passive stance in regard to teaching.[51] Socratic irony dissembles knowledge to stimulate the activity of the learner and listener, who must put forth effort to find this truth that the master will not plainly and simply assert. The *Heptameron*'s claim to nonintervention in the representation of reality, its subservience to the lessons of experience, is no more accurate an account of Marguerite's composition than is Socrates' apparent need for help in finding the answer to the problems he raises. But the claim to be a mere account of veritable history, without rhetorical modification, *is* a fundamental key to the textual functioning of novella as systematized by Marguerite, who has arrived at her irony (which, of course, she does not label as such) in a way completely opposed to Socrates.[52] Her irony is based on what her characters call *grace*, and she elaborates a hierarchy that actually undermines all ranks.

The repeated emphasis on the giving of *exemples* in the *Heptameron* reveals a sense of the rupture between the external world and spiritual meaning, a schism familiar to us through Foucault's works. In Marguerite de Navarre's text, however, the radical separation that will appear in Descartes has not occurred. As Pascal will say later in speaking of imagination, untrustworthy appearances are all the more dangerous because they are not always false. A similar situation obtains in the *Heptameron*, where the violent, the vicious, and the false can be redeemed, at times, as signposts toward the greatest of good. The representation of the good and holy, on the other hand, can become traps, luring the audience into an illusion of power through the specious equation of will and achievement. Most radically, the *Heptameron* establishes the basic alienation of the self from the external images by which the self is guided and represented. Whether one places oneself before an example as model for knowledge and conduct, or whether one attempts to transform a subjective sense of experience into a model that can support a generalization applicable to others, the failure of coherence between the "I"—source of a transcendent wisdom—and a "they" (or "he" or "she")—as narrative subject in history/story—sets the conditions for the isolation that Benjamin has so aptly described as the situation of the novelist. The novel as genre arises with "the solitary individual, who is no longer able to express himself by giving *examples* of his most important concerns, is himself uncounseled, and cannot counsel others."[53]

CHAPTER III

Montaigne and the Economy of Example

Ces exemples estrangers ne sont pas estranges. (I.23)

—Montaigne

Quod crebro videt, non miratur, etiam si cur fiat nescit. Quod ante
non vidit, id, si evenerit, ostentum esse censet

—Cicero

WHEN MONTAIGNE, in 1576, had a medal struck to bear the emblem that he had chosen, he united the form of a coin with the image of the instrument used for both justice and mercantile exchange: the balance.[1] Although this emblem is sometimes seen as a mere projection of the motto, "What do I know?" ("Que sais-je?"), Montaigne's personal balancing between affirmations is bound up with the evaluation of the affirmations and examples of others. The emblematic medal thus represents an exchange in which the weighing of opinions and anecdotes is a major preoccupation. The balance is symbolic of all those passages in which Montaigne makes metaphoric reference to texts that are "exemplary and weighty" (*exemplaires et poisans*). The medal itself is part of the claim of substantiality. More than a surface, the medal or *jeton* can be grasped and weighed. Although a medal is not officially money (*monnaie*), Montaigne distributed his medal to friends, thus putting it in circulation.

Montaigne's examples are, like this medal, the result and the embodiment of a weighing and a circulation. Into the balance, to determine the value of an example, go considerations of rarity, surface appearance, the density that underlies the surface, and the exchange value that comes from opinions on the honesty of the maker—or issuer—of the text from which the example comes. Montaigne collected examples of the strange and unusual. In measuring the stockpile that led to the writing of the *Essais*, he elaborated an economics of exemplarity from perceptions of rarity, production, consumption, and display of example.[2] Montaigne's textual self is the center of a commerce in which he is a consumer, broker, and increasingly a producer of examples, commenting throughout on the strange enterprise of readers and writers situating themselves in the exemplary tradition.

Montaigne's major contribution to the literature of example is a fusion of the ethical and the aesthetic in a demonstration of our constant imaginative activity of perceiving and formulating examples. Although Montaigne, like Machiavelli, begins with a traditional corpus of "exemplary" figures from antiquity and modern history, he emphatically shows that exemplarity is not an inherent characteristic of persons or incidents but the result of our way of speaking about them. Examples, in their content, are both good and bad, both to be praised and to be censured, but the *effect* of the example does not depend on the moral quality of the content. Montaigne is much more concerned with example's power to interest us, even to fascinate and astonish us, than in a purely ethical or even demonstrative value. Indeed, Montaigne's emphatic comments on example in the concluding essay, "Of Experience,"[3] state that examples do not provide useful information about permanent pattern to human life:

> Multiplication of our imaginary cases will never equal the variety of the real examples. Add to them a hundred times as many more: and still no future event will be found to correspond. . . . There is little relation between our actions, which are in perpetual mutation, and fixed and immutable laws. (1066/816)

Yet somehow writers can always bend and fold laws and examples so that there is some kind of a fit between discursive generalizations and the instances we propose to support them:

> All things hold by some similarity; every example is lame, and the comparison that is drawn from experience is always faulty and imperfect; however, we fasten together our comparisons by some corner. Thus the laws serve, and thus adapt themselves to each of our affairs, by some round-about, forced and biased interpretation. (1070/819)

Readers of Montaigne have long been aware of the structural and quantitative importance of examples in the *Essais*, but have not generally seen the consistency with which he approaches example from the first to the last of his 107 essays. Repeatedly Montaigne gives examples of examples, in which characters find or make an example. Various effects, ranging from pure astonishment to sexual excitement, are ascribed to examples, and these effects are most often based on the unusual quality of an event. Examples work in terms of supply and demand in the *Essais*. The unusual is thus promoted to a high place while ordinary events are devalued accordingly. Montaigne even goes beyond metaphors of economy to accounts of how people can earn money if they have something really unusual to display. The insistence on rarity, on the atypical rather than the typical, is a direct attack on the unexamined conception of example as the norm, as a selection of the usual or the representative.[4] Reversal and paradox, by producing examples that are unexpected, confer the character of rarity and make an example worthwhile.

RARITY

The first essay, "By diverse means we arrive at the same end," quickly brings up an example. By the third sentence of the *Essais* Montaigne is illustrating a general rule—or rather two contradictory rules—with a brief narrative:

> Edward, prince of Wales, the one who governed our Guienne so long (a person whose traits and fortune have in them many notable elements of greatness), having suffered much harm from the Limousins, and taking their city by force, could not be halted by the cries of the people and of the women and children abandoned to the butchery, who implored his mercy and threw themselves at his feet—until, going farther and farther into the city, he saw three French gentlemen who with incredible boldness were holding out alone against the assault of his victorious army. Consideration and respect for such remarkable valor first took the edge off his anger; and he began with these three men to show mercy to all the inhabitants of the city. (7/3)

Edward's example is the counterexample of the first rule and the example of the second rule. In terms of proof, this is an odd situation, for Montaigne has secured his position by taking both sides—proof hardly seems necessary in such a case. But the example can do something different from proving; it can both fascinate and display fascination. Edward is, in conventional terms, the principal figure of this story—his name comes first, and he is the only named character; he holds the balance of power and controls the outcome. Yet in the part of the story told here Edward is also a spectator. He remains passive before the pleadings of the victims, and he is the internal audience for the hopeless fighting of the three Frenchmen. These fighters are alone (*seuls*) and fighting against overwhelming odds. Their bravery could justifiably be called exemplary. We have here an example within an example, an example of courage framed by an example of the unpredictable effects of such courage. Edward does not surrender to the Frenchmen, but he does surrender to the impression they make on him. Their combat is uncharacteristic of the population around them, uncharacteristic even in more general terms of people who want to get some concessions from a victor. Montaigne calls this bravery "unbelievable." Edward apparently agrees, and his astonishment illustrates the effect of the unusual and incredible in examples.

This example is so typical of most of those in the *Essais* that we can easily become accustomed to such cases. But what is typical of Montaigne's writing is not, in a broader sense, any more typical of social norm than the happy ending of a fairy tale is typical of real life. As actors in the "unbelievable" event that Edward, as internal audience, beholds, these gentlemen manifest the spectacular character of examples, which stand on the threshold of fact and fiction. What is rare in "real life" is typical in fiction. The discrepancy between the rare and the typical is itself a motivating factor in the use of the example, just as the rarity of the Frenchmen's courage motivates the reversal in Edward's own action.

If Montaigne looks for rare and astonishing examples, fragmentation and discontinuity are means of accentuating those qualities by controlling expectations and the perception of a norm.[5] Examples are discrete units imported into or interpolated into a text perceived as the ongoing continuous whole.[6] Discontinuity, however, is not merely a spatial quality, not only a way of measuring the length of *exempla* and the quantity of quotations. The difference between what we expect and what we find is also a form of discontinuity. In distinguishing between Plutarch and Seneca, Montaigne points to the difference between Seneca's ethic and common practice. The Roman has opinions that are "Stoic and Epicurean, more remote from common use [*plus esloignées de l'usage commun*], but in my opinion more suitable for private life and more sturdy" (II.10:413/300). The departure from common practice, far from being a defect, renders Seneca somehow more interesting than Plutarch's opinions, which are "mild and accommodated to civil society." Generally novelty and strangeness are sources of value.[7] Montaigne presents these qualities in a defense of his own writing at the beginning of "Of the affection of fathers for their children" (II.8) in addressing Madame d'Estissac: "if strangeness and novelty, which customarily give value to things, do not save me, I shall never get out of this stupid enterprise with honor" (385/278).

This preference takes on the proportions of a general doctrine in the essay "That our desire is increased by difficulty" (II.15), where Montaigne makes an important connection between the unusual and all forms of desire, uniting intellectual curiosity with erotic attraction, *libido cognoscendi* with *libido sentiendi*. For Montaigne "there is nothing naturally so contrary to our enjoyment as the satiety that comes from facility, nor anything that whets it so much as rarity and difficulty" (612/464). Lycurgus, according to Montaigne's example, forbade sexual encounters between married persons, to give marital sexuality much more zest. This principle soon appears as a universal maxim, for the devout Italians make their pilgrimages to the distant shrine of Saint James at Compostella in Spain while the Spanish who live near Compostella travel all the way to Loretto. The inhabitants of Liège ignore the celebrated nearby baths of Spa in preference for the springs of Lucca and Aspa. Even military defense follows this paradoxical wisdom, for Montaigne points to his own château as being not only unusual but entirely unique among noble French houses in being without modern fortification: "Amid so many fortified houses, I alone of my rank in France, as far as I know, have entrusted purely to heaven the protection of mine. . . . I have still lasted long enough to make my duration worthy of remark and of record. How so? It is a good thirty years" (617/468).

The principle of rarity also governs the relationship between knowledge and belief.[8] In beginning the essay "We should meddle soberly with judging divine ordinances" (1.32), Montaigne declares,

> The true field and subject of imposture are things unknown. Because in the first place strangeness itself lends credit; and then, not being subject to our ordinary reasoning, such things take away our means of combating them. For this reason, says Plato, it is much easier to give satisfaction when speaking of the nature of the gods than when speaking of the nature of men, because the ignorance of one's audience affords a fine broad range and full liberty in handling so obscure a subject. (215/159)

Far from basing his rhetoric on the assumption that people believe in the things they know best, Montaigne takes the extreme opposite stance. Strangeness itself is persuasive; people are more inclined toward belief than toward disbelief. If this is the case, it will certainly affect the use of example, for the ordinary and everyday will breed disbelief as well as boredom. Montaigne adds, "Thence it happens that nothing is so firmly believed as what is least known, nor are any people so confident as those who tell us fables, such as alchemists, prognosticators, astrologers, palmists, doctors . . . " Montaigne gives examples of this key to persuasion through the unbelievable. The least verifiable assertions are the more fervently held, as religion shows, though Montaigne cautions against the effects of this tendency. It is not desirable, he notes, to assume a simple relation between prosperity and disaster, as they appear in the world, and God's favor or disfavor.

Hence, the Protestants' use of the victory at Rochelabeille as a sign of divine endorsement is not persuasive because the many battles won by their opponents do not shake their belief that God still favors the reformed religion. So far, nothing seems particularly unusual in all this. But Montaigne's next examples defy any attempt to reduce them to typical experience. The heresiarch Arrius and his schismatic pope Leo died during a battle; does this prove that God opposed them? The details of their deaths, however, give a particular piquancy to the purported intervention of God in human affairs, for Arrius and Leo died while a battle was raging, but their deaths were due to a violent attack of diarrhea. The emperor Heliogabalus also died in a toilet, but so did the orthodox Christian Irenaeus. These examples undermine any attempt at a direct hermeneutics of history, but they are clearly not chosen from any list of representative reversals of religious factions. Instead, they are bizarre, obscure, paradoxical in their own right. How many popes can you name who died while defecating?

The inverse proportion of belief to knowledge is similar to the proportion of knowledge to language in the area of sexuality. The most widely known words are the least said:

> For it is a good one that the words least in use, least written and most hushed up, are the best known and most generally familiar. No age, no type of character, is ignorant of them, any more than of the word "bread." They impress themselves on everyone without being expressed, without voice and without form. (III.5:847/644)

These unspoken words concern the genitals. In addition to these words, many examples in the *Essais* come from other domains that are subject to a certain restraint, particularly the excremental. It would be hard to find an example more unusual than the one near the beginning of "Of vanity" (III.9) concerning the gentleman who collected his excrements and displayed them in basins at his house.

Montaigne analyzes the tactics of groups and individual historical figures in their bid to become exemplary by reaching a status of exception. In "Of glory," the truly exceptional, the basis for example, is revealed to be *the exception created by discourse itself*, even at the debased level of publicity. "We call it making our name great to spread and sow it in many mouths," says Montaigne (626/474). Many succeed in obtaining this verbal greatness, for they became characters in Montaigne's stock of classical and medieval examples. Montaigne's description of the way such exemplary status was achieved removes, however, some of their luster. In the essay "That the taste of good and evil depends in large part on the opinion we have of them" (I.14), Montaigne undermines the examples left by groups, such as philosophers, which claim superiority over ordinary people. Quantitative and qualitative analysis are combined with the description of example as spectacle in a series of instances of people attempting to shift themselves from the norm into a glorious atypicality.

Language reveals the price that Posidonius the Stoic was willing to pay for renown:

> When Posidonius was extremely tormented by an acute and painful malady, Pompey went to see him, and excused himself for having chosen so poor a time to hear him talk about philosophy. "God forbid," said Posidonius, "that pain should gain such power over me as to keep me from such a subject!" And he threw himself into this same topic, the contempt of pain. But meanwhile it was playing its part and pressing him incessantly. At which he cried: "You may do your worst, pain, yet I will not say that you are an evil." (55/37)

The force of this example derives from a dialogue in which the suffering body tempts the speaker to deviate from his indifference and admit that suffering is more real than words. As Montaigne goes on to point out, only the difficulty of Posidonius's performance of "non-suffering," that is, of a superiority over suffering created for an audience (Pompeius) gives the episode any interest at all. And this interest is generated by the contradiction and self-destructive nature of the example: "This tale that they make so much of [*qu'ils font tant valoir*], what has it to do with contempt of pain? He is only arguing about the word: and meanwhile if these pains do not move him, why does he interrupt his talk for their sake? Why does he think he is doing a lot by not calling pain an evil?" Only because suffering *is* bad does Posidonius's refusal to say so become a *conte* or example. The value as spectacle can be fully appreciated only by someone aware that the words conceal something and destroy the unity of inside and out, words and things.

Both Posidonius, in presenting his spectacle of endurance to Pompeius, and the authors who have appropriated the story of Posidonius are aware that an "example" is being created here by human will, according to a recognizable convention of spectacle and merit or value (writers, notes Montaigne, *font tant valoir* this story—literally, give it so much value, a continuation of the economics of example). The suffering and death of Christ would seem to transcend this convention, in a Christian context. To find that Christ appears as example near the center of essay I.14 in its final form is striking. Montaigne introduces "the example of our holy guide" (80/41) in a somewhat scandalous context, however, after two cases of frivolous self-mutilation as spectacle. One case is that of a girl who stabs herself "four or five" times in the arm to prove her constancy, breaking her skin and causing considerable bleeding. In the other example, Turks slash themselves and then cauterize their wounds to impress their ladies, "and, so that the mark shall remain, they instantly apply fire to the wound and hold it there an incredibly long time to stop the blood and form the scar" (60/41). Montaigne adds that one can also find Turks willing to pierce their arms and thighs to earn small change.

This is hardly an edifying context in which to bring up religious suffering accepted willingly for the purpose of redemption. Once again the term *exemple* occurs at a peculiarly sensitive moment, linked with the name of Christ, whose function in Christian exemplarity is at least twofold. Christ is an example of the love of the Father, one manifestation of his goodness toward humanity, a projection of the love of God. But Christ is also an example of the life a Christian should lead, and is, in this sense, a projection of the law of God. In this latter function, Christ is the founding example for the *imitatio Christi*, an example *for* as well as an example *of*. Given this highly charged religious concept of example as *the* Example, which transcends and surpasses all others, it is difficult to ignore the trivializing context that Montaigne has created in the immediately preceding and immediately following examples. For the kinds of behavior that Montaigne attaches to the example of Christ do not have much more dignity than the Turkish practices immediately prior:

> We learn by a witness most worthy of belief that King Louis the Saint wore the hair shirt until, in his old age, his confessor gave him dispensation; and that every Friday he had his priest flog his shoulders with five little iron chains, which he always carried about for that purpose in a box. William, our last duke of Guienne, father of the Eleanor who transmitted that duchy to the houses of France and England, wore continually, for the last ten or twelve years of his life, a corselet under a monk's habit, for penance. Foulques, count of Anjou, went all the way to Jerusalem to have himself scourged there by two of his servants, a rope around his neck, before the sepulcher of Our Lord. (60/41)

However "private" these penitential practices may be in principle, they are known to the public. They are more representations or spectacles of humility than humility itself. (Tartuffe is not far away!) It is important for several reasons that Guillaume wears his *cuirasse* under and not over a religious habit. First, hiding his uncomfortable accoutrement demonstrates that he does not want to "show off" and receive public acclaim. Second, such a hiding can be only part (the signifier) of a sign of humility since it is unlikely that this concealment could be effective; it therefore amounts to something like saying "My armor, which I am wearing to mortify myself, isn't showing, is it?" Third, the habit/armor relationship is a reversal of the normal practice for the laity of bearing a "Christian spirit" inside while carrying out the world's work outside in the appearances of everyday life.

Like the Turks who show their ladies how manly they are in their scorn for pain, these Christians perform a ritual of suffering and humiliation for man as well as God. They are examples of the reproduction of an example—we can recognize the kind of symbolism of origin that so heavily characterizes example in Machiavelli. Within their story (or within their own *mise-en-scène*), these medieval Christians are enacting examples of faith. Finally, Montaigne says that on Good Friday some of the penitential performance is done for hire (61/41).

This instance returns full circle to the Turks, displaying the economic basis of religious suffering and self-mutilation. From St. Louis to the professional penitent there is a progression toward ever more public and theatrical display. St. Louis at first wore a hair shirt, then extended his devotion to involve other people when he required his confessor to whip him. Guillaume wore his "hidden" armor everywhere and continuously for ten or twelve years. Foulques requires an authentic setting and two valets to perform his imitation of Christ. Finally, the wealthy devout spare themselves suffering by paying others to put on the spectacle for them. Yet a revealing constant of the paragraph is the presence of terms of vision and witnessing: *les tesmoins nous sont plus à main, tesmoignage tres-digne de foy, ne voit-on encore, ay-je vu souvent*. Seeing is not believing, however, because seeing alone cannot prove that the Turks who wound themselves are really devoted to a lady, since they may also do it for money. Seeing Christians flagellating themselves does not prove that they do so from a desire to follow the example of Christ. Within Montaigne's essay, these examples show that the long tradition of Christian example does not prove much at all, precisely because of its spectacular nature and its uncertainty as sign. Flagellation is *not* the outward sign of an inward faith if it can be a service rendered for money.

Once we make a connection between the performance of exemplary acts and the themes of class difference, a whole network appears. Class distinctions not only modify the "taste" of sufferings, they also modify the external perception of those sufferings.[9] Example is largely a product of a class struggle as perceived by the upper class:

> Opinion is a powerful performer, bold and immoderate. Who ever with such hunger sought security and repose as Alexander and Caesar sought unrest and difficulties? Teres, the father of Sitalces, was wont to say that when he was not making war it seemed to him that there was no difference between him and his groom. (61/42)

Although opinion is "without measure"—presumably in the sense of being without limit—there is a criterion expressed in this paragraph based on a comparison between great men and their servants. Teres describes himself as in a contest with his groom for "difference." Besides scorn for his servant, Teres's remark evinces certain anxiety over the general lack of distinction between them. In this paragraph the opposition between the generalized *qui* and the specific names of Alexander and Caesar seems to play on the presupposition that *qui* as generic "the man who . . . " or "one" represents the norm, which requires seeking safety and repose, in opposition to the glorious but unusual or deviant tastes of the great warriors for worry and difficulty. Those who sacrifice things conventionally assigned great value (i.e., sought by the greatest number of persons) become exceptional and gain social value. Alexander and Caesar "buy" their distinction by giving up what others seek. Montaigne returns to the case of Caesar to state explicitly that Caesar is an economic entity, not only a "person" in the most natural sense of the term:

> How many good men have cast away all their security, and do so every day, to pursue the wind of royal favor and of fortune. Caesar went into debt for more than a million in gold beyond what he was worth, to become Caesar. (63/43)

The "Caesar" that is the subject of this sentence is not the same "Caesar" that appears as predicate of the verb *devenir*. This second Caesar is the creation of all those acts and investments that fabricate a hero. The distinction of these figures who appear so often in Montaigne's examples is not only the result of an economy of acts, but also of a monetary economy.

Other sacrifices or exchanges are part of the economy of Montaigne's examples in this essay. This quantification of human suffering (e.g., the girl who stabbed herself "four or five" times with a needle, the indication of the cost of hiring a Turk to slice himself up, the availability of mercenary flagellants), culminates with the description of how the death of children can also earn a place of distinction for their father. Montaigne gives a list of well-known Romans whose children died:

> Quintus Maximus buried his son, a consul; M. Cato his, a prae-tor-elect; and L. Paulus both of his, within a few days, with a calm face that bore no sign of grief. Once in my time I said of someone jokingly that he had cheated divine justice: for the violent death of three grown-up children having been sent him in one day as a bitter scourge, as may well be believed, he all but took it as a fa-vor. And I have lost two or three (but while they were still nurs-ing), if not without grief, at least without repining. (61/42)

This series of examples is carefully arranged, starting with the death of individual children, then moving to the death of two children, then the death of three. An "economics of death" is set in place, determin-ing the value of the death of a son or daughter by taking into account several factors: the age of the child, the political eminence he had at-tained, the timing of the loss (losing several within a brief period is worse), and—implicitly—the sex of the child. Counterbalancing the value of the loss is the reaction of the father. In all the cases given here, Montaigne evokes the "Romanity" or stoicism of the father, who treats the losses as if they were nothing, thereby denying the standard value of the loss of the child. The father thereby purchases, so to speak, a status of singularity (justifying his role in history as an exemplar) according to the discrepancy between the standard value of the loss and the value the father admits. One could even create a formula, similar to Genette's formula for verisimilitude: Value of Child (C) minus Fa-ther's Display of Grief (F) equals Exemplary Distinction (E), or $C - F = E$.[10]

The rarity toward which exemplary figures aspire appears also in Montaigne's comments on the way we learn history through texts. Montaigne recognizes that even the most ordinary kind of example is in fact an exception, not the rule. All historiography is a filtering or gleaning to such an extent that what appears ordinary in the stories we receive about battles and other great events constitutes the rare survival from a larger mass.[11] Thus *any* anecdote taken from classical or mod-ern sources is already unusual because few actions of valor are actually recorded: "in a whole battle in which ten thousand men are maimed or killed, there are not fifteen that are talked about. It must be some very eminent greatness, or some important consequence that fortune has attached to it, that gives prominence to an individual action, not only a musketeer's but even a general's" (II.16:627/475). History, which may present itself as a whole in the accounts we have of it, is actually what remains after passage through the sieve of memory. Most events do not reach us for lack of a record (*registre*). The discontinuity that Montaigne prefers in his authors, the gaps in his own failing memory, the forgetfulness of the world's history—these all turn out to be part of a universal structure of discourse (that is, of knowledge, belief, and speech). The rarefaction of historical memory, which is itself so selective, is subject to still greater reduction and separation when writers go about selecting the examples to use in their texts, for these are necessarily examples from examples, or even examples of examples. Montaigne draws attention to the arbitrary character of this process by saying that if he knew the unknown events of world history he could easily "supplant those that are known, in every kind of examples [*en toute espece d'exemples*]" (627/476).[12]

The rarity of examples is often because of their survival from remote times. The incidents that get our attention are the few historical facts that remain:

Even if all that has come down to us by report from the past should be true and known by someone, it would be less than nothing compared with what is unknown. And of this very image of the world which glides along while we live on it, how puny and limited is the knowledge of even the most curious! Not only of particular events which fortune often renders exemplary and weighty [*exemplaires et poisans*], but of the state of great governments and nations, there escapes us a hundred times more than comes to our knowledge. (908/692)

Not only is history lost this way, but that kind of history that is, so to speak, heavy history, those things that are "exemplary and weighty" among the actions of individuals.

Whole civilizations also take on an imposing quality of rarity when used in certain examples. In "Of coaches" (III.6), Montaigne shows how the discovery of America opened a new source of unusual information, facts filtered through separation in space, not time. Our acceptance of certain things as normal is shaken by accounts that cast our normal patterns as exceptional and portray the exceptions to our life as normal. In terms of the rare and the unusual, the relation between the title and the subject is particularly pertinent in "Of coaches."[13] The essay largely concerns the new world and the great Indian nations discovered there. From a European point of view, one of the conspicuous absences in American civilization is the coach, a vehicle widespread in Europe. The essay therefore is constructed around an exemplary absence, that is, the absence of a certain ordinary object within the example of American life. This surprising absence of a necessary object is merely ordinary life to the Americans. In other words, the European viewpoint creates an absence where there is only the fullness of real life to those who live in the new world. The conclusion is particularly striking:

> Let us fall back to our coaches. Instead of these or any other form of transport, they had themselves carried by men, and on their shoulders. That last king of Peru, the day that he was taken, was thus carried on shafts of gold, seated in a chair of gold, in the midst of his army. As many of these carriers as they killed to make him fall—for they wanted to take him alive—so many others vied to take the place of the dead ones, so that they never could bring him down, however great a slaughter they made of those people, until a horseman seized him around the body and pulled him to the ground. (915/698)

This example, from a European point of view, is full of the unusual, in regard to things and to actions. The enormous quantities of gold are emphasized by repetition, as is the decimation of the bearers and the surprising willingness of others to take their place. Yet these aspects of American life are of no particular note within the civilization in which they occur. On the other hand, a perfectly ordinary European gesture unseats the king because horses are unknown to the Americans. What is remarkable, that is, what is worth mentioning, in this story is the mutual discovery of ordinary things from contrasting points of view. The story Montaigne is telling happens in a place that was unknown, inexistent for classical European knowledge and discourse. The absence of coaches is exemplary because of this other, much larger absence of America, and demonstrates the way in which example is posed on the borders between language and silence, knowledge and nonknowledge.[14] Only what becomes known to us can be an example, but only something that conflicts with what we are accustomed to is worthy of being an example. The absence of the coach, which structures the vision of the new world, is representative of the mysterious absence that is at the heart of example.[15]

Appearances

If Montaigne sees struggling to fit laws to examples as more typical than finding examples that neatly illustrate laws, then it is not surprising that examples are something of a mystery. They are like pictures without captions. We speculate about their meaning and what may be behind them. Montaigne makes many examples out of displays that seem provocatively to conceal other things, appearances that we cannot penetrate, classify, or label. Like Edward of Wales, the reader is cast into the role of spectator of something astonishing, which does not fit a pattern he can name.

Here is one example of a fascinating concealment, a provocation to say what words can adequately explain the phenomenon:

> I must add this other example, as remarkable for the present consideration as any of the preceding ones. Emperor Maximilian, the great-grandfather of the present King Philip, was a prince superabundantly endowed with great qualities, and among others with singular bodily beauty. But among his humors was this one, very contrary to that of the princes who to dispatch their most important affairs make their throne of their toilet seat: that he never had a personal servant so familiar that he would allow him to see him in his privy. He would hide to make water, as scrupulous as a virgin not to uncover, either to a doctor or to anyone else whatever, the parts that are customarily kept hidden. . . . he ordered in so many words in his will that they should put underdrawers on him when he was dead. He should have added a codicil that the man who put them on should be blindfolded. (1.3:18–19/11)

Montaigne does not speculate on what moved Maximilian to this unusual modesty, so extreme that it finishes by producing the opposite effect of drawing attention to his body. In an age when, as Montaigne reminds us, princes did not have private acts but only selectively public ones, in which the intimacy of revelation was a political sign of privilege, Maximilian's conduct is exceptional and bizarre. His modesty sexualizes, though without eroticizing, his body in a special way. Suspicion appears about the feminine characteristics of the emperor, who is unusual in his bodily concealment as in his beauty. The frontier between genders, however, is only one aspect of Maximilian's mystery in an essay that concerns another major frontier in the spectacle princes offer to the world—death. Maximilian's story appears in the essay "Our feelings reach out beyond us [Nos affections s'emportent au delà de nous]" (1.3), where the concern we have for our reputation after our deaths is a major topic. On one hand, death is the moment when all interiority is surrendered and when our survival becomes purely external and verbal. Montaigne points with approval to nations in which the actions of a dead prince are examined after his death and the good actions separated from the bad. Only then, when the prince can no longer control what is said of him, can his acts be spoken of frankly. At this point the life of the prince becomes a matter of what we can tell about him, rending chronology into nontemporal classifications of good acts, bad acts, clever ploys, diplomatic successes—in short a whole range of paradigms.[16] This survival of the past—"survival" taken with a grain of salt because the prince's past in the mouths of the living becomes a creation of those who have truly survived by outliving the prince—is neatly symbolized by the example of Edward I of England, who ordered that his corpse be boiled so that his bones could be carried with the army in all its battles against the Scots, "As if destiny had fatally attached victory to his limbs" (18/11). These disembodied bones remain as royal relics without the connecting flesh. They are the fragments of the past with which the English army can stimulate its valor. They are without life except the life brought to them by those who use them. At the same time the bones refer to something missing; the relics have a quality of sacredness because the flesh is gone and because Edward is no longer a king but a symbol of past glory. Like Rolandine in Marguerite de Navarre's tale, Edward becomes an example when he is no longer a speaker but an object.

In the case of this king and the emperor Maximilian, the ruler is attempting to determine the future by controlling the spectacle of death and entombment. Both know power lies in the way they will be perceived; both wish to remove something from the control of their subjects: control over how their bodies are disposed of, and the sight of their flesh. Maximilian in this respect is especially interesting because he maintains in his death a form of inwardness, no longer thought or feeling but merely an invisibility created artificially so that there would always be something *behind* the spectacle. This removal of part of himself from the eyes of all, a removal proclaimed to the public in the codicil to his will, is a discursive transformation of a corpse into a spectacle. Maximilian's flesh, unseen though it may be, is guaranteed a role in what people say about the spectacle of the prince.

Of such matter is example itself, the way in which life is transformed into that which appears to others. "Exemplary" figures offer the most useful and colorful stories for building our discourse. A struggle emerges, in Montaigne's text, between simple openness or visibility and gaining attention through concealment. Maximilian is interesting because of what he conceals, but this concealment is only useful to Montaigne because it is a known concealment. Likewise, whenever Montaigne comments on the value of the private life and the avoidance of excessive public responsibilities, there is the paradox that the private can only exist in a text or in speech by becoming public. The examples from the ancients who praise modesty and concealment are all inherently contradictory. They reveal the failure, perhaps deliberate, to attain the obscurity they preached. In "Of glory" (II.16), Epicurus's motto, Conceal Your Life, appears ironically not far from an example of how Epicurus staged his death. Dictating a letter shortly before dying, the philosopher permits his disciples to see his pleasure, supposedly internal, at the memory of the discoveries he made in philosophy during his life. Montaigne comments, however, that this pleasure concerned not only the memory that Epicurus had of his discoveries but the memory he hoped to leave among other philosophers. Such an interpretation is justified by Epicurus's testament, says Montaigne, in which he left money for an annual banquet in his honor. Montaigne is surely right in seeing a contradiction between the doctrine of concealment and the availability of evidence of such a concealment in the example itself.

Montaigne is endlessly preoccupied with the gap between the stories told about us and our being. This gap provides Marguerite de Navarre with an argument for mankind's fall from grace, while for Montaigne it is the condition and source of writing, the motivation for multiplying language hopelessly—but not unhappily—in an attempt to account for the hollowness of things. "Of glory" begins with the celebrated distinction between the name and the thing:

> There is the name and the thing. The name is a sound which designates and signifies the thing; the name is not a part of the thing or of the substance, it is an extraneous piece attached to the thing and outside of it. (618/468)

Everything said about us is external to us and useless. In this appeal to traditional Christian modesty, Montaigne elaborates a theory of the emptiness of exemplary discourse. What is said about us is separate from us and insubstantial (*de vent et de voix*), mere wind. It signifies us but thereby only points to an empty thing, "we are all hollow and empty" (*nous sommes tous creux et vuides*), and hence all true discourse about humanity must take into account this hollowness. How can an emptiness appear? Only by a process of a purely external verbal elaboration, one which never really touches the thing. This questioning is not limited to words but extends to all those outward or perceptible things by which we attempt to grasp or to fabricate a consistent entity out of the hollowness of humanity. In "Of the inconsistency of our actions" (II.1), the discontinuous and inconsistent behavior of human beings makes the assumption of a unified core seem especially risky. Montaigne's metaphor is particularly revealing; our actions are so contradictory that it does not seem possible that they are "from the same store" (*parties de mesme boutique*). The unity writers give to historical characters is therefore fabrication, a creation of our textual needs to make something solid out of the shiftiness of human life:

> And who would believe that it was Nero, that living image of cruelty, who said, when they brought him in customary fashion the sentence of a condemned criminal to sign: "Would to God I had never learned to write!" So much his heart was wrung at condemning a man to death! Everything is so full of such examples—everyone, in fact, can supply himself with so many—that I find it strange to see intelligent men sometimes going to great pains to match these pieces . . . There is some justification for basing a judgment of a man on the most ordinary acts of his life; but in view of the natural instability of our conduct and opinions, it has often seemed to me that even good authors are wrong to insist on fashioning a consistent and solid fabric out of us. They choose one general characteristic, and go and arrange and interpret all a man's actions to fit their picture; and if they cannot twist them enough, they go and set them down to dissimulation. (332/239)

The repeated use of the term *image* here shows that Montaigne does not merely regret the difficulty in touching some solid base in the true person. Instead he shows that in examples we are dealing with the product of a process of simplification, an "external," flat entity called "Nero." The "true image of cruelty" results from the tradition of depicting Nero quasi-allegorically as symbol of a spiritual quality. Nero himself, as living human entity, would also be an abstraction, we can infer, because we could not grasp his hollowness. Instead we use a linguistic creation, the name "Nero," to try to stabilize this flux. But even language turns out to be inconsistent. The simplified, linguistic Nero still ends up contradicting some of the stories told about him. This is what history is made of, an almost arbitrarily chosen image that serves as key to the representation of characters. If a surplus of actions exists, something that cannot be made to fit the image, it is not historical discourse that has failed, it is the character who is dishonest! This is a form of the "return of the living dead," for the dishonesty is not apparently attributed to the textual entity—for example, "Nero"—but to the original, ungraspable human character who is now competing with the textual character whose elaborate consistency he is violating. Dissimulation therefore becomes a double vice. Not only is it simply wrong in real life to deceive people, it is wrong (or even worse, annoying) to present obstacles to the literary use of one's external, public gestures.

Nero is useful in examples because he is the "true image of cruelty." In *this* example, however, Nero serves to exemplify something that is even more profoundly connected with the process of exemplification: the tension between inside and outside, between image and a posited reality behind that image. This example is inconsistent with the other exemplary uses of the figure Nero. A gap appears not only between Nero and "Nero" but between one textual "Nero" and other "Neros." Through this gap we glimpse a hidden center, one that could be attributed to any or all of these proliferating Neros, the intersection where they are supposed to cohere around some historical moment. There are two approaches we can use to deal with this hidden center. One is to assume that Nero is dissimulating and to read Montaigne's question "And who could believe that it was Nero . . . ?" as an invitation to see the words of regret as insincere, as hypocrisy, or as a bad joke. On the other hand, we could read Montaigne's question as directing us to view Nero's words as being entirely sincere, a manifestation of true grief at the thought of another condemnation to death. In the former case we would end up by reconstructing a new instance of the same exemplary "Nero," still performing his cruel pranks on the condemned and on historians alike. In such a case Nero justifies the historians who want to accuse him of dissimulation, but he undermines Montaigne's use of his name to exemplify inconsistency. On the other hand, if Nero was entirely sincere, he was not really the "true image of cruelty," and he weakens the traditional exemplary use of his name while he serves Montaigne's purposes in arguing for almost universal inconsistency.

There is a strong link between exemplarity and the ontology of the "image," as Montaigne uses the term. Montaigne describes a textualized culture, one in which there is an almost universal collaboration in producing consumable units of behavior in the form of examples of various qualities. In the remarks on Nero's inconsistency, it seems that the historians create these images. In the *Essais* as a whole, however, it seems that historical figures often manipulate appearances to become examples. Epicurus, Maximilian, Nero, Caesar, Edward I, and others all take into account the way in which their actions and sayings will be recorded and glossed after their deaths. When Montaigne says in "Of the inconsistency of our actions" that we can furnish examples of inconsistency from our own experience (or from our own actions—*Tout est si plein de tels exemples, voire chacun en peut tant fournir à soy-mesme . . .*), he supposes (even in this early A passage) that his readers are practiced in the process of example formation, that they are capable of producing an "image" or dominant representation of themselves or others, which will then contrast with the minority or atypical representation. In other words, Montaigne assumes we are familiar with the creation of a discursive consistency that can then be used to locate those things that subsequently refuse to "fit" and can be labeled inconsistent. This is a "discursive consistency" because it is not immediate and spontaneous but the result of a dialogic process—it takes two interlocutors to produce a representation—but any reader of the *Essais* can learn to dialogue inwardly to locate such consistency. For this reason Montaigne speaks of "furnishing" examples to oneself; each reader serves as giver and receiver when examples are thus furnished, rehearsing the consistency we wish to maintain in our presentation of self to the social world. Montaigne says much later in his book that he engages in fitting inside and outside together in considering his friends: "So I reveal to my friends, by their outward manifestations, their inward inclinations" (III.13:1076).

The preoccupation with this external representation and perception of our actions so penetrates the *Essais* that Montaigne is on both sides. He denounces the obsession with appearing to others and preparing an image for future discourse while he nonetheless practices writing as a way of converting even his contradictions into some kind of whole, repairing the porosity of his own memory. Montaigne, believing we are "hollow and empty," denounces the search for glory in public and creates a book to compensate for the hollowness, a book consubstantial with the author. In both cases humanity is depicted as engaged in a constant self-representation, which must always assume a disparity and separation between exterior and interior (where "exterior" is the domain of representation of all sorts, in words and other images). Spectators of ourselves, we are split into the two parts necessary for appreciation of our manifest qualities. Perhaps Nero was having fun thinking of how merciful he was appearing when he signed the order for execution.

The most extreme case of the display of qualities, the conversion of life into a spectacle in which we are alternately seen and seeing, is monstrosity, which is repeatedly a source of examples in Montaigne's *Essais*. The word *monstre* itself is derived from and continually associated with the verb *monstrer* (*montrer*, "to show").[17] The little man from Nantes, of whom Montaigne writes in "Of custom, and not easily changing an accepted law" (I.23), earns a living from showing his dexterity in the use of his feet. He has no hands. "He earns his living showing himself" (*à se faire voir*) writes Montaigne in a paragraph that conveys the interest the author took in such exhibitions, which he also evokes in "Of a monstrous child" (II.30). The monster combines the twin characteristics of exemplarity—rarity and exteriority—because the monster is unusual, a disruption of normality, and the monster can only be known from the outside, as spectacle. Montaigne emphasizes the visual nature of his experience of the Siamese twin in II.30 by relentlessly describing the child in terms of the verb "to see": *Je vis avant hier un enfant; vous voyez, au dessoubs le nombril; le nombril de l'imparfait ne se pouvoit voir*. The adults with the child earn money by showing him, "to get a penny or so from showing him, because of his strangeness." Immediately after describing the child, Montaigne tells of another "monster," again in visual terms, but with one crucial difference: "I have just seen a shepherd in Médoc, thirty years old or thereabouts, who has no sign of genital parts. He has three holes by which he continually makes water. He is bearded, has desire, and likes to touch women" (713/539). Once again *voir* and *montre* are the indications of Montaigne's knowledge of this individual, but the enigma of what it is like to be a monster appears in reference to the monster's desire. With the concise *a desir*, Montaigne questions what is behind the appearance, what is there *inside* a monster. The shepherd's case is puzzling because he shows no sign of genitals but he has desire just the same. There is, therefore, something invisible that does not fit. If the shepherd were merely sexless, he or it would form a striking contrast to normal humanity. But in addition to this difference, which makes the monster rare and interesting because of the gap between it and us, there is a difference between the inside and the outside of the monster itself—desire on the inside but no instrument or sign of desire on the outside. In some ways this monster is an inverted image of ourselves, for we are "hollow and empty" but we manage to produce a good appearance, while the shepherd has desire inside but nothing to show for it outside.

Montaigne deals with the concept of exemplary rarity in this essay by using exteriority to neutralize it. We pay to see monsters because they arc different from us, exceptions to the rule. But in God's eyes there are no exceptions: "What we call monsters are not so to God, who sees in the immensity of his work the infinity of forms that he has comprised in it; and it is for us to believe that this figure that astonishes us is related and linked to some other figure of the same kind unknown to man . . . but we do not see its arrangement and relationship" (713/539). Difference is here converted into an effect of distance. Life becomes a kind of gigantic anamorphic painting that we can never see from the proper distance. The proper insertion of the apparent exception into the appropriate serial continuity can be understood metaphorically as an effect of perspective, and, appropriately, Montaigne invokes God here as he did in "Of glory" to mark the relationship between appearance and inward reality. Just as God sees the hollowness of the glorious individual, so too He sees the normality of the monster.

CIRCULATION AND EXCHANGE

If Montaigne had been able to assume such a divine perspective, the *Essais* would not exist, for only the disparities and differences of this world provide a structure for his work, a structure that is in fact an economy. Any system based on rarity is potentially economic, ready to generate movement on the basis of supply. The monsters who exhibit themselves do so because other people will pay to see them. Authors lay up wholesale stores of quotations and *exempla* for redistribution—retail—to the readers; recognition of this approach to writing justifies critics' classification of Montaigne's book as "compilation-literature."[18]

Of course, examples are not traded on an exchange as are stocks today, but they do circulate from text to text, and the choice of a valuable example rather than a valueless one can make the difference in the general merit of a book as a whole. Montaigne himself uses the monetary metaphor to describe Jean Bodin's criticism of example in Plutarch. Bodin had accused Plutarch of writing "incredible and entirely fabulous things" (II.32:722/546). Montaigne protests that Bodin insults Plutarch by claiming that the Greek writer believed things that were not true:

> But to charge him with having taken incredible and impossible things as genuine coin [*pour argent content*] is to accuse the most judicious author in the world of lack of judgment. And here is his example: "As," he says, "when he relates that a Lacedaemonian boy let his whole stomach be torn up by a young fox he had stolen, and kept it hidden under his robe until he died, rather than disclose his theft. In the first place, I find this example badly chosen, since it is very hard to assign bounds to the achievements of the faculties of the soul, whereas we have more chance to assign limits to physical powers and to know them. And for this reason, if it had been for me to do, I would have chosen rather an example of this second sort. And there are some of these that are less credible, as, among others, what he relates of Pyrrhus. (722–723/546)

The cliché *prendre pour argent comptant* fits the context in which examples are shown to be transportable and exchangeable. Bodin does not give Plutarch proper credit, protests Montaigne, but the Greek author's credit is quite good with Montaigne. The writer of the *Essais* has taken an example from Bodin who took an example from the Greek—an example of an example—thus demonstrating the way in which examples pass from text to text and take on a special value from the process by which they circulate. Moreover, at the center of the contention between Bodin and Montaigne is the question of the worth of different examples. Something simply "fabulous"—fictive and unreal—has a worth different from an example that is rare but still within the range of believability. To evaluate we must be familiar with the issuer of the example as well as with the stock of similar examples.

The line between what is fabulous, hence not worth believing, and what is entirely ordinary, hence not worth noticing, is a fine one. What seemed so far-fetched as to be beyond belief to Bodin, seems to Montaigne to be ordinary, but *within Plutarch*. In other words, what is not really typical of "everyday experience" can be characteristic of certain sources of examples. Yet these examples, taken from their normal context and introduced to us in contrast to our modern or local expectations, retain their rarity and value. On this topic Montaigne juxtaposes two revealing statements:

> I am so steeped in the greatness of those people that not only does Plutarch's story not seem incredible to me, as it does to Bodin, but I do not find it even rare and strange. Spartan history is full of a thousand more cruel and uncommon examples: by this standard [*à ce pris*] it is all miracle. (723/547)

In other words, Plutarch and others who write of Spartan history are so full of rare things that ordinary things in Sparta are rare things for us. Hence Spartan history becomes a treasure of exemplarity for writers such as Montaigne. The reappearance of the metaphor of commerce, *à ce pris*, does not seem to be fortuitous in Montaigne's argument at this point. Value and rarity are intimately related, and they require attention to source and means of transmission.

Montaigne's essay "Of the power of the imagination" (1.21) contains a commentary on the way we use examples in our exchanges with others. For this reason it is especially striking to find, within one of the examples, a circulating gold medal, an object that has become, in effect, a currency of belief.[19] Sexuality, especially male sexual performance, is a frequent theme in Montaigne. In 1.21 Montaigne tells of the wedding of a friend whose family worried that the groom's virility might be impaired by a magic spell cast by an unsuccessful rival. Montaigne proposes to help by giving the groom a medal with magical properties and instructs him on its use. The medal in question had been given to Montaigne himself by Jacques Peletier to protect him against sunstroke and headache. Montaigne comments that the emptiness of the use of such objects, combined with certain bizarre ceremonies, is what gives them weight: "These monkey tricks are the main part of the business, our mind being unable to get free of the idea that such strange means must come from some abstruse science. Their inanity gives them weight and reverence [Leur inanité leur donne poids et reverence]" (101/71). We do not know from whom Peletier had received the medal, but we detect a whole chain of *singeries*, in which the hollowness of both object and procedures gives them an inverse weightiness. Montaigne indicates that we are attracted also by the strangeness of the ceremony, so that the magical currency is guaranteed by the mystery of its origin. The newlywed trusted Montaigne, as Montaigne trusted Peletier (though perhaps with a certain skepticism—but he *did* keep the medal with him), so that effect is dependent on a dialectic between the strangeness of the incantations and the familiar authority of the person who passes on the medal.

The circulation of this medal is part of a complex economy of sexuality, concerning the groom's attention or lack of attention to his own performance and the role of women in establishing a hierarchy of virility among males. As Montaigne says in introducing the example of the bridegroom, an *excess* of desire can produce an apparent *absence* of desire. An aging man, who had experienced impotence because of an excessive eagerness and virility, may become a better sexual partner because the weakening of desire weakens the impediment to achievement—"who with age finds himself less impotent through being less potent" (100/70). Therefore the groom, being distracted by the hocus-pocus of the medal, allows his body to perform its function. The medal produces a curious *absent*-mindedness in the groom; the medal and its procedures of use are empty, says Montaigne, and the weighty effect of this emptiness (its *poids et reverence*) is a desirable emptiness in the groom, a lack of preoccupation with certain thoughts.[20] It is paradoxical, but ultimately quite reasonable, that a gold medal should be a way of venting or providing a catharsis for some kind of excess (thus justifying the introduction of the groom's story by a reference to degrees of potency in aging), for monetary economies also confer on symbolic objects the ability to produce absence.[21] Once a certain type of object has been selected as valuable—gold, coin, paper certificate—other objects are correspondingly devalued. Even in the case of the valued object an excess, by inflation, can produce an absence of value. By focusing on the medal, Montaigne provides the groom with an outlet to his preoccupation with the sexual act and allows the marital act to regain a beneficial and "natural" indifference.[22]

The medal circulates among the men of this example, but so does desire for the bride. Because she had been courted by someone else present at the wedding, the groom is afraid of a spell. The bride is thus subject to a potential exchange (in the way commodity futures are traded), and the groom and his family are apparently preoccupied with his having a "debt" of some kind to the unsuccessful suitor. In this conjunction Montaigne's treasure, taken from his *coffres*, relieves the groom's fear by supplying a spare potency (*un miracle, qui estoit en ma puissance*) if the groom takes the medal and also Montaigne's bathrobe, which he would wear to bed and use to cover himself and his bride. Montaigne's friendly participation in the wedding night thus dispels— or expels—the rival's unfriendly intervention between bride and groom.

Now, although this is an example, it may seem that the economy of imagination and desire constitutes a digression from a study of exemplarity per se. Throughout "Of the power of the imagination," however, Montaigne unites examples of belief with the belief in examples. By telling each other these tales, we affect one another in the most profound and physical ways. Montaigne seems to believe the tales of contagion and spells originating in the imagination of other people. Not only can we become ill by believing we are ill (e.g., the woman who believed she had swallowed a pin and became well again when she believed, falsely, she had vomited it), but the evil eye can affect us. The imagination of women can leave visible marks on the bodies of the children they bear in their womb. All these things happen in a circulation of imagination, to which Montaigne compares other illnesses, "just as a body passes on its sickness to its neighbor, as is seen in the plague, the pox, and soreness of the eyes, which are transmitted from one body to the other" (104/74).

After commenting on the way the imagination of others can affect our bodies, Montaigne passes explicitly to the circulation of examples taken from antecedent texts, from conversation, and from our personal stock of examples. Montaigne says that as long as he can use them, he does not worry about the original truth of the statement, "for I refer the stories that I borrow to the conscience of those from whom I take them" (105/75). The concluding paragraph of "Of the power of the imagination" is a discussion of the equivalency of real and imaginary examples. What matters is the use of examples, not their origin in an external, material, and temporal reality. Significantly, the example of the bridegroom and the concluding theoretical reflection are additions occurring after 1588, which deny the intrinsic value of objects of exchange and conversely affirm the *social* and collective use-value of miraculous medals and examples alike. Declaring that the commentary on the examples is the only thing that Montaigne vouches for personally ("The reflections are my own, and depend on the proofs of reason, not of experience . . . [Les discours sont à moy, et se tienent par la preuve de la raison, non de l'expérience . . .]," 105/75), Montaigne proposes a dual social process of exemplification. Given a certain example or series of examples, everyone can elaborate a commentary: "If I do not comment [*comme*] well let another comment for me." On the other hand, given a proposition, each one of us, he says, can provide examples: "everyone can add his own examples to them."

The most explicit statement of the use-value of examples in circulation begins,

> So in the study that I am making of our behavior and motives, fabulous testimonies, provided they are possible, serve like true ones. Whether they have happened or no, in Paris or in Rome, to John or Peter, they exemplify, at all events, some human potentiality [*l'humaine capacité*], and thus their telling imparts useful information to me. I see it and profit from it just as well in shadow as in substance. And of the different readings that histories often give, I take for my use the one that is most rare and memorable [*la plus rare et mémorable*]. (105/75)

Rarity is again accentuated, while historical veracity is set aside, to permit the free use of examples provided by the traditional supply or by contemporary conversation. Curiously, while Montaigne attaches little importance to the veracity of the stories that serve as examples, he proclaims his absolute fidelity to the integrity of the examples as he receives them: "In the examples that I bring in here of what I have heard, done, or said, I have forbidden myself to dare to alter even the slightest and most inconsequential circumstances. My conscience does not falsify one iota; my knowledge, I don't know" (106/76). Montaigne shows respect for the social and conventional nature of examples. The example itself is not internally altered, but it can be used for different transactions within the discourse of the person who appropriates it. That the examples come from elsewhere actually facilitates the task of the writer, who is not responsible for the content of the examples but only for their transmission. Montaigne says that he thinks it is easier to write the history of the past than the history of the present, since the writer of the former "has only to give an account of a borrowed truth" (106/76). In this connection the monetary metaphor reappears to indicate that in writing the history of the past an author does not really guarantee the material reality of the statements he transmits: "How be responsible for the thoughts of persons unknown and give their conjectures as coin of the realm [*donner pour argent contant leurs conjectures*]" (106/76)?

PROCESS

Examples, like the objects mankind uses as monetary tokens, are not of value in themselves but for the kind of activity surrounding them: creation, exchange, evaluation, accumulation. The adjective "exemplary" (*exemplaire*) distinguishes things of value, and Montaigne uses this adjective inside an example from his work as a jurist in which the activity, not the product, is stressed. "Let us take an example from ourselves," he writes:

> To treat matters diversely is as good as to treat them uniformly, and better: to wit, more copiously and usefully. Let us take an example from ourselves. Judicial sentences form the ultimate point of dogmatic and decisive speaking. Yet the most exemplary ones which our highest courts present to the people, fitted to foster in them the reverence they owe to the dignity of those bodies, principally because of the ability of the persons who form them, derive their beauty, not so much from the conclusion, which to them is everyday, and which is common to every judge, as from the discussion and stirring up of the diverse and contrary reasonings [*la disceptation et agitation des diverses et contraires ratiocinations*] which the matter of the law allows. (509/377–8)

The value of parliamentary judgments is not the conclusion or sentence but the exhibit of the activity of judging. There is a parallel between Montaigne's skepticism about the truth of many of his examples and his condescension about court decrees. In both cases the thoughts provoking the story or decision are more important (though undoubtedly not to the person judged) than an objective reality. Montaigne finds value in this *disceptation et agitation*.[23]

The example of Democritus and the figs, which follows immediately, seconds this comment on the exemplary judgments. Democritus, having eaten some figs that tasted of honey, decided to find out how they had acquired that flavor. As he was going out to see where they had grown, his servant told him it was not worth investigating because she had simply put the figs in a container that had earlier held honey: "He was vexed she had deprived him of this occasion for research and robbed him of matter for curiosity: 'Go along,' he said to her, 'you have made me angry; I will not for all that give up seeking the cause as if it was a natural one.' And he willfully sought and found some 'true' reason for a false and supposed effect" (510–11/378). Montaigne generalizes the pleasure of investigation, supposition, and discourse. This is not the philosopher's alone, but can be shared by others if they are exposed to an exemplary, rather than a dogmatic, rhetoric.[24]

Stimulating ratiocination, examples take on an ethical and aesthetic quality. Characteristically Montaigne does not seem to be concerned with a "lesson" so much as with participating in the imaginative recreation of a heroic life. In "Of Cato the Younger" (1.37), after decrying the attribution of less-than-heroic intentions to a figure like Cato, Montaigne says:

> The same pains that they take to detract from these great names, and the same license, I would willingly take to lend them a shoulder to raise them higher. These great figures, whom the consensus of the wise has selected as examples to the world, I shall not hesitate to restore to their places of honor, as far as my ingenuity allows me to interpret them in a favorable light. But we are forced to believe that our powers of conception are far beneath their merit. (231/170)

These exemplars are clearly a form of social fiction. Their historical foundation seems irrelevant. Montaigne does not engage in a historiographical dispute with those who deflate the exemplary figures; instead, he concentrates on the relation between those figures and ourselves, not on the circumstances in which they related to their own time. (Pascal takes the opposite approach, see chapter 4.) Their place in our tradition is not an automatic or objective product of the facts of their lives but the result of an agreement of certain authors, the *consentement des sages*. Moreover, their place in our lives depends on our efforts, not on theirs. Montaigne, and others, by producing more laudatory discourse and by redepicting the heroes, increase their merit. When he says "it is necessary to believe" that our attempts to conceive their merit are beneath that merit, a first reading might lead us to think that Montaigne means that they really *must* objectively have been better. But in view of Montaigne's complex skepticism, another meaning offers itself. "It is necessary to believe" that our attempts at imagining the merit of the heroes are inadequate because we need an absent ideal, not for the benefit of that ideal but for our own benefit.[25] This view, fitting Montaigne's comment about helping the exemplary figures achieve greater status, provides the bridge between the ethical and the aesthetic that the essay requires. ·

"Of Cato the Younger" begins by setting Montaigne in opposition to the common error of judging others by oneself. The essayist says, "I easily believe that another man may have qualities different from mine. Because I feel myself tied down to one form, I do not oblige everybody to espouse it, as all others do" (229/169). This point of departure concerns knowledge and ethics, since it sets up a standard for our way of knowing and judging others. In other words, it deals first with our descriptive assumptions about what others have done and why, and second with our normative assumptions about what they should have done. The essay ends, however, with the sketch of a theory of literature and of literary criticism, including quotations from five Latin poets, from Martial to Virgil. In passing from the ethical/epistemological concerns of the beginning to the aesthetic questions of the end, the essay reveals the common ground of these matters in the process of representation. Believing in the exemplary figures takes an effort of the imagination, a suspension of our familiar, too familiar, experiential standard.

Here Montaigne presents a direct contrast between the exemplary attitude and its opposite, for there *is* an exemplary attitude. It consists of a willingness to accept and even actively to create difference. It is based on cultivating alienation. "Alienation" here means the de-centering that occurs when we measure ourselves by a foreign, external standard, a standard that is artificial or idealist (and that we even recognize as being largely fictitious), rather than by our own strength and experience. The opposite attitude holds to a belief in continuity and resemblance. Montaigne contrasts his own tendency to accept unlikeness with other people's presumption of sameness: "[I] conceive a thousand contrary ways of life; and in contrast with the common run of men, I more easily admit difference than resemblance between us" (229/169). The attitude of refusing otherness, which appears notably in Bodin's criticism of Plutarch in II.32, deprives us of the diverse possibilities available through examples. Use of examples, however, requires an effort that involves aesthetic options, pricking our imagination to remove us from our narrow thought and experience. This form of alienation appears in the poets named in the last paragraphs of "Of Cato the Younger." Such a poetic doctrine, with definite elements of what will be known to the following century as the sublime, requires of the highest poetry that it transport us out of ourselves, just as the exemplary figures require us to leave behind our familiar judgments of human intention:

But the good, supreme, divine poetry is above the rules and reason. Whoever discerns its beauty with a firm, sedate gaze does not see it, any more than he sees the splendor of a lightning flash. It does not persuade our judgment, it ravishes and overwhelms it. (231–2/171)[26]

Exemplarity and sublime poetry therefore have an intimate connection, both requiring a capacity to leave the self and to experience, in some way, an ideal that is outside. Montaigne astutely combines this form of aesthetic alienation with disclaimers of belief in the objective existence of such absolutes. Even though the thrust of this essay is to open the self to contact with difference, Montaigne's remarks make it clear that this difference is a product of the self. In other words, we make the heroes. Our help, our *tour d'espaule*, makes the exemplary figures so powerful, permits us to suspend our familiar standards and to look for something other than resemblance to ourselves.

The Place of the Subject

Montaigne combines the elaboration of his textual self with the apparently opposite exaltation of otherness. Montaigne's self is tied closely to the use and production of examples. Even a declaration as ringing as "I do not care so much what I am to others as I care what I am to myself. I want to be rich by myself, not by borrowing. Strangers see only the results and outward appearances" (II.16:625/474) bears the mark of a comparative exercise, the effort of making a distinction between self-perception and the appearance one presents to others.

The concern for the self and its powers, based in both Christian and Stoic influences, requires a definition of the self, a definition that can only come from a knowledge of what is not-self or different. As Regosin observes about Montaigne's metaphoric use of the expression "the book of the world," "Truth does not reside outside, in signs, but inside in relation to the touchstone of the self."[27] The description of sublime poetry transporting the self outside confirms this interior/exterior dichotomy, and an example, located in others, draws the borders of the self. One of Montaigne's preoccupations is the final boundary of his self, death. He contrasts our attitude toward our own death with our vision of the death of others in "Of judging of the death of others" (II.13): "When we judge of the assurance of other men in dying, which is without doubt the most noteworthy action of human life, we must be mindful of one thing: that people do not easily believe that they reached that point" (605/458). Our vision of the self is thus an open-ended one, despite a rational conviction that we must die, for we never can *see* our own death as we do that of others. Montaigne joins Machiavelli and Marguerite de Navarre in emphasizing the general tendency to see everything as measured from our own position, and he compares the dying man to a traveler in a boat who seems to see the mountains, fields, sky, coastline, and cities moving at the rate he is moving.

Montaigne seeks to represent the self without falling into the naïveté of these nondialectical illusions. Because the historical example is *of* someone else and is based on an indirect source, it is doubly separate from Montaigne himself. On the other hand, unlike a quotation, in which Montaigne borrows the words of another writer, the example is told in Montaigne's own words, so that it has a somewhat floating character, neither entirely Montaigne's nor entirely another's.[28] In the case of the quotations, which are in a foreign language, and of paraphrases, Montaigne measures himself mostly as object, that is, as an entity sharing the characteristics of the narrative characters of whom the example is being told.

Because example is a statement that links a general or abstract statement to a specific instance or subgroup, what is at issue in many of the essays is whether Montaigne, as he defines himself in the words of his book, is like or unlike the specific instances he gives. Does he too fit under the general statement in question? Montaigne is not simply comparing himself to other *people*, he is comparing himself to other *examples*. A person is not an example, since examples are formed only in language.[29] Montaigne, creating a word-self or textual existence, is comparing his word-self with other word-beings. Therefore Montaigne does not compare himself—as ultimate biological or historical entity—to Alexander, Epaminondas, Cato, or La Boétie, but compares the literary character "Michel de Montaigne" with other literary characters. In using the very name, he hesitates about the relationship between his "je" and this outward, verbal character (e.g., II.16:626/474). As Rigolot says of intertextuality and autobiography in the *Essais*, "the observer [Montaigne] looks at himself obliquely, through the discourse of the 'authors,' from the necessary margin of classical culture, which, paradoxically, liberates the *moy* from authority and from alterity."[30]

Although Montaigne professes to be concerned only with what he is in himself—*quel je sois en moy mesme*—the *Essais* show through the examples that the *moy mesme* is a unit dependent on others for its fictions and its reality.[31] If examples are in some way models *of* behavior (though not necessarily models *for* behavior), the essays progressively become themselves the model of Montaigne's behavior, an exterior by which Montaigne finds himself bound progressively. The verbal construction of the *Essais*, by its proliferation, calls for more words precisely because the structure of exemplarity itself, in Montaigne's view, posits an unstable relationship, an exceptional situation, and a hollowness in the thing (*chose*) that cannot be filled by the word (*nom*). Just as the opening examples in "Par divers moyens" (I. I) set in motion a spiral of opposites—everything calling for a counterexample in a structure that depends for its central meaning on contradiction itself—so the enunciation of a discourse by an "I" requires answers to the question, "What is it that cannot be said by me of the 'I'?"[32] This question entails others: questions of what cannot be said with certainty of any person, of what cannot be said by the "I" about itself even though it can be observed and said *by* others, and of what can be said only *of* others. The frontier between "I" and Other is verbal, in our glosses of one another. In the interpretation of the *Essais*, as Auerbach observed, we are constantly invited as readers to adjudicate between the two sides, *les autres* and *le particulier*, thus echoing the process of Montaigne's writing.[33]

Many readers have seen that book III devotes even more intense scrutiny to the self/other relationship than the earlier books.[34] Yet the last book of the *Essais* differs from the first two by the reduced role of traditional *exempla*, no longer displayed in such quantity or in the same conspicuous position at the beginning of essays. If the *exempla* have moved from the beginning to the center of the essay as text, perhaps this is because example, in an ever more complex construction, has moved to the center of the Montaignian representation of self. We should turn inside out a perceptive remark of Jean Starobinski, who sees the classical figures in the *exempla* as being actual models for Montaigne to imitate.[35] Instead, as the *Essais* develop, Montaigne questions this movement from outside to inside, from model to imitation. The lucid comments that Montaigne added to "Of Cato the Younger" after 1588—and which form the bulk of that essay—demonstrate a growing persuasion that the "exemplarity" of classical figures comes from our appropriation of them in our own language, not from an objective, atemporal quality of the patrimony of heroism. The consent of the wise elders who have fabricated the canon of classical models is not sufficient without our own active use of these models to create an otherness for ourselves. In sexuality as well, we must think less about ourselves. This alienation through forgetfulness is not a static, pre-existent state, but requires our participation. Without his collaboration, for instance, the gold medal of "Of the power of the imagination"

(1.21) would have been useless to the bridegroom (perhaps significantly, this example also entered the *Essais* after 1588).

The general characteristics of Renaissance exemplarity appear in Montaigne's comments about his own case. His text becomes an exterior in which a certain whole "Montaigne" (*mon estre universel, comme Michel de Montaigne*, 805/611), like a certain "Nero," will be perceived. Some people, like those who pay to see monsters, will pay for the privilege of examining this Montaigne. But, like monsters and all examples of unfamiliar things, Montaigne's book assumes value with distance:

> And in this humble example [*en ce bas exemple*] you may see an image of greater ones. In my region of Gascony they think it a joke to see me in print. The farther from my lair the knowledge of me spreads, the more I am valued. I buy printers in Guienne, elsewhere they buy me. On this phenomenon those people base their hopes who hide themselves while alive and present, to gain favor when dead and gone. I would rather have less of it (III.2:808/614).

Montaigne explains how he disappears physically from the social world to appear in it as the character of his book. While explaining that he is all on the outside (*je suis tout au dehors et en evidence, nay à la societé et à l'amitié*), Montaigne declares in "Of three kinds of association." (III.3) that he withdraws into himself when he is in a crowd but opens up when he is alone:

> Solitude of place . . . rather makes me stretch and expand outward; I throw myself into affairs of state and into the world more readily when I am alone. At the Louvre and in the crowd I withdraw and contract into my skin; the crowd drives me back to myself. (823/625)

If Montaigne was born to be in evidence and on the outside yet can only be in evidence when he is alone in his library, then Montaigne was born to be a book. Such a pronouncement is consonant with the frequent claims of consubstantiality with his book. At the same time it reinforces the relationship between the writer's self-representation and the exteriority of all exemplification.

Montaigne is not establishing himself as an example for others in the sense of being a model for imitation, but on the other hand, examples depend on another unit of discourse as examples *of*.[36] Since the consensus of those who have discussed example in Montaigne is that examples, and particularly *exempla*, in the *Essais* do not teach any lesson, how can one define the "of what" in Montaigne's examples? Another way to arrive at the problem of how the textual "I" can figure in examples is to recall that there is nothing natural or inevitable about the habit of understanding narratives and other statements as examples. Most of the stories that figure in the *Essais* could be read, if they were extracted from the context Montaigne has provided, without any need to see them as examples. After all, restored to their original context, narratives from Tacitus, for instance, would link together to form a historical continuity (Montaigne, as we have noted, found Tacitus too interested in this continuous or horizontal dimension of narrative). So, that Montaigne did not fortify his house during the religious wars could simply be a historical or biographical statement. The consensus that such narrative statements constitute exemplary material indicates that readers do react to the way Montaigne frames narratives with more general statements.

It may seem strange to refer to abstraction in a book that so emphasizes concrete, physical topics. But such concrete references are striking because they are framed by abstractions and commonplaces. Between Montaigne and his body there is already a gap that will become the foundation of method in Descartes. Unlike Descartes, however, for whom the body as experienced (not as the anatomical abstraction it becomes in studies of the pineal gland and the eye) was primarily to be avoided as both object of study and instrument of study, Montaigne sees the body as the focus and laboratory of a series of conceptual issues. Even after subjecting the body as instrument of understanding to severe and damning criticism in the "Apology for Raymond Sebond," Montaigne returns constantly to the body as example of cultural and ethical rules and pretensions. Anthony Wilden, who also perceives a division between self and self in Montaigne, believes that Montaigne finally rejected this division.[37] Wilden's belief in the final unification of self in Montaigne, however, seems to assume that only an essentialist position requires such a division. Montaigne, in this view, would arrive at an existential understanding that rejects the alienating, divisive, ideal.

Exemplarity, as discursive practice, maintains a dimension of abstraction that transcends essence/existence dichotomies. If Montaigne can use examples of himself, he must have the habit of fragmenting and interrupting narrative with a more general discourse.[38] The humble example-cluster shows such disruption:

> It is bad manners, besides being harmful to health and even to pleasure to eat greedily, as I do. I often bite my tongue and some-

times my fingers, in my haste. Diogenes, coming upon a boy who was eating that way, gave his tutor a box on the ear for it. There were men at Rome who taught people to chew, as well as to walk, gracefully. By this I lose the leisure for talking, which is such a sweet seasoning for the dinner table, provided the remarks are appropriate, pleasant, and brief.
[C'est indecence, outre ce qu'il nuit à la santé, voire et au plaisir, de manger goulument, comme je fais: je mors souvent ma langue, par fois mes doits, de hastiveté. Diogenes, rencontrant un enfant qui mangeoit ainsin, en donna un soufflet à son precepteur. Il y avoit à Rome des gens qui enseignoyent à mascher, comme à marcher, de bonne grace. J'en pers le loisir de parler, qui est un si doux assaisonnement des tables, pourveu que ce soyent des propos de mesme, plaisans et courts.] (III.13:1105–06/848–49)

The structure of this example requires Montaigne to occupy three discursive positions overtly (maker of the general statement, narrator of the first-person narrative, narrator of the third-person narrative) and three indirect or metaphoric positions to which he is compared: the good teacher (like Diogenes), the bad teacher, and the child who eats too fast. One generality, or maxim, is supported by the two narrative examples, followed by a second maxim ("le parler . . . est un si doux assaisonnement . . .") linked to the first-person narrative but without an example to support it (that is, there is no example of the pleasure of talking during a meal). In this way the depiction of Montaigne as character is disrupted and framed by generalities and parallel narratives. Montaigne presents a simple piece of information about how he eats through a matrix of maxim and example. This practice is typical of the way in which Montaigne represents his textual self at the boundary between generalization and concrete instances. Montaigne is directly presented here in only two statements ("je mors souvent ma langue, par fois mes doits, de hastiveté" and "J'en pers le loisir de parler"), but he is presented indirectly through both maxim and example. One maxim begins and one maxim ends the passage quoted while the classical examples form the core, and the "I"-statements serve as transition between the maxim and the exemplary core. The "I"-statements are actually a continuous layer, a single example of gluttonous eating, into which the example of the child is placed as a *mise-en-abîme* of such eating. As discursive mediating character, the "I" is good and bad, observer and observed. It is worth noting that in this passage the first maxim is presented in negative terms ("C'est indecence . . .") while the second maxim is given in positive terms ("le loisir de parler [qui] est un si doux assaisonnement," etc.).

The habit of framing his own self-description in relation to maxims is not an innovation of Montaigne's. These generalizations can be viewed as a conservative element in his writing, but they are nonetheless essential to the particular "I" of the *Essais*, with its almost obsessive attempts to limit and particularize while at the same time generalizing and finding universal applications for the results of self-study and self-definition. Because this habit makes Montaigne always a divided subject/object, it creates an almost limitless series of *personae* to whom the figure of Montaigne can be related.

The relative decline in classical examples in the later essays has led to the question of whether Montaigne decreases his use of example as the *Essais* unfold. Cottrell argues that Montaigne renounces exemplarity as the years pass: "The movement from *exempla* to anti-*exempla* is of a piece with the movement from *reigle* to *registre*. It is a 'reflexive movement' that leads back to a unique, unexemplary 'I,' to the 'I' that fashions itself by the act of writing."[39] This movement "away from exemplarity" is associated with the abandonment of a voluntaristic struggle against external forces in favor of a more passive stance in the first-person examples. In at least one way this description of a change is perfectly correct. The later examples do not associate exemplarity with imitation in a positive sense. "Exemplary" as an adjective cannot serve as a synomym for "good" in an opposition between good and bad. Early *Essais*, however, abandon the opposition between good and bad as a simple moralistic framework. The appropriation of classical models of conduct (that is, "exemplary" figures in the didactic/injunctive sense) early assumes a writing-oriented playful quality. Nero, the true image of cruelty, is more interesting to Montaigne as an opportunity to explore the folds and recesses of that image than as an object lesson in the need to shun cruelty. In this respect the *reigle* is already neglected in favor of the *registre* before 1588, for the triumph of the will over circumstance is already less interesting to Montaigne than the perception of human diversity.

The increased emphasis on direct self-depiction in book III marks a change in the source of examples but not a reduction in their importance. On the contrary, Montaigne finds examples proliferating and is less concerned with holding a stockpile of examples gleaned from others now that he has fully understood the process of making examples. If we cannot find a positive example, we can always make a negative one, even if the topic is ourselves:

It is a practice of our justice to condemn some as a warning to others. To condemn them because they have done wrong would be stupidity, as Plato says; for what is done cannot be undone. But they are condemned so that they may not do the same wrong again, or so that others may avoid the example of their wrongdoing.

We do not correct the man we hang; we correct others through him. I do the same. My errors are by now natural and incorrigible; but the good that worthy men do the public by making themselves imitable, I shall perhaps do by making myself evitable. . . . By my publishing and accusing my imperfections, someone will learn to fear them. The parts that I most esteem in myself derive more honor from self-accusation than from self-commendation. That is why I fall back into the former and dwell on it more often. But when all is said and done, you never speak about yourself without loss. Your self-condemnation is always accredited, your self-praise discredited.

There may be some people of my temperament, I who learn better by contrast than by example, and by flight than by pursuit. (III. 8:921–22/703)

Within this brief passage Montaigne illustrates two uses of the word "example" (*exemple*): as model to imitate (*mieux par contrarieté que par exemple*) and as model to flee (*l'exemple de leur faute*). What is a loss to some is a gain to others, and Montaigne classifies the *Essais* here as a loss to himself in an economic system of which the example is the basic unit. He looks for negative examples and gives them in his turn. Such a circulation is the law of example, for we cannot profit from our own examples but only from the examples of others. Montaigne thus moves from a position close to Machiavelli's, where the writer is broker of examples of history, toward a role glimpsed in the *Heptameron*, when storytellers reveal their own faults. As producer of negative examples, Montaigne may instruct others, but the risks of Montaigne's exemplary marketplace seem as great as those of Marguerite de Navarre's theology of grace. After all, the example must find a taker to be useful, and this taker cannot be Montaigne but must be *like* him, of his temperament ("Il en peut estre aucuns de ma complexion"). This need to be alike but different in order to use examples leads directly from Montaigne's active, gregarious, and, overall, happy economy of example to the austere and troubled examples of Descartes and Pascal.

CHAPTER IV

Descartes and Pascal: Self-Centered Examples

saepe licet res veras per
falsa exempla illustrare   —Descartes

En un mot le moi a deux qualités. Il est injuste en soi en ce qu'il se
fait centre de tout. Il est incommode aux autres en ce q'il les veut
asservir.   —Pascal

THE ORDINARY CONVERSATIONS OF LIFE

Descartes and Pascal take up example where Montaigne leaves it. Montaigne's shift of emphasis from classical textual examples to the universal formation of example from the everyday provides a background to the almost total elimination of classical example in the *Discourse on Method* and in the *Pensées*. Pascal is explicit in praising in the *Essais* Montaigne's habit of taking ordinary subjects, *les entretiens ordinaires de la vie*, as his starting point.[1] Yet example becomes a source of problems in the work of both Descartes and Pascal because of the importance they attach to the role of the perceiver, the self, in viewing examples. Since example permits a speaker to move from his unsupported discourse to a common source of external instances, which will bridge the gap between the subjective assertion of the speaker and the belief of the audience, there is always some tension between example and the self. Moreover, the two authors' differing conceptions of the self lead them to place sharply different values on the knowledge derivable from the social supply of observable appearances. For Descartes knowledge culled from "example and custom" can be only negative: it can teach what not to believe. For Pascal these examples are a primary source of the knowledge available to purely human reason.

The rejection of example as knowledge by one and the embrace of example by the other should not obscure the many similarities in Descartes's and Pascal's views. They both view history as misleading rather than enlightening when used for purposes of example. They avoid the rare examples favored by Machiavelli and Montaigne and instead stress the repetitious quality of the common contemporary example. Most important of all, they both view the imitability of example as either dangerous or impossible. These similarities stem from a withdrawal of immediate significance from the world of appearances. Even though Descartes may be classified as a deductivist and Pascal an empiricist (to the extent that his argumentation appeals to social experience), they each locate the redeeming force of enlightenment within the individual and thus outside the manifest world open to all people. Whether it be the certainty of the Cogito or the gift of grace, this inner force will direct the actions of the elect, not the attractive power of a reproducible earlier instance.

Paradoxically the attempt to find a universal truth for humanity leads to an emphasis on the individual subject or self. Already apparent in Montaigne, this tendency is accentuated in Descartes and Pascal, for whom the solitary individual—whether it is Pascal's thinker who *cannot* remain alone in his room, or the protagonist of Descartes's *Discourse* who *does* remain alone in a heated room to discover truth—is central to all knowledge of mankind. This subject, this self, divides in two. For Descartes there is a fallen, exemplary self of external appearance distinct from the true self that exists within thought. This true inner self, the self that follows from the Cogito, uses the outer self as temporary mask to protect the scientific project from the dangerous scrutiny and interruptions of society. For Pascal the outer self is the vehicle of the only truths that can be obtained by human reason, though only a particularly deep inner self can adhere to the knowledge of the surface.

Although Descartes and Pascal try to determine the boundaries between self and nonself, each for his own reasons, the self is at least as problematical as the world from which it must be divided. Only careful scrutiny, even a kind of radical intellectual reduction, of the individual can produce a credible concept of the self. How can example begin with the self when the self is doubtful or at best a kind of theoretical construction? How can the self use examples without deforming them through its limited point of view? Representation *of* the self for others and representation *from* the point of view of the self are, besides, contradictory activities. As Machiavelli showed, the exemplary individual, the prince, cannot see himself. Perspective requires the invisibility of the observer. A point of view is what we see *from* when we look at something *else*. The points an observer can see are not those he occupies at the moment of seeing; they are, at best, points of view he has occupied or will occupy at other moments. Yet study of a moment past or future is, for Descartes and Pascal, a dangerous experiment in fiction, one that permits the observer to be deluded about his immediate, present capacities. Both Descartes and Pascal emphasize knowledge in the present, but they understand that the immediate is out of reach. Only the mediate, the product of a mediation, can approximate the present active perceiving self. If the attempt to represent the self and the attempt to represent from the point of view of the self are the first steps in knowledge, the third step—communicating this knowledge *to* the other self of the reader—is the most complex and treacherous step of all.[2] The techniques of discovery invoked by Descartes and Pascal indicate the danger of losing oneself in the image of others. To attempt a presentation of self to the other, the act of a writer to a public, runs the risk of betraying the writer—to attract and seduce the reader—or of betraying the reader, who may surrender to the alluring text rather than withdraw into true self-discovery.

The Exemplarity of the *Discourse on Method*

Descartes's basic problem is how to spread his method among other people without losing his proprietary rights over it. The ultimate vision of the author of the *Discourse on Method* is to establish a scientific institute to be directed by a single knowledgeable individual. Therefore one basic thing must be reserved to Descartes: establishing a method. This is not something that he wants others to imitate. Yet if nothing he did could be imitated, what he describes in the text would be no method at all, merely the idiosyncrasies of a creative individual. As author, Descartes wants to set forth what he himself has done as an example and yet withhold part of the example, preventing others from imitating the entirety of what he has done. In the scientific institute no volunteers will be permitted. The will of a single person, the methodologist, must prevail. Only workers paid by the master, and therefore under his complete and personal control—extensions of himself—should be allowed to work there. The tension between presentation of an imitable example and the withholding of that example begins early in the *Discourse*. The exemplary and anti-exemplary appear in every facet of the text, from the anonymous author's account of his experiences in school to his creation of several subtly different images of the "I."

Complicating the author's task is the *anonymity* of the *Discourse*. If readers attempt to conform to the relationship of anonymity explicitly established by the author, they must ask what gives the author the right to their attention and what kind of text this is. Rather than inviting obedience, the author seems to aim at inspiring imitation of a certain conduct by giving an exemplary narrative, centered on an "I" who passes from ignorance to enlightenment. Such a happy partnership of exemplification and imitation involves, however, a complex interplay of roles assigned to each party. In order to narrate, the writer must claim some status as an author or else must indicate some source of authority. In order to use the example given in the narrative, the reader must know how to understand and evaluate such narratives and how to determine the boundary between himself or herself and the narrative model. In order to be useful, the model provided must suppose certain things in common between reader and protagonist of the narrative. All of these conditions create a series of roles for the "I" of the *Discourse* and impose on the reader differing relationships to that "I."

The problem of the roles of reader and author appears at the start of the *Discourse*: "Good sense is mankind's most equitably divided endowment."[3] This sentence is so brutally direct that it has long puzzled commentators.[4] Yet it is utterly within the nature of a rhetoric of method. A certain impersonality is necessary for the exchange of roles, for the imitation or performance by the reader of the series of acts established by the author. The first paragraph contains no instance of the first-person singular (it is instead a conflation of the first-person plural and the third-person plural). Only in the second paragraph does the subject appear in his individuality. This individuality is addressed in a paradoxical way. Having fused the persons to legitimize *method*, the author must now disengage his subjectivity from this sharing to authorize his speaking. The concept—*accident*—by which Descartes accomplishes this rhetorical separation is borrowed from scholastic philosophy, but the context gives it an entirely new function. "As for myself," writes Descartes, "I have never supposed that my mind was above the ordinary" (126/2). Since Descartes must present a universal potentiality—or commutability with the reader—he can only make the difference come from outside his being as human being. There is no difference in his capacity to reason, "because as far as reason is concerned, it is the only thing which makes us men and distinguishes us from the animals, and I am therefore satisfied that it is fully present in each one of us. In this I follow the general opinion of philosophers, who say that there are differences in degree only in the *accidental* qualities, and not in the *essential* qualities or natures of individuals of the same species [car pour la raison ou le sens, d'autant qu'elle est la seule chose qui nous distingue des bêtes, je veux croire qu'elle est tout entière en un chacun, et suivre en ceci l'opinion commune des philosophes qui disent qu'il n'y a du plus ou du moins qu'entre les *accidents*, and non point entre les *formes* ou natures des *individus* d'une même espèce]"[5] Descartes's use of the term *accident* is followed by a sentence explaining the kind of difference that may exist between himself and members of his species. For Descartes this difference seems to be historical chance, something that his experience has imposed upon the initially undistinguished subject. Accident, the difference between members of a species, apparently has become in Descartes's case *an* accident: "But I do not hesitate to claim the good fortune of having stumbled, in my youth, upon certain paths which led me to certain considerations and maxims from which I formed a method . . . [Mais je ne craindrai pas de dire que je pense avoir eu beaucoup d'heur de m'être rencontré dès ma jeunesse en certains chemins, qui m'ont conduit à des considérations et des maximes, dont j'ai formé une méthode . . .]" (126/2).

If the Cogito can be considered the foundation of Cartesian metaphysics, Accident seems to be the foundation of Cartesian rhetoric. It is the concept that mediates between commonness and individuality. It allows the anonymous author of the *Discourse* to assert his right to speak out. Whereas the previous passage on *bon sens* establishes the public as having timeless qualities in common with the speaker, the "good fortune" (*heur* derived from *augurium*) of happening upon certain paths establishes the speaker's difference on a historical basis. By appropriating the scholastic accident, Descartes has found the way out of the apparent contradiction with which he begins the *Discourse*. The authority of the speaker in direct discourse is rescued from the impersonality, supposed by method, displayed in the opening paragraphs. The link between discourse and method has been forged through history.[6] The narrative that begins three paragraphs further is thus not free stylistic choice but is instead determined by Descartes's already formed relationship to his reader.

The problem of beginning the *Discourse* can be compared to Lucretius's conception of the swerve that permitted creation. Lucretius's swerve allowed the formation of difference out of sameness. Descartes's *heur* similarly allows the subject to take on a contingent, historical authority to exposit method without losing his resemblance to his readers. The relationship between history and method is fundamentally a problem of the relationship between author and reader, between a historical difference that can be transformed into an ahistorical sameness. Here *path* provides a concept permitting the expression both of authority (difference) and exchange (potential sameness). Within the first three paragraphs of the text this figure is copiously displayed: "we use different approaches [nous conduisons nos pensées par diverses *voies*]"; "those who walk slowly can, if they follow the right path, go much farther than those who run rapidly in the wrong direction [ceux qui ne marchent que fort lentement peuvent avancer beaucoup davantage, s'ils suivent toujours le droit *chemin*]"; and finally the "certain paths [certains *chemins*]" discovered by the author. Though open to all, and thus fully compatible with the notion of method, the path in question is one actually traveled by a subject otherwise like all other individuals. The discovery of the path belongs to history; its description, to discourse; its performance, to method.

Although the author's difference justifies his writing, it does not, in Descartes's terms, justify teaching. The final part of this tripartite scheme, the performance, is ascribed to a freely acting reader. At the receiving side, the problem of difference and sameness reappears, for Descartes asks the reader to decide whether to follow the same path as the author:

> So it is not my intention to present a method which everyone ought to follow in order to think well, but only to show how I have made the attempt myself. Those who counsel others must consider themselves superior to those whom they counsel, and if they fall short in the least detail they are to blame. I only propose this writing as a history [*histoire*], or, if you prefer, as a fable [*fable*], in which you may possibly find some examples [*exemples*] of conduct which you might see fit to imitate, as well as several others which you would have no reason to follow. I hope that it will prove useful to some without being harmful to any, and that all will take my frankness [*franchise*] kindly. (127/3)[7]

To interpret a text, the reader must decide what kind of text it is and what claims it makes. Readers will approach a sonnet differently from a treatise on optics. Here Descartes mentions two possible genres, *histoire* and *fable*, but leaves the choice between them to the reader (*si vous l'aimez mieux*). At the same time the author, whose claim in the title of the text is to publish a "discourse on the method of directing one's reason and seeking truth in the sciences," escapes the privileged role that seemed to distinguish him from others and returns to the level of exchange of roles with his reader. The coordinate structure of the sentences with their regular oppositions (teach/show; everyone/I; give/receive; fail/blame; history/fable; imitate/not imitate; useful/harmful) concludes with an indication of the single quality that the author claims in a non-paired structure: "que tous me sauront gré de ma franchise."[8] It is difficult to see how the reader could evaluate and appreciate the anonymous author's sincerity.[9] In such a context the older sense of the term *franchise* seems to impose itself—a limit on sovereign authority. The responsibility for the choice of examples to imitate, like that of generic classification, is not assumed by the author. He limits his authority. He grants a franchise to the reader.

If the reader here assumes much of the responsibility of an author, the author, within the narrative, continues the exchange of roles by depicting himself as a reader. Among the disciplines that he studied in school, he notes, had been letters, which are divided into reading and writing. Reading is covered by several terms: "I knew that the languages which one learns there are necessary to understand the works of the ancients; and that the delicacy of fables enlivens the mind; that famous deeds of history ennoble it and, if read with discretion, aid in maturing one's judgment; that the reading of all the great books is like conversing with the best people of earlier times . . ." (128/4). In rejecting this curriculum based on reading, Descartes returns to a problem of the author-reader relationship. Reading tends to estrange the reader from his own time and place. Reading is like traveling:

> But I thought that I had already spent enough time on languages, and even on reading the works of the ancients, and their histories and fables. For conversing with the ancients is much like traveling. It is good to know something of the customs of various peoples, in order to judge our own more objectively, and so that we do not make the mistake of the untraveled in supposing that everything contrary to our customs is ridiculous and irrational. But when one spends too much time traveling, one becomes at last a stranger at home; and those who are too interested in things which occurred in past centuries are often remarkably ignorant of what is going on today. (129/4–5)

Both exercises are on the whole negative. They do not bring a positive knowledge but only a precautionary experience of otherness that can become positive only at the moment of return. It is as if texts and voyages were mirrors, but empty mirrors. The reader, like the traveler, unlearns. But because he unlearns through otherness, the student or seeker risks losing himself in a total estrangement from here (in reading) and from now (in traveling). Descartes refers here to old books, *livres anciens*, but his second objection to reading shows that the estrangement of reading is not simply a matter of old texts as against new texts. Readers may surrender themselves to texts: "fables make us imagine a number of events as possible which are really impossible, and even the most faithful histories, if they do not alter or embroider episodes to make them more worth reading, almost always omit the meanest and least illustrious circumstances so that the remainder is distorted."

Descartes does not claim that representation is impossible for theoretical reasons. Texts give a distorted view of the world on practical grounds. Authors want to attract readers by giving an image of things that is more in keeping with a certain canon of worthwhile subjects (*dignes d'être lues*). The value of texts is determined by the value of the things represented (*la valeur des choses*), and this value is in its turn determined by the reader's sense of what is worth reading. Descartes's expression for this phenomenon underlines the false transparency of texts by noting that the reader finds the *things* worthy (*la valeur des choses, pour les rendre plus dignes d'être lues*) and becomes unconscious of the transformations and omissions in the most faithful histories. The nature of histories is to give a sense of reality that corresponds to the reader's expectations and desire. Descartes's description of reading runs against the grain by restoring a sense of the text as result of an act of writing—an act not centered on reference to an objective reality but on the rhetorical relationship. *Fictive* texts (fables as opposed to *les histoires les plus fidèles*) are not the only ones in question. Fable and history, ancient and modern, have in common that they mislead the reader about himself by exalting his imagination of his powers.

After the coupled terms *fable* and *histoire*, Descartes mentions romance (*roman*) as the genre that includes within itself the example of aberrations due to reading: "those who regulate their behavior by the examples they find in books are apt to fall into the extravagances of the knights of romances [*romans*], and undertake projects which it is beyond their ability to complete" (129/5). By concluding his series of allusions to literary genres with *roman*, Descartes underlines what history and fable have in common—giving the reader illusions about his or her own nature—and not what might separate them into direct and indirect representations of the world. The choice of the term *roman* sets this problem within the social history of reading.[10] Romance is the genre most concerned with the loss of an object that must be recovered and with the loss of roads or pathways back to an origin or toward a goal. Within this plot, romance in the Renaissance emphasized the problems of illusion and levels of reality inherited from such antecedents as the Arthurian romances.[11] This movement culminates in seventeenth-century France with an almost obsessive concern for the production of illusions by romance itself. The popularity of *Don Quixote* in France and the success of Sorel's *Le Berger extravagant* indicate this preoccupation. The authority of the written text is no longer a value but a danger. The reader may lose his self-consciousness by surrendering to the persuasions of a flattering text.

The "I" of the *Discourse* gives an example of one attitude that can be adopted toward reading. The protagonist turned his back on the texts of the school because he felt estranged from his own situation. Traveling was an alternative, studying the "great book of the world" (131/6) that appealed to Montaigne. Strangely enough Descartes already disposed of this alternative in an allusion before treating it directly. Traveling already served as a comparison to reading in order to undercut reading. Both are estrangements from one's own situation. Both are dangerous forms of loss. The circle of the comparison is completed by the simile of the world as book, both antithesis and complement of the book as world (i.e., as autonomous reality rather than as reference). This circle of comparison is also a circle in the reader's experience of the *Discourse*. We follow the author through his argument twice. There is no surprise in finding that the paragraph, filled with hope, about the freedom from the "subjection of my teachers," is followed immediately by disappointment. Descartes had already warned his reader about hoping to find help in the experience and words of others. "It is true," he writes, "that while I did nothing but observe the customs of other men, I found nothing there to satisfy me, and I noted just about as much difference of opinion as I had previously remarked among philosophers" (131–32/7). Diversity, of course, is for Descartes almost a synonym for error, and the experience of the world is only the experience of things from which we should withhold belief.[12]

The negative charge of this passage strikes a devastating blow to one form of learning—*example*: "I became acquainted with customs generally approved and accepted by other great peoples that would appear extravagant and ridiculous among ourselves, and so I learned not to believe too firmly what I learned only from example and custom" (132/7). The term *example* appears both in the commentary on reading literal books and in reading the metaphorical great book of the world. Because we go astray if we imitate others (e.g., *ceux qui règlent leurs moeurs par les exemples* . . .), the value of reading is purely "cathartic," purely a purgation of preconception. This is a negative, albeit real, value, which sends the reader back to himself.

Only a second negation, the rejection of the negative experience that is reading, can provide a positive value, the value of studying in oneself or, rather, of studying in *myself*. The reader of the *Discourse* might object that to base one's own evaluation of reading on the example of the Cartesian protagonist is to violate the lesson that the narrative seems to propose. To refuse example entirely we must refuse Descartes's example and the reading of the *Discourse*. But rhetoric should not be confused with logic, and the circularity of this argument may make it stronger, not weaker. The conclusion of part 1—by returning to the notion of example—is linked to Descartes's prefatory insistence on *not* presenting a method and to its statement that the narrative contains examples worth imitating (*exemples qu'on peut imiter*) and others that should not be imitated (*quelques autres qu'on aura raison de ne pas suivre*, 127/3). The reader is left, both at the beginning and the end of the narrative of part 1, with the task of deciding how to read and how to use examples.

The reader has, however, another relationship to the author-subject in this part of the *Discourse*. Following the sequential order of the narrative, the reader is brought closer to the author-character in a kind of complicity. The repetition of the protagonist's disappointment, in two chronologically successive episodes, and the anticipatory analogy of reading as traveling allow the reader to arrive at the second episode of disappointment with a foreknowledge of the impending failure. The reader is thus brought closer to the knowing "I" of the narrator and given a superiority over the "I" as protagonist of the narrative. The protagonist expected the book of the world to teach him what the books of the school did not. But the reader knows that reading and traveling are alike in their estrangement from one's own circumstances and powers. Anticipation, circularity, and repetition allow the reader to be in some sense fused with the enlightened subject-narrator of the *Discourse*. The reader may choose to compare himself with the enlightened narrator or with the neophyte protagonist. This possibility of comparative identification is further enriched by the display of other figures to whom the "I" is juxtaposed.

These secondary figures, intertwined with such earlier comparisons as reading and traveling, anticipate the roles of the author and the reader of the *Discourse*. The teacher appears at the point of contact between the two halves of the reading/traveling sequence: "This is why I gave up my studies entirely as soon as I reached the age when I was no longer under the control of my teachers [*la sujétion de mes précepteurs*]" (131/6). The mention of the teacher concludes the review of the school curriculum, which the teacher embodies. Through him the protagonist's relationship to reading is transformed from a matter of knowledge into matter of power. The school is based on subjection of the student, whereas the conclusion of part 1 makes the protagonist as subject—both a matter to study (*en moi-même*, "in myself") and a free consciousness that chooses its studies. The correlation between the teacher and the student protagonist, on the one hand, and between the author and the reader of the *Discourse*, on the other, is made through the author's careful disclaimer of the school model. The refusal to give *préceptes* (127/3) at the outset of the narrative in favor of examples to be chosen by the reader parallels the student's escape from his subjection to the "preceptors" as he rushes to choose examples from among those offered in the book of the world. The preceptor is a negative image of the author of the *Discourse*; the "I" is nonpreceptor. Does that mean that the reader can fail to revolt and need not flee?

Once the teacher is disposed of, another negative figure appears— the man of letters, the writer. Writing appears in the *Discourse* as a practice that escapes method. It is an inherent talent of the individual and could be taught neither by the protagonist's former teachers nor by the *Discourse on Method*: "I esteemed eloquence highly, and loved poetry, but I felt that both were gifts of nature rather than fruits of study. Those who reason most cogently, and work over their thoughts to make them clear and intelligible, are always the most persuasive, even if they speak only a provincial language and have never studied rhetoric" (129–30/5). Unmethodical, solitary, the practice of writing cannot belong to the mass evoked at the beginning of the *Discourse*. But writing reappears in the same paragraph as the preceptor, when the protagonist rejects also the reasonings of "a man of letters in his study, concerned with speculations which produce no effect, and which have no consequences to him except perhaps that the farther they are removed from common sense, the more they titillate his vanity, since he needs so much more wit and skill to make them seem plausible [*vraisemblables*]" (131/7).

The author of the *Discourse* vigorously rejects much of this characterization, particularly in part 6. The *Discourse* claims to be derived from common sense and aspires to a social effect through practical modifications of knowledge. The image of the man of letters is another negative image of the "I," a counterpoint to both the young protagonist going off to study the book of the world and the author of the eminently practical text in our hands. By locating this passage, however, two paragraphs before the protagonist's retreat to a heated room to give up the book of the world and the conversation of others, Descartes makes it seem in some ways an anticipation of the stance of the "I" of the *Discourse* in parts 2 and 3.[13]

While Descartes rejects reading and traveling, writing and teaching, he still makes the "I" of his story especially concrete, providing numerous narrative details that seem without purpose in presenting a method. By attaching us to the "I" who went to the wars in Germany ("I was then in Germany . . . ") are we meant to identify with an autobiographical "fable"? Is this the "I" whose example we might imitate? Descartes seems to lull us into the acceptance of this narrative first person, who went to school and to war, before shattering this "I" into two others, who define themselves by a completely contradictory approach to example and imitation. Three "I" 's must be distinguished:

the autobiographical subject (especially in part 2), the ethical subject (dominant in part 3), and the metaphysical subject (revealed in part 4).

The autobiographical fable begins by situating the subject within a tradition: "From my childhood I lived in a world of books [J'ai été nourri aux lettres dès mon enfance . . .]." The device appears familiar; the writer will present some concrete details, some "accidents" in the entirely scholastic sense, which ground him in a historical reality that we can recognize. The subject takes on a special kind of authority by the kind of history he gives himself, for his infancy proceeds from letters. He is the nursling of letters. Life and letters are fused from the beginning in a formula that has the ring of a cliché. But this cliché takes on force from its negation; letters are invoked only to be renounced.

This opening fusion is not a stylistic luxury. The subject's performance of his *ascesis* must begin by a moment of fullness. Only by establishing the value of his education and of his place in that traditional education can the subject give value to his revolt.[14] The eminent position of the "I" as representative of the scholastic and humanist traditions gives a more spectacular power to the external "I" 's annihilation in radical doubt. Descartes's immolation of the concrete external "I" recalls the Machiavellian examples of sacrifice, in which the killing of an individual allows a lesson to appear. Descartes builds toward doubt and the Cogito by accentuating apparently autobiographical details.[15]

The inner self will suspend certainty and be irresolute in its judgments while the outer self, described in part 3 of the *Discourse*, will be resolute in its actions. The latter, the ethical, socially visible subject, is resolute only at the cost of surrender to the moral rules and the example of others. The movement of the Accident earlier in the *Discourse* is here inverted. The ethical subject submits himself to the indistinction that his personal history had allowed him to flee. All of the arbitrariness of customary conduct, formed of a pure historical contingency, is accepted by the protagonist who had determined not to follow example and custom in part 1. The inner "I," concerned with the pure distinction between true and false, does not have a social conduct but only an intellectual one and rejects example. This distinction appears in the comparison of the temporary shelter:

> In planning to rebuild one's house it is not enough to draw up the plans for the new dwelling, tear down the old one, and provide materials and obtain workmen for the task. We must see that we are provided with a comfortable place to stay while the work of rebuilding is going on. Similarly in my own case; while reason

obliged me to be irresolute in my beliefs, there was no reason why
I should be so in my actions. In order to live as happily as possible
during the interval I prepared a provisional code of morality for
myself, consisting of three or four maxims which I here set forth.
(140–41/15)

The "I" that will be resolute in its actions during the destruction and
reconstruction of the definitive subject is deliberately set aside from
even the most minimal attempt at certainty and rationality. It is surrendered to the ethic of others while the deliberative "I" sets itself totally
apart from the conduct and examples of others. The ethical, provisional "I" is cut off from the central Cartesian project. It is the "I" of
the others, in its acceptance of the prevailing moral code without even
the modest corrections brought about by the experience of traveling,
and it will simply cease when the definitive, self-assured "I" has been
constructed from within. The two subjects are antithetical and nondialectical; no synthesis between provisional "I" and metaphysical "I" is
projected.

The writer's refusal to recommend the imitation of the examples set
forth in the narrative (127/3) assigned responsibility to the reader. He
was supposed to select and, at his peril, perform the protagonist's actions, or some of them. Now, when the alienated subject of the provisional ethic is constructed, Descartes bases it on imitation, that is, on
the performance of actions already performed by another. He creates a
mimetic "I" that adopts the wisest of the others as exemplary. In the
definition of his own subject, the writer of the *Discourse* has installed a
group having qualities and experiences similar to those of a potential
reader "among ourselves" (*parmi nous*, 141/15), *inside* the narrative.
Meanwhile the subject has become a performer of examples, rather
than a creator of examples.

In determining the role of the ethical subject, Descartes seizes upon
the actions of others and not upon their words.[16] People's *example* is
external, divorced from the discourse of those acting, and simply displayed to the inquiring intelligence which assigns it a new and higher
significance. The continuity of everyday life is broken by Descartes's
insistence on retaining the actions and discarding the words. He underlines the symmetry between the wily Cartesian imitator and those
imitated. His own *persona* is split into an inside and an outside, as is
theirs; their actions do not correspond to their beliefs, his do not correspond to his doubts.

The reader, the reasonable public, is waiting on the "I" 's path. The
reader and the author-subject are imitators of examples. It is tempting

to speak of a mirroring of reader in protagonist and of protagonist in reader, but this formulation would distort the temporal aspect of the relationship. The reader's example is only adopted provisionally, justified only as an external protection for the solitary, deliberative "I": "I should not have been content for one instant to rely on the opinions of others if I had not planned to use my own judgment at the proper time" (144/18). The specular and the mimetic—concepts frequently merged in our tradition—are opposed in the *Discourse*. The reader does not find his opinions mirrored in the Cartesian truths, nor does the protagonist discover much in common with those he meets in his travels.[17] Instead of a mirror providing mutual self-discovery, the contact proposed by the *Discourse* is mimetic. Mimesis serves as *camouflage* for the author in part 3, and mimesis appears as method—at the reader's own risk—throughout.[18]

Having built his cocoon, the protagonist can prepare in solitude the new, metaphysically founded "I." Logically the Cogito could begin without preamble. The rhetorical effect of the Cogito, however, depends on its position in the *Discourse* as culmination of a particularly concrete series of narrative detail.[19] It not only serves as the beginning of certainty but as the end of the preparatory journey and the destruction of error. Shifting out of the external reality of example, the speaker of the *Discourse* here moves into a nonexemplary pure assertion of the "I." The subject of the Cogito has no body, no past, no relationship to others, no project or method, no location in historical space. The Cogito is a momentary and solitary act that places the "I" outside of the iterative realm of Aristotelian example.[20] While a similar thought may occur to the same thinker at another time or to another thinker, that it has occurred once does not give any greater weight to another occurrence. The Cogito has no quality of precedence or history. The historical and serial quality of example, by which Aristotle defines *paradeigma*, is not compatible with an act that has no past and no future. The argument of the great king (see introduction) supposed that what has happened in the past is likely to happen again. The Cogito has no past and supposes no future.

Arriving at the Cogito, the reader of the *Discourse on Method* must relate to the new metaphysical "I" that has resulted from the splitting of the narrative protagonist. The Cogito has several characteristics that affect this relationship:

1. The performance of this act gives the performer certainty of being. This certainty cannot come from a narration, even from

narration of that act. The "I" of the Cogito is distinct in its truth-status from the "I" of its narration.

2. The performance of the Cogito, besides being covered by the general warning that some of the "history or fable" may not be wise to imitate, is not an imitable performance. Since the Cogito is an act of radical solitude, it can only occur authentically by refusal of all that comes from outside the subject, including models.

3. Since the Cogito seems to elude the reader who may attempt to imitate it, and since its form of truth does not come from narrative (i.e., it is not a historical witness to the truth of some event), it seems to serve entirely to give the speaker the right to speak. It is a foundation for the author's authority, told "afin qu'on puisse juger si les fondements que j'ai pris sont assez fermes" (147/20).

The Cogito returns from history to discourse by coming back to the pure *word* of the speaker. The metaphysical "I" speaks entirely outside of history. The Cogito and the earlier Accident both concern the right to speak, but the Accident asserted an authority on the basis of history, "the good fortune of having stumbled, in my youth upon certain paths," while the Cogito asserts that authority beyond history. The truths that will appear in the last three parts of the *Discourse* come from a transcendental subject, one that can speak with certainty grounded in absolute truth and not only narrate an individual itinerary.

The suspicion of example underlying the review of the school curriculum moved Descartes to flee from imitating others in his search for truth. Transferring to the reader the responsibility for deciding whether to imitate examples does not resolve the problem. If the basis of truth and learning is not in the external historical realm but in the absolute certainty of individual consciousness, then the reader cannot reach such truth by observing Descartes. This split between truth and example appears in the first part of the *Discourse* as a liberating discovery, by which the protagonist is released into his own reason. At the end of the *Discourse*, however, the writer discovers the paralyzing effect of this failure of example. His own text cannot enlighten the reader. Descartes asserts his own superiority as reader and critic of the text ("I have hardly ever met a critic of my opinions who did not appear to me to be either less rigorous or less equitable than myself," 173/44). If other readers are inferior in their ability to discern the strengths and weaknesses of the *Discourse*, then the value of their choice of the examples to imitate and the examples to shun, mentioned at the opening, will be highly doubtful. They will choose less well than the writer. In fact, the reader will simply not *understand* the truths embodied in Descartes's text: "although I have often explained some of my opinions to very intelligent people, who seemed to understand them very distinctly while I was speaking, nevertheless when they retold them I have noticed that they have almost always so changed them that I could no longer accept them as my own" (173/45). The danger of reading, earlier mentioned by Descartes, was that the reader might lose himself in the text, might identify too completely with a figure that would estrange him from himself and finish like the *extravagant* hero of a romance. Here, in part 6, the author expresses the opposite fear—that the reader may modify the text according to his own understanding. The reader who transforms the opinions to suit himself has avoided the danger of surrender to a text, but now the author fears a loss. The reader's opinions are no longer those of the author.[21]

As methodical philosopher, Descartes insists on the uniqueness of his discovery and on the profitability for all of a reduction of the plurality of paths to a single path toward knowledge. But at the same time Descartes hesitates at the point of recommending or even imposing imitation within a method that had so relegated imitation to an inferior position. Imitation belongs, in the realm of knowledge, to an obsolete and negative moment. In the realm of conduct, it belongs to expediency, bad faith, uncertainty, and diversity. Rhetorically the whole *Discourse* is based on the movement away from the disappointments and the self-estrangement that come from imitation. The *Discourse* is completely penetrated by the subject's refusal to imitate except within the provisional ethic.

Descartes's provisional ethic, in which the protagonist mimes the behavior of others, is a bridge to Pascal's observation of what people *do*, not what they pretend to do or think they are doing. Pascal's humanity seems unable to do other than perform according to a determined pattern. The resolute Cartesian self, which inwardly refuses example while the outer "I" espouses it, corresponds to the Pascalian "wise man" (or *habile*) and to his "perfect Christian." But while these characters are inwardly aware of the foolish outward nature of what they do, the difference is a difference of awareness, not of performance. All provide examples that mark of defective humanity, but not everyone can view them as examples. The speaker of the *Discourse* cannot integrate the examples provided by the readers except at the level of camouflage, while proffering a pure "I" that seems unexemplary because of its dubious imitability. In the *Pensées*, on the other hand, example can only work as a means for one defective "I" to inspect itself through the experiences of another similarly imperfect creature. Pascal's argument needs the deforming effect of exposure to other people in order to exploit the exteriority of example, but he must fragment this exterior to provoke questions about what is behind it.

THE RHETORIC OF DISRUPTION

The apparently disordered fragments of Pascal's *Pensées* are more than the accident of an unfinished manuscript. Pascal's rhetoric requires that the unbeliever see disorder in a world to which he has become accustomed and in which he has seen order. As Pascal wrote, "I will write my thoughts here without order and not, perhaps, in an unplanned confusion. This is the true order which will always designate my object by means of disorder itself" (532).[22] Such is the dialectical situation of the opening of Pascal's apology for the Christian religion, an apology that has been given intense scrutiny over the past several decades in a quest to unlock the riddle of Pascal's argumentation.[23] In building his argument, Pascal leaves a trail of examples or what appear to be the makings of examples: "Perseus, king of Macedonia. Paulus Aemilius. They reproached Perseus for not killing himself" (15). A reader of the *Pensées* can soon recognize Pascal's shorthand in certain of these names or combinations of names. Perseus and Paulus Aemilius are examples in Pascal's argument concerning the peculiar sense of disinheritance or disgrace felt by a king who falls from his office:

> For who considers himself unfortunate for not being king except a king dethroned. Did they think Paulus Aemilius unfortunate when he was not consul? on the contrary, everyone thought that he was fortunate for having been consul, since his state was not to be consul forever. But they considered Perseus so wretched no longer to be king, because his state was to be king forever, that they thought it strange that he could stand to be alive. Who considers himself unfortunate to have only one mouth and who would not find himself unfortunate to have only one eye. (117)

"Perseus" is thus, on the level of Pascal's discourse, a *synecdoche* for the argument of the fallen king. Perseus, the king, is, on the level of the content of Pascal's argument, a *metonym* for the state of fallenness.[24] And, once the mention of Perseus is inserted into its argumentative context, what happened to Perseus is an *example* of the difference between falling from one's condition and simply passing from one phase to another within one's condition. In reading the *Pensées* we become used to finding these synecdoches, which are the nucleus of an example. Such synecdoches are of use primarily to Pascal as an economical means of organizing his argument. In reading we must convert them into examples to restore or construct meaning, but the synecdoches cannot be restored to full narrative continuity without losing the framed discontinuity that makes example what it is. A certain incoherence must remain to distinguish history and example.

Such incoherence appears in a major way in the long fragment on imagination (44), in which Pascal provides examples of the nonrational order of society and of all human conduct. Imagination and reason are contrasted, and imagination is shown to be dominant in human life. This argument is not built on purely assertive or theoretical grounds; at every step Pascal presents a verisimilar event from everyday life to secure assent:

> Would you not say that this magistrate, whose venerable age makes him respected throughout the nation, acts in accordance with a pure and sublime reason and that he judges things by their nature without pausing to consider these vain circumstances that touch the imagination only of the weak minded. Watch him go to hear a sermon, to which he brings a devout zele reinforcing the solidity of his reason with his ardent charity; there he is ready to listen with an exemplary respect. Let the preacher come forth, if nature gave him a hoarse voice and an odd face, if his barber shaved him badly, and if perchance he is besmirched as well, however great may be the truths he proposes I wager that our senator will lose his grave mein.

Everything here seems to belong to the rhetoric of *enargeia*, the oratory of the "vivid picture."[25] The magistrate is presented as if he were before our eyes, available for presentation in a gesture of pointing, "ce magistrat . . . ," and with the verb *voir*, "to see." Pascal is appealing to his interlocutor with evidence that cannot be denied, because it is present and it has, so far, no apparent meaning except its very presence. It is assumed that the interlocutor will not object to Pascal's presentation because it appeals to a sense of solidarity in the perception of the everyday world. The magistrate is not, of course, a physical object, not even a biological entity, not even a name. Even if Pascal were standing on a streetcorner pointing to a historical person, Pascal's language would already be transforming that person into a personnage, into a character.[26] The magistrate is marked by a series of qualities that belong to a convention of the type: he is mature, reasonable, respected, impartial, devout. In seeing "the magistrate," we are subject to conventions of how to see a magistrate. He is the embodiment of reason and plays a special role in a passage concerning the triumph of imagination over reason. All of the qualities that seem to set him above imagination culminate in the adjective that describes the social fiction by which such characters are created: *exemplaire*. The "exemplary respect" that he is ready to show in church during the sermon sets this adjective at the pivotal point of the example of the magistrate, just before Pascal begins to describe the preacher.

The preacher, like the magistrate, is presented as a spectacle. But, whereas the magistrate was a spectacle for the reader ("voyez-le entrer dans un sermon"), the preacher is a spectacle for the magistrate as well. The contact between the description of the two characters is brutal. The evocation of the magistrate culminates with the expression of his positive exemplarity (the magistrate is everything a magistrate should be), which borders on the introduction of the preacher, who is many things a preacher should not be. Both characters are primarily appearances. Their faces, bearing, and costume are marks that should reflect the rational dignity of their roles. In the first case this expectation is met; in the second it is not. Imagination controls response by giving more weight to the image, to the mark, than to the hidden or abstract verity that reason should detect. The assumed response to the magistrate is appropriate, though determined by the image of the magistrate. The magistrate's response to the hypothetical preacher is not appropriate, though governed by the same power that creates veneration for the magistrate.

The correspondence between the qualities of "ce magistrat" and the conventional model of a magistrate is so perfect that he may aptly be called exemplary, for the completely adequate example corresponds to the concept that it renders palpable. Because the magistrate embodies reason, gravity, and respect, he can serve as an example of the hollowness of those qualities when confronted with an image of their opposite. The magistrate manifests the duplicity of example through the rapid passage from positive exemplarity to negative exemplarity (that is, the embodiment of how one should not, ideally, react to a sermon). This duplicity alerts us to the danger of the belief in the exemplarity of social perception.[27] The combination of these two aspects (outwardly grave and reasonable magistrate, inwardly subject to irrationality; outwardly ludicrous and unworthy preacher, inwardly bearing the word of God) forms the message of Pascal's example, which undermines the conventional exemplarity of a complacent Christian society. Characteristically Pascal disrupts the "exemplary" surface of society through the use of an example.

Because example is exterior, that is, because it concerns what all can see, it is related in Pascal's rhetoric to the movement of the imagination. The fragment within which this passage appears not only proposes imagination as the dominant faculty in man but as a faculty not always untrue. The magistrate is not necessarily a fraud in his appearance of rationality and gravity. By representing these qualities in their highest degree, the magistrate can create the tension necessary to manifest the supreme power of imagination, which is able to overcome the mediocre person and the most wise. The magistrate is both embodiment and victim of imagination, as appearance and as receiver of appearances, which have been socially codified (the example of the magistrate, the anti-example of the preacher). Nonetheless, nothing can certify that there is a truth in the example shown us, for it all depends on appearance, the domain of imagination itself.[28]

Imagination is not a stable marker of error or truth. Since examples, containing representations of an event or object we perceive, are within the realm of the image—and thus of imagination—we cannot be certain of anything that is taught by example.[29] It is right to find or locate dignity in a magistrate, but the appearance that leads toward this dignity is untrustworthy. The magistrate serves as an example of the true marking of a hidden quality, yet our reasons for perceiving this quality are riddled with error. As an example, the magistrate leads us toward a truth, but only by undermining the rhetoric of *enargeia*, of the picture, by which we are first attracted to that truth. The *Pensées*, in the earlier sections particularly, repeatedly attack the limitations of mankind's interpretive capabilities. The example of the magistrate and many others in fragment 44 work by reversing appearances—a syncopated reversal in which the reversal usually works but does not always, so that there is a missing reversal (a syncope) defeating rational interpretation by allowing an appearance to be an authentic revelation of what seems to appear.[30]

Pascal stresses the instability of these outward appearances as signs. Despite an apparently simple binary system in which things are classified within a differential grid of clarity and obscurity, such opposition cannot provide a key to the semiotics of society. What is clear and what is unclear change places unpredictably in such a way as to require a dialogue, always shifting to locate the blindspot of the interlocutor/adversary. Pascal uses effects of proximity to make the clear obscure and to defamiliarize the everyday through an excessive and unexpected magnification.

FIGURE

Pascal's purpose in describing the human condition in the examples of the early sections of the *Pensées* is clarified by his discussion of the rhetoric of scripture. In the sections on "Figurative Law" and "Prophecies," Pascal speaks several times of example alongside the concept of biblical exegesis called *figure*.[31] Figure and example are related rhetorical instruments that differ in their relationship to time and to their audience. By "figure" Pascal means the signs given by God to mankind in the prophecies and miracles recorded in Scripture.[32] In dealing with the Bible Pascal has simplified most tropological and figurative rhetoric to the single term of figure. Here again Pascal uses a binary system, in which different pairs are at various times in opposition. The principal opposition is between figure and reality, or "thing" (*chose*):

> To learn whether the law and the sacrifices are reality or figure it is necessary to see whether the prophets, in speaking of these things, fixed their view and their thought on them in such a way as to see in them only this old covenant, or if they see [*sic*] there something else of which this covenant was the painting. For in a portrait one sees the thing as figure.
> [Pour savoir si la loi et les sacrifices sont réalité ou figure il faut voir si les prophètes en parlant de ces choses y arrêtaient leur vue et leur pensée, en sorte qu'ils n'y vissent que cette ancienne alliance, ou s'ils y voient quelque autre chose dont elle fut la peinture. Car dans un portrait on voit la chose figurée.] (260)

The emphasis throughout is on the absence or invisibility of the reality, in contrast with the abundant visibility of the figure. The whole interpretive process depends on the decision to see many events and details in the Old Testament as literally untrue in order to justify a reading of them as spiritually or figuratively true: "When the word of God, which is truthful, is literally false it is true spiritually" (272).[33] At other moments Pascal does not insist on the falseness of the biblical literal meaning, but simply refers to the Hebrew interpretation of certain things as being "carnal," and not penetrating to the hidden spiritual sense. By undercutting the materiality of the Old Testament, Pascal obtains an effect similar to the disconcerting magnification of examples in profane experience. In both cases something that would be taken for granted in its materiality and familiarity is cast in a new light as surface or appearance behind which an absent meaning lurks. Pascal mentions the importance of the prophets' looking *through* the law and the sacrifices to see something of which these would be only a "painting." Moreover, the whole Old Testament is broken, exegetically, into successive patches of spiritual and carnal meaning, for Pascal does not present the Old Testament as a whole to serve as a figure but only portions. He mentions two erroneous readings of the Scripture: "Two errors. 1. to take everything literally. 2. to take everything spiritually"

(252). The significant and the insignificant must be segregated, and this supposes an operation akin to the choice of elements to create an example series, keeping only what will correspond to the general truth that is being evidenced.

"Figure" in the Pascalian sense and the examples of everyday experience presented earlier in the *Pensées* have in common a certain availability to the interlocutor or reader.[34] Example is constructed to appeal to the listener's sense of prior knowlege, as when Pascal speaks of gambling, hunt, and the "conversation of women." These are activities presumably known to the listener, and when they are built into an example they remain themselves and do not need to be translated into something different. Metaphor, on the other hand, produces statements that seem incompatible with earlier factual knowledge, as when "suns" become the eyes of the beloved. Pascal himself reflected on how examples work within the knowledge of the listener:

> Examples that one takes to prove something else, if one wanted to prove the examples one would take the other things to be the examples. For as one always believes that the difficulty is in what one wants to prove one finds the examples clearer and helpful in showing that thing.
>
> Thus when one wishes to show a general thing one must give the particular rule of a case, but if one wishes to show a particular thing one must begin with the (general) rule. For one always finds the thing that one wants to prove obscure and the thing that one uses for the proof clear, since in proposing a thing to prove one fills oneself with the imaginary idea that this thing is obscure and that, on the contrary, the thing that is supposed to prove it is clear, and thus one easily understands it.
>
> [Les exemples qu'on prend pour prouver d'autres choses, si on voulait prouver les exemples on prendrait les autres choses pour en être les exemples. Car comme on croit toujours que la difficulté est à ce qu'on veut prouver on trouve les exemples plus clairs et aidant à le montrer.
>
> Ainsi quand on veut montrer une chose générale il faut en donner la règle particulière d'un cas, mais si on veut montrer un particulier il faudra commencer par la règle (générale). Car on trouve toujours obscure la chose que l'on veut prouver et claire celle qu'on emploie à la preuve, car quand on propose une chose à prouver, d'abord on se remplit de cette imagination qu'elle est donc obscure, et au contraire que celle qui la doit prouver est claire, et ainsi on l'entend aisément.] (527)

The union between prophecy and the accomplishment of the prophecy is as close and necessary as that between the parts of any sign (signifier and signified) and of any example (exemplifier and exemplified). There is a necessary deferral to the enigma that prophecy constitutes. Only the fulfillment of a prophecy makes it clear that the utterance in question was a prophecy to begin with, and not simply a practical or carnal utterance, as most Jews, according to Pascal, believed. Not all prophecies are predictions, that is, not all prophecies are directed, at the moment of their utterance, at a future event. Only retrospectively can the prophecies be widely recognized. Prophecies are split in time. Whether an act waits thousands of years for its meaning to be revealed in *figure*, or whether a prediction waits for an act to fulfill it, message and act are temporally separate.[35]

Figure's difference in time may obscure its kinship with example. Both of these configurations in the Pascalian system correlate an abstract, nonvisible, or "spiritual" message with a visible occurrence in the material, historical world. Both of them take as their visible element events from the continuum of social life that are strikingly inconsequential and of no inherent difference from other similar events. In both cases, the possessors of the abstract message are able to perceive significance where other people are not. In figure, the message is given before the event; the two are typically separated by thousands of years. In example, as Pascal uses it in the early parts of the *Pensées*, events are present to us, constantly occurring or recurring, while the meaning is also being presented. Even the historical example has no special privilege by virtue of its pastness. It is merely *chose vue*. If anything, the historical character of an example gets in the way of our perceiving it as an example.

Christians and Jews understand figures differently because they situate them in different times. For the Jews, the prophecy is available without its confirmation. For the Christians, the prophecy is already confirmed by the New Testament. In this sense Christianity for Pascal appears as a religion transcending history, or with its history closed at the time of the accomplishment of the prophecies. The Jews, as a whole, did not recognize, in the Christian view, this closure of history because they failed to see in the concrete events of the New Testament the correlative of the prophecies. This gap between prophecy and accomplishment—a diachronic distinction—is analogous to the gap between perception and understanding in example, a synchronic distinction.

Whereas prophetic figure requires the pairing of moments in a diachronic structure, example requires not merely the closure of history but the deflation of presumed historical difference. All the prestige of what is ancient, a great source of Pascal's faith in the Judeo-Christian tradition, gets in the way of understanding the lives of the saints as "examples." Pascal takes a position of returning the past to its everyday quality, studying longstanding phenomena that appear only when the patina of History is removed from history:

> What keeps us from comparing the things that happened in the church's past to what one sees now is that ordinarily we consider Saint Athanasius, Saint Theresa and the others as crowned with glory and with years, judged before us like gods. Now that time has clarified things this is how it appears, but at the time when they persecuted him this great saint was a man who was called Athanasius and Saint Theresa was a girl. Elias was a man like us and subject to the same passions as we, said Saint Peter to keep Christians from that erroneous conception which causes us to reject the *example* of the saints as disproportionate to our state. They were saints, we say to ourselves, they were not like us. (598)[36]

Although history appears to clarify things (*éclaircir*), distortion imposed by the historical perspective actually prevents mankind from seeing things as they were; hence it prevents men from obtaining any sense of proportion. Because the saints are always before us—in the sense of chronological priority and of being proposed to us, set before our eyes for our edification—humanity can only grasp sanctity as a temporal absence. In this passage the retreat of sanctity into constantly receding past is echoed by Saint Peter's comment about Elias. *Figure* and *example* are here incompatible, for the figure takes on its meaning only with the passage of time; example, on the contrary, loses its meaning with the passage of time. To understand an example, we must try to remove the historical dimension to make the individual case available for imitation. We must understand the case as being not unique but as manifesting a timeless rule or pattern that can recur. To understand figure, on the other hand, the reader of the Bible must avoid conceiving the event or utterance in its native concreteness. If Elias were to serve as figure, rather than as example, we would have to avoid seeing him as "a man like us" and would try to see him as bearing a unique meaning for the history of redemption, as a signifier of which the signified has been revealed in such a way as to complete or saturate the sense of Elias as sign.

Example and prophecy (figure) operate by creating a *découpage* or segmentation of worldly knowledge and by showing that the "reality" men think they have grasped is somehow insubstantial, mere covering or chaff, beyond which or through which they can reach substance. Pascal's brief reflections on example indicate that he sees this figure in terms of a dialectic between clarity and obscurity, precisely the opposition with which he defines the general concept of figure in the fragments on prophecy and miracles. The "thing to be proven" (*la chose à prouver*) at first seems obscure, whereas the "thing to prove it" (*celle qui la doit prouver*) is clear. Pascal points out that both individual cases and general rules can be variously obscure or clear, so that it is not possible to assume that the generality will be the "thing to be proven" and the individual instance the more accessible instrument by which agreement is reached on the generality. We may encounter instances or phenomena difficult to understand until set in the framework of a general rule, but we may also propose a general rule difficult to accept until clarified by specific instances.

Pascal locates the clarity and the obscurity differently in discussing and using example and figure. In the examples used earlier to shake the unbeliever out of an easy familiarity with everyday habits, Pascal adduced clear instances of familiar activities and feelings to move toward an extremely obscure, probably incredible, generality: that the condition of mankind can only be explained by the hypothesis of a fall from grace. In the case of the prophecies, a series of apparently contradictory statements and events seem obscure or without religious significance until the clarity of a Christian message is applied to the series of figures. The original obscurity of the scriptural text is not accidental but deliberate, for only a portion of mankind has the exceptional privilege of understanding.[37] Pascal states the apparent incoherence of the Scriptures in a fragment entitled "Contradiction" (257).[38] Failure to adopt the figural reading, Pascal contends in this passage, would result in an incoherence so general that not only the Old Testament as a whole but even individual chapters would be incomprehensible.[39]

The distinction between clear and obscure, which appears in the fragment on the use of example, does not depend on an objective quality of texts or of concepts. What is clear or obscure depends on who is trying to interpret. Pascal's hermeneutic stresses the subjective in the interpretation of biblical figure as it does for everyday example. The Old Testament utterances were evidently familiar to the Jews. The term used by Pascal, in the sense of material and with a pejorative connotation (*charnel*), indicates a relaxed familiarity, an easy understanding of the prophecies.[40] What Pascal finds contradictory, the Old Testament Jews found acceptable and without inconsistency. To make his interpretation and persuasion work, Pascal must awaken in the reader a sense of contradiction. He must draw out of the Old Testament itself sources of discontinuity, which break the apparent narrative smoothness of the Bible story. One way of doing this is to locate interpretive guidelines in the prophecies themselves. In this way he locates the counsel to reduce the apparent meaning to the status of a veil within the Old Testament: "The prophets said clearly that Israel would always be loved by God and that the law would be eternal and they said that one would not understand their meaning and that it was veiled" (260). Another way to disturb the interpretation of the Bible is to split it into successive units that seem inconsistent. By doing this, Pascal creates a syntagmatic or horizontal discontinuity rather than a paradigmatic or vertical one.

What retrospectively appears "obscure" to the Christian apologist must have appeared clear to the Jews; and what must have appeared obscure to them, the coming of the Messiah, appears clear to Pascal as Christian. The alternation of obscurity and clarity is an active and constantly shifting concept. The general rule illuminates the particular case—as Pascal says of examples—and the state of the particular case before the change or discovery of the general rule must subsequently seem to have been obscure. Since Pascal is not writing for Old Testament Jews but for a contemporary unbeliever, the whole question moves to a different level. Pascal now considers why the Jews did not realize the obscurity of the prophecies. Paradoxically, what is clear must be obscure and what is obscure must be clear for the Jansenist God's plan to be accomplished:

> But God, not having wished to reveal these things to this people which was unworthy and yet having wished nonetheless to bring these things about so that they would be believed, predicted the time clearly and expressed these things at times clearly but with abundant figures so that those who loved the figuring things would stop at them and so that those who loved the things figured would see them. (270)

There is a complicity between mankind and God in the creation of the hidden face of everyday things in mankind's refusal to ask why men do what they do. Likewise, there is a responsibility placed on the "carnal" Jews for not having seen what the "spiritual" Jews saw in the prophecies. The phrase "d'abord on se remplit de cette imagination qu'elle est donc obscure [we first fill ourselves with that imaginary idea that it is obscure]" is a reminder that persons decide where they will situate the relative obscurity, allocating it between case and general rule.

Although Pascal's apology has moved considerably from the sec-

tions "Ennui," "Raisons des effets," and "Divertissement," when it arrives at "Loi figurative" and "Rabbinage," the underlying principles
are the same in regard to revelation. The same process of withdrawing
from appearance to be open to the discovery of something hidden
works in contemporary life just as it does in the Bible or in hagiogra-
phy:

> The ordinary life of men is like that of the saints. They all seek
> satisfaction and differ only in regard to the object *in which they
> locate* satisfaction. They call enemies those who keep them from
> it, etc. God has thus shown the power that he has to give invisible
> goods by the power that he has manifested over the visible ones.
> (275)

The miracles and prophecies that occur in the whole history of God's
relation to his people (the Jews as the holy people, the saints) manifest
the visible/invisible pairing that permits discovery only to those who
realize that there is something to discover. The "where" of "où ils la
placent" refers to the hidden dimension that exists for the saints who
see something *behind* appearance (a paradigmatic or substitutive relationship) as opposed to the flat life of ordinary men who look only for
the succession of visible things. "What is coming next?" the latter
might ask, rather than, "What does this mean?" Yet, in both cases, as
Pascal says, they would be dealing with the same outward life and the
same everyday words (e.g., "enemies"). The introduction of this detail
from the language common to saints and others is an example following from the general statement made in the first sentence of the passage
("La vie ordinaire des hommes . . . "). It is, like most examples, part
of a series, which is here elliptical in form ("etc."). Although the apparent purpose of the example is to show that God can make revelations in material ways by rewarding his chosen people as he did at the
time of the Flood and in Egypt, it also shows the problem of interpreting such material signs. The first of these is about the interpretation made by the people who receive the benefit from God and their
decision about *where* to locate the significance of worldly good and
evil. The second concerns the problem for those who perceive both
saints and non-saints and who cannot really tell the difference, since
their ordinary life is similar. In reading the Old Testament, it is difficult for a non-saint to see why the apparently profane events in the
history of the Jews should have something other than a profane significance. The saint/ordinary person distinction, which at first operates
only "within" the text—that is, seems to be a difference among persons or events of the Bible—actually spreads to include the reader of

the Bible, since different readers will locate the significance in a different place. Some will see the surface; others will see something behind
the surface. In relating the New Testament to modern life, Pascal also
points out the similarity of appearances in cases where there is a crucial
difference in what is hidden:

> As J. C. has remained unknown among men; so truth dwells
> among common opinions without difference on the outside. So
> the Eucharist is among common bread. (225)

The contrast in external and internal meaning in what is perceived
corresponds to a division within the perceiver as Pascal describes him.
The simile of the portrait or painting introduces the concept of the
place of the human perceiver in dealing with appearances. The many
fragments that mention the interior and the exterior are part of a spatial
analogy that unites the perceiver and the perceived in the process of
discovering, or of failing to discover, what lies behind the surface. Understanding the relation between the seen and the unseen is basic to
example, but such a relation depends on situating the observer in
space. The division of Old Testament figures into surface and depth,
veil and truth, is parallel to the division of everyday example into what
is seen on the surface (by the people or the half-wise *demi-habile*) or
through that surface (by the perfect Christian). The difference in interpretation depends on the interpreter, as conceived in terms of depth
and proximity:

> If one is too young one does not judge well, too old the same . . .
> So also pictures seen from too far away and from too close. And
> there is only one indivisible point which is the true place. The
> others are too near, too far, too high or too low. Perspective as-
> signs this point in the art of painting, but in truth and in ethics,
> who will assign it? (21)

Whether treating it as the tyrannical and unjust center of human society in the form of the *moi* or praising it in the description of the perfect
Christian with a thought from "behind the head," Pascal gives special
attention to the subjective self—its abilities, its location (in a metaphoric sense), and its relations to other subjects.

Christians and Christianity are associated with the proper relationship between surface and depth: "Only the Christian religion is pro-
portioned to all, being a mix of outside and inside."[41] The well-known
Pascalian metaphor of the "pensée de derrière la tête"—the "thought
from behind the head"—indicates that people's understanding, as well
as the things they perceive, can be divided into inside and out. The

depth of worldly phenomena can be perceived only by a "deep" person, that is, someone who has something "behind." This "behindness" is the final term in a series of gradations that move from the people's entirely superficial thought. Pascal's use of the gradations of profundity in thought, however, pairs surface and depth and ridicules the intermediate positions. The common people and the "habiles" have explicit spatial qualities. It is revealing that Pascal should link the "thought from behind the head" with knowledge gained from the most superficial phenomena. The people honor those who are well dressed, have many livried servants, and so on, and judge by the surface. But, as Pascal says, "it is not a mere surface nor a mere trapping to have several servants . . . Being brave is showing one's force" (95). Paying attention to appearance and according it the proper weight is the great question of knowledge. Those who turn away from the knowledge of everyday superficial activities are the "demi-habiles," who are inferior to the people.[42]

This view of the relation between the appearance and the significance of examples produces paradoxical observations, such as "Respect is: Inconvenience yourself. That is apparently vain (*vain*) but quite just" (80). Here the metaphor of the hollowness of appearance (*vain*, *vanus*), which underlies all of the exemplarity of everyday life in the early sections of the *Pensées*, is placed face to face with the characterization of the perceiver. What appears hollow is not hollow, for the wise observer knows that hollowness is significant. The depth of the perceiver, his distance from the ordinary perception of life, determines the depth of what is perceived. By the reversal that makes of the humblest and most superficial phenomena objects worthy of the attention of the deepest and wisest people, everyday life becomes a source of learning in example. The learning available in this way, however, is meaning only in proportion to the interior gift of the perceiver. To the half-wise, the "demi-habiles," everyday life is only the object of scorn.

One of Pascal's recurrent examples demonstrates the different levels of perception that function in regard to everyday life:

> That is marvelous: not wanting me to pay respect to a man dressed in brocade and followed by seven or eight servants. And why not? he will have me whipped if I don't greet him respectfully. His way of dressing is a force. It is just like a well harnessed horse compared to another. Montaigne is amusing in not seeing the difference that there is and in being puzzled that people find a difference and in asking what the reason of it is. In truth, says he, how does it happen, etc. (89)[43]

This imagined encounter with the well-dressed man and his servants is an example not only of the reality of the difference in power symbolized by the apparently inoffensive and irrelevant brocade but of the inability of the half-wise to see the difference. The rich man with his lackeys and the horse with a rich harness had already been plucked out of a purely narrative or descriptive context and set forth, by Montaigne, as instances of human error. Pascal accepts Montaigne's division of life into examples, and gathered many of his examples from the *Essais*, but Pascal approaches the notion of difference with a much stronger belief in system. For Montaigne, observation of phenomena constructed or reconstructed into examples is a largely decentered activity, which is given coherence, if at all, from the writing self. Even the "self" of Montaigne is held together and shaped by the activity of writing. In the process certain local differences appear between Montaigne and others, but on the whole there is a skeptical reduction of difference. Things may be less dissimilar than they appear, thinks Montaigne, and the difference is located most often in a contrast between appearance and the content of that appearance. Understanding, or rather writing, permits the verbal filling of that content with the writer's more or less manageable—though unendingly productive and prolix—insights. Pascal, far from wanting to reduce difference and to fill the hollows behind appearance, accepts a fundamental and systematic dualism for which the basic distinctive criteria are located outside of our consciousness, in God's grace. Man should therefore believe in difference and attach great importance to it, but cannot ever be sure of having located the difference. Surrendering to undifferentiated appearance is the paradoxical way to assure ourselves of possibly possessing within our soul, but outside of our consciousness, the mark of the only difference that matters—grace.

The elect or initiate are systematically and self-consciously different in their inward and outward selves. Pascal defines the proper position of the wise as being a stance of outward similarity to the people with an inward thought "behind the head," "Il faut avoir une pensée de derrière, et juger de tout par là, en parlant cependant comme le peuple" (91). This declaration, which provides the basis for Pascal's ethical position as well as for his epistemological position, corresponds to what Lucien Goldmann describes quite appropriately as the "worldly refusal of the world [le refus intramondain du monde]."[44] The refusal of the world by one living in the world creates a state of permanent ironic suspension in the believer, a fragmentation of the self that is both cause of the perception of the world as fragmented and the product of such a perception.

TURNING ASIDE

Pascal describes mankind as endlessly avoiding the obvious. The hidden is, in part, a creation or secretion of humanity in its desire not to see. *Divertissement*, or diversion, is the general category under which this *turning aside* is presented in the *Pensées*. Once again, as with Montaigne and Machiavelli, the relation between appearance and the submerged content of an example is what counts, but for Pascal the turning aside itself is, at least in the early stage of his argument, as important as what is concealed. The examples in section 8 of the *Pensées*, entitled *Divertissement*, are examples of turning aside, so that what readers see is this swerve itself in activities like hunting and gambling. In these human pastimes everything seems to be on the surface. What can be hidden in hunting a hare, except the hare? It seems that men want to find and catch this hare, but this is not entirely so, as Pascal argues. The discovery of the hare defeats or at least deflates the game. Only the hidden hare is interesting. The example of hunting, like others in this section, concerns the division of life into inside and out, apparent and concealed. The examples are constructed around an absence, and, on the purely profane level, only the *absence*, not the *absent*, is really interesting:

> For this reason gaming and the conversation of women, war, and high appointments are so much sought after. It is not because there is in reality happiness, nor that people think that real contentment comes from having the money that can be won in gambling or from having the hare that is hunted; people would not want these things if they were freely offered. This soft and peaceful enjoyment which allows us to think of our wretched condition is not what people are looking for, nor the dangers of war, nor the burden of office, but rather the agitation that turns us away from such thoughts and diverts us. Reason why we prefer the hunt to the capture.
>
> [De là vient que le jeu et la conversation des femmes, la guerre, les grands emplois sont si recherchés. Ce n'est pas qu'il y ait en effet du bonheur, ni qu'on s'imagine que la vraie béatitude soit d'avoir l'argent qu'on peut gagner au jeu, ou dans le lièvre qu'on court; on n'en voudrait pas s'il était offert. Ce n'est pas cet usage mol et paisible et qui nous laisse penser à notre malheureuse condition qu'on recherche, ni les dangers de la guerre, ni la peine des emplois, mais c'est le tracas qui nous détourne d'y penser et nous divertit. Raison pourquoi on aime mieux la chasse que la prise.]

In the "*y*"—suspended at a tantalizing distance from its antecedent in "our wretched condition"—lies the thing that the characters in the examples are not looking at or for. The example functions at the intersection of two different seekings: the exemplary characters are pursuing the money or hare that they do not want to obtain, turning aside from an awareness of their own actions. We, as readers, are invited not to pursue the hare but to inspect the relationship between the hunter and the hunted. What is obscured to the hunter by the fact that he is a hunter is revealed to those who witness the hunt.

Because example is always based on a breaking apart of things we are used to seeing in a different connectedness (for example provides another, more self-conscious connectedness), the series of examples in the *Divertissement* section make visible to the reader what is not visible to the player-hunter. The player does not know what he is doing because that knowledge would likely stop the game. By believing that he wants to win, the gambler can find pleasure in a game that would be otherwise mortally boring. The stakes of the game in themselves and the game in itself are equally unimportant—yet neither could function without the other. The relation between the two can be discovered by Pascal and the ideal reader by a process of standing outside the game while at the same time having a profound and sincere sense of what it is like to be inside the game. From inside the game you cannot see it, but if you are without any understanding of the importance of the stakes in gambling or the hare in hunting, it would be impossible to understand how these activities could effectively block thinking about the human condition. Those who criticize such activities concentrate, like the gambler or hunter, on the prey or stakes.[45] From within the hunt or game you cannot see the turning aside that is the essence of such an activity. Yet from too far this turning aside becomes equally invisible. The philosopher who supposes that these activities are vain because of the object (the money, the hare) has misplaced his attention as much as the player because such a philosopher or "demi-habile" does not perceive the turning aside as the principal characteristic of these activities.

The game (in this case specifically gambling) is already in itself a suspension or disconnection of activity from ordinary life. Rules are imposed that justify otherwise incomprehensible sequence and set aside the stakes or "pot" from ordinary monetary circulation. The example of gambling is a double disconnection, which, like a double negative, forces a kind of reconnection—setting the game into a larger picture within which the suspensive quality of gaming becomes apparent.

In the suspension of the game operated in Pascal's example, the objects on which the player and the philosopher are fixated are shown to be peripheral. The example, by the disconnection proper to this figure, separates the observer from the apparent object of the hunt or game so that he can see what is hidden by that object. The hare turns out to be a sign of something else, a metonymic sign, which works because it is associated with the never-ending story of the hunt. By prying loose the sign from what it covers, we discover the distance from sign to thing, the nontransparency of this sign. But the "thing" of which this is the sign is missing, or rather it is a negative thing. From outside the activity, we can see that the hare hides the motivation of the hunt, that is, the fear of repose and introspection. Once the function of the hare as sign is revealed, a whole chain of signification is available, for in each case the fear of seeking signifies the hidden object of that avoided search, God.

The Pascalian version of the exteriority of example is amply displayed in these passages on diversion. To understand the hunt we must be able to imagine ourselves both inside and outside it. For the disdainful philosopher looking on with scorn at the wasteful fury directed at an unworthy object, the hunt cannot reveal its necessary and universal meaning (Pascal elsewhere argues that the philosophers themselves misplace the value of life by setting up vain "sovereign goods"). We must be able to feel the lure of the chase while remaining temporarily out of its power. Pascal has dealt with this question of viewpoint by placing within the hunt a character both *within* it and completely *exterior* to it: the *piqueur* or "beater" who chases the prey out of hiding for the hunter: "The gentleman sincerely believes that the hunt is a great pleasure and a royal pleasure, but his beater is not of that opinion." The nobleman's activity differs little from that of the beater except that one gets to keep the capture, which he does not need for food, while the other participates in the activity purely as labor. The beater would not be able to respond to the example of the hunt as would the middle-class or aristocratic reader to whom Pascal is directing himself. On the other hand, the reader is outside the hunt as viewer or receiver of this example, but he is expected to be able to respond with a sense of what the *interior* of the activity means for the hunter.

The example allows us to perceive the hiding that is hidden by diversion. Fracturing the unexamined continuity of social reality and then juxtaposing these fragments, the serial character of example isolates what the instances have in common. Diversion is that essential element. Yet diversion only indicates that mankind is creating, by its turning away, an area of shadow. The examples do not show what is in that shadow.

Pascal's use of example in this section introduces a theologically defined rhetoric of exemplarity, a rhetoric that places the onus of nondiscovery on humanity, as represented by Pascal's interlocutor, for the nondiscovered is hidden by a failure to seek. In the passage last quoted the verb *chercher*, "to seek," appears obsessively to emphasize that what is not seen is the result of humanity's improper relationship, in both active and passive ways, to the search for happiness. On the one hand, men create the area of shadow by a blind concern for frivolous objects. On the other hand, they fail to seek the most important thing in life, an answer to the question of why they are in this condition in the order of the universe. So mankind is responsible for the existence of the hidden despite the doctrine of salvation by grace alone. Even though they cannot discover the true faith by their own acts and even though discovery of the truth of religion does not in itself bring salvation, men's active flight from the search for knowledge permits Pascal to present a demonstration of human responsibility for the existence of the hidden. Mankind *secretes*, so to speak, the secret. Examined from the point of view of the persuaded believer, the failure to search will appear as a lack of grace, something for which the unsaved are responsible even though they did not cause this lack of grace. But when the argument of diversion is presented to the unbeliever, he cannot avail himself of such a complex, and even duplicitous, religious argument because he is not yet supposed to understand such doctrines. The responsibility for the misplaced object of the search can remain only, in the unbeliever's eyes, with himself. In Pascal's argument what men see does not always serve to lead them toward salvation but, on occasion, to justify their damnation (in the section on miracles, Pascal writes, "Les miracles ne servent pas à convertir mais à condamner," 379).

If we accept the argument that men are hiding something, that they are all engaged in some form of turning aside, we have already taken a step toward understanding the order of Pascalian rhetoric. Hugh Davidson has succinctly described this approach as Pascal's "backward-looking" procedure, by which Pascal first establishes an agreement about suppositions and then moves backward toward the presuppositions that may correspond to those suppositions. This movement differs from a logical establishment of axioms or of a major premise to which a minor premise is joined in view of moving toward a conclusion. Or, as Davidson puts it, in his discussion of Pascalian proofs, "we should ordinarily be inclined to say that a proof is an organism consisting of two parts, an antecedent and a consequent. However, as Pascal uses the word, *preuve* refers to the former, the presupposition, rather than to the latter, to the certifying part rather than to the whole instance of reasoning."[46]

This notion of moving backward suits Pascal's argument from example especially because in this section of the *Pensées* the examples he uses are not simply illustrations of a principle.[47] Rather than forming a satisfying match of principle and illustration, the examples destabilize both the fabric of social existence and the knowledge derived from the appearances that permitted this social critique.

CONSTRUCTING THE SELF

Pascal's statement that all the unhappiness of men comes from the inability to stay alone in a room is among the best-known passages in the *Pensées*:

> When I have at times begun to consider the diverse perturbations of mankind, and the dangers and the sufferings to which men subject themselves at Court and at war, whence come so many quarrels, passions, bold and often bad undertakings, etc., I have often said that all the misfortune of men comes from one single thing, and that is from not being able to stay still in a room. (136)

Pascal adds immediately afterwards that such a retreat would not free us from unhappiness but would do the opposite, since our human condition is so wretched that "nothing can console us when we think carefully about it." This fragment from the beginning of the consideration of *divertissement* introduces the question of what or who is in fact diverted. The hypothesis of an individual in retreat from the world founds the Pascalian vision of the self, the subject who perceives, conceives, and judges things. Pascal's explicit denunciation of the self, the *moi*, declared to be hateful (597), seems to block both Montaignian introspection and Cartesian monologue. Yet most of the examples in "Raisons des effets" and "Divertissment" appeal to similarity between the actors or *personae* within the examples and the reader's self-image. The unbeliever's self-perception is central to the whole process of persuasion, for he must draw on his own internal sense of what it is to be a hunter and what it is to be a disinherited king. Even more important is the *place* of the viewer. As in the case of the hunt, being too close to a certain activity prevents seeing what is happening.

At the same time, one self must be sufficiently distanced from an activity to be able to perceive what is invisible to that other self who is plunged blindly into diversion. With this in mind the following passage becomes highly significant:

> Seeing the blindness and the misery of man, seeing the whole universe silent and man without knowledge abandoned to himself, and as if lost in this corner of the universe without knowing who put him there, what he has come there to do, what will become of him after death, incapable of all knowledge, I become afraid like a man carried asleep onto a deserted and frightful island, and who wakes up without knowing and without a means of escape. And thereupon I marvel that one does not become desperate in such a wretched state. I see other people around me of a similar nature. I ask them if they are more knowledgeable than I. They tell me that they are not and thereupon these lost wretches, having looked around and seen some attractive objects surrender themselves to these objects and become attached to them. For my part I have not been able to attach myself and considering that it seems more likely that there is something more than that which I see I have inquired if this God might not have left some sign of himself. (198)

The speaker portrays a society of monadic individuals similar in their nature but different in the degree to which they can detach themselves from their surroundings. These individuals are measured from the self of the speaker who finds these people "near me," "of a similar nature [to mine]," and not "better informed than I." Out of this initial suppression of all social organization and all accidents of differentiation, comes the initial impulse to seek, an impulse that is expressed in a return to the self "Pour moi . . . " Sight and appearance serve positively and negatively to persuade the speaker that what appears in the world is only distraction, diversion, or alienation from a possible explanation of this state. The other selves appear for this speaker in the *Pensées* as negative versions of the self in a preparatory phase of seeking. This step is much like the negative moment in Descartes's exemplarity, when the diversity of the practices and beliefs of mankind causes him to renounce the study of books and the world.

The conceptualization of the self takes a more explicit form in fragment 597, which begins, "The self is hateful. You, Miton, you cover it up, but you don't get rid of it." In this attack on the *honnête homme*, Pascal indicates the danger of cultivating a surface of modesty to facilitate social life. In making life with others agreeable, gentlemanly accommodation prevents them from hating us and spares us the pain of being the object of hate. Nonetheless, the self sees itself as the center of everything and only disguises itself outwardly to allow others to forget the tyranny that the self would impose ("car chaque moi est l'ennemi et voudrait être le tyran de tous les autres"). Pascal's reasons for attacking a system that makes social life more bearable are not difficult to reconstruct. Since the observation of man in society is a major source of discovery about the gap between inside and outside, any convention that blocks the discovery of the inward viciousness of mankind gets in the way of Pascalian exemplification. A refined and polished *moi* is not sufficiently threatening to disturb and thus to disaggregate society into the repellent monads on whom Pascal's argument from social examples works. This monadic system is established, in the fragment on the sleeper (198), as being a source of observation of the other individuals of a similar nature. The hatred one feels for the self must be a hatred felt for the nature of man in general, since one seeks in the others a replica of the self—a basic condition for the acceptance of any human example. The gentlemanly, social *moi* provides an outward falsification of the inward self, creating the illusion that the self can be tamed, can be rendered nontyrannical, and can become pleasant. In this way social cohesion persuades each self of the nonhatefulness of the self: "Thus you do not make it [the *moi*] pleasing to those who hate injustice. You make it pleasing only to the unjust who no longer perceive in it their enemy. Thus you remain unjust and you can only please the unjust" (597). The agreement existing between the "unjust" can occur only because each self is working hard to maintain a seductive exterior in order to dominate the others, taking them off guard. If the self, on the other hand, recognized its hatefulness, it would not seek to enslave others by falsification, since that falsification is part and parcel of the original hatefulness. From this self-discovery would be born a society of nonseductive, and even nonattractive, individuals who could recognize in others the replica of their self in the other hateful selves.[48]

It is not difficult to extrapolate a social aesthetic or etiquette on this Jansenist/Puritan model, an etiquette of worldly solitaries. Love of neighbor is not the primary thrust of Pascal's writing. In fact, the simultaneous alienation from both self and other is necessary for the *Apology* to direct the unbeliever elsewhere. Despite the clear differences, there are potential or latent resemblances between the Pascalian and the Cartesian structuring of the self.

Cartesian introspection does produce a vision of the world centered on the "I" or self, but this self is so radically reduced that it is a self alienated from most of the attributes of self. Without assurance of possessing its body, deprived of its opinions, habits, emotions, the Cartesian self can only assure itself of its existence by conceiving a God who would not deceive it. Although the Cartesian self moves toward certainty by exclusion of other selves, and so differs from the Pascalian study of disharmony and conflict, this exclusion occurs after a preparatory survey of the deplorable state of human diversity not unlike Pascal's vision of the *"misérables égarés"* who have no idea where they are going.[49] While the Cartesian self is preoccupied by the distinction between the nonextended, purely rational, and perhaps undoubtable "I" and the extended, material, and perhaps imaginary attributes like the body, the Pascalian self is concerned with the dialectic of hatred and hatefulness uncovered by being similar to, but always despising and struggling with, other selves.

Pascal seems aware of the political and rhetorical dangers presented by Descartes's *Discourse*, and he explicitly associates the notion of tyranny with that of the self (597). Their incompatibility, which proves an insurmountable problem for Descartes, is the source of all of Pascal's initiating or introductory exemplarity. Like Descartes, Pascal introduces a gap within the self, but this gap is not conceivable in terms of a duality between mind and body, or reason and extension.[50] The *Pensées* explicitly renounce the anatomy of the human person.[51] Instead the treatment of other selves as exemplary of what we are leads to sufficient dissatisfaction for a complete breakdown of human self-sufficiency. Example on the purely human level collapses after having served its preparatory function, but it collapses completely, leaving no "I" as potential exemplar to replace the discredited diversity of selves. In what could be called a "poly-decentered" view of humanity, each self is led to see itself mirrored in other selves and to be revulsed equally by this specular image and by the "original" self.

This mirroring is a constant comparative activity, in which the self reveals its dependent nature. Man's ability to remain solitary leads to constant friction and struggle over the signs of relative wealth, power, beauty, prowess, and so on, in a commerce that is entirely based on signs, appearances. "He has four lackeys" is an example of the kind of sign that is used in the social display of difference. The fragment in which the observation about the lackeys initially appears in the *Pensées* is not in the first person but in the third person, revealing the perception of an onlooker who is not talking with the employer of the four servants but watching, counting, and, undoubtedly, pondering the signficance of that number. Pascal exploits this comparative activity by using the hatred generated by the self's contradictory but irresistible tendency to seek confirmation of its own "tyranny"—that is, to construct a critical and reflexive image of the self—by inspecting the condition of the others. The self is always trying to become the center of the world but never entirely succeeding. Yet the self cannot tolerate the much greater anguish of confronting questions that transcend the petty comparisons of human interaction. The profusion of examples, the lack of a single, stable instance that could serve to fix our attention, leads to this poly-decentered exemplarity of a self able neither to contain itself nor to submit itself to another but always moving back and forth.

If we trust Pascal's contemporary, Filleau de la Chaise, whose summary of the *Apology* purports to be based on oral remarks by Pascal himself, the diversity between selves would have figured in Pascal's argument as a negative example, as it did in the opening pages of Descartes' *Discourse*:

> Why, for example, that strange diversity among men, who are all of the same nature? How can the simplest thing in the world, the soul or thought, be so varied? . . . and that with so much difference and mixture of these qualities with one another and even of qualities that are opposed, there are not two men in the world who resemble each other nor even a man who is not different from himself from one moment to the next? If the soul passes from fathers to children, as philosophers believed, where can such diversity come from?[52]

This diversity, which for Descartes is a defect that could be solved as well as an indication of a mistake to avoid, does not play the same role in Pascal's rhetoric. For the diversity of mankind in the *Pensées* is not at all to be remedied; in fact, the attempt to remedy it (which is, in part, the goal of the codes of conduct and communication that form *honnêteté*) throws an obstacle in the path of transcendence of human illusion. Attention to the *visible* diversity of humanity also threatens an eclipse of the hidden diversity, which is the really important difference. The saints, exemplary figures if there are any, raise this problem of the hidden difference:

> External works. There is nothing so dangerous as what pleases God and men, for the states that please God and men have one feature that pleases God and another that pleases men, like the greatness of Saint Theresa. What pleases God is her deep humility in her revealed knowledge; what pleases men is her knowledge. Thus we kill ourselves to imitate her words thinking that we are imitating her state and departing from what God loves and from placing oneself in the state that God loves. (928)

Authorizing himself to speak for God, Pascal here gives an example of the split between human perception of the surface and divine perception of the inward spiritual value. In one way Pascal is close to Descartes here: both would agree that phenomenal, apparent reality does not give any certainty. But for Descartes the inward evidence of his own Cogito authorizes him to set himself forth as regulator of the conduct of others—making of Descartes a kind of Saint Theresa of science. For Pascal, on the other hand, the self of the saint is entirely inward and not humanly imitable, except by a paradoxical inversion beyond those not inspired by grace. Echoing Marguerite de Navarre, Pascal adds to this fragment, "It is better not to fast and therefore to be humiliated than to fast and to be complacent." Imitation of the Saint's *visible* acts or qualities would lead to a direct violation of the most important quality, which is internal and consists in humiliation. On the other hand, public failure to imitate her external qualities would lead to humiliation and so lay the basis for a replication of her internal state. The best imitation of such an exemplar is non-imitation; the more we use the appearance of the saints to nourish a sense of diversity and irremediable incoherence in human commerce, the better we can prepare ourselves for the invisible reception of grace.

Pascal's reduction of the compliant reader/interlocutor to the state of passive receptiveness is highly reminiscent of the Cartesian elaboration of the provisional ethical "I," the subject that pliantly acts out the least critical social pattern of conduct while inwardly pursuing a different line of inquiry, subverting the outward actions. In contrast to the inward Cartesian active self, however, the Pascalian inward self is also passive. The "thought from behind the head" does not permit the subject to assume that any inquiry will lead to a positive outcome. The heart of man is, to use Montaigne's phrase, *creux et vuide*—"hollow and empty"—and the wise man of the *Pensées* can only attain a consciousness of passivity raised to a second degree.

The image of the man alone in his room is a point of contact between Cartesian and Pascalian conceptions of the self. For Descartes in the *Discourse* the withdrawal into the self in the Cogito was an attempt to transcend time and history, sources of alienation and error, to discover the present of a true contact with the self. This present, however, was only meant to be a ground for a return to a renewed temporal succession of methodological inquiry in the intersubjective, social world, within which organized groups of people perform successive operations of experiment and verification. In this way the Cogito is not the end or goal of inquiry, or properly the beginning. It is a phase between the negative and unsure history of inquiry and the renewed history of inquiry that will follow. The Cogito is a kind of "hinge" in history, a moment that reverses the direction and value of the successive study of the external world. In the *Pensées* the withdrawal into the self in the closed room is never achieved, because it is impossible for human nature to reach the heroic goal of baring and bearing the hateful self. For Descartes the self of the Cogito is outside of the social and historical world, and the self of the Cogito is not comparable to other selves. Yet the Cogito is not necessarily atemporal, for it is a presence of the self to itself in a *present*. The Cogito is both an example of the method of inquiry and the basis of the method. It may be imitated, but without really entering the order of successive, diachronic inquiry. It is always an attempt at starting again, always an attempt at attaining presence of the self to the self, despite the haunting of the ghost of the earlier Cogito, which deprives later enactments of their attempt at pure presence. The retreat into the room in the *Pensées* is outside of historical succession yet rigorously tied to history. It is not only synchronic (or an attempt at synchronicity), but it transcends the distinction between past and present. The retreat is an ideal that cannot be accomplished but stands outside and beside historical social life as a measure of the *failure* of human life. The retreat into the room stands as a reminder of the force of repulsion and anguish that throws the self into the diversion of everyday life and thus into contact with other hated selves. The example of these selves is not proposed *to be imitated*, but it is inevitably, automatically "imitated" or rather replicated (for "imitation" supposes a will to enact or reenact).

The Pascalian self measures what it sees in the world of temporal existence—hunting for the hare, gambling for the stakes—against an atemporal ideal. It measures itself in a mirror through the gap or distance created by the figure of an impossible, inverted self. This inverted self remains inside the head of the wise man as he contemplates the social and temporal totality from which he cannot free himself, even provisionally. In this way example in the *Pensées* thrives as a nonimitative and purely cognitive concept. The image of the man alone in the room can now be addressed as something more precise than an image; Pascal is here creating a specific type of example, the example of what is not possible. From the beginnings of example theory in ancient times, the fictive example is recognized as entirely "legitimate," despite its lesser authority in the minds of audiences. There is, however, something remarkable about the example of the solitary thinker in the *Pensées*. It is not a negative example (in the sense of a conduct that the listener is urged to avoid imitating), and it is not merely a fictive example (in the sense of something that is not real but is plausible and could have happened). The solitary is rather a *fabulous* example (in the sense of something that has not happened and could not have happened). But even this description is not adequate, for the fable has only a superficial impossibility. Animals, for instance, may not speak and behave as Aesop has them do, but people *do* behave in that way. A simple translation or decoding yields a perfectly historical example. Pascal's impossible example instead produces a "hole" in our experience of the social examples that are so deliberately banal, so much a part of "les entretiens ordinaires de la vie."[53] In the gap between the impossible example and the historical example lies the indication for a need to escape from exemplarity into grace. The impossible example of the solitary performs the disruptive function usually attributable to the maxim or the general discourse that example supports.

By presenting the self with alternate images of itself, one purely imaginary and the others all historically and socially available, Pascal's disruptive rhetoric creates not only a discontinuity between examples but a discontinuity in the self-perception of the interlocutor. Once again Descartes appears as a possible reference of Pascal's critique of the impossiblity of self-presence. The belief in the possibility of solitary self-presence is a Cartesian notion that exalts the strength of the self. But the Cartesian self can only achieve the experience of self-presence by constructing a self that only exists fleetingly and momentarily and cannot pretend to any historical durability. It can exist only as an exclusive totality—a totality of bad faith, knowing that there is more than itself but refusing to recognize this—while the Pascalian self exists as part of a larger, an exhaustive totality. But in the *Pensées*, to experience this larger totality and experience the self as part of the whole, gaps, holes, and discontinuity are necessary and inevitable.

Knowing oneself as part of the whole requires acknowledging one's inability to exist other than as part of a social experience of hateful "sameness in difference," as part of a world that is postscriptural and so without external signs of difference. This postscriptural world of exemplarity projects the temporal difference of the two Testaments into the consciousness of the individual Christian, the believer, who can never rely on the temporal closure of a series of events, but must trust in a difference created out of simultaneity by grace. This conflict between the events of history and the difference of an experience that transcends history—or wishes to transcend history—is the acute problem raised by the work of Pascal's contemporary, Madame de Lafayette.

Marie de Lafayette: From Image to Act

L'auteur a une grande connaissance de la Cour. L'on ne peut rien de
plus vif, ni de plus ressemblant que la peinture qu'il en fait.

—Valincour

FOR AN EXAMPLE to function, it is not enough that it contain an accurate representation of an event or an object. It must link that event or object through language to time. The most accurate reproduction or model is useless if it is not clearly situated as finished or continuing or future. Aristotle based the effect of *paradeigma* on history and its cycles. On the other hand, Marguerite de Navarre, whose *Heptameron* is explicitly referred to in Lafayette's *La Princesse de Clèves*, directly challenged history and its examples to assert the priority of the word in the inner experience of salvation. Lafayette goes even further than Marguerite de Navarre to split the exact representation of the world from the word that could, if not redeem it, at least render the image of the world useful for a practical knowledge. It should be no surprise that both Lafayette and her readers were quickly caught up in a controversy over time and the fidelity of images.

In the celebrated letter denying her authorship of *La Princesse de Clèves*, Lafayette says of the novel, "what I find there is a perfect representation of the world of the Court and of the way one lives there. There is nothing romanesque and elevated about it; in fact, it is not a romance: it is, properly speaking, a memoir and this was, from what I have been told, the title of the book, but it was changed [ce que j'y trouve, c'est une parfaite imitation du monde de la cour et de la façon dont on y vit. Il n'a rien de romanesque et de grimpé; aussi n'est-ce pas un roman: c'est proprement des mémoires et c'était, à ce que l'on m'a dit, le titre du livre, mais on l'a changé]."[1] In these two sentences Lafayette establishes a series of theoretical problems with which critics are still coping more than three centuries later: the denial of authorship, the claim of a perfect representation, the distinction between romance (*roman*) and the nonromance that will come to be known as novel (*roman*), and, not least of all, the question of the temporality of the literary text. This last may be the most important, despite the off-hand way in which the time of *La Princesse de Clèves* is mentioned. As a perfect representation of the court, the text seems to claim a direct historical reference, a depiction of the "way things were." Yet the verb Lafayette uses to make this claim for the book she denies having written is in the present tense, *la façon dont on y vit. La Princesse de Clèves* was published in 1678 under Louis XIV, in a court that was self-consciously and aggressively different from other courts. But the novel takes as its setting the court of Henri II in 1558, one hundred twenty years before. If historical exactness is a principal quality of the book, one should write in the past tense of *la façon dont on y vécut.* Either Lafayette's letter is claiming for the novel a coding of the *roman à clef* variety (a trivial claim that could be applied to innumerable works of the period), or she is saying something more important: that the way one lives in the court is beyond the distinction in time and tense and is permanent, essential. *Vit* would thus be a present tense of generalization of the sort found in the La Rochefoucauld's maxims. This distinction is an important one, for the conflation of "lives" and "lived" concerns the very being of the world as represented in the text.

The most important, most astute, and most hostile critic of *La Princesse de Clèves* did not let this problem slip by. Valincour, in his *Lettres à Madame la Marquise *** sur le sujet de la Princesse de Clèves* (1678), protested—claimed to be "extremely surprised"—that the first sentence of the novel contained a similar error in the tense of the verb *paraître*, "to appear." The novel begins, "Magnificence and gallantry have never appeared with such brilliance as in the last years of the reign of Henri II [La magnificence et la galanterie n'ont jamais paru en France avec tant d'éclat que dans les dernières années du règne de Henri second]."[2] In Valincour's eyes (or in his critic/character's eyes) the first sentence should have been rewritten in part as "had never yet appeared in France with such brilliance [n'avoient encore jamais paru en France avec tant d'éclat . . .]."[3] This rewording would have satisfied an ideology of representation dominant at the court of 1678, for, according to Valincour, Lafayette's evaluation of the court of 1558 was an insult (an *injure*) to the court of Louis XIV. Valincour explains this mistake as a forgetfulness on the author's part, for it does not seem possible, he argues, that someone who knows the court of Louis XIV as well as the author seems to, could have made a similar error in representing the true relationship between the two courts.

Time and representation are tightly linked by Valincour and Lafayette. Fidelity of representation is, in turn, the touchstone of generic classification and rules. Lafayette claims that the book is not "romanesque," and that it is not a *roman*. On the other hand, Bussy-Rabutin wrote, shortly after publication, that the story contained things which "smacked of romance [sent le roman]."[4] Bussy's comment is provoked by an incident in the novel which strikes him as being incredible, that is, as lacking in verisimilitude (*vraisemblance*). Romance is thus associated with the unbelievable, with a kind of narrative that is not reflective of the world as it is expected to be.

Valincour sets forth some of the generic expectations against which Lafayette's work was judged. According to Valincour's first letter, in fiction treating matters about which the reader is likely to have no knowledge, the author can invent freely. The signals of temporal and spatial setting—the medieval past or an exotic orient, for example— give a text a status entirely exempt from the comparison between the reader's society and the world of the narrative. Thus, according to one figure in Valincour's text, the author of *La Princesse de Clèves* could have indulged freely in a departure from normal conduct if only she had given the story a different setting:

> I would advise the author to make up all the names as he must have invented the whole story; or, if he was so eager to write a history of France I would pray him to set it at the time of Pharamond or Clodion le Chevelu, so that what he made up could be more easily hidden in the obscurity of that distant period and so that his readers would be spared the continual discovery of incidents that clash with truth.[5]

The discussion of the two types of fiction—pure fiction and fiction that involves historical truths known to the reader—depends on the division of common belief into two categories, one called *vérité* or truth, and the other called *vraisemblance* or verisimilitude. Avoiding noticeable factual untruths helps lull the reader into accepting the plot as a whole. Hence, the highly critical Monsieur ★★★ in Valincour's first letter declares that he was shocked "to find at the Court of Henri II a Mademoiselle de Chartres, who never really existed; a Grand Prior of the Order of Malta, who wants to marry her; a Duke of Clèves who does marry her, though in reality he was never married." Monsieur ★★★ declares in exasperation, "Everything in it is false, and from the Court of a King of France we are thrown suddenly into the Kingdom of Amadis, among unknown people and unlikely adventures [*des aventures peu vray-semblables*]."[6] This passage shows the way Valincour passes from a standard depending strictly on fact to a standard of verisimilitude as the overall governing principle, one which, in a highly ideological way, subordinates fact to a sense of the fitting, proper, and believable. In practice, Valincour implies, the facts (*vérité*) are themselves signals for the application of social value, decorum, or expectation. What is considered verisimilar enough in the *Aeneid* or in Tasso's *Gerusalemme Liberata*—works approved by Valincour's interlocutor—would not pass as believable for a story set within proximate historical times.[7] By setting the narrative in a court about which readers in 1678 had reasonably ample factual knowledge and to which they might wish to compare their own, the author was apparently inviting the reader to expect a parallel in social norm between reader and character. Valincour combs *La Princesse de Clèves* for events and situations lacking in verisimilitude, and he makes clear, in his second letter, that checking historical facts is only a first step in reading. A reader should next try to place a fictional text in one of the two categories (merely verisimilar or true and verisimilar), deciding whether the more restrictive standard of truth/verisimilitude is actually respected by the work in question.

The two types of works are roughly equivalent to romance and novella (though these are not the terms Valincour himself uses). His contemporary Du Plaisir sees the *nouvelle* as the genre that eliminates the fabulous in favor of *vraisemblance*.[8] In like manner Segrais, under whose name *Zayde* first appeared, places in his collection, *Les Nouvelles françaises* (1656–1657), the distinction:

> It seems to me that the difference between the romance and the novella is that the romance presents things as manners dictate and in a poetic fashion, but that the novella must be closer to history and aim rather at giving images of things as we ordinarily see them happen rather than as we imagine them.[9]

Thus, the novella is closely connected with reality and norm and opposed to a literature of free imagination and desire. Both Lafayette and her critics agree that history and the law, not the principle of pleasure, are the defining characteristics of the genre (whether novella or memoir) to which *La Princesse de Clèves* claims allegiance.

The copious debates among contemporary readers whether people really did or should behave like the Princess, amply attested in documents of the period, leave no doubt that respect of standards of "normal" behavior was paramount for the public of 1678 and that the respect of factual truth was secondary or merely instrumental.[10] For Valincour and others such as Bussy-Rabutin, the generic signal given by the historical allusions in *La Princesse de Clèves* upsets the scale of verisimilitude. Judged as pure fiction (*roman*), the text was set improperly—it was not sufficiently distant. Judged as a form of novella (*nou-*

velle historique), the work failed to depict conduct that seemed to represent the real, historical norm—it was not sufficiently close.

Lafayette probably intended to contradict the generic signal, refusing both the ideal world of the romance and the notion of predictable normality implicit in the novella. Lafayette fashions a new kind of text by modifying the novella's traditional truth-claim or ontology and its traditional narrative structure.

Concerning truth, novella, usually appearing in a series or novella collection, is inherently critical. The novella (from the *Quinze joies de mariage* to the *Heptaméron*) aims at representing the world or "reality" by proposing a pattern of conduct and incident (the way things *are*—an ontological claim) and at evaluating this pattern as basis for future conduct (the way things *will* or *should be*—an ethical claim). These two claims of the novella discourse join to form a circle that could be called the "discourse of wisdom," a discourse that rises from and then applies itself to an image of reality. Its effect is to urge certain actions in view of how the world is and how it will continue to be. It assumes a repetition and a predictability that the wise can use to their advantage. The novella collection forms the bridge between romance and history by being a fictive, yet in some way a representational and critical text.

Basic to the novella is the relationship between image and action. Valincour echoes the narrator of *La Princesse de Clèves* when he says the text contains a depiction or painting (*une peinture*) of the court. The question of what the court is or was like is all bound up in the metaphors of visual representation. In both of Lafayette's major works, *La Princesse de Clèves* and *Zayde*, paintings—in the literal sense—are made, altered, lost, stolen, and appropriated in unusual ways. These incidents of plot are also a figural embodiment of the deviations and misappropriations of representation of the royal court and its characters. Since Valincour and Lafayette agree that *La Princesse de Clèves* is an exact representation—or a painting—of the court, it is important to understand the role of such representations within Lafayette's texts.

ZAYDE

Lafayette's *Zayde* (a "Spanish story" or *histoire espagnole* published in 1669 under Segrais's name) consists of a series of exemplary tales bound together in the framework of the adventures of Consalve, a Spanish nobleman.[11] Not only does Consalve, along with numerous other characters, propose general statements, which are then tested against narratives of experience, but these examples (that is, principle-narrative pairs) concern the very process of trying to pin down the variability of appearance with neat formulas and predictions. The foundation of example is shaken by three recurring problems throughout *Zayde*. First, the characters' general statements about life fail repeatedly to coincide with events. Second, the past, present, and future do not cohere when the characters try to relate them and to use the past to predict what will happen. Third, distinguishing between what is specific to an individual and what is characteristic of larger categories poses real problems for Consalve and the others. Uniqueness, after all, defeats example by preventing imitation and analogy. If a character is unlike all others, then no generalizations can be made on the basis of his experiences. Anything that prevents decisions regarding unicity and shared features paralyzes the process of exemplification. On the other hand, if no individual can be represented concretely, is *any* representation possible, or must language remain in pure abstraction? If abstraction dominates, then the movement from principle to concrete instance is blocked, and example also fails.

This third problem appears in *Zayde* in conjunction with the general theme of representation, and thus three problems close to form a triangle. After all, the concept of a general statement, the first problem of this series, supposes that language can actually contain or refer to concrete things. And the concept of a unique representation also concerns such connection between conventional signs and the outside of the sign convention. Lafayette makes it clear that more than human language in the narrow sense is in question by introducing painting as a metaphor for signs that refer to concrete entities. Painting, and especially portrait painting, leads the characters in *Zayde* to become lost in the labyrinths of human identity. In particular for the male characters, not having a clear conception of the self leads to insoluble problems of forming rules about human behavior.

The three problems appear in the early pages of *Zayde* in Consalve's account of his experience of love. Looking back from an isolated refuge near Tarragona, the hero tells a chance encounter, Alphonse, of what happened to him at the court of Leon, where he had defended different ideas about love from those of his friends Ramire and the prince Don Garcie. The three men set forth the necessary conditions for falling in love with a woman. This exchange sets up a number of general principles or maxims against which the following actions of the three characters can be measured as examples of those maxims. To make this point more obvious, Consalve comments, "I would not have told you about this conversation . . . but you will see in a while that it foreshadowed everything that has happened since [Je ne vous aurais pas fait le récit de cette conversation . . . mais vous verrez par la suite qu'elle fut un présage de tout ce qui arriva depuis]" (p. 56). The three characters each adopt different combinations of two basic claims. As set forth in their positive forms, the first of these maxims (all expressed from the male point of view) is that falling in love depends on knowing the woman well for a long time. As Consalve says, "You will never convince me that you are in love with someone whom you can hardly recognize and whom you wouldn't even know if you saw her someplace besides the window where you are used to seeing her" (p. 53). The "gallantry" of the Spanish court is in his opinion not love because love is based on knowledge. The negative form, so to speak, of this equation between love and knowledge is given by Don Garcie in perfectly formed maxim like La Rochefoucauld's: "surprise awakens and increases love; those who know their mistresses before loving them are so used to their beauty and their wit that they no longer notice these qualities when they are loved [la surprise augmente et réveille l'amour; au lieu que ceux qui connaissent leurs maîtresses avant que de les aimer sont tellement accoutumés à leur beauté et à leur esprit qu'ils n'y sont plus sensibles quand ils sont aimés]." As his second requisite for love, Consalve declares that the woman must not have any existing attachment to another lover (p. 54).

On the basis of these two variables—knowledge and previous attachment—the three characters present three positions or dispositions toward love. In contrast to Consalve's position requiring previous knowledge and a lack of previous attachment, Don Garcie equates love with surprise; he could only love a woman he did not previously know, but he agrees he would prefer that the woman not be in love already. Ramire, on the other hand, insists that the woman be in love with another man, but seems to agree with Consalve that intimate knowledge of the woman is a condition for falling in love with her. In Ramire's combination of the need for a rival and the need for knowledge, the two conditions are closely and necessarily linked by the desire to observe, in a voyeuristic way, the rival's progressive expulsion from the woman's affections: "I would be more convinced of a woman's love for me if I had seen it begin in the moment of her most ardent attachment to another man." The three attitudes are used to elucidate the feelings of the three characters toward Nugna Bella, a lady who will soon become Consalve's lover. Don Garcie knows Nugna Bella too well to love her; there is no element of surprise. Ramire cannot love her because Nugna Bella is not yet in love with anyone else and, therefore, there is no element of rivalry. Consalve does not love Nugna Bella because he does not know her well enough—though he admits that he could love her if he knew her better.

In Consalve's tale of his rivalry with Ramire for Nugna Bella, the whole narrative is built along the lines of the maxim/example dichotomy. Don Garcie's and Ramire's relationships with women exemplify their opening statements. Once Consalve is Nugna Bella's lover, Ramire can love Nugna Bella. Meanwhile the arrival of Consalve's sister, Hermensilde, who is totally unknown to all courtiers, provides Don Garcie with the surprise he feels is necessary for love.

Consalve's case is more perplexing. He spent a good deal of time with Nugna Bella and seemed to know her quite well. She also had no previous attachment. Yet the subsequent undoing of that love, when Nugna Bella replaces him with Ramire in a liaison favored by Don Garcie, calls into question the whole project of *knowing*, which is the first and essential requirement set forth by Consalve. The hero falls in love with a woman because he thinks that he knows her, but right from the start there are indications that Consalve is wrong. Even though Consalve is the narrator of his experiences at court, the indications of his lack of knowledge do not appear as retrospective commentary on his part, but are built into information he had at the time, as various comments in his narrative reveal. Consalve's narrative establishes a principle that goes far beyond the relationship between men and women, since it demonstrates that Consalve was ignorant of Nugna Bella's nature and also of his male friends. This failure of knowing is linked to the second principle of love, the requirement that the woman not have a previous attachment to another man. Consalve is not able to trace the frontiers of male otherness—that is, to establish who is a rival and who is not—because he is incapable of knowing other males just as he is unable to know the woman with whom he is in love.

Consalve's story, as he tells it, demonstrates this failure to establish the boundaries of his own identity. He adopts Ramire as his protégé and furthers his career at court, giving him access to the prince, Don Garcie, and to Consalve's lover, Nugna Bella. Although Consalve distinguishes Ramire "from all the others" at the court, Consalve does not distinguish Ramire from Consalve himself, and instead associates him in the fortunes of the family. Ramire is living off the reputation and status of Consalve, becoming his brother/double, and eventually replacing him entirely in the court structure. Failure to know the other, woman, and failure to know the self in its boundaries with other male selves are the two flaws that lead to Consalve's downfall and to the exile in which he finds himself at the beginning of *Zayde*.

Although Consalve's requirements for love seem to be proven by his narrative—knowing the woman and knowing that she was unattached do lead him to fall in love—the fulfillment of these conditions was

based on an illusion. Consalve's example thus differs from Don Garcie's and Ramire's by not providing full confirmation of the general
principles he set forth. The structure of the tale leaves no doubt that it
is an exemplary narrative, though it provides evidence for and against
the principles that it exemplifies. This internal narrative, the "Story of
Consalve," paradoxically serves the function usually performed by the
frame-narrative in novellas, for it proposes the general rules that the
narratives either confirm or disprove. The doubtful relationship between Consalve's beliefs about love and his experience of love turns
into a frank opposition between belief and experience in the surrounding narrative, in which Consalve and Alphonse have already given
shelter and care to two foreign women whose ship was wrecked off
the Catalan coast.

Consalve falls in love with the first of the two women to be found,
a woman wearing Arab dress but speaking a language neither Arabic
nor Spanish. It seems, from the conversation between the two women,
that the object of Consalve's attentions is named Zayde, but Consalve
can determine with certainty nothing else about her. Nonetheless,
from the way Zayde looks at him and gestures toward him while talking with her companion, Consalve infers that he resembles someone
Zayde has known, and he believes this person is Zayde's lover. As
Consalve describes his situation to Alphonse, every affectionate glance
cast by Zayde in Consalve's direction signifies to him her rejection of
Consalve:

> Zayde is mourning some lover who has been shipwrecked; that's
> why she goes to the seashore every day; she goes to weep at the
> spot where she believes her lover died; I love Zayde and Zayde
> loves someone else; and of all misfortunes this is the one I thought
> I was safest from … . and, Alphonse, what seems to me even
> more cruel than all I have just said, I resemble the man she loves.
> She noticed it during her walk. I saw the joy in her eyes when she
> saw something that reminded her of him. She showed me dozens
> of times to Félime; she had her look closely at my features; she
> looked at me all day long, but she doesn't see me or think of me.
> When she looks at me, I remind her of the only thing I would like
> to make her forget; I even lose the pleasure of seeing her beautiful
> eyes turned towards me; she can't look at me any more without
> making me jealous.
> [Quand elle me regarde, je la fais souvenir de la seule chose que je
> voudrais lui faire oublier; je suis même privé du plaisir de voir ses

beaux yeux tournés sur moi; et elle ne peut plus me regarder sans me donner de la jalousie.] (p. 51)

Consalve's relationship with Zayde is the opposite of his earlier one with Nugna Bella. His love flourishes in the absence of knowledge. Zayde is only an appearance to him, an appearance or empty repository in which Consalve can place his imaginings or his guesswork. In this part of the novel all information that the reader has about Zayde comes from the general narrator's description of her appearance, dress, gestures, and the incomprehensible words she utters, or from Consalve's parallel attempts to capture in words for himself or for Alphonse the outward marks upon which can be constructed a fragile hypothesis about Zayde's origin, past, and present feelings. The parallel thus created between the general narrator and Consalve is not accidental, for the hero is a "writer" or "author" himself, making up stories about Zayde, stories that tell more about Consalve than about her. The difference between the general narrator and Consalve is that he is a more aggressive and complete storyteller, for he does not content himself with recounting appearances but converts them into signifiers for a highly uncertain signified situation.

Consalve's role as interpreter of Zayde and his role as character in the "Story of Consalve" demonstrate together that the hero is not a reliable interpreter of appearances. When telling how his sister, his best friend, his mistress, and his prince—persons he had more than ample opportunity to observe and speak with—deceived him entirely about their emotions and intentions, Consalve shows that even the optimal circumstances for reaching certain knowledge about human conduct are not sufficient to allow him to reach such knowledge. How secure, therefore, is his hypothesis about Zayde's relationship to an earlier lover and hence to Consalve as double or signifier of that lover?

The "Story of Consalve" is an exemplary tale on the two general principles about male love, principles that concern the variables of knowledge and rivalry. His passion for Zayde completely contradicts the conditions needed for love as he had established them before his disappointing experience with Nugna Bella. In the absence of all knowledge about her and with the certainty that she is already attached emotionally to another man, Consalve falls more in love with her than he had previously with Nugna Bella. Consalve, adopting the absolute form of the principles of knowledge and rivalry, is the example of an extreme, against the background of Don Garcie's and Ramire's compromise or combination. Although their experience of love seems to conform to the principles they establish in advance, Consalve's experience at the court of Leon leads to a doubtful outcome. As long as his experience is limited to his story about the court, one could suppose that his principle of knowledge being necessary was a correct description of his own needs for true love; perhaps the required degree of knowledge had simply not been reached. When the earlier experience is linked with Consalve's passion for Zayde, however, it becomes clear that Consalve is exemplary of a completely mistaken principle. Knowledge of the woman is not necessary for Consalve to fall in love. He is, therefore, at first an apparent example of the general principle that love without knowledge can be no more than an ephemeral gallantry (as his relationship with Nugna Bella showed), and he is later exemplary of the failure of self-knowledge: Consalve did not know himself well enough to determine the conditions under which he would fall in love. Consalve thus passes from the first extreme position to a second extreme position, traversing in one leap the intermediate ground held by Don Garcie and Ramire, who had held to a more "realistic" correspondence between rule and exemplary narrative experience.

Consalve's mute passion for Zayde, however, raises a far vaster question about the linking of general statements and life. If we remained within the "Story of Consalve," we might believe that the thrust of *Zayde* concerned merely Consalve's need to "grow up" and learn about love so that he is equal to the gallant "men of the world," Don Garcie and Ramire. The glimpse back to this failure to connect words with acts, however, sets up a question of how to link general principles with acts in Consalve's ongoing pursuit of Zayde (which lasts until the very end of *Zayde*), the "Story of Alphonse," the "Story of Alamir," and the "Story of Zayde and of Félime." When Consalve meets Zayde in his rustic retreat, great attention is concentrated on the problem of putting knowledge into signs.

Because language, written or spoken, cannot bridge the gap between Zayde and Consalve, other forms of representation have to serve the purpose. Consalve hits on the stratagem of using a picture to tell Zayde what he understands of her situation and what he feels. A painter had been asked to paint the sea as seen from one of the windows of Alphonse's house, and, in keeping with the instructions of his employer, the painter had created the scene of a storm with a shipwreck, with corpses lying on the shore and some survivors still swimming toward land. Consalve asks the painter to modify the canvas in order to present his hypothesis about Zayde's absent lover, whom Consalve presumes dead:

This storm made Consalve think of Zayde's shipwreck and gave him an idea of how to let her know what he thought of her sadness. He told the painter to add some figures to his painting and to put a beautiful young woman leaning over the body of a dead man on the sandy surface of one of the rocky outcroppings. She should be weeping while looking at him. There should be another man at her knees trying to make her move away from the corpse, and the woman, without looking at the man who was speaking to her, should push him away with one hand while she wiped away her tears with the other.

[Cette tempête fit souvenir Consalve du naufrage de Zayde et lui mit dans l'esprit un moyen de lui faire connaître ce qu'il pensait de son affliction. Il dit au peintre qu'il fallait ajouter encore quelques figures dans son tableau, et mettre sur un des rochers qui y étaient représentés une jeune et belle personne penchée sur le corps d'un homme mort, étendu sur le sable; qu'il fallait qu'elle pleurât en le regardant; qu'il y eût un autre homme à ses genoux qui essayât de l'ôter d'auprès de ce mort; que cette belle personne, sans tourner les yeux du côté de celui qui lui parlait, le repoussât d'une main et que, de l'autre, elle parût essuyer ses larmes.] (pp. 94–95)

Showing the painting to Zayde, Consalve guides her viewing of it, distinguishing the figures and indicating the principal characters, finally resorting to writing on the painting with a crayon the names Zayde and Théodoric (Consalve's pseudonym in his exile) over the last two figures. Since Zayde does not read Spanish and Consalve does not yet know that her language is Greek, it is fortuitous that the initial letter of the two names would be the same in both Roman and Greek alphabets, and thus she understands the link Consalve wishes to make.[12] Zayde responds to Consalve's gestures by taking the brush and removing the figure of the dead man:

she took a brush and wiped away the dead man, understanding that Consalve accused her of mourning him. Although he realized that he had made Zayde angry, Consalve was happy to see her paint out the man he thought she loved. Even though he realized that Zayde's gesture could be a sign of her pride more than a proof that she was not mourning anyone, he thought that after he had shown his love for her she was granting him a favor by not wanting him to believe that she loved someone else.

[elle prit un pinceau et effaça entièrement cet homme mort, qu'elle jugea bien que Consalve l'accusait de pleurer. Quoiqu'il connût aisément qu'il avait fâché Zayde, il ne laissa pas d'avoir une joie

sensible de lui voir effacer celui qu'il croyait aimé. Encore qu'il
pût s'imaginer que cette action de Zayde fût plutôt un effet de sa
fierté qu'une preuve qu'elle ne regrettait personne, il trouvait
néanmoins qu'après l'amour qu'il lui avait témoigné elle lui faisait
une faveur de ne vouloir pas lui laisser croire qu'elle en aimât un
autre.] (p. 96)

One of the limitations of painting is that it lacks the signs of negation.
Another is that its temporal aspect is extremely difficult to control,
since what is in the picture is always in the present. A sequence of
paintings thus is a sequence of presents, which can be interpreted as
before and after only in reference to other scenes in the sequence. A
third limitation is that the painting cannot make a distinct ontological
claim. It cannot, by itself, assert that the scene belongs to the realm of
historical reality as opposed to fiction or fantasy. By removing the
dead man from the painting Zayde intends to communicate something; but what? Consalve's two interpretations are basically one:
Zayde does not admit that she loves someone else. He merely hesitates,
at first, over whether this "statement" is a true or false one and over
the motivation of her communication.

Later Consalve realizes that the removal of the image of the dead
man can lead to a different interpretation, one he finds troubling. Perhaps Zayde has a lover who is not dead. She would thus assert, by
removing the dead man from the painting, that she loves no "dead
man." If Zayde weeps for a lover who resembles Consalve, that lover
escapes the containing power of painterly representation to become an
omnipresent threat: "She was right to remove the image of the dead
man," says Consalve to Alphonse, "she knew that the one she wept for
was still alive" (p. 98). The dead man's escape, so to speak, requires a
closer inspection of what is really being represented in the painting.
Zayde is flanked by two men, the one she is looking *at*, but who cannot
look at her because he is dead, and the one from whom she is turning
but who is looking at her. The two figures in the painting able to see
and looking at someone are meant to represent the two people who
are looking at the painting, Consalve (Théodoric) and Zayde. In the
painting, Zayde refuses to look at Consalve and keeps her gaze fas-
tened on the man who cannot see her, the dead lover. This is one way
of presenting the problem that Consalve has in "real" life, that is, life
outside the painting. Zayde looks in his direction or even *at* him, but
she only sees the dead man, for Consalve has become—this is his explanation of the situation—the image of the absent lover. As he has told
Alphonse, Zayde does not see him ("enfin elle m'a regardé tout le jour,

mais ce n'est pas moi qu'elle voit ni à qui elle pense") but finds in him only a likeness. By separating himself as Théodoric from the absent lover, Consalve conveys to Zayde the distinction between himself and the one he represents. By letting Zayde look at the dead man in the painting, the hero gives her an alternative image for that lover, and Consalve can resume his being as something other than an image for the absent, disembodied lover. When the painted image is removed, Consalve is, in a way, deprived of his own image, since he again becomes the representation of his rival. What might, in another novel, have been merely a clever aesthetic device is in *Zayde* demonstrably part of a systematic concern with the containment of likeness in signs. Throughout the rest of the story, after Zayde's departure from the Catalan retreat, Consalve is obsessed by the need to rediscover the *ménage à trois* that had occupied the center of the painting. He needs to find Zayde and the man who resembles him.

Example is in some way always the outside of discourse, always a movement to find confirmation by grasping at a support that does not come from the speaker's subjective verbal affirmation. The "internal narrative" of Consalve, and later the similar stories of Alphonse and Alamir, though "internal" in the sense of being placed within the framework of *Zayde* as a whole, are attempts to juxtapose *a priori* affirmation on the part of a single character with the intersubjective or social experience of the fictive events of the novel. Consalve's tale of what happened to him proceeds by gradually reducing the discrepancy between what he believed and what the other characters knew. The gap between his opening claims about knowledge and rivalry in love and the account he gives is the structure of an example, but an example that undercuts its original proposition, a counter-example. The story of Consalve is, therefore, an attempt to move from internal or subjective certainty to objective or external certainty and to reveal the deception that occurs when this external support fails.[13]

As we know, evidence is related to seeing—"seeing is believing"—in its descent from *ex-videre*. We see something on the outside, from the outside. The use of the painting to convey Consalve's understanding of his relationship to Zayde also concerns an attempt to deal with the outside of language. In some ways the painting, used in this way, is an attempt to replace language with its own "outside," the realm over which language holds dominion by its control of the functions of asserting what is, negating, and specifying temporal assignment. Language, in the earlier case of the story of Consalve and its maxim/example structure, posits a general principle that awaits confirmation or disconfirmation from specific instances, things that happen in a certain moment and in a certain place. In the painting, however, things are reversed. The painting is the generality; it can portray *any* shipwreck, with *any* woman on the shore, next to *any* corpse, and *any* other man. Indeed, we are told that the painter created a shipwreck, not in reference to any wreck that had taken place, but merely to make the painting more "pleasant" (*agréable*, p. 94). To specify that the woman is meant to stand for Zayde and the man to stand for Consalve, he must write names into the painting.

This reversal loosens Consalve's grasp over the whole concept of knowledge as basis of love, for without the relationship of word to thing, or more specifically, of *name* to thing, it is impossible to verify that any general principles exist, that experience can be contained within the boundaries of some rules permitting prediction and explanation, and that love itself can be anything other than a solipsistic fantasy. Another way to put this is to say that Consalve's quest not only illustrates the pair of maxims he so boldly maintained before having any experience on which to defend them, but also makes palpable the problematical relationship between the general and the specific on which the operation of examples is based.[14]

The split between language and vision is one boundary that runs throughout *Zayde* to separate discourse from all outside it. The way in which naming is particularly associated with this boundary line is significant because this function ties together representation with the rather doubtful maxims that Consalve presented in the "Story of Consalve." Knowledge of the woman and avoidance of rivalry with another man were his key precepts, but in his pursuit of Zayde, Consalve discovers that he is in love with a woman he cannot know and that he is himself his own rival. Although he can *see* Zayde he cannot know her, and although she looks at him she can neither *see* nor *know* him, for when she looks at him she sees someone else. Of course, this last proposition, that Zayde sees someone else when she looks at Consalve, is Consalve's interpretation of the thoughts and perceptions of a woman he admits he does not know. Seeing seems possible as an act independent of knowing, but knowing must consist of both vision and language, of the capture of vision by language.

Consalve thinks he has a rival because of the split between his name and his painted image. At the end of the novel, we learn that her father Zuléma had shown her a portrait of a young man whom she was to marry. This happened during a visit to an astrologer:

> Since the Greeks hold astrology in high regard and since young
> people are very curious about the future, Zayde repeatedly asked

this famous astrologer to tell her something about her destiny.
But he always refused. The few moments that he could spare from
his studies he spent with Zulema, and he seemed to avoid displaying his extraordinary knowledge . . . she demanded more insis-
tently . . . that he consult the stars about her future. "I don't have
to study the stars," he told her with a smile, "to assure you that
you are destined to marry the man whose portrait Zulema showed
you." . . . Zulema told Zayde, with all the authority of a father,
that she would never marry anyone but the man for whom that
portrait had been made. (p. 207)

The portrait, as it turns out, not only resembled Consalve but *was*
Consalve's portrait. The image unites successfully with the name, an
operation that had been clumsily and incompletely attempted when
the name "Théodoric" was written in desperation on the canvas. The
dangers of visual representation are nowhere more apparent than in
this wandering and alienated likeness that fell into Zuléma's hands as
booty of war. Zuléma meant that Zayde should marry the prince of
Fez, whose portrait he believes it to be. When all discover that Consalve is the man he resembled (as Zayde had wished when she admit-
ted, "I wished that you could be the one you resemble [j'ai souhaité
que vous pussiez être celui à qui vous ressembliez]," p. 232), this identification removes the barrier to his marriage as it does to his love.
Although the woman, Zayde, had had an earlier attachment to another
man, the other man was himself.

When language and vision are reconnected, the abstraction of the
painting yields to the concreteness of being in time. More than the
name of the subject of the portrait is at stake. Zayde had asked the
astrologer to tell her something about her own future, despite his reluctance to let his knowledge appear (*faire paraître son savoir*). The appearance of knowledge from within the hiding place of the astrologer's
mind coincides with his decision not to consult the stars but to make a
statement about the portrait, to recover for discourse an image that had
merely been gathered by chance. We learn later that this statement was
a banal result of common sense, of the kind of common sense from
which arise the maxims that Don Garcie, Ramire, and Consalve had
exchanged at the beginning of Consalve's adventures.[15]

This entirely ordinary assertion about the way things would turn
out, however, turns out to be right only because of a mistake. The
astrologer's words are correct, but his intended meaning was incor-
rect—and what is correct and what is erroneous depend strictly and
narrowly on the adhesion of words to images. But the words also de-

pend on the fitting of present assertion to future occurrence, as do Consalve's words earlier about the requisites for loving a woman. There is a correspondence between attempts to control pictures through words and the attempt to control the future through words. And in both cases the success with which language coincides with the vision is apparently random and without general pattern.

In *Zayde* words not only fail to relate past and future, but prove insufficient to discover self-knowledge by tracing the boundary between self and other. This inability, which is experienced by all the important male characters in *Zayde*, is connected with Consalve's second requirement for falling in love. Lafayette's hero wanted to be the woman's first lover, but as it happens, Consalve is replaced by another man (Ramire) he helped to fashion to resemble him in many ways. In contrast to Consalve's failure to recognize Ramire as an external threat, Lafayette places Alphonse and Alamir, who are constantly fearful of other men.

The "Story of Alphonse" is a second narrative example of the two principles that Consalve has set forth in his earlier story. Like Consalve, Alphonse wants to avoid finding himself in competition with another man for the love of a woman; like Consalve, he attaches greater value to knowledge than to surprise. Alphonse considers himself impervious to surprise because of a supposed general knowledge that he has of the female sex. What he calls "my knowledge of women" (*connaissance que j'avais des femmes*) makes him see womanly beauty as an appearance under which there are no surprises, only more of what he has already known. He decides never to marry a beautiful woman so that he will suffer less from the inevitable betrayal.

Alphonse falls in love with a woman who fits precisely the criteria set forth by Consalve. She has never loved another man and she is willing to tell her most personal thoughts, feelings, and actions. Bélasire had been courted by many men, but none had apparently awakened in her any response. She is so exceptional that Alphonse inquires into her unusual refusal of attachments. What he finds reassures him that Bélasire is the kind of woman with whom he could form a secure relationship. She says that she could not marry anyone she did not love passionately. She has remained unattached. Feeling that Bélasire makes an exception for him, he declares that he loves her. The result is a balance of two skepticisms. The male skepticism about womanly virtue and honesty is matched by Bélasire's distrust of her suitor.[16] When she admits her love, Bélasire exemplifies Don Garcie's principle that surprise, not knowledge, is the condition for love. "How charming it was for me," says Alphonse, "to discover Bélasire's surprise at not being in control of her feelings [Quel charme c'était pour moi de connaître l'étonnement qu'avait Bélasire de n'être plus maîtresse d'elle-même]."

On the other hand, Alphonse, who believes he knows all about women, is puzzled by Bélasire, since she does not fit his maxims about how women behave. She seems exceptional, she behaves in a way that is "completely different" from other women. In what follows in the story of his betrothal, Alphonse seems to be trying to reduce Bélasire to his general description of women, for one day he asks her what her other suitors had done to try to win her affection: "I enjoyed seeing the difference in the way she treated me from the way she had treated other men. She told me the names of all the men who had loved her; she told me what they had done to win her favor. She told me that the ones who had been the most persistent were the ones she disliked the most and that she had never been attracted to the Count de Lare, who had loved her up until his death" (p. 111).

Alphonse probes for two things. First, he is learning about Bélasire and her past, trying to determine the point at which she has changed. Second, through the difference in the way he is treated by Bélasire, he is finding how he differs (how his experience differs) from a number of other men. Certain implications of this quest for a dual knowledge are obviously psychological. Alphonse can be described as a narcissistic seeker for the perfect mirror of his difference from other men, and as suffering from an imperfect passage through the ego formation that would permit him to do without a constant and prurient inquiry into the distinction between himself and his image. He can determine neither the extent to which other men are truly distinct from himself nor the line between himself and his "mirror" in the woman. The resentment he develops later results in part from Bélasire's inability to produce the ultimate reassurance that he is indeed different; the more she offers proof of her exceptional frankness, the more Alphonse fears that Bélasire is or has been in love with someone else. Truly, as Alphonse tells Consalve, the fault is in himself. The psychological—or inward—importance of this inquiry for Alphonse cannot be separated, though, from the broader questions of knowledge.

One of these questions concerns the structuring of the world by the type of inquiry we undertake. Alphonse's quest is not an unbiased one. He has a stake in confirming his earlier knowledge about women and their infidelity. Alphonse's general principle protects him against his own desires. If Bélasire violates the role to which she has been consigned, as either exception to all desire or mere example of womanly infidelity, Alphonse risks losing control of himself and failing in his resolves.

Bélasire thus becomes a kind of surrogate for Alphonse, who expects her to maintain his self-control for him by confirming the knowledge that Alphonse and others have already decided must be the stable norm. "Women betray men in all love relationships" is the maxim that Alphonse bases on his knowledge of women; Bélasire is incapable of loving men, and therefore she does not betray them. She is therefore the exception that confirms the rule by being exceptional and noncontradictory at the same time. Alphonse in his own right lays claim to a status of exception, for he has chosen the strange tactic of avoiding jealousy by avoiding all thought of marrying a beautiful woman. Between Alphonse and Bélasire, two exceptional persons, the conversation is extraordinary (*extraordinaire*, p. 107). There is, however, no room in Alphonse's plan for a necessary modification if Bélasire falls in love with him, as she does. By loving a man, Bélasire moves from being a noncontradictory exception to being potentially a contradiction or a confirmation of the original maxim. For Alphonse to surrender the original "wisdom" as false, on the other hand, would mean abandoning his claim to knowledge (*la connaissance que j'avais des femmes*, p. 106) and accepting the opposite of knowledge, as it is established here by Don Garcie and Bélasire, surprise. Alphonse sets up a veritable inquisition into Bélasire's past, driven by the logic of the maxim/example pairing, looking for a historically specific instance to confirm his principle. The general principle thus structures the narrative forthcoming, focusing on what is sought and discarding or ignoring the rest, the excess of the example. As surrogate for Alphonse, Bélasire is coerced into the role of narrator, telling the story that is supposed to fit the maxim. She not only tells him stories orally, but writes out an account of her conduct with Lare. Alphonse comments:

> although she had already told me these things a thousand times, I thought with pleasure of having her write them. The following day she sent me what she had promised. I found a very exact account of what the Count de Lare had done to please her and of everything she had done to cure him of his passion, along with all the details necessary to persuade me of the truth of what she said. [quoique ce fussent des choses qu'elle m'avait déjà dites mille fois, j'eus du plaisir de m'imaginer que je les verrais écrites de sa main. Le jour suivant elle m'envoya ce qu'elle m'avait promis: j'y trouvai une narration fort exacte de ce que le comte de Lare avait fait pour lui plaire et de tout ce qu'elle avait fait pour le guérir de sa passion, avec toutes les raisons qui pouvaient me persuader que ce qu'elle me disait était véritable.] (p. 115)

Alphonse engages in a curious form of literary criticism in his unhappiness with Bélasire's writing.[17] Writing make Bélasire think about her dead suitor (Alphonse thus recognizes that he is pushing Bélasire to fulfill the prediction that is inherent in his "knowledge of women"), and leaves Alphonse unsatisfied since the narrative is excessive and deficient at the same time: "The passages in her story where she entered into detail were intolerable to me; I thought that she remembered too well the actions of a man who had been of no importance to her. The incidents that she skipped over lightly convinced me that there were things she didn't dare tell me . . . [Les endroits de son récit où elle entrait dans le détail m'étaient insupportables; je trouvais qu'elle avait bien de la mémoire pour les actions d'un homme qui lui avait été indifférent. Ceux qu'elle avait passés légèrement me persuadaient qu'il y avait des choses qu'elle ne m'avait osé dire . . .]" (p. 115). The opposition in signifiers (presence versus absence of detail in the narrative) points to identity in the signified: Bélasire loved the count de Lare. Any evidence of Bélasire's fondness for the count would confirm Alphonse's "knowledge" about women, but no amount of information can ever disprove it. Likewise for Consalve the depiction of the dead lover and the removal of the corpse from the painting seem to point in the same direction: toward a lover whom Zayde is mourning or missing. A similar problem of evidence confronts the principal Islamic character, Alamir.

This third male character to be the subject of a series of internal narratives suffers from a combination of Consalve's and Alphonse's afflictions: obsessive jealousy and inability to determine the limits of his own male identity as represented externally. Alamir, the prince of Tharse, is also the proponent of a specific rule about the way women behave: he feels that women are only able to love wealth and power. Alamir has, thanks to his rule about women, an image of how women "are." But in fact Alamir is less preoccupied with making this abstraction coincide with specific instances than with obtaining an image of himself through women. Rather than practice Alphonse's brutal frankness with his form of negative seduction, Alamir seeks merely to enact the conventional male courtship in order to awaken a corresponding but "real" passion in women. His previous conduct is described by Félime, who is desperately in love with him:

> He had never been truly in love; yet, though without passion himself, he knew so well how to appear passionate that he had succeeded in convincing every woman he had deigned to court. It is true that during the time when he wanted to attract a woman, the

desire to be loved gave him a sort of ardor that one could take for passion. But, as soon as he was loved, since he had nothing left to desire and since he was not amorous enough to derive pleasure from love alone, without the difficulties and mysteries of the pursuit, he thought of nothing but breaking off with the woman he had loved and getting another to fall in love with him. (p. 175)

Alamir serves as a singularly complete exemplary character. He is a condensation into one character of the multiplicity of example; a series of nearly identical incidents supports a single rule. The mechanically repetitive quality of Alamir's behavior provides a series that resembles one created out of the stories of many men. This sense of the discontinuity of Alamir's acts—the passion that breaks off abruptly when the woman's love appears to be assured, the rapid location of another object of pursuit—renders Alamir a fragmentary collection of highly specialized acts. Alamir's continual return as paradigmatic entity (the "lover") in the syntax of pursuit appears in Félime's paired temporal descriptors (*dans le temps/sitôt*) indicating the two phases of Alamir's life. The only thing maintaining the first phase is the "difficulty," "mystery," or "obstacles." The woman's role in Alamir's life is to maintain these obstacles that prevent his falling into the nonbeing of the automatic *sitôt*, the need to find a new object.

This temporal cycle is based on the problem of appearance. Like Consalve and Alphonse, Alamir believes that the woman he is courting loves another man. In Alamir's case the other man is the Prince of Tharse. Since Alamir *is* the Prince of Tharse, this form of jealousy results from a split in Alamir's own self-image. This split is a permanent, atemporal feature of his personality, and love of pursuit permits him to project an atemporal feature into a temporal sequence. In attempting to be loved for "himself" and not as "Prince of Tharse," Alamir devises situations in which he courts a woman without revealing his rank and then, as soon as he is secure in the woman's love, he discloses his full identity. At this point the emergence of the "Prince of Tharse" coincides with the disappearance of the obstacle on the part of the woman, and Alamir as "himself" is eclipsed. The disappearance of Alamir's semblance of love coincides with his belief that the woman no longer sees Alamir himself, but the Prince of Tharse.[18]

Alamir is like Consalve in this play of appearance and interpretation. He takes the signs of love addressed *to* him as signs addressed *through* him to the Prince of Tharse, just as Consalve assumes that the loving glances bestowed on him are addressed to the man he resembles. Coldness is desired, warmth feared. All the signs of love reverse their va-

lence because Alamir is not sure who he appears to be. This disturbance in the image of himself renders all empirical knowledge
impossible. The inductive process requires a stable interpretation of
appearances. A chemist cannot confirm a hypothesis if he is uncertain
whether the two substances combined to produce a reaction are the
same substances or only appear to be the same substances that similarly
combined on an earlier occasion. Likewise Alamir cannot be at all certain what the woman's response means if he is not certain whether the
man to whom she is responding is the *same* man. If example is a rhetorical induction, in Aristotle's terms, then the discontinuity of appearance and essence destroys any conviction that example could produce. Alamir's belief or maxim that women love the most powerful
and most wealthy man of Tharse because of his power and wealth cannot be disconfirmed by example. Therefore, confirmation by example
is also insecure.

INIMITABLE EXAMPLES

Undercutting the ability of appearance, as example, to support general
statement is a major characteristic of *La Princesse de Clèves*. The heroine, Mademoiselle de Chartres, later Princess de Clèves, does not attempt to impose maxims of her own on the world around her. Instead
she serves as receiver or audience for a number of maxim-example
pairs proposed by other characters. Her role is clearer when placed in
the context of the generic filiation of *La Princesse de Clèves*. Seen as a
novella, Lafayette's work constitutes a change of proportion rather
than a completely new pattern. The novella collection usually consists
of a framework of commentary sharply distinguished from a series of
narratives. In *La Princesse de Clèves* and *Zayde* the frame-narratives expand while the internal narratives contract. The reader's interest is thus
guided toward the amplified "frame" functions of receiving and comparing the internal narratives and of detecting patterns in them rather
than toward the narratives themselves. The protagonist of *La Princesse
de Clèves*—like her analogues in the novella collections—hears all of the
internal narratives. We, the readers of Lafayette's text, do not accede
to these narratives except as they are available to the heroine. Yet the
seventeenth-century audience did not want to accentuate the protagonist's role as internal audience. Traditionally these internal—or "intercalated"—narratives are considered four in number: the stories told
about Diane de Poitiers (p. 265), Madame de Tournon (p. 81), Anne
Boleyn (p. 299), and the Vidame de Chartres (p. 314). There is also the
story of Marie de Lorraine told by Mary Stuart (p. 256). In the first of

his *Lettres à Madame la Marquise* ★★★, Valincour describes the stories of Madame de Tournon and Diane de Poitiers as extraneous and as defects in the overall narrative structure: "For it seems to me that the mark of excellence in a work is to have nothing absolutely useless in it; and I cannot imagine what purpose is served by the stories of Madame de Tournon and of Anne Boleyn, or by several other details of the history of France that are placed here and there" (p. 23). While the story of the Vidame appears necessary to Valincour, he denounces the mother's narrative about Diane de Poitiers and "the whole story of the former court" (p. 18). Valincour returns several times to the problem of these narratives later in his *Lettres*. Addressing his reader the Marquise, he says, for instance:

> You are not the only one who found the story of Madame de Tournon digressive and twice as long as it should be. Perhaps Monsieur de Clèves was right to tell it to his wife at Coulommiers to entertain her and she was not bored listening to it; but it is just the opposite when an author tells the story in a book, and the readers, who only want to hear the story of Madame de Clèves, find in their way the story of a woman who doesn't interest them in the least. Even if the author had secret reasons for not omitting this story, he should have shortened it and tied it in better with the rest of his book. (pp. 158–59)

While pointing out the Princess's great interest in this narrative, Valincour assumes that the reader's interest must diverge from the heroine's, so that the result is a breakdown in the linkage between this internal narrative and the frame-narrative or story of the Princess.

Only with the passage of centuries has the exemplary nature of these narratives been emphasized. As Pierre Malandain writes of these stories, "they all have, ultimately, a single addressee, the heroine. Even when they are not directly communicated to her, they end up being known to her and their effect on her is underlined, whether they contribute to her apprenticeship in the life of the court and in the dangers of amatory intrigues that take place there or whether they place her in a direct relationship and as the goal of the passion that she inspires and that she feels."[19] Hence these narratives, in the view of the twentieth-century reader, constitute, at least in part, an education of the protagonist and put at her disposal—and ours—a repertory of models of human conduct subsequently available to motivate her own conduct.

Madame de Lafayette's contemporaries, however, were practiced readers of *romans* and *nouvelles*. When Valincour says he does not understand the value of most of the internal narratives, his puzzlement is not without reason. It may give us a clue to the principal problematic of Lafayette's novel. The author has suppressed traditional mechanisms for the integration of frame and internal story. The abundant commentary of romances like *L'Astrée*, where the intercalated stories give rise to lengthy "debates" and even to judicial proceedings, is absent in *La Princesse de Clèves* and *Zayde*. Lafayette's texts also lack the commentaries of the frame-narrative of the *Nouvelles françaises* (or the *Decameron*). They lack even the minimal statement of a theme that opens each of the four narratives of Madame de Villedieu's *Les Désordres de l'amour* (1675) where the reader knows in advance what truth the narrative example will demonstrate. In *La Princesse de Clèves* a single element common to all of the tales is not singled out, and the internal audience frequently contents herself with simple thanks to the narrator of each tale. As a consequence the reader is confronted with a number of rich narrative examples of human conduct from which a number of thematic models can be constructed.

In attempting to find a principle that will give unity to the series of internal stories, the reader will turn for guidance to the other narrative level, the story of the Princess. However tenuous may be the direct link from any one of the stories to another, we may assume that they have in common a certain influence on the protagonist. And the reader must suppose that as he sifts the narratives to find some kind of pattern the young Mademoiselle de Chartres, the internal audience, is similarly seeking pattern to human conduct in her apprenticeship at the court of Henri II. But in the heroine's reaction to the internal narratives we see a frequent turning aside from the apparent examples of the nature and risks of love. Instead, only after falling into the traps about which she has been warned does she recognize them in what she hears. The lessons contained in the Vidame's letter, for example, are only available to the interpreter/heroine as a vision of her own already-experienced suffering from jealousy. The complex story of Sancerre earlier in the novel, one that could have been seen as the most quintessential and insoluble case of jealousy, does not lead her to beware of this horrible outcome of love. Instead of seeing Sancerre's fate as a potential image of her own, she reacts only to her husband's statement that he could assume the role of counselor should his wife love another. Thereafter, when the Prince comes to tell her what happened to the unhappy Sancerre, "she was not very curious about the rest of that adventure. She was so preoccupied by what had just happened that she could scarcely conceal her distraction" (p. 294). Thus the narrator explicitly shows a blockage between the protagonist's thought and the monitory incident. Only after the episode of the Vidame's letter does the Princess have, in an experiential sense, the category "jealousy" at her disposal for further interpretation of the narrative presented to her. Similarly the heroine's attention turns from the monitory center of the narrative about Anne Boleyn toward questions about Elizabeth, of whom the heroine is jealous.

Finally, with the Vidame's letter, the Princess seems to have understood the perils of love and the resulting jealousy. But the narrator carefully disconnects the protagonist from the full content of the letter. Her immediate reaction to it is described thus:

> Madame de Clèves read and reread the letter without realizing what she had read. She saw only that M. de Nemours did not love her as she had thought and that he loved other women whom he deceived like her. What evidence and what knowledge for a person of her temperament, with a violent passion, who had just shown her passion to a man she judged unworthy . . . (p. 310)

Her conclusions about the source of her emotions are judged false by the narrator: "But she was mistaken. This suffering, which she found unbearable, was jealousy, with all the horrors that it brings."

The story of the Vidame de Chartres and his letter displays a complex and ironic relationship among the three levels or voices of the narration—internal narrative (including the letter itself), the heroine's thoughts, and the narrator's commentary. The Vidame's letter is a rich narrative example of a highly formalized relationship between the sexes, based on the control of the signs of love and of what has been called the mimesis of desire. The story contained in the letter displays the woman's triumph, for her ability to manipulate the signs of emotion allowed her to regain an ascendancy over the Vidame de Chartres. Yet the Princess's relationship to the letter is not directed toward the full explanation of the relationship between the woman and the man, whom she assumes to be Nemours, but only to the information that Nemours loved another. The conclusion of her meditation on the letter is that "she would be completely cured of her love for that prince" (p. 311). The narrative voice, which has already pointed out the heroine's failure to provide a correct explanation of her emotion on reading the letter, also contradicts the heroine's conclusion about being cured of love: "she was far from the calm that brings sleep" (p. 311).

Although the protagonist has the same access to the internal narratives that the reader has, the narrator takes care to indicate the protagonist's limited perception when she—with the reader—first learns of them. The reader is thus challenged to find in the narrative more than the Princess does. The internal narratives thus take on a fullness that is always in disaccord with the moment of the novel in which they appear.

Something of the heroine's blindness was apparent to the author's contemporaries. Valincour commented that it was a pity that the heroine was so "simple" and that her mother's counsel was wasted on her.[20] Yet, as a thematic of Lafayette's work, this kind of blindness is not simply that of a naïve Agnès in a tragic key, for the protagonists of *Zayde* are similar, if not more patently resistant to the truth that lies before them. For them the only wisdom is what comes always too late, or too soon. Consalve has no sooner renounced love because of the universal betrayal of which he was victim than he falls in love with Zayde, a woman so totally unknown to him that he does not know what language she speaks. What wisdom should he draw from his previous experience—that love leads inevitably to betrayal? or the countermaxim of his previous error—that one must love only the unknown? Likewise the hero of *Zayde* shows a remarkable ability to neglect the tremendously rich contents of all the tales he hears "along the way" in his obsessive quest to learn the identity of Zayde's mysterious lover. For while Consalve goes forward seeking resemblance in a single character, the tales are all in some sense tales of resemblance and repetition in human passion.

The protagonists of both of Lafayette's novels are thus deliberately flawed interpreters moving through an enormous quantity of narration. This discontinuity between the internal narratives and the first-level narrative provokes commentary absent from the text. It creates discomfort at the lack of integration and calls for a voice that can englobe the two levels. It undermines, at the same time, the reader's confidence in the heroine's ability to learn from the narratives of others, for she can only use them, as she does in the Vidame de Chartres's case, to learn what she already knows.

This characteristic relationship of the protagonist to the internal narratives is one indication of a way in which the narrator also assigns a specific role to the reader of the novel. Faced with the protagonist's failure in *La Princesse de Clèves*—and in *Zayde*—to integrate the different levels of narration, the reader is called to perform that integration. The ironic reader thus projected by the text watches over the protagonist not merely with that superiority of knowledge supposed by any irony, but with a specific superiority in interpretation. Madame de Lafayette molds the reader by use of the inherent structural property of the traditional novella collection—its requirement of an active interpretive voice situated outside of each discrete narrative unit. She projects this role simultaneously upon the protagonist, who fails in this role, and upon the reader of the novel. The functioning, or dysfunctioning, of the protagonist determines therefore the functioning of the reader. In turn the protagonist is shaped by the specific problematic central to Lafayette's texts: the search for a principle of coherence in human affairs.

The search for this coherence is related, in the early pages of the novel, to a doctrine of language set forth in a brief account of the Princess's education:

> Mme de Chartres was of a contrary opinion. She often described love to her daughter. She showed her its pleasant side in order to persuade her more surely of the dangers that she taught. She told her about men's lack of sincerity, their deceit and their faithlessness, and about the conjugal unhappiness that affairs bring. And she showed her, on the other hand, the calm life that an honest woman has and how much virtue, combined with beauty and high birth, gives brilliance and distinction. But she also showed her how difficult it was to keep that virtue, attainable only by an extreme suspicion of oneself and by a great persistence in the only thing that can bring happiness to a woman—to love one's husband and to be loved by him.
>
> [Mme de Chartres avait une opinion opposée; elle faisait souvent à sa fille des peintures de l'amour; elle lui montrait ce qu'il a d'agréable pour la persuader plus aisément sur ce qu'elle lui en apprenait de dangereux; elle lui contait le peu de sincérité des hommes, leurs tromperies et leur infidélité, les malheurs domestiques où plongent les engagements; et elle lui faisait voir, d'un autre côté, quelle tranquillité suivait la vie d'une honnête femme, et combien la vertu donnait d'éclat et d'élévation à une personne qui avait de la beauté et de la naissance; mais elle lui faisait voir aussi combien il était difficile de conserver cette vertu, que par une extrême défiance de soi-même et par un grand soin de s'attacher à ce qui seul peut faire le bonheur d'une femme, qui est d'aimer son mari et d'en être aimée.] (p. 248)

Most mothers use silence where this mother uses speech, an antidote against the ignorance through which the daughter might succumb. The mother makes a description of love, *une peinture*, where she *shows* the pleasant and *shows* the dangerous. Her teaching is based on convincing the daughter of the reality of this vision of love, its correspondence to the world, and thus differs from a pedagogy based on the communication of an ideal, the revelation of a system of conduct deduced from otherworldly requirements. In other words, the mother chooses the method of example over the method of pure rule or discursive assertion. But by teaching in this way, by *showing*, the mother is teaching the heroine how to *see* what she is looking at, or how to *look at* what she sees. It is a lesson in how to draw from appearances a knowledge of what is.

Thus formed by her mother, the heroine of the novel becomes a figure of the interpreter, of the spectator-reader, just as the mother is a figure of the narrator-commentator. The mother shows her daughter pictures of the court; the narrator shows us pictures of the court. On both levels the showing takes the force of accentuated contrasts that break the smooth surface of normality. Just as the narrator, in the second sentence of the novel, introduces the most powerful woman at the court—Diane de Poitiers—as an exception to the rules of love, so the mother points toward the happiness of the woman who escapes the world dominated by masculine infidelity. In both cases the speaker is drawing attention to the exception. And in the doctrine of Madame de Chartres to see the world is to be able to interpret, to draw the norm even from images of the exception, to be suspicious of appearances as one is suspicious of the silence which allows a vision to exist without the interpretive discourse that redeems it. But the internal narrator is, according to the general narrator, already herself exceptional. Madame de Chartres is not a mother like the others. Is this the general narrator's way of disavowing the practice of Madame de Chartres as internal narrator? Or does the narrator instead point to the mother's successful escape from a tradition of silence?

From the beginning of *La Princesse de Clèves*, Lafayette creates a dynamic of the exceptional, where the energy of the narrative comes from failures of what is experienced to coincide with what is said about experience. The character of the heroine is, like us, the readers, one who tries to make from the succession of events a discursive coherence. And this effort or this function occurs according to the two directions indicated by the mother: along the axis of external empiricism (*le peu de sincérité des hommes*, etc.) and the axis of internal empiricism (*une extrême défiance de soi-même*).

Following this impulsion, the heroine must not accept silence but instead seek, invite, and appreciate the discourse of wisdom as it isolates and emphasizes examples of conduct. For she must know how the world *is*. But this knowledge will derive from the other characters' efforts to tell stories, to take appearances and give them the density of isolated, punctual events. Yet these events must also have the significance of iterative, hence recognizable patterns. An event, or the accumulation of actions and qualities attributed to a character in such a way as to constitute a "story," falls into the hands of others, so to speak, to become something that means (a signifier) and not just something meant (signified). But the second direction the heroine will follow, the axis that leads her toward suspicion of herself, is also the search of a signifier in something that, without the formation received from Madame de Chartres, she would have taken as a *signified*. She becomes a story for herself. She becomes able to compare what she finds in the stories of others with what she finds in herself. Just as the stories of the other characters—the internal narratives—must not simply remain there, inert and isolated, but must join together to say something about human nature, what the heroine sees in her own actions must say something about her own emotional state as it reflects collective human experience.

This suspicion of oneself not only grounds a way of reading oneself into the representations of the experience of others but creates a need for such representations.[21] For the internal doubling of the character of the Princess—the doubling created precisely by the doctrine of self-suspicion—makes it necessary to have a constantly renewed relationship with someone who can put into words the examples (thus *make* examples, since an example is not an example until it is selected and said as such) and with someone who can listen to the story of the Princess herself. To be virtuous according to Madame de Chartres's doctrine is to be engaged in a certain kind of discourse. Where other mothers imagine that silence suffices, the heroine's mother refuses silence, as her own role, and would refuse it to her daughter as well. She urges her daughter to "confide in her all the amorous advances men might make [lui faire confidence de toutes les galanteries qu'on lui dirait]" (p. 253). The first indication of her daughter's dangerous inclination for Nemours is, for the mother, that the Princess no longer speaks about what she is experiencing. "But," says the narrator, "Madame de Chartres saw it only too well" (p. 270).

The problems raised by the internal narratives can now be considered in the light of the heroine's role as internal audience, an audience that attempts to execute a particular interpretive program. Such a reconsideration reveals the narrator's implicit criticism of the mother's doctrine and clarifies the ironic role assigned to the reader of the novel. By having available within *La Princesse de Clèves* the centralizing and problematizing image of an audience, we can explore the significance of discrepancies and inconsistencies that to Valincour were only mistakes. For if Valincour can claim that the stories of Diane de Poitiers, Madame de Tournon, and Anne Boleyn are of no conceivable use, this is because he neglects the internal receiver of these narrations. Instead he is concerned only with the external receiver, the reader, and with this external reader's unmediated reaction to the internal narratives. But if we suppose, on the contrary, that the effort of making sense out of the internal narratives may have its own value, then we can overturn the whole perspective of reading that underlies Valincour's way of looking at the novel.

We have seen that the mother gives the heroine a certain key to the relationship between language and reality (i.e., human or courtier nature), between reality and conduct, between conduct and language. But in addition to giving this key to unlock the meaning of what she witnesses at court, the mother also gives an *example* by telling one of the internal stories. This is the story of Diane de Poitiers, mistress of François Ier and of Henri II. Diane de Poitiers is the first woman mentioned in the novel, the most powerful, and the one whose historical factuality is the most established. One would expect the story of Diane, as told by the mother-pedagogue, to be a mere demonstration (a mere "showing") of the generalities outlined in the mother's earlier presentation of the reality of life. But this story does something different.

The mother's narrative is provoked by two expressions of the daughter's belief about the reality of the court. The Princess was at that age "when one believes that a woman cannot be loved when she is over twenty-five" (p. 263), and she also believed that the Connétable de Montmorency was much loved by the Queen. The first of these expressions is based on a common opinion that conflicts with an observation: "[she] was astonished at the king's love for the duchess." The second error is based on an observation that the heroine believes without invoking the corrective knowledge of the Court. This error calls for the interpretive precept from Madame de Chartres: "If you judge by appearances in the court . . . you will often be wrong: what appears is almost never true" (p. 265).

Taken together the two errors call into question the mother's whole educational system. The story of Diane de Poitiers breaks down the wisdom of Madame de Chartres and forces her to admit something that is real even though it is not likely; it does not correspond to the models of human conduct that she had set forth:

It's true, she replied, that neither her qualities nor her faithfulness made the king fall in love with her nor do they keep his love alive. And that is why his passion is inexcusable. For if that woman were young and beautiful, in addition to being of high birth, and if she had merited his love by never having loved anyone else, and if she had been entirely faithful to the king, loving him only for himself and not for his power and his wealth, and if she had never made use of his power except for good reasons or ones pleasing to the king himself, one would have to praise the king for loving her. (p. 264)

Madame de Chartres judges this passion not in relationship to a utilitarian ethic—the happiness of the two lovers—or in terms of a Christian morality—for in this case no amount of merit on Diane's part would justify the adultery—but instead in terms of a code of the passions, which itself had been represented earlier as an *empirical discourse*. Madame de Chartres had already presented a conduct different from Diane's in the context of the representation of adulterous love and masculine conduct. She had *shown* her daughter the unhappiness that awaits any woman who participates in nonmarital passion. In attempting to correct the common but false conception held by her daughter— that a woman of Diane de Poitiers's age cannot count on the love of a man—Madame de Chartres must expose a fault in the discourse of wisdom earlier set forth. In this way an ethical fault (Diane's relationship with the king) becomes an *ontological* flaw: the *real* triumphs over the discourse that had tried to capture and limit it. This royal passion does not conform to the conditions abstracted from habitual courtly conduct, yet the king's passion *is* and endures. This is a case where appearance becomes one with being and thus escapes the corrective powers of language.

The second circumstance to call for this story about Diane de Poitiers is an exactly contrary error on the heroine's part: the queen's apparent friendship for the Connétable de Montmorency. In exordium, the mother presents the precept that what appears is almost never the truth, appearance is almost never joined with, or equal to, being. Only an instrument of translation furnished by the discourse of wisdom, by "what everyone should know," can allow one to pass from the appearance to being. The character who serves as the occasion and the illustration of the precept is queen *and* Italian, therefore, according to the common wisdom, both jealous *and* deceiving (pp. 241–42). Once one understands the codes of the court, one can easily interpret the gestures of the queen and of others. Here discourse and appearance correct each other mutually to provide a highly predictable reading of the court.

The internal narrative about Diane consecrates her as the paradigm of the exceptional. The king's love—as Madame de Chartres tells it— grows with age instead of declining. Those who try to tell the king of Diane's infidelities perish in the enterprise. Jealousy, "which is bitter

and violent in all other men, is sweet and moderate [in Henri II] because of the extreme respect that he has for his mistress." The Comte
de Taix, having informed the king of Diane's affair with Brissac, is
disgraced, removed from his post, and replaced by . . . Brissac!

This internal narrative therefore does not evidently reinforce the
mother's earlier lessons. It undermines, instead, her ethical and epistemological doctrines. A man can have a lasting passion: a woman's
fidelity and merit do not seem to be the only key to happiness; jealousy
can be *douce* (in a man, of course, seen from the feminine point of
view). All of this, as unlikely (*invraisemblable*) as it is, is real and apparent at the same time.

The story of Madame de Tournon and Sancerre follows quickly
upon the story of Diane de Poitiers. It is told by Monsieur de Clèves
who succeeds Madame de Chartres as teacher of the ways of the court
and later as confidant. This narrative pursues and complicates the
problematic of the story of Diane. Like Diane de Poitiers, Madame de
Tournon stands out from the rest of the court. She is distinguished by
her exemplarity. The Princess says that Madame de Tournon was "in
the entire court one of the people who appealed the most to me and
who seemed to have as much prudence as virtue" (p. 279). Madame de
Tournon, like Diane de Poitiers, has become a verbal figure inhabiting
the discourse of the court to such an extent that, as the Princess says
after her death, "I would have been affected by her death even if I had
not known her . . . " But while Diane represents the union of appearance and being in opposition to the doctrines of Madame de Chartres,
Madame de Tournon confirms the scission between the two but also
undercuts the corrective powers of language to read this duality and
thus to tame it. The epistemology of inversion is thus amply justified
but rendered useless. Where does one begin—with what appearances?
Known at first as the model of austere virtue by her absolute refusal of
love during her widowhood, she becomes, in a first reversal of this
appearance, the model of the woman as faithful and tender lover. This
is so much the case that the Prince de Clèves, once he has become
Sancerre's confidant, gives his wife the impression that there is no
woman at the court whom he esteems more than Madame de Tournon. Once more, however, that appearance is reversed to make Madame de Tournon the extreme model of the deceiving woman:
"Skilled dissimulation . . . could not reach a greater extreme" (p. 289).
Thus the model has been reversed, twice, and has become the symmetrical anti-model, each time outdistancing the powers of language
to separate truth from appearance and to integrate the examples thus
formed into its discourse of wisdom. Finally, however, at the moment

when the story of Madame de Tournon enters the text known as *La Princesse de Clèves*, it is fixed. It will not change anymore. Moreover, it is not we who have been deceived. We, the readers, learn of Madame de Tournon's exemplarity as virtuous widow by means of the same sequence of internal narrative that shows her to be the opposite. It is, rather, the bearer of the didactic message who admits to having failed in earlier descriptions of Madame de Tournon and the figure of the internal audience, the Princess, who admits to having been deceived by Tournon's reputation as a figure in the world of discourse that constitutes the court.

The problems of the discourse of wisdom intersect those of the narrative structure of the novel in a brief internal narrative that seems very different, at first glance, from the stories of Diane de Poitiers and Madame de Tournon. The episode of the king's horoscope (p. 296) might be quickly described as a means of preparing the major political event of the novel, the death of Henri II and its resultant redistribution of power, and of using this courtly matter as a background for the heroine's most urgent individual concern. Yet the story of the horoscope raises an epistemological problem common to all of these narratives—the problem of application or predictability. The other stories, including that of Marie de Lorraine told by Mary Stuart, are retrospective but hold forth the possibility of the repetition of a pattern (e.g., will Nemours's passion fade as does the Vidame's? does the physical resemblance between Marie de Lorraine and Mary Stuart portend resemblance in destiny?). The horoscope story, as told by the king, has a similar structure. The astrologer correctly identified the king from among the nobles present. Does this judgment that was retrospectively true lend weight to the astrologer's claim to tell the future?

The king's story occurs in a discussion about horoscopes. One part of the court shares the queen's opinion that horoscopes should be heeded. Another group takes the contrary view. The king sets forth his belief, which, like so much of the discourse of wisdom in Lafayette's works, is composed of two opinions occurring in temporal succession: " 'I used to be very curious about the future,' said the king, 'but I was told so many false and improbable things that I ended up convinced that we can't know anything true' " (p. 296). The prediction that he gives as an example sets a doctrine of verisimilitude—the belief in a certain set of norms or *apparences*—against the eventual truth of the novel. "There is little likelihood that I'll be killed in a duel," says Henri II. The king's opinion determines the opinion of the court: "Those who had defended astrology gave up and agreed that we should not believe in it."

This episode is extremely important for its display of the function of the discourse of wisdom. The oracular statement, a particularly banal motif of the baroque imagination, here serves as pretext for a three-fold criticism of the wisdom of the court. First, this discourse is shown to be connotatively determined. Proclaiming belief or disbelief in horoscopes is a way of declaring adherence to the queen's or to the king's faction. This connotative use is taken a step further by M. de Nemours in an aside to the heroine when he uses belief and disbelief to make an amorous declaration. Second, the discussion of the king's horoscope continues the schism between appearance (*vraisemblance*) and being (*vérité*) that haunts the discourse of wisdom. There seems to be little likelihood that Henri II will be killed in a duel. Such a conclusion is dictated by a whole complex of certainties, including the temperament of Henri II and the conventions of the period (i.e., a king does not have singular combat except with another king). Nonetheless, a seventeenth-century French reader knew, and any reader will know within a few pages, that the historical and novelistic truth will belie this initial probability. Finally, the discussion surrounding the king's horoscope undermines the value of collective wisdom, just as the astrologer's prediction in *Zayde* manifested the failure of "common sense." Not only does the consensus form for reasons that are connotative (or rhetorical) rather than denotative, but the constant reversal in the discourse of wisdom demonstrates its fragile and aleatory quality. Some courtiers believed in oracles; some did not. The king believed once; the king no longer believes. Consensus is formed around the king's negation of the value of oracles. The king and the consensus, however, are wrong. The king does die in a duel.

The case of the king's horoscope, like the story of Madame de Tournon, illustrates the failure of the courtly discourse of wisdom to contain reality within norms and examples. But there is still another much more important example of this failure: the Princesse de Clèves herself. The Princess is the object of attempts to contain her and her behavior in this discourse. Repeatedly the Princess is shown to act contrary to what the others consider normal. Even the mother, upon hearing that her daughter did not want to attend a certain ball, "argued for a while against her daughter's opinion, finding it unusual [*particulière*]" (p. 273). Later Mary Stuart tells the Princess how odd she is: "you are the only woman in the world who confides everything in her husband" (p. 327). Her husband uses her peculiarities as a guide to controlling her. As he says, "given your character, I confine you more by leaving you your freedom that I could by establishing rules" (p. 340). On another occasion the husband is offended by the Princess's refusal to see M. de

Nemours and says, "From someone like you, madame, everything is a sign of favor except indifference" (p. 362). The confession in the garden appears extraordinary to everyone, including the Princess herself. She points out to Clèves that hers is "A confession that has never been made to a husband" (p. 333), and he admits that her gesture is "the greatest proof of faithfulness that a wife has ever given her husband" (p. 334). The invisible spectator of this scene, Nemours, also finds the confession *extraordinaire* and has still more reason to consider the Princess "a woman so different from all those of her sex" (p. 337).

Given the repeated ability of the other characters and of the Princess herself to fit her into opinions of normality, one can perhaps best describe the Princess as a figure of rhetoric that runs against the discourse of wisdom as commonly practiced. This figure is the *paradox*, the paradoxa. Is there something about Lafayette's view of wisdom and its creation and transmission in language that lends itself to the construction of a text drawing its energy from this kind of continuing opposition? We could, of course, with Lukács speak of the ironic nature of the novel as genre. But the irony of *La Princesse de Clèves* is not simply the irony of the hero's ideal opposed to the hostile reality, but rather irony that has split the protagonist from her conception of herself and the world, and the world (the place of the discourse of wisdom) from itself and from her.

In the appeal to paradox as principal force of her rhetoric, Lafayette is far from isolated in her period. And as paradox, the heroine is not alone in the context of the novel, for there is another form that functions in a similar way: the *maxime*. There is nothing new in noting that such forms exist in Lafayette's novels. They have been noted in part because of the claims that La Rochefoucauld collaborated in the writing of the novel. One scholar has counted fifty-two utterances found in *La Princesse de Clèves* that might be considered maxims.[22] This listing highlights a tendency to place statements of abstraction in prominent positions in the novel. It thus emphasizes one of the aspects of the discourse of wisdom as practiced collectively at the court. But, in the type in which it comes to our attention in the seventeenth century—as the Rochefoucauldian maxim—the maxim is not simply a statement in the present tense made by an unnamed speaker and said of an impersonal or collective entity. It erupts, either from the unusual whiteness of the page of aphorisms or from within the discourse into which it does not recede. Its nature as the assertion of a generality upon which the reader must already have some opinion—*les hommes*, *l'amour*, *les femmes*, *la folie*, *la sagesse*—demands that it obtain either the assent or dissent of the reader. Yet its very impersonality, rather than inviting an indifferent, somewhat distant reaction from the reader, engages him, on the contrary, to react with violence in order not to yield to that lulling commonality of vision that pretends to include him. Unlike the proverb, to which it is often compared, the maxim is a polemical form. It sets up numerous dichotomies, one of which is between those who agree, the enlightened, and the others. The proverb, on the other hand, may simply have a phatic function or signal a non-divisive belonging to the largest collectivity.

Lafayette makes brilliant use of the dichotomous, paradoxical structure of the maxim. In *Zayde*, the maxim functions to manifest the disjunction between the characters' initial, faulty conception of human nature and their subsequent experience. But the structure of *Zayde* interests the reader of *La Princesse de Clèves* not so much because the hero-narrators proffer maxims or openly reject the maxims of others, but because the maxims introduce the larger factor of negation by which the plot echoes the maxim structure itself. While the heroes at first use the maxim to contradict the prevailing wisdom of the world of the novel, their narratives in turn contradict this initial assertion.[23]

In both *La Princesse de Clèves* and *Zayde*, the hero's conduct is set directly contrary to the wisdom of the other characters, and, at least in *Zayde*, the hero's action and/or utterance are formed by the negation of the societal discourse. In *Zayde* the protagonist's narration in turn disproves the protagonist's initial paradox, his initial stand against societal wisdom. The narrative seems to set the hero up in order to crush him in a literary gesture that confirms the totalizing power of societal discourse to contain all conduct within its norms.

In *La Princesse de Clèves*, however, the structure of paradox remains, and the heroine does not conform to the prevailing social norm. While it is true that the Princess fails utterly to attain the earthly happiness that seemed to be the goal of her mother's lesson, she does not, in an act of self-narration, confess her failure and accept the contrary wisdom. Instead, the final pages of the novel accentuate the problematic of the protagonist's deliberately inverted reading of the discourse of wisdom.[24] In these final pages, including the interview with Nemours, the recourse to schematic formulations (including maxims) increases but becomes interrogative. "But do men continue to love in a lasting relationship? [Mais les hommes conservent-ils de la passion dans ces engagements éternels?]," the Princess asks Nemours (p. 397). As it becomes more and more difficult to distinguish between narrative voice and indirect internal voice of the heroine, it also becomes more difficult to detect the closure that could mark the end of the balancing between different views of the heroine's ethical role (e.g., "a duty that exists only in my imagination" in contrast to "the strict rules that my duty imposes upon me") and of masculine nature. Only the intervention of a third force, illness, which modifies the point of view on earthly reality, breaking the repetitive pattern of example, allows an escape from this stalemate. But this ending is not a resolution of the established dynamics of the scission between the heroine and the discourse of wisdom. Neither the heroine nor the reader will find an answer to her question about Nemours's fidelity. We do not know whether he would be an exception, like Henri II, or would confirm the courtly norm, like the Vidame de Chartres. By the end of the novel the ability of the discourse of wisdom to set forth a representation of reality and to make a prescription for dealing with reality thus represented has been reduced virtually to an aporia.

Lafayette has broken the cycle of example. Her heroine has heard several stories about the past related in various ways to the future, that is, to the way things are supposed to happen again. She refuses, however, to enter into the cycle of example by choosing to illustrate in her own conduct either a confirmation or a challenge to a statement of general truth. With her move out of the courtly narrative, where the past and the present seem to mirror one another, she interrupts the series required for example. In a way, Lafayette has rephrased the problem that was so agonizing for the main characters of *Zayde*, the difficulty of attaching an image to the time-dominated world of act. When Consalve realized that he could not connect the image of the dead lover with the past, present, or future of a verbal statement (e.g., "She does not *have* a lover, but she *had* a lover," etc.), he discovered that even the most accurate likeness does not guarantee knowledge. Lafayette points to this general weakness in the European conception of the sign, and especially of example, at crucial moments of the novel. This is what is in question in the whole debate over the tense of the opening sentences of *La Princesse de Clèves*, as Valincour, at least in part, detected. Moreover, the link to *Zayde*, with its literal treatment of the problem of the image, is made by the term for the mother's stories about the court, "a painting" (*une peinture*).[25]

A painting exists in a form of perpetual present. But a painting is not the only kind of representation fixed in such a present.[26] The maxim is also proposed in the present tense and pretends to a universality that eliminates difference, both synchronic and diachronic. The characters in *Zayde* repeatedly set forth maxims allegedly valid for all time and every occasion. Even in the cases in which general statements are qualified so that they apply only to one character (for instance, Consalve's claims about his own nature and the necessary conditions for him to fall in love), those statements are made in the present tense and with reference to the future. These characters are not the only ones to confront the limitations of such general representation. In *La Princesse de Clèves*, the mother's lesson contains maxims that pretend to universal and permanent validity. Such maxims are supposedly grounded in the mother's depiction of the court and are condensed forms of that depiction, just as Alphonse's vaunted "knowledge of women" in *Zayde* was a composite "picture" of all the women he had known. When the Princess arrives at the crucial moment of seeing Nemours for the last time, she presents the limitation of maxims and, implicitly, of all representations that pretend to a supratemporal validity. She places the maxim about the infidelity of men in the interrogative: "Mais les hommes conservent-ils de la passion dans ces engagements éternels?" This maxim-turned-question directly poses the question of the temporality of the maxim and of the representations subsumed by it. The belief that a man is not able to continue to love a woman once the woman has "surrendered" to his pursuit is founded on the cumulative representation of male conduct.

The problem with this representation of a general nature, the maxim, is that it ignores differences in persons and times to produce an absolute truth. On the other hand, the partial representations on which it is based are, precisely, only partial. As *La Princesse de Clèves* and *Zayde* demonstrate repeatedly, passage from a partial, concrete representation to a general rule or from a general rule to a partial, concrete representation is an act of fiction. By attempting to tell in advance what Nemours will do, on the basis of his own earlier acts as represented in what is said about him at the court and of the maxim about male conduct, the Princess is doing what the characters of *Zayde* did: suppressing difference and assuming a perfect correspondence of maxim and example. This approach links the situations of Consalve and the Princess to the most ancient rhetorical assumptions. The past, says Aristotle in recommending the use of examples, tends to resemble the future.

In Lafayette's works, however, the Aristotelian rhetorical assumption is not accepted. The examples do not prove the rule, no more than the paintings provide union with being, with an affirmation about the nature of reality in time. A major irony of the novel is that at this moment Lafayette reminds us of the relationship between the *nouvelle* tradition and the rhetoric of instruction by example. Precisely the last clause of the text attaches the work as a whole to the tradition of the example conceived as model of conduct, while Lafayette bars that model: "her life, which was not long, left examples of inimitable virtue

[sa vie, qui fut assez courte, laissa des exemples de vertu inimitables]"
(p. 395).

In linking the term *inimitable* with *examples*, Lafayette combines a
reference to the search for a model of conduct with the contrary valorization, well-established in the example tradition, for the extraordinary and the uncommon. The Machiavellian insistence on acts that
leave *radi esempli*, few copies or imitations, likewise selectively emphasizes acts that exceed the ability of society to assimilate them. This
exaltation of the excessive is sometimes treated by readers of Lafayette's work as mere indulgence in a love for superlatives, in other
words, as a stylistic tic of little conceptual consequence. Yet, after seeing how example functions in several other early modern authors, we
can perceive the conformity of Lafayette's concluding sentence with
two characteristics of exemplary textuality. The word *example* appears
in the plural in her text, in keeping with its usually multiple textual
manifestation. The redundancy of examples points to a general statement capable of subsuming all of the instances. In this case the Princess's virtue is thus being attested. Second, the examples in question
are elliptical; they are not specified but only alluded to in all their latent
richness.

The crucial importance of this elliptical quality of *La Princesse de
Clèves* has only recently been described with theoretical and historical
rigor. Joan De Jean has demonstrated that Lafayette makes of ellipsis—
suppression of authorial identity, elimination of proper names at significant points in the text, the heroine's renunciation of the world of
the court—a mark of female self-assertion.[27] Ellipsis as it appears in De
Jean's study is a figure that appears at various levels and governs phenomena often described separately in such a way that the similarity and
interaction of these levels does not appear. For instance, the absence of
proper nouns would be assigned to stylistics while the study of the way
the heroine "elides" herself from the court at the end of the novel
would be attributed to narratology or psychology. By fitting these levels back together, De Jean is able to reveal a coherent strategy and to
account for the response of such contemporary readers as Valincour.
Of the problematic concluding sentence, the following remark is a key
to Lafayette's use of example:

> The very vocabulary with which the princess' gestures toward
> self-possession are characterized—"extraordinary," "singular,"
> "inimitable," "without precedent,"—signals Lafayette's fidelity to
> the ideals of her century's most powerful female voices. These
> hyperbolic affirmations of female superiority, of woman's ad-

vancement beyond previous norms and thereby outside narrative, are the language of *préciosité*, the exclusively female literary movement with which Lafayette was associated in her youth, whose adherents both lived apart from society and defined a separate space for *écriture féminine*.[28]

Far from being a "mere" stylistic habit, the concepts of exceeding or transcending the tradition of representation and the tradition of behavioral replication—imitation of conduct—unite in Lafayette's invocation of the concept of example at this culminating point of the text. Significantly the final examples of virtue, which the heroine left, are not specified in the text. They are what we have earlier referred to as elliptical examples, examples not less but perhaps even more forceful by their absence. Ellipsis, example, and paradox are thus the converging figures that describe the structure of Lafayette's work. The coherence of this concluding gesture might well be envied by other authors, like Descartes, whose *Discourse* is a useful point of comparison against which to appreciate the originality of Lafayette's exemplarity.

The *Discourse* is marked by the inability to reconcile exemplarity with the transference of responsibility and judgment to the reader, or in other words, the inability to shift between example as original, nonimitable transcendent event and example as copy of an already enacted event. Lafayette simply does not become involved in a politics of replication, as does Descartes. While Lafayette, like Descartes, rejects "what I learned only from example and custom," and while her protagonist also takes up a position outside the world of the court, Lafayette does not seek to establish the protagonist's act as a founding moment, an admirable eccentric act that justifies surrender to a model. This difference can be seen in the position of the example of retreat as gesture in the unfolding of the *Discourse* and of *La Princesse de Clèves*. The nameless protagonist of the Cartesian *Discourse* withdraws into his heated room to perform a Cogito, which is then published to the world in a fable. What had been a desired invisibility becomes a kind of theatrical spectacle, the heated room almost a stage on which our attention is focused to observe the intimate detail of the verbal and epistemological performance of discovery. Even if the retreat and the Cogito are not to be imitated, they confer an authority which legitimizes the subsequent "fruits" of the method and allows the author of the *Discourse* to codify the procedures of research over which he will preside, employing workers who "would do, in the hope of gain, which is a very effective motive, precisely what they were told."[29]

The Princess's retreat, with its elliptical examples, is the concluding moment of Lafayette's text and occurs at the end rather than close to the beginning as Descartes's retreat does. Rather than construct a new exemplarity to take the place of the failed exemplarity of history and observation of the world, Lafayette more consistently rejects the example/example, model/copy pair that had for two millenia constituted the basis of exemplary rhetoric. While Descartes effectively noted the alienation that occurs when a reader allowed the textual persona to dominate the reader to the exclusion of self-awareness, Descartes nonetheless ends by proposing an alienation consisting of subservience of worker to master. Lafayette remains faithful to the radical insight that so troubled Descartes.

Moving outside the politics and rhetoric of replication and predictability, Lafayette undercuts the association of example with the cyclical return of the past that Aristotle established as the basis for *paradeigma*. In the concluding sentence of her novel, Lafayette enunciates the most concise and radical doubt about the whole doctrine of exemplary instruction. In concluding upon the rhetorical procedure that had troubled, fascinated, and preoccupied some of the most innovative writers of the sixteenth and seventeenth centuries, Lafayette sets face to face the concepts of representation and imitation in her reference to these inimitable examples.

Thus the text concludes by underlining a disjunction between representation, bearer of examples, and the life of experience and action. The schism here displayed has appeared throughout *Zayde* and *La Princesse de Clèves*; it is latent in the term *imitation* itself, which straddles with difficulty two concepts. Imitation signifies, on the one hand, the representation of being in text (sometimes called *mimesis*) and, on the other, the representation of a text in our own being, in our ethical conduct (as in such expressions as *imitatio Christi* or *imitatio sanctorum*). In the former case (*mimesis*), the text becomes the model *of* reality; in the latter (imitation), the text becomes a model *for* reality. The heroine of *La Princesse de Clèves* witnesses the failure of this combined model, for the internal narratives do not support the unified theory of conduct presented by her mother. Her own actions run through the novel in contradiction to the norms of conduct that constitute the discourse of the court. With this sundering of discourse and experience, silence and retreat are the most coherent existential responses; the novel, not the *roman* or the traditional *nouvelle*, the most coherent literary response.

CONCLUSION

THIS STUDY has aimed to show that example is more than a minor "technical" feature of literary texts in French and Italian literature of the sixteenth and seventeenth centuries. Anyone who has followed this far will probably have been surprised at times by the entailments of example as they have been traced here, but I hope that the examples I have given have been persuasive and have permitted the kind of play between inside and outside views of example that Machiavelli, in his simile of the artist, describes as necessary for knowledge.

To claim a limit for example by arguing that it functions merely to alter the behavior of readers is to neglect its role of organizing a type of knowledge. Particularly in the major prose authors of the sixteenth and seventeenth centuries, example serves as an instrument for relating the individual to sources of authoritative knowledge. Both use of and reflection upon example, in the texts of this period, are especially interesting because of the crisis in this relationship. Without retracing the path through all the texts discussed above, it is worth pausing to emphasize the situation of early modern authors in respect to example. In the transition from heavy reliance on textual authority to emphasis on observation and introspection, both the role of the giver of an example and the role of the receiver change. Since the exemplary material—the source of concrete instances to support a general statement—must still be somehow available to the receiver as objective confirmation of the speaker's assertion, there is a shift from evidence from the past, available only in texts, to evidence from the present, visible in the everyday world. But this shift from past to present, though seemingly of secondary importance (after all, what does the source of evidence matter as long as the public is persuaded?), undermined example as the figure that tied past to future through the present. From Machiavelli to Lafayette there is an increasing doubt that what has happened before will necessarily happen again, a doubt given a peculiar twist by Descartes and Pascal. For them the repetition of the past in the future is not itself in question. But mere repetition, the iterativity of example, is split off from meaning, which is withdrawn from the outside world into the subjective realm.

At the same time, both the giver and the receiver of examples, confronted with a growing field from which example materials can be selected, are faced with the problem of determining whether any given example is actually applicable to them. The proliferation of potential examples parallels a growing autonomy of individuals, or at least a growing puzzlement as to the exact limits of the individual. This trend, strikingly embodied in Lafayette's works, has economic, broadly social, and religious foundations, but its outcome was to doom whole literary genres based on the categorization of persons within relatively rigid limits. The novella as practiced from the thirteenth to the sixteenth centuries thus yields to the novel. The commentary, which can still be seen as vestigial form in the *Essais*, yields to the discourse, as written by Descartes. Both of these broad and impressive generic shifts are related to the change in that sometimes unnoticed figure, the example.

Each of the authors discussed here not only used example but devoted much attention to its suppositions and effects. Over the century and a half from Machiavelli's work to Lafayette's, example declined as a source of knowledge and as a means of persuasion. Although this decline was already beginning in Machiavelli's work, by the mid-seventeenth century authors devoted more time explaining why example should be treated as mask and left to the people, than using example to convince the discriminating and coequal reader. The separation between discourse and example grew to the point at which example was no longer example, that is, no longer appearance subordinated to an explanatory and classifying statement. Such statements were still possible and, indeed, are present in the work of Descartes, Pascal, and Lafayette, but the speaker who can make them and fit them to the surrounding representations of the world retreats. The authority of general statement is no longer imposed on the world of historical appearance. Instead, general statements are merely juxtaposed to the "exemplary" material, offering the reader a choice of how to relate the two utterances. Machiavelli claimed to offer the Prince a distilled wisdom otherwise unavailable to him. Marguerite de Navarre cautioned readers against the snares of example, and Montaigne explored ways of withdrawing example from the historical domain and into a highly personal and subjective one, where the statement/example pair tilted decisively toward the speaker and away from the common ground of socially accepted objectivity. With Descartes, Pascal, and Lafayette the reader is shown a model of appearances next to which are general statements, but these statements are always separated in some way from the appearance that could substantiate it. The speaker (and the main character) of the texts of the seventeenth-century writers reach the extreme of retreat from the publically rhetorical situation in which example flourished in antiquity. They are themselves unconvinced by the positive inductive evidence around them.

The rise of irony and the appearance of the reader as free agent removed from example not only its imitative or injunctive force but even its role as embodiment of abstract truth. No longer part of a canon of exemplary passages or figures and broken off from practical rhetorical discipline, the literary example became an enigma and even an embarrassment to which criticism is only now beginning to respond.

Although the chapters above have related specific authors to problems of their time, the question remains why, in a general way, example should be such a preoccupation and a problem for writers of the early modern period. Burckhardt's classic description of Renaissance individualism, despite its optimistic approach, points properly in the direction of a crisis based on the important claims of individuals.[1] With the rise of individual figures as the center of learned attention comes a crisis in shared knowledge. The heroic individual must be separate from the mass, and the comments of Machiavelli, Montaigne, and Descartes stress that this status of exceptional power and knowledge is not a projection of the community but a calculating imposition by the successful individual. This isolation results in problems of discourse. Machiavelli's Prince, like Descartes's Philosopher-Methodologist, communicates with the multitude by gesturing toward shared external evidence, rendering visible a power that is latent or potential in him. Breaking away from a belief in the stable already-proffered appearances of the natural world—perhaps last represented in Raymond Sebond's *Natural Theology*, translated by Montaigne—the Prince and the Philosopher arrange and institute these appearances.[2] Whether staging a spectacular execution or merely counterfeiting the behavior and speech of those around them, such modern orators are themselves aware of the artifice required for using examples and framing them with appropriate language.[3] They also know, because they claim for themselves an exceptional status, that example is based on the exceptional and the rare—even though such categories are the artificial result of the creation of economies and rules in discourse.

Against the background of these affirmative users of example stand the skeptics, who are just as cognizant as the Prince and the Philosopher of the unstable basis of appearance but who draw more radical conclusions. For the theologically inclined current, from Marguerite de Navarre through Pascal and Lafayette, the discourse of salvation renders vain and useless a rhetorical figure based on external appearance and external works. Meditation on such appearances can only be a preparation for surrender to a "higher law" beyond the undecidability of experience. Whether this appeal to an invisible force be called grace, wager, or retreat, it marks the withdrawal of the Logos from worldly phenomena.[4]

With the rise of a scientific discourse at the end of the seventeenth century, example will blend into the general inductive trend of thought, and many of the doubts of the early modern literary culture will fade—perhaps too easily. The acceptance of language claiming to be based on a direct representation of empirical reality is nothing but a return to the naïve belief in the neutrality of example, a neutrality that explains its separation from studies of figural rhetoric. While simile and metaphor have been seen as inventive and worthy of study, example has assumed an innocence at radical variance from the rhetorical awareness of early modern Europe.

1. *Novantiqua*, chap. 2, "The Commonplace as the Common Place," pp. 19–60.

INTRODUCTION

1. Du Cange, *Glossarium* 3:356–58. The second of the three definitions of *exemplum* given is, "The same as *exartum, essartis* [French *essarts*]; woods or brush cleared for cultivation."

2. Cf. Jonathan Culler's comment, "Any figure can be read referentially or rhetorically. 'My love is a red, red rose,' tells us, referentially, of desirable qualities that the beloved possesses. Read rhetorically, in its figurality, it indicates a desire to see her as she is not: as a rose . . ." ("Prolegomena to a Theory of Reading," in Suleiman and Crosman, *The Reader in the Text*, p. 65). Richard A. Lanham more prudently observes, "The Western self has from the beginning been composed of a shifting and perpetually uneasy combination of *homo rhetoricus* and *homo seriosus*, of a social self and a central self" (*The Motives of Eloquence*, p. 6).

3. Most notably the studies of Derrida; La Capra ("Reading Exemplars: *Wittgenstein's Vienna* and Wittgenstein's *Tractatus*," in *Rethinking Intellectual History*, pp. 84–144); Stierle ("L'Histoire comme exemple, l'exemple comme histoire"); Suleiman ("Le Récit exemplaire"); Gélas ("La Fiction manipulatrice"); Warminski ("Reading for Example"); Regosin ("Le Miroüer Vague"); Gelley ("Frame, Instance, Dialogue"); Struever ("Pasquier's *Recherches de la France*"); and principal sections of the International Association for Philosophy and Literature devoted to example in 1986 and 1988 (not published).

4. One indication of the lack of interest in example as rhetorical figure is the absence of an entry for *example* in indexes and word-lists of contemporary treatises. Siegel's *Rhetoric and Philosophy*, for instance, has entries for such items as *metaphor, imitation, induction*, and *negation*, but not for *example*. Similarly Rice and Schofer's *Rhetorical Poetics*, Fontanier's *Les Figures du discours*, Winterowd's *Rhetoric: A Synthesis*, Dupriez's *Gradus*, etc., all lack entries for *example*. The *Princeton Encyclopedia of Poetry and Poetics* does have an entry for *exemplum*, though in the limited sense discussed below. Lanham's *A Handlist of Rhetorical Terms* also has an entry for *exemplum*, properly defined as equivalent to *paradeigma*, but no entry for *example*. Barthes, in "L'Ancienne Rhétorique," provides entries on *exemplum, imago*, and *argumentum* (pp. 200–201). Curiously—and, given Barthes's self-consciousness, no doubt deliberately—on these very pages Barthes contrasts the terms *exemplum* and *exemple* without indicating whether the ancient figure was related to the modern figure (e.g.,

p. 200), note "Exemple d'*exemplum* donné par Quintilien . . ."). The treatises that specify *example* as a topic or index entry, like Miller et al., in *Readings in Medieval Rhetoric*, are decidedly in the minority. A notable exception is the work of Perelman and Olbrechts-Tyteca, including their *The New Rhetoric*. In spite of their work, *example* has practically no standing in contemporary rhetoric, especially in any application to literary texts.

5. *Rhetoric* 2.20.1394a. For Aristotle's *Rhetoric*, I have used two editions: *Rhétorique*, ed. and trans. Médéric Dufour; and *The "Art" of Rhetoric*, ed. and trans. John Henry Freese (Loeb Classical Library). Subsequent references to Aristotle's *Rhetoric* are from the Loeb Classical Library edition.

6. White, *Tropics of Discourse*, p. 91.

7. White, only a few pages from the passage establishing a certain equivalency between historical narrative and metaphor, writes, "Now, I am not interested in forcing the analogy between psychotherapy and historiography; I use the *example* merely to illustrate a point about the fictive component in historical narration" (White, *Tropics of Discourse*, p. 87, emphasis mine). It is ironic that White should so neglect example, given that he contributes a concept that may prove useful in the study of example, the "hypotactical." White's conception of the "hypotactical" as a discourse about reality that is "conceptually overdetermined," and hence opposed to the "paratactical" as the "conceptually underdetermined" (p. 4), leads toward "example," which is the extreme case of hypotaxis. Although many discourses may purport to represent reality while in fact using that representation to express patent doctrinal or ideological conceptions, example appears in discourse explicitly and—ostensibly, at least—solely to support a certain conception. The ideal example would present an overdetermined view of reality by controlling every element of that view so that there was no "excess" or leftover reality that did not fit the conception presented.

8. *De inventione* 1.19, ed. H. M. Hubbell (Loeb Classical Library).

9. Quintilian also makes this tripartite division (*Institutio oratoria* 2.4, ed. H. E. Butler [Loeb Classical Library]).

10. "*Simile* has a force not unlike that of *example*, more especially when drawn from things nearly equal without any admixture of metaphor [Proximas exempli vires habet similitudo, praecipue illa, quae ducitur citra ullam translationum mixturam ex rebus paene paribus]." Quintilian contrasts this quasi-exemplary simile with the nonexemplary simile equivalent to the Greek *parabole*, translated by Cicero, he notes, as *collatio*. This nonexemplary simile consists of such comparisons as the members of a body to the parts of a society.

11. *Inst.* 12.4.

12. "Every artificial proof consists either of indications [*signa*], arguments, or examples," Quintilian writes (*Inst.* 5.9). At first the distinction might lead one to suppose that examples are necessarily narrative in form, whereas indications are not. But the usefulness of the indication or sign is for proving a single case by an observation not especially applicable to other cases, whereas the example, for Quintilian, transcends the immediate or synchronic situation

to create a diachronic historical series. An indication would be the use of a "bloodstained garment, a shriek," etc., says Quintilian, to prove a crime. As *signum* (Greek *semeion*) this type of proof is still artful or technical—and therefore interesting for rhetorical theory—because there is still room for argumentative maneuver. The bloodstain does not necessarily indicate a crime; it could result from a nosebleed. This distinguishes the *signum* from the *signum insolubile* (Greek *tekmerion*), which is an incontrovertible indication of a fact leaving no room for dispute or interpretation and hence of no interest for the rhetorician (*Inst.* 5.9).

13. "With regard to rumour and common report, one party will call them the verdict of public opinion and the testimony of the world at large; the other will describe them as vague talk based on no sure authority, to which malignity has given birth and credulity increase, an ill to which even the most innocent of men may be exposed by the deliberate dissemination of falsehood on the part of their enemies. It will be easy for both parties to produce precedents to support their arguments [*Exempla utrinque non deerunt*]" (*Inst.* 5.3).

14. Cf. Battaglia's summary of the situation of example in Roman rhetoric. Noting that Quintilian uses *exemplum* to mean both *parabole* and *paradeigma*, he notes, "I Romani hanno quasi tutti preferito il termine *similitudine* o *comparazione*, che in greco corrisponde propriamente a *parabola*, e chiamano *esempio* ciò che si fonda sul vero e sull'accaduto, che in greco si dice *paradigma*" (*La coscienza letteraria del Medioevo*, p. 458). Battaglia traces Quintilian's role in establishing example as a unifying concept for subsequent rhetoric. Although the division into such figures as *historia, argumentum*, and *fabula* persists through the Middle Ages, many different strands are most frequently woven together in what will globally be called *exemplum*. See Battaglia, *La coscienza letteraria del Medioevo*, p. 473.

15. The single most substantial study of *exemplum* remains Welter's *L'Exemplum dans la littérature religieuse et didactique du moyen âge*. The earliest use of *exemplum* as a term of vernacular literary criticism or history that I have been able to locate in Welter's work is by Paul Meyer in 1889 (quoted by Welter, p. 1), followed by Crane in 1890. Welter, after noting that everyone who studies the *exemplum* gives his own definition, adds to this series by proposing the following: "Par le mot *exemplum*, on entendait, au sens large du terme, un récit ou une historiette, une fable ou une parabole, une moralité ou une description pouvant servir de preuve à l'appui d'un exposé doctrinal, religieux, ou moral" (p. 1). Welter's wisdom in providing such a broad definition is not usually followed by subsequent writers. Most striking is Welter's proper reluctance to define *exemplum* (1) as having an exclusively narrative form (he includes descriptions); (2) as proposing a model for direct imitation (he merely stipulates that the *exemplum* support a statement or *exposé*); and (3) as being concerned exclusively with ethical instruction (he includes doctrinal and religious statements as well).

16. One reason for appealing to the term *exemplum* with caution is that scholars who have dealt at length with the history of the *exemplum* are, in gen-

eral, little inclined to see it as a stable generic entity. The major popularizer of the concept of the *exemplum* in English-language criticism was Crane in his anthology, *The Exempla or Illustrative Stories from the Sermones Vulgares of Jacques de Vitry* (1890). Crane, however, points out the broad range of meanings assumed by the word *exemplum*, even in the clerical milieu:

> The word *exemplum* is employed by the ecclesiastical writers in two meanings, first our "example" in a general sense; second, an illustrative story. This second meaning of the word is, I think, not earlier than the end of the twelfth or the beginning of the thirteenth century. The two meanings of the word may easily be confused, and give rise to incorrect inferences, as, for instance, where Gregory in one of his homilies . . . says: "Sed quia nunnunquam mentes audientium plus exempla fidelium quam docentium verba convertunt" [But because sometimes the examples of the faithful affect the minds of the listeners more than the words of the teachers do]. This passage was later taken as an authority for the use of *exempla* in the restricted sense of illustrative story. (Crane, p. xviii, note)

Crane points out that the habit of anthologizing *exempla* from popular sermons is not founded on a strict definition of *exemplum*, for such a definition did not exist. Makers of the *exempla* collections choose widely different materials: "Sometimes moral reflexions, etc., are considered *exempla*, and sometimes mere references to biographical or historical fact are so treated" (Crane, p. xlvii). Some collections are made of narrative material without discursive or commentative text. In this case the surface structure of the text considered an *exemplum*, and even its illustrative purpose, varies greatly: "the *exemplum* was a story which had no independent value, and was usually given in a very concise form to be expanded at the preacher's will" (Crane, p. lxxx).

The more recent and more systematic inventory of *exempla* made by Tubach pushes even further the questioning of what constitutes an *exemplum*, to the point that even Crane does not escape the accusation of having elevated heterogeneous material to the status of a genre. The *exemplum*, in Tubach's treatment, becomes a narrative unit of widely varying form, which is subjected to a common rhetorical purpose:

> Divergent as this material may be in its content and origin, the exemplum is an attempt to discover in each narrative event, character, situation or act a paradigmatic sign that would either substantiate religious beliefs and Church dogma or delineate social ills and human foibles. (Tubach, *Index exemplorum*, p. 523)

With such a definition, under which *any* narrative can be considered an *exemplum* if it is interpreted in certain ways, it is not surprising that Tubach's primary difficulty in compiling his *Index exemplorum* was finding grounds for exclusion of narrative material. His inventory reveals what narrative materials preachers used, without regard to formal distinctions or even to distinctions of content.

More recently and still more radically, Vitale-Brovarone has attacked the very possibility of providing a definition for the medieval *exemplum*. "Non è possibile," he writes, ". . . definire . . . tipologicamente il 'vero' *exemplum*, a meno che non si voglia introdurre una *fictio* di procedura metodologica" ("Persuasione e narrazione," p. 95). Refusing any evolutionary definition of the *exemplum*, he evokes the great adaptability of *exemplum*, "una variatissima possibilità di adattamento . . . una gamma di virtualità che possono realizzarsi in qualsiasi momento," and warns against the creation of a provisional definition of *exemplum* in view of the danger of such provisional definitions solidifying into permanent ones (as in the case of Bédier's definition of the *fabliau*), pp. 95–96. Geremek also comments, "Sur le plan typologique, les *exempla* montrent une immense diversité. On y voit des légendes, des contes orientaux, des récits miraculeux, des fables antiques, des récits conventuels, des anecdotes, des récits bibliques et des paraboles, des miracles, des observations qui relèvent de l'histoire naturelle, des narrations mythologiques" ("L'*Exemplum*," p. 177). This recognition of the nongeneric quality of *exemplum*, the inability to furnish a typology, has the practical effect, according to Vitale-Brovarone, of obliging the critic to use different approaches according to the different form that the *exemplum* assumes—narrative analysis when the *exemplum* is narrative, cultural anthropology when the *exemplum* is formed of comparisons with objects, animals, etc. In this broad vision of *exemplum* even the consecrated link between *exemplum* and narrative is called into question: "Ho già detto sopra quanto poco mi senta incline a vedere nella narrazione esemplaria il solo *exemplum* a pieno titolo, e quanto invece senta la mancanza di una documentazione più completa della altre forme esemplarie (iconografiche, drammatiche, gestuali ed altre) che svolgono, a mio giudizio, la stessa funzione" (p. 108).

17. apRoberts, "Exemplum," p. 264. apRoberts continues: "The term is applied chiefly to the stories used in medieval sermons, though the illustrative anecdote is still, perhaps, the commonest feature of public speaking. Chaucer's *Pardoner's Tale* furnishes an example; not only the main story but many lesser narratives are used as *exempla* of the Pardoner's text." This entirely typical definition (apRoberts is not to be faulted for any of its contradictions, for he provides an exact description of usage), on the one hand, limits the use of the term *exemplum* to illustrations of a *moral* point, without accounting for the illustration of other points, while, on the other, it extends the term to cover "illustrative anecdotes" in modern as well as medieval usage. Presumably, therefore, illustrations of nonmoral points are not *exempla* but merely "examples." The definition continues by giving an "example" in Chaucer, but this example is presumably not, in apRoberts's text, an *exemplum*.

18. The eminent Ernst Robert Curtius did little to dispel the confusion. He wrote: "Like the *sententiae*, the examples of human excellence and weakness that the Middle Ages found in antique authors served it for edification. *Exemplum* (*paradeigma*) is a technical term of antique rhetoric from Aristotle onwards and means 'an interpolated anecdote serving as an example.' A different form of rhetorical *exemplum* was added later (*ca.* 100 B.C.), one which was of great importance for after times: the 'exemplary figure' (*eikon, imago*), i.e., 'the

incarnation of a quality': 'Cato ille virtutem viva imago' " (*European Literature*, pp. 59–60). Curtius's representation of Aristotle's *paradeigma* is a tendentious retrospective harmonization of the ancient with the medieval practice. Aristotle does not define example as an interpolated anecdote. The basic definition of *exemplum* that Curtius gives, however, receives such wide approval that certain scholars now make generic comparisons between the *exemplum* and other "genres" without feeling the need to provide any definition of this genre.

19. Cottrell, *Sexuality/Textuality*, p. 58: "An *exemplum* is in fact a literary genre that is based on the adage, the *sententia*, the maxim, the common place, which in the Renaissance was a subliterary genre—more a device than a genre, really—that was intended to communicate commonly held values and to transmit culture." Regosin has also significantly widened the scope of *exemplum* by treating it as example in the full sense ("Le Miroüer Vague," pp. 73–86).

20. The use of the term *exemplum* seems appropriate in two circumstances: when it is defined as heuristic instrument of literary analysis and when *exemplum* is a verifiable discursive practice of a specific, and most often chronologically limited, textual tradition. A transtextual and transtemporal consistency cannot be presumed for the term *exemplum*, even though, in dealing with certain specific texts, the knowledge of a circumscribed canon of *exempla* is necessary to appreciate intertextual gestures.

21. Du Cange, *Glossarium* 3:356–58. The second of the three definitions of *exemplum* given is, "The same as *exartum, essartis* [French *essarts*]; woods or brush cleared for cultivation."

22. *Paradeigma* is associated with *eikon* etymologically in Greek, but this association does not come to the fore in Aristotle's discussions of *paradeigma*.

23. It is highly appropriate that *exemplum* should, in its career in late antiquity, assume the sense of image, picture, thus rejoining its Greek counterpart in emphasizing visibility.

24. Du Cange gives several citations of *exemplum* used to denote pictorial representation. These include two quotations from a letter of Anastasius to Leo III, concerning images in marble inlay in pavement, "Et in pavimento marmoreis Exemplis stratis . . ." Du Cange refers to a treatise in which the layering or covering (*stratus*, from *sterno*) of floors with images (*exemplis*) is discussed with reference to Greek usage. Thus *exemplum* is related specifically to visual representation, and it seems significant that the *exemplum* is inlaid into a larger setting. It is a detail of decoration just as it is, in discourse, a detail brought forth from one context into a new, argumentative one. Moreover, the force of marble images presents an aspect of what one could call the rhetoric of pictures, since it concerns the effect of the image on its viewer. Marble images can be expected to have a certain authority as well as longevity; their durability gives them the power of what is handed down literally *in stone*.

25. Among the early medieval definitions cited by Vitale-Brovarone is the following significant one from the *Ars grammatica* (3.3) of Carisius: "paradigma est enarratio exempli vel rei praeteritae relatio significans adhortationem vel dehortationem [paradigma is the narration of example or the reference to an

event of the past signifying urging towards or urging against]." As Vitale-Brovarone observes, "Non pare un'alternativa sinonimica ma una vera e propria distinzione fra due campi precisi, vale a dire quello della *res praeterita* che ha il suo vigore . . . nell'autorità dei *maiores* . . . e il campo dell'*exemplum*, che non trae autorità da una *res praeterita* in quanto tale, ma da un suo valore esemplare intrinseco, tale da dover essere narrato (*ennaratio exempli*) piuttosto che riferito o allegato (*rei praeteritae relatio*)" ("Persuasione e narrazione," p. 98).

26. Geremek sees an evolution of exemplum away from the function of example (in the sense of pattern of ethical perfection) during the course of the thirteenth century itself. This evolution produced, in Geremek's view, a complex narration of human destinies, where attention is given to the psychology of the individual and to the social situation ("L'*Exemplum*," p. 157).

Many narrations used in sermons were apparently not directed at illustrating the points of morality or faith that were the overall purpose of the sermon, but were aesthetic interludes intended to win the audience's good feeling—*captatio benevolentiae*—or simply to wake them up. Jacques de Vitry, in the preface to his *Sermones vulgares*, describes the purpose of such narration: "With these, for the most part, popular examples [*vulgaria exempla*] should be interspersed to stimulate and amuse the laity, that they may have some edification; perhaps it will be objected that it was prophesied: 'they have told me evil stories [*fabulationes*], but not according to your law . . .' Believe on the basis of experience: sometimes when I was drawing out the sermon and have seen more of the people bored and sleepy, with one little word all have been awakened and given renewed interest for listening. For example [*exempli gratia*] once I remember having said, 'That man sleeping over there will not reveal my secrets or my plan.' Everyone, thinking that I meant him, opened his eyes, and, once the hubbub died down, they listened in attentive silence to serious words: 'Wisdom therefore is justified by her children' " (Crane, pp. xli–xlii, note, and xlii–xliii, note). Vitry returns often to the rhetorical purpose of *fabulosis exemplis* and their effect on a congregation of lay persons and simple persons, insisting that such *exempla* are not only for edification but for recreation—"non solum ad edificationem sed ad recreationem, maxime quando fatigati et tedio affecti incipiunt dormitare" (Crane, p. xlii, note).

27. See Gilmore, *Humanists and Jurists*.

28. Olschki writes, "Together with the quotation of classical authors, the allegation of examples became one of the most current and abused elements of the humanistic style. It had its justification in the general inclination to avoid abstract generalities and to embody ideas and ideals in living symbols and impressive personifications" (*Machiavelli the Scientist*, pp. 43–44).

29. The whole realm of Renaissance imitation theory as influence on writing is so large a topic that it must be studied separately from example as rhetorical device.

30. Kahn, p. 9. Or, as Montgomery puts it, "The most persistent aim of poetry [in the Renaissance] was understood to be an influence over audience behavior . . ." (*The Reader's Eye*, p. 181).

31. Polydore Virgil, *De rerum inventoribus* (1499), 1.10 (p. 29).

32. Weinberg, in his *History of Literary Criticism*, comments on the Platonizing interpretations of Aristotle (pp. 59–60). Noting elsewhere the difficulty of distinguishing Horatian and Platonic versions of poetics in the Renaissance vulgate, Weinberg writes of sixteenth-century critics of Dante: "When . . . vaguer reference is made to pleasure and utility, with little specification of the latter or with a simple indication that moral examples are provided, then a Horatian system seems to be involved. Perhaps, also, the great concern over the audience, not only in the early but also in the later period, betrays a predominantly Horatian and rhetorical orientation. For a number of critics wishing to judge the *Divina Commedia*, it becomes imperative to decide whether the audience is made up of the masses or of an élite . . ." (p. 874). This concern with the difference between a popular or an elite audience is bound up with the long-standing belief that examples are a particularly popular, or vulgar, figure of thought.

33. Weinberg, *History of Literary Criticism*, p. 36. Emphasis mine.

34. One of the simplest declarations of the immediately imitable quality of literary example is made by Orazio Toscanella, writing in 1562 on the purpose of comedy: "La Comedia primieramente fù ritrovata, accioche le persone moderassero i loro desiderii con lo essempio di altri, & si facessero migliori" (quoted in Weinberg, *History of Literary Criticism*, p. 167). Similarly Leonard Salviati, in the *Infarinato secondo* (1588), declares in defense of *Orlando Furioso*: "E in che altro, che nell'*esemplo* consiste il profitto dell'Epopeia? E à che altro, che all'esemplo, che debba trarsene dagli ascoltanti, risguardano gli ammaestramenti, e le leggi della bontà del costume nelle poesie introdotto?" (cited in Weinberg, *History of Literary Criticism*, p. 1041).

35. The concept of decorum needs no extensive documentation here. A typical case is the simplified poetics of example presented by Andrea Menechini in his *Delle lodi della poesia, d'Omero, et di Virgilio* (1572). Weinberg summarizes Menechini's position: "Examples of these kinds are deduced from the actions narrated by the poet, which are much more effective than those told by the historian since they are relieved of dross and imperfection" (*History of Literary Criticism*, p. 191).

36. One paraphrase of Aristotle's *Poetics* therefore notes this departure from the rule of verisimilitude: "Although characters are to be portrayed as similar, nevertheless it is necessary, like the painters, to add something to them [*addere illis aliquid*], each in its own kind, whether the poet imitates good or less good characters . . . so that they may appear as examples [*specimen*] of the virtues and the vices" (Ellebodius, *In Aristotelis librum de poetica paraphrasis* [ca. 1572, manuscript], quoted by Weinberg, *History of Literary Criticism*, p. 523).

37. Kibédi-Varga, *Rhétorique et littérature*, p. 130.

38. Furetière gives a series of more detailed definitions with greater distinction among different meanings. His first definition, "Modèle de conduite; action vicieuse ou vertueuse qui est proposéé à imiter," is similar to the Academy's, but with emphasis on the action rather than the decorum of its selection.

His second definition at first seems to be a neutral rhetorical/dialectical one: "Comparaison qui aide à concevoir, à imaginer." The kind of conception that he uses to illustrate example, however, returns to the authoritarian: "Quand on veut instruire par des paroles, le chemin est long, il est bien plus court par les exemples. On dit, Faire un exemple sur des gens de neant; pour dire, en punir quelques-uns des moins considerables, pour porter exemple aux autres." Furetière continues with two strictly pedagogical definitions; *exemple* is used to signify a line of writing for pupils to imitate and also to signify the copies that the pupils make (in these senses, *exemple* is feminine in grammatical gender). Richelet, in 1706, gives definitions similar to Furetière, with the addition of an explicit recognition that example is a rhetorical figure, "*Exemple . . .* Terme de *Rhétorique.*"

When the Academy defines the adjective *exemplaire* (exemplary), it strongly implies the quality of example as ideal model: "EXEMPLAIRE adj. de tout genre. Qui donne exemple, qui peut estre proposé pour exemple. *Vertu, piété exemplaire, vie exemplaire, chastiment exemplaire.*"

Cotgrave's French-English dictionary has few surprises in its definition of the constellation of terms relating to example: "Exemple: m. *An example, sample, patterne, or president* [sic] *to follow; a copie, or counterpane of a writing; one thing alledged to prove, or inforce, another that resembles it.*" But in the translation from English to French, there is a significant addition: "An Example. *Exemple, exemplaire; Monstre.* To take example by. Patronner." The French word *monstre* introduces the visual character of example while at the same time preserving the link between "spectacle" and "monster." The words *monstre* and *montre* are in turn translated back into English: "Monstre: m. A monster; a deformed creature; a thing thats [sic] fashioned or bred contrarie to nature," and "Montre: f. A patterne, scantling, proofe, example, essay; also, a muster, view, shew or sight; the countenance, representation, or outward appearance of a thing; a demonstration; also, a watch or little clock that strikes not; also the glass box that stands on the stalls of Goldsmithes, Cutlers, & c; and generally, any thing that shewes, or points at another thing; whence. *La monstre d'un horologe.* The hand of a clocke. *La monstre d'un maquignon de chevaux.* The place wherein a horse-scourser shewes his commodities." Although the entries for *montre* and *monstre* are separate, the word *montre* is given as *monstre,* indicating that they are actually homonyms at the time. This kinship has important consequences for the description of example in the sixteenth and seventeenth centuries, and especially for Montaigne.

39. *De copia* or *De duplici copia verborum ac rerum commentarii duo,* translated into English by Betty I. Knott as *Copia: Foundations of the Abundant Style,* is included in *Collected Works of Erasmus,* ed. James K. McKonica *et al.* (Toronto: University of Toronto Press, 1978).

40. Cave, *The Cornucopian Text,* especially chap. 1, "Copia," pp. 3–34. Cave retraces this preoccupation to Quintilian, *Inst.* 10, where the amassing of material is treated (pp. 126ff.).

41. For broad yet detailed consideration of imitation theory in the Renais-

sance, see Greene's *The Light in Troy*. Greene considers the doctrine of "extraction" of models in ancient theory in chap. 4, "Themes of Ancient Theory," especially pp. 62ff.

42. Machiavelli, *Opere*, ed. Ezio Raimondi, p. 5. The relevant passage from Erasmus reads: "Itaque studiosus ille velut apicula diligens, per omnes auctorum hortos volitabit, flosculis omnibus adsultabit, undique succi nonnihil colligens, quod in suum deferat alvearium. Et quoniam tanta est in his rerum foecunditas, ut omnia decerpi non possint: certe praecipua deliger, & ad operis sui structuram accomodabit" (*De utraque verborum ac rerum copia*, in *Opera Omnia*, p. 271).

43. The borderline status of these texts in respect to the "traditional" or respected textual genres is not surprising when one considers that example is on the borderline of disciplines and textual traditions since classical antiquity. Battaglia notes of example/*exemplum* in the Middle Ages that it depicted what the literature of "genres" and of "schools" did not permit. Example thus constitutes what Battaglia calls a "subliterature" or *sottoletteratura* (*La coscienza letteraria del Medioevo*, p. 481).

44. "Le Récit exemplaire." A complete reversal of this point of view appears in Perelman and Olbrechts-Tyteca, who divide the "resort to the particular case" into example, illustration, and model (*The New Rhetoric*, pp. 350ff). In their terminology only the model is used to influence conduct by encouraging imitation.

45. The choice of parable as starting point for the study of example leads to many problems. Chief among these is the allegorical nature of most parables. Short of equating example and allegory, most New Testament parables would fail to qualify as example because of their replacement of the literal sense of their constitutive terms.

46. "La fonction de ces fables n'est donc nullement de communiquer des valeurs qui puissent servir à construire une éthique (ou même une pragmatique) mais simplement de dépeindre, sans illusions, le monde comme il va" ("Le Récit exemplaire," p. 483).

47. "La Fiction manipulatrice."

48. "Ce qu'implique l'*exemplum* (ce à quoi il introduit) n'est pas seulement ou pas prioritairement une règle, mais la croyance en ce que son rapport à la règle est exactement celui qui articule une manifestation anecdotique à une vérité transcendantale. En ce sens, il n'y a d'exemplarisation possible que sur le fond d'un accord sur une *théorie de la manifestation* qui est aussi bien la théorie d'une lecture" (p. 82).

49. "Coupé de toute possibilité de formuler un judgment de vérité . . . amené à délaisser la situation initiale pour focaliser sa performance interprétative sur la seule histoire rapportée . . . contraint, enfin, à admettre implicitement l'adéquation de cette histoire à une règle d'action" (p. 84).

50. In this respect example shares with quotation, and particularly with "pseudo-quotation," the distancing of its content from the rest of the text. In quotation this distancing changes the enunciator; in example there is a change

in the level of concreteness (from the general to the particular) or a movement from like to like (from the story of one prince to the story of another prince, etc.).

51. The *OED* divides its definition of example into closely related meanings: 1) "A typical instance; a fact, incident, quotation, etc. that illustrates or forms a particular case of; a general principle, rule, state of things, etc.; a person or thing that may be taken as an illustration of a certain quality." 2) "(Logic) . . . The species of argument in which the major premiss of a syllogism is assumed from a particular instance." 3) "A signal instance of punishment intended to have a deterrent effect; a warning, caution; a person whose fate serves as a deterrent to others." 4) "A parallel case in the past." 5) "A precedent appealed to, to justify or authorize any course of action." 6) "A person's action or conduct regarded as an object of imitation." This series of meanings provides an "ordinary language" basis for refinement into a description of example as rhetorical and conceptual implement.

52. Genette, *Figures* 3:145–67. Example can be considered within the framework of *aspect*, as Genette has codified it for the study of narrative. Although aspect is used primarily to describe the temporality of verbs in terms of frequency of occurrence, it is not difficult to see that examples, even when they exist in a kind of perpetual present, exist as a kind of event—of which the most extreme case would be an event that takes place permanently and without apparent end. The narrative of events can be described, in Genette's terms, as being *singulative, repetitive,* and *iterative*. Recalling briefly Genette's definition of these terms, we can say that the singulative narrative tells each event once (tells *n* times what happened *n* times). The repetitive narrative tells each event more than once (tells *n* times what happened one time). And the iterative tells each event less than once by condensing a whole series of similar events into a single verbal event, telling one time what happened *n* times (e.g., "For a long time I always went to bed early . . . ,"). It is important to note that here *n* is always assumed to be greater than one. Genette's study of frequency thus constructs a set of proportions or ratios between the narrative form (*récit*) and the story (*histoire*).

If we use Genette's aspectual ratio to describe for each example the relationship between the number of times a thing is told and the number of times it happened, we can highlight some interesting characteristics of the textual manifestation of example. The "events" occurring in examples stand for themselves as events and for like events as potential. To take Aristotle's historical example above: in purely narratological terms this brief narrative is singulative. It tells twice what happened twice, first in the case of Darius and then in the case of Xerxes. It adds, but again in the singulative, what *will* happen in the case of the present Great King. Therefore, it tells three times what happened three times. Yet this unproblematically singulative narration, once accepted within the domain of exemplary textuality, is perhaps not singulative after all. Aristotle has told three times what has or will happen *more than three times*, that is, what will happen every time the Great King crosses over into

Egypt. Considered in this way, the apparent singulative becomes iterative—it tells an event fewer times than the event occurs. Genette states his definition of the iterative in terms of the proportion $1R/nH$, where R = *récit* and H = *histoire*. The case presented by Aristotle's example retains this proportion, when it is seen as projecting into the future, in that he tells $3R/nH$, where $n>3$. Hence our preference is for the awkward paraphrase of Genette, "telling each event less than once,"—an apparent impossibility except in the case of ellipsis and example. This difference in description occurs because Genette is concerned almost exclusively with narrative dealing with events as past (even science fiction, as he points out, is almost always told in this way), whereas example, even when the events specifically mentioned are past, concerns the future. As Aristotle notes, "while the lessons conveyed by fables are easier to provide, those derived from facts are more useful for deliberative oratory, because as a rule the future resembles the past" (2.20.1394a).

53. *The New Rhetoric*, p. 353.

54. To push this subordination to its extreme, we could create a number of sentences that would traditionally be perceived as heterodox. For instance, "Allah is an example of (a) God" indicates that Allah is not unique. Even without naming other gods, the term *example* indicates the possibility of inserting Allah into a series of gods. Similarly, but without using the term *example*, one can perform the same act by saying, "Allah and Jesus are gods." In both cases we have established an exemplary presupposition concerning the open-ended series "god" and created a form of distance between the reader and the entity signified, in first instance (e.g., Allah), for the reader knows that the larger import of the text will most likely concern not Allah but gods or religious belief generally.

55. The insistence that an entity cited as an example must represent itself distinguishes example from metaphor. Example is always literal (even when, as in Aesopian fable, it can have another *added* meaning). In metaphor, the common properties of things justify the replacement of the term for one of the things by the term used for the other thing. The tension between the two things remains in our perception, as we attempt to locate the common properties, but the term present in the text (the tenor or *phoros*) is not meant to be understood "literally" (that is, in all its properties) but only in respect to a small number of those properties. In example, one thing is never "replaced" by another:

Metaphor: Cassandra is a rose.
Example: Cassandra is an example of a seer.
             Cassandra and a rose are both examples of
               living things.

Assuming that Cassandra is not a plant but a person, the first of these sentences is a metaphor, within which common properties of the two things, rose and woman, are sufficient to justify replacing the name of one with the name of the other. In making a metaphor, one must replace the principal semic element of one of the two terms (either Cassandra is not a rose, and therefore we recognize the expression as a metaphor; or Cassandra is a rose, and the sentence is merely informing us of another type of rose, which may be new to us). In the second sentence, "seer" is a term that entirely includes Cassandra. There is no "literal" incompatibility with Cassandra's being both of those things at once, since Cassandra would not be herself if she were not a "seer." In the third sentence, both Cassandra and a rose are themselves; neither is replaced by the term for the other, but both are included under a larger class, which is specified. If the central semic properties of both entities are incompatible with the larger class, the example is not properly formed. Though metaphor and quotation are rarely compared, they are on the boundaries of example in their conceptual premises. It is not at all an accident that such rhetoricians as Geoffroi de Vinsauf place example/*exemplum* between "similitude" and "image," while literary critics such as Hugo Friedrich speak of quotation and example side by side in describing Montaigne's style. Janus-like, example has one face turned toward referential support in history and in the concrete, accepted world of experience or sensation, and the other face toward a fictive world of words within which there are plausible but never actualized events. It is thus situated between metaphor, which does not rely on history or social consensus but on the play of words, and quotation, which does require historical basis. With the possible exception of the pseudoquotation (the distancing of a phrase by use of graphic markers), quoting requires some preceding utterance of the same words. It involves a gesture with a necessary foundation in the past, and thus implies a view of temporal linearity, most often associated with a high valorization of the past and its wisdom. Even if a quotation is made for the purpose of negative evaluation or even ridicule, however, the act of quoting sets discourses and texts in a privileged temporal order. Metaphor, on the other hand, does not have an essential bias toward such a historical view of discourse.

56. *De oratore* (Loeb Classical Library) 34, p. 303.

57. On *evidentia* see Cave, *The Cornucopian Text*, pp. 26–30 and 262–63, and Norton, *The Ideology and Language of Translation in the Renaissance*, pp. 55ff. On the visibility of example, it is worth noting the distinction made in one of the medieval glossaries between *exemplum* as that which we imitate or avoid and *exemplar* as that which we copy, having seen it with our eyes: "*Exemplum* est quod sequamur aut vitemus; exemplar ex quo simile faciamus. Illud animo aestimatur, istud oculis conspicitur" (Pirie and Lindsay, eds., *Glossaria Latina*, quoted in Battaglia, *La coscienza letteraria del Medioevo*, p. 448, note).

58. The sense of a gesture "outside" discourse in example relates it closely to evidence or *enargeia*. Quintilian makes an interesting distinction between "being seen" and "showing" (gesturing toward): "*enargeia*, which Cicero calls illustration and evidence, which seems not so much to say as to display . . . [*enargeia*, quae a Cicerone illustratio et evidentia nominatur, quae non tam dicere videtur quam ostendere; et adfectus non aliter, quam si rebus ipsis intersimus, sequentur]" (*Inst.* 6.2.32).

59. Warminski, "Reading for Example," p. 92.

60. Compagnon, *La Seconde Main*, pp. 246–47.

61. "L'allégation et la citation, si elles sont toutes deux des relations entre le texte et le hors-texte, fonctionnent cependant en sens inverse l'une de l'autre; leurs orientations sont opposées. L'allégation va du texte vers l'extérieur; la citation va de l'extérieur vers le texte comme vers un enfermement, une emprise. L'allégation et la citation sont encore comme l'ouvert et le fermé: le texte de l'allégation est ouvert sur ses marges, il déborde de son cadre; le texte de la citation comprend son hors-texte, il ne laisse rien dépasser et se clôt sur lui-même" (Compagnon, *La Seconde Main*, p. 282).

62. The brief *Webster's Seventh New Collegiate Dictionary* defines the verb *allege* as "to declare as if under oath but without proof," "to assert without proof or before proving," and gives as "archaic" the meaning "to adduce or bring forward (as source of authority)." The *Robert* dictionary (1977), while recognizing a drift similar to what has happened in American English, designates as merely "vieilli" (but not as archaic) the meaning "Citer comme autorité, comme preuve de ce qu'on affirme; donner pour raison, pour argument." On the other hand, the contemporary sense is given by the *Robert* as "Mettre en avant," and the dictionary cites as usage: "Alléguer des raisons, des excuses, des prétextes. Alléguer un droit, des exemples (*sic!*)." As Compagnon reminds us, in antiquity allegation meant a reference to proof that did not depend on the citing of a specific individual authority, whereas quotation or citation did (*La Seconde Main*, p. 281).

63. "These misappropriated fables [in the *Libro de Buen Amor*] are the product of a devious author figure calculated to create a distance between the didacticism of the tale itself and the enunciator of the tale—so as to make the attentive reader question the discernment of the enunciating subject, to underscore (like the rift separating what they practice from what they preach) their own unexemplary status" (Marina S. Brownlee, *The Status of the Reading Subject*, p. 96).

CHAPTER I

1. Given his emphasis on demystification and reorientation of the view of the past, it is surprising that Machiavelli is frequently accused of having idealized Livy and the ancient Romans and of having viewed Livy uncritically. Machiavelli neither concerns himself with matters of veracity in Livy's account, nor tries to cut the Romans down to a modern size. Machiavelli's critical attention is drawn, not to objective or referential accuracy, but to the proper formation, use, and reception of examples as sources of power in the present. His consideration thus goes far beyond the commonplace of history learned from examples and moves into the more abstract or preliminary question of what makes an example possible. As Felix Gilbert points out, the belief in "history taught by example" was a commonplace among Machiavelli's contemporaries, including Guicciardini (*Machiavelli and Guicciardini*, p. 230).

2. Olschki says, notably, that factual material from Livy is not Machiavelli's

major concern because "his [Machiavelli's] idealization [of Rome] is an abstract one and has a marked intellectual and functional character. For that reason all the fables, legends, and stories told in the first decades of Livy's narrative are as valuable, instructive, and authoritative as the more authentic episodes and details" (*Machiavelli the Scientist*, p. 48). Strauss argues that Livy replaces the Bible as a sacred, authoritative text for Machiavelli, and that Machiavelli then turns against Livy in *Discourses* 2. Strauss specifically notes that one Machiavellian tactic consists of transforming "the Roman ruling class as it was into a ruling class as, according to him, it should have been" ("Machiavelli and Classical Literature," p. 24). The most detailed consideration of Machiavelli's idealization of the Romans through Livy is Whitfield's article, "Machiavelli's Use of Livy." Whitfield describes Machiavelli's appreciation of Livy as uncritical and contrasts this attitude with Guicciardini's. As Whitfield says, "an idealist is one . . . who looks for perfection; nor is it surprising . . . that Machiavelli sees it, on the basis of Livy's account, in ancient Rome" (pp. 85–86).

3. The argument whether Machiavelli's reasoning is predominantly deductive or inductive seems to me to have been largely unproductive. The difficulty of distinguishing between Machiavelli's exposition of his ideas (the *ordo docendi*) and the actual conduct of his thought (the *ordo cognoscendi*) leads to vigorous confrontational positions that are unlikely to lead to any resolution. Bondanella, for instance, sees the term *illustrative* as diminishing the importance of example in Machiavelli, saying, "These quotations show that Machiavelli considered the actions of these 'most striking exempla' to be essential to his arguments: they are not simply illustrations of his ideas but are themselves the source of his inspiration" (*Machiavelli and the Art of Renaissance History*, p. 52). Examples may well be essential to Machiavelli's "inspiration," that is, to some internal workings of Machiavelli's mind before the composition of his text, with or without being essential to the argument ultimately set forth by the writer. Similarly, when Olschki says that Machiavelli's "examples are paradigms of experience and starting points for his inductive generalizations" (*Machiavelli the Scientist*, p. 47), Olschki neglects the distinction between experience and paradigm. Paradigm (example) is not a "starting point" in any pure sense, for paradigms themselves are fabricated and projected *upon* experience. Far from reducing the importance of Machiavelli's examples by seeing them as creations of his discourse, we believe that only the study of his discourse can explain their importance.

4. Felix Gilbert, *Machiavelli and Guicciardini*, p. 170. Barberi-Squarotti echoes this sentiment: "l'elemento concreto, l'accadimento, la nozione obiettiva, non sono all'origine, ma costituiscono pura materia del discorso, punto di reiferimento per il facile orientamento di chi legge . . ." (*La forma tragica del "Principe,"* p. 115.)

5. "The treatise [*Il Principe*] is finally not a referential text. It initially gestures toward validating itself by invoking its foundations in a world of transtextual, 'real events.' But these gestures are often empty . . ." (McCanles, *The Discourse of Il Principe*, p. xv).

6. Machiavelli's recognition of the irrational in history and of the usefulness of techniques like the exemplary sacrifice has caused him to be described himself as irrational, ambiguous, and confused. For a statement of this view, see Anglo, *Machiavelli: A Dissection*.

7. These two claimed "newnesses" must be circumscribed. Machiavelli is quick to say that seizing power is not unknown in history. He points out the commonness of such events in all times and places. The originality of Machiavelli's observations or even his discursive genre has also been challenged (Allan H. Gilbert, *Machiavelli's Prince and its Forerunners*; a spirited defense of Machiavelli's newness appears in Strauss, *Thoughts on Machiavelli*, pp. 232–34). But Machiavelli presents himself as teaching a *new* and unpopular doctrine, and even Felix Gilbert emphasizes that Machiavelli's explicit concern for the "new prince" is a departure from the traditional medieval pattern of treatises on ideal rulers (*Machiavelli and Guicciardini*, p. 163). Prezzolini, in *The Legacy of Italy*, claims that the title of *The Prince* is misleading because the book is "just a special study of the general conditions facing the 'new rulers' " (p. 135).

8. *The Discourses*, 73/103. References to the *Discorsi* are indicated by "*D*." English translations of the *Discorsi* are from the Modern Library edition of *The Prince* and *The Discourses*, with introduction by Max Lerner (New York: Random House, 1940); translations of passages from *The Prince* are from James B. Atkinson's translation (1976; reprint, Indianapolis: Bobbs-Merrill, "The Library of Liberal Arts," 1977). Quotations from *Il Principe* are indicated in the text as "*P*." The page reference to the Italian text precedes the page number of the translation.

9. Machiavelli's emphasis on foundings has as its background the humanist preoccupation with origins. Florentines were particularly involved in a controversy about the identity of the founder of their city—whether it was Caesar or veterans of Sulla's army. See Baron, *Humanistic and Political Literature*, pp. 18–30. In *The Prince*, Romulus is one of the four great "armed prophets" (with Moses, Cyrus, and Theseus) who seem to be great manifestations of *virtù* or political efficacy and skill. I will make no attempt here to examine the extraordinary ramifications of the problem of *virtù* in Machiavelli's work, but a succinct discussion and selective bibliography can be found in the introduction to Atkinson's translation of *The Prince*.

10. The best study of the "founding foundlings" is the chapter on "The Founder" in Pitkin's *Fortune is a Woman*, pp. 52–79.

11. Machiavelli's campaign against hereditary succession marks the whole of the *Discourses* and forms one of the most original characteristics of the *Life of Castruccio Castracane*, the historical account (or romance) about a foundling who became prince of Lucca but abstained from marrying in order not to produce heirs.

12. In view of Machiavelli's use of Livy as source and authorization, it is interesting to note how the sixteenth century perceived Machiavelli and Tacitus. The relations between antiquity and modernity were so reversed, according to Toffanin (*Machiavelli e il "Tacitismo"*), that Tacitus became a "palimp-

sest" behind which the thought of Machiavelli was read by Pope Paul III and others. When Paul IV ordered *Il Principe* burned, says Toffanin, "distruggeva l'origine perché restasse in onore soltanto quel palinsesto" (p. 129).

13. Pitkin properly notes that the founders are not parricides but foundlings. She goes on to argue that the founders are, in fact, marked by an exceptional piety and cites Titus Manlius's protection of his father (p. 61). It seems to me however, that Pitkin here neglects the distinction between the founder and other exemplary figures, like T. Manlius, who are not founders.

14. See Mattingly, "Machiavelli's Prince." Mattingly particularly notes the hostility between Giuliano de' Medici, the initial dedicatee of *The Prince*, and Cesare Borgia (p. 490).

15. The distinction between "true history" and basic record of event was common in Machiavelli's day. As Felix Gilbert says, "the humanists knew of two kinds of historical writings: the true history which was to be composed on the pattern of Livy or Sallust; and the reports about historical events which provided the material from which the true history would be constructed" (*Machiavelli and Guicciardini*, p. 223). Machiavelli is therefore writing a genre one step beyond true history, for he is basing himself on something already recognized as such and refining upon it.

16. Latin would be more likely to use the word *minuere* for "to reduce" in the contemporary English sense.

17. It is important to note the gesture of giving the fragment, which becomes the symbol of a double authority—the authority both of antiquity and of the patron who is now the proprietor of something rescued from antiquity.

18. Atkinson, note to *The Prince*, p. 254.

19. Here in the English translation "display" has been given for *usare* in the translator's attempt to condense into this word all the visual terms of the Italian.

20. In this complex sentence, Machiavelli has woven together the work of those acting in society, those who found societies and give them laws, and those who analyze societies. Temporally, the founder of society must project forward an experience of evils that have not yet occurred in that society (*presuppore*). The analyst of societies, says Machiavelli, can show, looking back, that such a looking forward is necessary. The sentence concludes that time itself uncovers both the hidden evil and the reasons for which that evil was hidden. The analyst and the social man have to look backward to discover the hidden. What analysts and others discover may be different, though Machiavelli's balanced phrase suggests that the ordinary person is more interested in the reasons for the concealment while the former is interested in what is being hidden: *quando alcuna malignità sta occulta un tempo, procede da una occulta cagione*. It is at least clear that there are two levels of concealment, and if the *occulta cagione* is a concealed general law belonging to the science of occasions, it concerns both the institutional and historical structures that permit revelations of human evil. The conclusion that time is the father of truth (an affirmation that does not altogether erase the fact that time also fosters or at least permits con-

cealment in the *sta occulto un tempo*) may give an impression of open-endedness to this view of human endeavor, but this interpretation would be erroneous. The truths that time reveals are the truths that must also be presupposed by the legislator, thus forming a circle of presupposition and historical revelation. Machiavelli here is close to the wheel of fortune, a conception of history that appears also in the proemium to *Discourses*, book 2.

Whatever *usually* appears is false. The student of history is in the paradoxical position of looking for appearances that manifest the unusual bursting forth of the evil always there. Machiavelli's study is thus based on a quest for reversals, by which ordinary appearance is shown to have no basis. Since it is a form of appearance, example is itself subject to doubtful scrutiny, for it can be the deceptive appearance of mankind's good behavior, another person's penetration of that appearance, or the interplay between the two. This last case is what Machiavelli requires as an example of the rule of concealment, since a man who is always apparently bad tends to subvert the rule, for any continuity of this sort undercuts the fundamental dichotomy of essence and appearance.

There is, then, a hierarchy of example, for examples of goodness and examples of badness only find their ultimate usefulness for the analyst in a higher level, where both exemplify the instability and untrustworthiness of what we perceive. This process of reversal could keep us from ever deciding whether any behavior was what it seemed, and even whether the worst behavior did not conceal something else (goodness?). Machiavelli is careful to try to stabilize appearances in a totality. This final wholeness is traced in the quantifiers of the first and last clauses of this long sentence: "all those who have written," "all history [*ogni istoria*]," "all truth." Moreover, Machiavelli, lauding the founder of civil laws, seems to emulate him in recommending a presupposition or axiom that badness is the ground of human nature. Once we have discovered that ground, we can remain more or less assured of having reached the truth. The answer to the objection we have just encountered on what could be concealed under the appearance of evil is given by Machiavelli elsewhere in the *Discourses*, in the story of Giovanpaolo Baglioni, a vicious man apparently without any further possible evil to conceal, who finally reveals the ultimate evil, weakness in the performance of the bad (*Discourses* 1.27).

21. Strauss, who is strongly persuaded that Machiavelli's omission of examples is determined by censorship, uses the term *exclusions* for these litotic examples. I prefer the term *litotic* because it indicates that the very absence of an example is a creation of the text. Exclusion supposes—in keeping with Strauss's view of the reality of the censored—that the example precedes its textual formulation (even as absence).

22. The paradox of joining these two apparently contradictory effects is not the least interesting aspect of Machiavelli's thought, but following the implications of a union based on a constitutive difference would take us out of the way.

23. Pitkin has noted that Machiavelli on other occasions renders historical

figures fiercer than they were in other accounts, e.g., Brutus (*Fortune is a Woman*, p. 60).

24. Barberi-Squarotti, *La forma tragica del "Principe,"* p. 152.

25. Apparently wishing to make Decius's death unique, Machiavelli does not note that one of the "rare examples" of similar sacrifice is Decius's own son in battle against the Gauls (Livy 10.28.12–18).

26. The introduction to book 3 is numbered as chapter (*capitolo*) 1. It has a form similar to the proemia of the first two books and therefore should be considered as a true introduction, with all that that implies for its prominence in Machiavelli's argument.

27. Olschki's claim that Machiavelli "believed that political achievements depend upon men and not upon institutions" (*Machiavelli the Scientist*, p. 36) seems to me to be one-sided, since institutions and men are mutually interdependent. Extrainstitutional action is unthinkable to Machiavelli, who sees institutions as immediately recuperating the actions of men.

28. *Discipline and Punish*, p. 95.

29. *Black's Law Dictionary* gives for this legal proverb a faulty reference to the *Institutes* of Justinian (*Inst.* 2.161). I have not been able to locate its source.

30. Livy indicates that Papirius's severity was debilitating to the morale of the army and not invigorating (Livy 8.36).

31. Such sacrifices may be motivated in part by a need to personalize political acts not only by representing an individual who is punished but, through the reenactment of the judging and execution, by returning society to an image of the founder, the *auctor*. Lefort notes, in a different context, a similar impulse: "On est tenté de dire que la fiction du pouvoir machiavélique est au service d'une double intention, celle de nommer la perte de la substance de la société et de l'homme, en donnant figure à la dissolution du lien qui unit le pouvoir avec la totalité de l'existence humaine, et celle de conjurer la menace de cette perte en donnant figure *dans* la société au Sujet dont la présence garantit par une action destructrice la croyance en son unité virtuelle" (*Le Travail de l'oeuvre: Machiavel*, p. 90).

32. Sacrifice as represented in literary texts has been most thoroughly treated by René Girard. Since Machiavelli describes executions in terms that are on the border of purely utilitarian and mystical motives, it is inevitable that we think of Girard's theses in *La Violence et le sacré* for a way of locating Machiavelli's thought in reference to the conception of the scapegoat or *pharmakos*. One point especially reminiscent of such scapegoating is the interchangeability of the good and bad man, the sacred king and the slave, in sacrificial ritual. Although many of the cases cited by Machiavelli can be given a coherent and plausible interpretation in accordance with the doctrine of the *pharmakos*, there are significant differences in the way Machiavelli uses these examples. For Machiavelli executions do not prevent social conflict through displacement of violence. Violence does not appear to lessen tension between clans in his view of history, and Machiavelli does not stress the unchanging ritual formulae of sacrifice (cf. Girard, *La Violence et le sacré*, p. 52). Though several of Ma-

chiavelli's executions show the passage from a sacrificial system to a judicial one, they show the judicial framework as weak in its normal functioning and as sustaining itself only by the irruption of the violent exception. For Girard the "outsider"—be he king, slave, or enemy—is eminently sacrificeable while members of the inside group are spared once they find a scapegoat. This seems to agree with Machiavelli's location of exceptional victims, persons outside the group because of their unusual goodness or evil. For Machiavelli, however, the exception most often is constituted *at the moment of the execution.* Decius and Mucius Scaevola, who "sacrifice" themselves, are placed outside the group only by that very act. The distinction between inside and outside, executable or not, is not a useful way of classifying persons in Machiavelli's doctrine of execution; since anyone can pass from one to the other, everyone is executable. The execution is therefore privileged at the expense of the executed—entirely within the logic of making examples by breaking into a continuum.

The temporal character of Machiavelli's executions differs from Girard's sacrifices and from his mimetic violence (vengeance) to which sacrifice puts an end. Girard's mimetism is a process by which one act of violence leads to a responding and similar act. A first clan commits a murder. The clan of the victim seeks revenge, causing the first clan in turn to seek revenge, and so on. This cycle of violence can be broken by a killing, which absorbs violence without calling for revenge, in order words, by a ritual sacrifice strongly surrounded by universal consent to its unifying, nondivisive quality. Before (or without) sacrificial ritual, society is in prey to a chain of historical alternation between groups, the initiative for violent revenge passing back and forth between opposing clans. In sacrifice, a neutral group (one that need not be revenged) provides a substitute for a victim from the opposing social group. For Girard, therefore, emphasis is on the synchronic opposition in social groupings. With Machiavelli's exemplary executions, however, emphasis is not on such opposing groups but on the diachronic succession of executions. At issue for Machiavelli is the mimesis of sacrifice itself, the ability of society to provide out of its unity an exceptional victim, to create an outsider from within the group, as a means of enacting a nonsynchronic opposition, the opposition between founding and decay.

In the case of Decius, it seems that Machiavelli is concerned with the kind of "enemy brother" situation that concerns Girard. In fact, it would be difficult to find more perfect symmetry or twinning than in the confrontation between the Romans and the Latins. Yet the role of violence in this episode is different from the confrontation of Eteocles and Polynices, which typifies such symmetry for Girard (*La Violence et le sacré,* p. 72). The two groups do not perpetuate violence but abolish it by fusing into one as a result of the Roman victory. Decius's "suicide" is not to abolish violence but to encourage it in his own army. This mimetic purpose, however, is not to give the other side a model for its vengeance. The synchronic opposition is important to Machiavelli primarily as a way of creating a diachronic difference, a founding moment in which a minimal or nonexistence difference in space—the symmetry between the two armies—yields to an enormous difference in time, the change from before to after the "most important battle in Roman history." Decius's "sacrifice," therefore, increases and encourages violence (unlike a sacrifice in Girard's terms) and does not figure in Machiavelli's text as a truly mimetic violence. Machiavelli does not, as he could have, depict Decius's act as a model for his soldiers to imitate. Instead he sets Decius's act apart as "rarely imitated" (having *radi esempli*). This lack of direct model and direct imitators sets Machiavelli's executions and self-executions apart. Such examples seem, in his thought, to lose their value if they are the result or cause of an imitation. They seem to refer to one another without reflecting or causing one another.

33. It is surprising that Pitkin, who has such perceptive things to say about the violence of foundations and has also noted Machiavelli's use of the metaphor of a "second birth" for this phenomenon of a renewal of the state (pp. 241–42), did not link the two concepts. The sacrifice of citizens could be seen as a reference to the violence of birth—something that would square with Pitkin's comments on Machiavelli's view of the mother.

34. This altogether typical sequence of examples with their intricate interconnections belies Barberi-Squarotti's insistence that Machiavelli's examples are only brief and rapid allusions "di rapido richiamò di una verità nota a tutti nell'ambito esterno" (*La forma tragica del "Principe,"* p. 145).

35. The use of augury makes a circle from the people back to the people, since augury allows them to continue believing what they want to believe. The belief that conditions were right for a Roman victory comes from soldiers and the consul. The Pollarius, unwilling to counter this desire to fight, attributes the desire to the gods, who have communicated through the sign of the chickens. The soldiers' desire is communicated by the Pollarius through the consul, making a circle (army [and consul]→Pollarius→ chickens [gods]→ Pollarius→ consul→ army), which allows the battle to proceed. This perfect circularity of the interpretive and symbolic process, however, cannot exorcise its own fallacy, its fragility. Machiavelli, in taking the example from Livy, remains close to the Latin text except that he condenses it to make the schema of interpretation clearer. In Machiavelli's text, the upsetting of this circular arrangement appears promptly, for no sooner has the consul started putting his squadrons in order than Spurius Papirius initiates a new circle, which runs (other Pollarius→ army→ consul's nephew→ consul→ army→ Pollarius [gods]→ consul→ army) from the army, which fears that the auspices are false, through various stages of report to the consul back to the army, which relearns what it already believed: the gods punish the sacrilegious. This circle once again purports to receive its ultimate message from the gods, but with a heightened element of sacrifice. In the earlier circle the message appears in the gods' motivation of the chickens' appetite for corn. In the second circle the sign is constituted by the death (or consumption) of the "liar," whose offering appeases the gods and whose death is explicitly linked to something that is part of mankind's reason for invoking the gods (*caso*, "chance"). But once again, the gods have had a little help. The gods here, like the historical text underlying Ma-

chiavelli's discourse, are what Watt has termed "passive authority": "Truth, knowledge, science, the law, or a written text, may all be called authoritative, but they cannot speak for themselves . . . In matters of knowledge, passive authorities (as they may be called) can speak only through active authorities" (*Authority*, p. 45). Just as the chief Pollarius interpreted the gods' message to suit the apparent military situation of the army, so the consul and the soldiers interpret the gods' will to suit the apparent spiritual situation of the army. Lucius Papirius places the Pollarii *so that* whatever happens to the Pollarius will follow the prediction. Machiavelli's text masterfully creates an ambiguity about which prognostication is to be realized, whether it is the consul's or the Pollarius's or both. The sequence of propositions—"it would come back upon him" and "so that the effect would follow"—seems to indicate that the effect in question (the punishment of the liar) will be better realized if the Pollarius is placed in danger, something in keeping with the overall supposition that the consul is perfectly cognizant at every moment of what is going on and intentionally determining the death of the Pollarius. Nonetheless, the effect in question may refer directly to the gods' will in response to lying, and the prognostication may be the Pollarius's illicit one. The circularity of the system is, at any rate, demonstrated by the fact that the Pollarius is killed by an arrow from the Roman side, so that the liar is killed by the army to whose desire he gave voice. It also seems plausible that Lucius Papirius may have had a hand in this misdirected arrow.

36. Another Appius appears in Machiavelli's text in connection with these sacred fowl when Appius Claudius argues to the people that the Tribunes can no longer be trusted since they show no concern for the chickens' dietary and other habits (*D*, 321/507).

37. Suleiman, "Le Récit exemplaire," pp. 468–89.

38. Strauss argues, with excessive optimism, that Machiavelli believes that followers of his system will be able to achieve systematically what the Romans achieved by blind chance ("Machiavelli and Classical Literature," p. 22).

39. See Chabod's discussion of Machiavelli's oppositional, "dilemmatic" technique, with its exclusion of the middle way: "Machiavelli's Method and Style" in *Machiavelli and the Renaissance*, pp. 126–48.

40. Barberi-Squarotti, *La forma tragica del "Principe,"* p. 112.

41. This declaration, however, sets the stage for Machiavelli's attempt to cancel the bad modern examples by returning to the example of Lucullus in his battle against Tigranes of Armenia.

42. Felix Gilbert pointed out the importance of Machiavelli's realization that "the dimension in which politics worked was history and that every political action had to be fitted into the context of historical change" (*Machiavelli and Guicciardini*, p. 198). But Machiavelli, it seems to me, while expressing the need for arriving at the appropriate cognizance of change, perceived the impossibility of both grasping fully the nature of that change and acting upon a realization of change. Gilbert's term of "instinctiveness" (p. 197) seems apt for

the only working quality of the political agent in Machiavelli's view of the world.

43. "The Perspective of Art," p. 188. See also Prezzolini's comparison of Machiavelli and Galileo, *The Legacy of Italy*, p. 129.

44. Proemium to *Discourses* 2 (177/270).

45. This phenomenon is related to mankind's inability to appreciate present advantage. For instance, freedom can be appreciated only after its loss (*D*, 109/ 161).

46. Mazzeo comments on the ambiguity of Machiavelli's thought (evident in this passage) by seeing it as a necessary element, almost a mimesis within Machiavelli's discursive approach of the strategy of the political leader: "The ambiguity of Machiavelli's thought is deliberate, and his universe of discourse precludes theoretical consistency simply because the prime requisite of effective political action is flexibility" (*Renaissance and Seventeenth-Century Studies*, p. 123).

47. We are led to agree with Barberi-Squarotti's assessment of Machiavelli's examples as "absolute examples, extreme forms defined a priori as sublime models of action, or rather, of being . . ." (*La forma tragica del "Principe,"* p. 146).

48. McCanles, *The Discourse of Il Principe*, p. xii.

Chapter II

1. For a discussion of this filiation of *exempla* and novella, see Pabst, *Novellentheorie und Novellendichtung*. A contrary vision of the origin of the novella is given by Ferrier, who sees novella as developing out of romance, in *Forerunners of the French Novel*.

2. Tetel, "Ambiguité chez Boccace et Marguerite de Navarre," and *Marguerite de Navarre's Heptaméron*. Ambiguity and hidden meanings were, interestingly, associated with the "Spiritual Libertines" who influenced Marguerite de Navarre through Briçonnet. Calvin wrote of them, "Non pas qu'ils n'usent des motz communs qu'ont les autres: mais ils en deguisent tellement la signification, que iamais on en sait quelle est le subject de la matiere dont ilz parlent . . ." (quoted in Heller, "Marguerite de Navarre and the Reformers of Meaux," p. 307.

3. 9/68. I have used the edition of the *Heptaméron* by Michel François in the Classiques Garnier (Paris: Garnier, 1967) and consulted Yves Le Hir's text in his *Nouvelles* of Marguerite de Navarre (Paris: Presses universitaires de France, 1967). Quotations given in translation are from *The Heptameron*, translated by P. A. Chilton (Harmondsworth: Penguin Books, 1984) with modifications (italics) by me to clarify points relevant to my argument. Pagination given refers first to the French text of François and then to the English.

4. The prologue of the *Heptameron* has been studied extensively. In conjunction with the prologue and the narrative frame generally, I have made use of Lajarte, "L'*Heptaméron* et la naissance du récit moderne," and "Le Prologue de l'*Heptaméron*," in *La Nouvelle française à la Renaissance*, ed. Lionello Sozzi,

pp. 397–423; and Norton's essay in the same volume, "Narrative Function in the 'Heptaméron' Frame-Story," pp. 435–47.

5. *The Cornucopian Text*, especially chap. 1, "Copia," pp. 3–34.

6. Boccaccio similarly alludes ironically to the *exemplum* tradition, it seems to me, when he writes in the proemium to the first day of the *Decameron* that women can take counsel from his stories and learn what forms of conduct should be imitated and what shunned: "delle quali le già dette donne, che queste leggeranno, parimente diletto, delle sollazzevoli cose in quelle mostrate e utile consiglio potranno pigliare, in quanto potranno cognoscere quello che sia da fuggire e che sia similmente da seguitare . . ." (*Decamerone*, p. 5).

7. Although Serrance does not seem to have been a Franciscan monastery, Marguerite de Navarre makes few or no distinctions and lumps all regular religious orders together with the Franciscans as hypocrites. "Pour Marguerite, tous les religieux sont de l'ordre de saint François!" writes Atance, "Les Religieux de l'*Heptaméron*: Marguerite de Navarre et les novateurs," p. 189, note. For detailed consideration of the Franciscans and French culture in the sixteenth century, see Krailsheimer, *Rabelais and the Franciscans*.

8. Kevin Brownlee, in an important forthcoming study of Faux Semblant, demonstrates convincingly that this complex character is of the highest philosophical and historical interest for an understanding of the discursive practices of the Dominicans and the Franciscans. Brownlee further elucidates a point of major interest to readers of the *Heptameron* by analyzing the way the *Roman de la Rose* uses a "false" character to make doctrinally "true" statements ("The Problem of Faux Semblant: Language, History and Truth in the *Roman de la Rose*" [unpublished]).

9. Lajarte, "L'*Heptaméron* et la naissance du récit moderne," and "Le Prologue de l'*Heptaméron*."

10. The tension between intense belief and an equally intense skepticism about the "objective" paths to truth is described by Defaux in reference to the attitudes of Erasmus, Lefèvre d'Etaples, and Marguerite de Navarre toward comprehension: "ce langage fidéiste et sceptique est aussi, et indéniablement, l'un des langages de l'Humanisme le plus authentique" (*Le Curieux*, p. 108).

11. Here the formal distinction between *récit d'histoire* and *discours*, familiar from the work of Emile Benveniste, parallels Aristotle's cognitive distinction between "what has happened" and "the kind of thing that *can* happen" (*Poetics* 51b1, trans. Else, p. 32).

12. Tetel, *Marguerite de Navarre's Heptaméron*, pp. 195–96.

13. Simonin-Grumbach, "Pour une typologie des discours," pp. 85–121.

14. Betty J. Davis, for instance, concentrates exclusively on the narrators in her *The Storytellers in Marguerite de Navarre's Heptaméron*. Though this thorough examination of one feature of the novella structure provides much useful information, such an approach cannot provide a full basis for interpretation unless the content of the novellas is connected with the analysis of the storytellers.

15. See Lilly, *An Introduction to the Law of Evidence*, secs. 23 and 82.

16. Benveniste, "La nature des pronoms," in *Problèmes de linguistique générale*, pp. 251–57.

17. The law of evidence admits statements of the parties to litigation, but interested declarations by a party are obviously not of great evidentiary weight. Statements made by a party before the present litigation have an entirely different value. See "The Hearsay Rule: Selected Exceptions," in Lilly, sec. 54.

18. In the *Digest* of Justinian, which I consulted in an edition published with *privilège du roi* of Henry II (*Corpus Iuris Civilis* [Geneva: Jean Vignon, 1614]), this rule of evidence is given in a slightly different form: "Nullus idoneus testis in re sua intelligitur" (*Digest* 22.5.10). Philippe de Rémi, Sieur de Beaumanoir, a thirteenth-century jurist, attests to this prohibition in his region, the Beauvoisis (*Les Coutumes du Beauvoisis* 1, chap. 39, sec. 35). Ullman gives a summary description of the function of the witness in medieval judicial practice (*The Medieval Idea of Law*, pp. 122–26), and Chénon shows the persistence of Frankish elements in the law of the witness in his *Histoire générale du droit français*. See also Lilly, chap. 4, sec. 23, p. 66; and Wigmore, *The Principles of Judicial Proof*, 2d ed., pp. 268–69. Other indications of the procedures of legal "instruction" in the courts of the period in France are given in Natalie Zemon Davis, *The Return of Martin Guerre*, and her *Fiction in the Archives*.

19. See Defaux, *Le Curieux*, pp. 104–10, on the link between self-doubt and humanism in the thought of Erasmus, Budé, Lefèvre d'Etaples, and especially in the milieu of Briçonnet and Marguerite de Navarre.

20. Initially her statement does not even refer explicitly to the woman but conveys the situation to du Mesnil metonymically. His place is taken; there is a disturbance in places and placings. This "metonymy" is at the frontier of the distinction between metaphor and metonymy since du Mesnil and the "other man" (in this case the bishop and not the husband) belong to the same paradigmatic group (male lovers) and they can be substituted or selected for one another in a sentence. The major disturbance, from the young lover's point of view, is in the function of combination (or predication) and not in the selection. The bishop is not taken for him, but the bishop has taken his *place*.

21. This is doubly so here, since the words of the servant are conveyed in the internal narrator's voice.

22. Marguerite recalls here the distinction between words and consummation in marriage. A marriage made only in words (the *verba de praesenti* or *paroles de présent*) was a valid marriage but could be dissolved for several reasons if acts had not followed, after which the marriage was indissoluble. Although this argument, in connection with the wife's love affair with the bishop, is parodic at most, Marguerite returns to this question of canon law in the story of Rolandine.

23. The young lover's speech, as "reported" indirectly to us, combines his own, self-interested claim of having been betrayed (paraphrasable as "I have been wronged"), his vision of the events of the night (paraphrasable as "The bishop came out of the house"—a perfectly factual witnessing), and the ironic

characterization of the interlocutor to convey the speaker's meaning (paraphrasable as "You are too holy, because you have touched holy things").

24. An example is much like a "case," except that exemplification always points toward the proving or disproving of a generality. Case, which is also subordinate statement, may be an entity to be understood and clarified by the application of one or more generalities. An entity can serve as both example and case; a case, when clarified and fully systematized, may subsequently be used as an example. I subscribe in large part to Jolles's distinction between example and case on the grounds that in a case the generality or norm is not immediately and clearly applicable (*Einfache Formen* [1930], translated into French as *Formes simples* by Marie Buguet, pp. 142–43). For Jolles a case indicates a conflict of generalities or laws. I would add that this conflict may only be, in some instances, a lack of certainty about which law applies. Once that doubt is resolved or a new generality formed, the case is available for use as an example.

25. This characteristic of the *Heptameron* is merely an emphasized feature of the novella in the Boccaccian tradition. The claim that the events are contemporary or recent is a generic marker strongly differentiating novella from fairy tale, for instance, where, as Jolles reminds us, events are situated "a long, long time ago."

26. A further similarity between the story in the novella and the working of the frame-narrative is the alternation between female and male in the judicial process. The wife (F) tells Neaufle (M) who tells the chancellor (M) who tells the Regent (F) who tells La Barre (M). After the trial is reported to the king (M), his sister (F) asks to have the sentence commuted. Although this series (F,M,M,F,M,M,F) is not identical with the alternation of storytellers, it does strengthen the institutional resemblance of novella and frame.

27. Among the reformers of Meaux, the cult of images in churches was attacked. These black magic images are in a way the inversion of ecclesiastical statuary. See Heller, "Marguerite de Navarre and the Reformers of Meaux," p. 271.

28. Vitale-Brovarone describes the separation of roles, which may be called into play by the person who exercises the function of teacher, in his study of late classical and medieval *exemplum* ("Persuasione e narrazione," p. 105).

29. Marguerite de Navarre, *Nouvelles*, ed. Le Hir, pp. 369–72.

30. There may be considerable significance in the choice of a bastard as spouse in this tale. Before the thirteenth century bastards were generally without civil rights, including the right to marry and the right to bear witness. Does Marguerite allude to some residual sense of impediment, which would make a bastard the last kind of man a woman would want to marry? See Chénon, *Histoire générale du droit français* 2, p. 75.

31. For the development in lyric poetry of the ramifications of Marguerite de Navarre's conception of God's word and human attempts at expression thereof, see Cottrell, *The Grammar of Silence*. The conditions for the validity

of marriage in canon law, and hence in the law of France, are succinctly presented by Chénon, *Histoire générale du droit français 2*, pp. 81ff.

32. Beneveniste, "Les Relations des temps dans le verbe français," in *Problèmes de linguistique générale*, pp. 237–57.

33. The way in which the heroine of this story disappears into it as third-person character contrasts with Lafayette's treatment of the seclusion of the heroine at the end of *La Princesse de Clèves*. As that conclusion is described by De Jean, "The princess comes to realize that in order to control her story she must suppress it" ("Lafayette's Ellipses," p. 898). Is Lafayette's ellipsis a conscious rewriting of Rolandine's destiny?

34. Unless one considers Longarine's general comment about "faiz si pesant" (174/253) as an allusion to Rolandine's sufferings.

35. In the eyes of the frame-narrators the only villain in the story seems to be the bastard, and, moreover, only one phase of the bastard's career is taken into account, his infidelity, something mentioned nine-tenths of the way through the text of the story, during most of which he is described as a patient, enduring, and resourceful lover. The lover's betrayal is necessary for the triumph of Rolandine. As Oisille comments, invoking a kind of literary *felix culpa*: "ce qui donne autant de lustre à sa fermeté, c'est la desloyaulté de son mary qui la voulloit laisser pour un autre" (174/253).

36. Chénon recalls that the law did not require the consent of parents for a marriage to be valid, even if it was illicitly contracted: "Il est à remarquer que le droit canonique n'exigeait pas le consentement des ascendants au mariage de leurs enfants, même mineurs, à peine de nullité: il prescrivait seulement aux fils et aux filles de famille de le demander en témoignage de respect . . . La conséquence . . . était la validité des mariages clandestins . . . " (*Histoire générale du droit français 2*, p. 88).

37. For a different interpretation of the character of Oisille, as representing a specifically "feminine" form of authority, see Sommers, "Feminine Authority in the *Heptaméron*: A Reading of Oysille," pp. 52–59.

38. This point echoes what Erasmus says in *De copia*: "some material can serve not only diverse but contrary uses . . . This same incident [Socrates' cheerful acceptance of the hemlock] can be turned to Socrates' praise or blame . . ." (*De copia*, trans. Betty I. Knott, p. 639).

39. The gentleman tells the king: "Si le secret du Roy est caché au serf, ce n'est pas raison que celluy du serf soit declaré au Roy; mais entendez vous que tous ceulx qui portent cornes n'ont pas le bonnet hors de la teste, car elles sont si doulces, qu'elles ne descoiffent personne; et celluy les porte plus legierement, qui ne les cuyde pas avoir" (26–27/88). The passage proposes a curious parallel to the perspective simile used by Machiavelli in the dedication of *The Prince*.

40. The stag's head is a combined representation of the king and the husband, both cuckolds, and has enunciatory features proper to each separately. While the stag's head is able to enunciate self-consciousness, as in the gentleman's case, it is also blind and on display, like the king.

41. Atance, "Les Religieux de l'*Heptaméron*," p. 195. Crane also sees the use of narrative in sermons as much increased by the foundation of the Franciscans and the Dominicans (*The Exempla or Illustrative Stories from the Sermones Vulgares of Jacques de Vitry*, pp. xix–xxi). Cf. Vitale-Brovarone ("Persuasione e narrazione," p. 110), who refers to the explosion of the phenomenon of *exemplum* in the thirteenth century because of the mendicant orders. See also Welter, *L'Exemplum dans la littérature religieuse et didactique du moyen âge*, pp. 42ff. Cazauran has located similarities between at least one of Marguerite de Navarre's tales and a Franciscan sermon of the sixteenth century. See "La Trentième Nouvelle," pp. 620–24.

42. Tubach: "it no longer seems practicable to organize a list according to the few basic types of characters in exempla, such as monk. Too many tales would have to be listed under this particular heading" (*Index exemplorum*, p. 518).

43. The representation of religious orders in the *Heptameron* cannot be considered merely a direct document of monastic conduct in the fifteenth and sixteenth centuries. Atance points out that the monks of these stories constitute an anomaly in Marguerite de Navarre's reference to contemporary society: "Marguerite présente un tableau convaincant et réaliste de ses contemporains sauf quand il s'agit des religieux. Après cette constatation, deux hypothèses semblent s'imposer: ou bien la reine ne connaissait aucun religieux digne d'être loué, ou bien, pour des raisons de polémique, elle n'a pas tenu à honorer dans son ouvrage ceux qui étaient vertueux et vivaient selon les règles de l'Eglise. Cette dernière hypothèse nous paraît la bonne" ("Les Religieux de l'*Heptaméron*," pp. 188–89). But Atance does not follow through with an explanation that takes into account the *literary* tradition of depicting monks. His conclusion that only "hatred" can explain the representation of the monks seems frankly naïve: "Qu'on le veuille ou non, l'attitude de Marguerite ici contraste péniblement avec tous ses autres écrits et même avec sa vie. Pour nous, le cas est clair: seule la haine peut expliquer cet acharnement et cet aveuglement" (p. 192). Marguerite de Navarre, I believe, is not so much interested in referring to actual, historically real monks as she is in using the connotation of monks to establish a specific position about the values of teaching. Connotation does not ignore social or referential reality, but it provides a richer explanation of reality by incorporating the kinds of discourse associated, in and outside texts, with the groups in question, i.e., the Franciscans and the Dominicans.

44. "Marguerite de Navarre and the Reformers of Meaux," p. 309.

45. In the story contained in this *proemio* to the fourth day of the *Decameron*, a young man is raised by his father away from society and does not know what women are. The effect of his discovery of them is even more powerful because of his innocence.

46. Cazauran ("La Trentième Nouvelle," p. 630) has specifically commented on this novella (number 30) for its similarity to a story told by Luther in his *Enarrationes in Genesin*.

47. This feature appears on all levels of the book—in the theological discus-

sions, in descriptions of illness, in the narrative form—thanks to what I will call the hydraulic mechanism. The basic metaphor here is that of water behind a dam: "Et, tout ainsy que l'eaue par force retenue court avecq plus d'impetuosité quant on la laisse aller, que celle qui court ordinairement, ainsy ceste pauvre dame tourna sa gloire à la contraincte qu'elle donnoit à son corps. Quant elle vint à descendre le premier degré de son honnesteté, se trouva soubdainement portée jusques au dernier" (230/318). This is the description of the good woman who sleeps with her son and whose shame is brought about by the austerity of her life, an austerity that represses nature to such an extent that still worse sins occur. This conception of the bursting forth of the constrained or hidden appears frequently in the passages of novellas in which lovers hide their passion: "parfaicte amour mene les gens à la mort, par trop estre celée et mescongneue" (53/119). Any strong emotion can produce a similar effect of increasing the hydraulic pressure. In story 10 the heroine, Floride, on hearing of the death of the man she loves secretly, held in her tears so completely that the tears "having been held into her heart by force, caused violent bleeding from the nose in such abundance that her life was almost lost" (69/137). Even when love is described as a flame (pyro-hydraulics?), the constraint in which it is kept makes it burn stronger (story 26, 217/301).

This metaphor in itself is extremely banal, but in the *Heptameron* it functions as part of a union between health and sin. By holding back her emotion in an attempt to conform obediently to her mother's wishes, Floride makes herself sick and almost dies. By trying to hide a true love that could not be satisfied in a socially acceptable marriage, the young gentleman of story 9 makes himself sick and dies. The incestuous mother is so austere in her sexual life that natural appetite cannot be satisfied except through the unnatural means of incest. By holding in emotion, you become sick; by holding in sinful but natural desire, you fall into a still graver sin. In both cases, the harm is done by human will and reason, and the stronger the will and the more ingenious the reason, the worse the damage. There is a surprising wisdom in sinning because by sinning you confess the fall of human nature and the danger of our attempts to improve our lot. Marguerite thus elaborates a hygienics of the passions based on what we would call the release of repressed desire: "Je voy que les folz, si on ne les tue, vivent plus longuement que les saiges, et n'y entendz que une raison, c'est qu'ilz ne dissimullent point leurs passions. S'ils sont courroucez, ilz frappent; s'ilz son joieulx, ilz rient; et ceulx qui cuydent estre saiges dissimulent tant leurs imperfections, qu'ilz en ont tous les cueurs empoisonnez" (249/339).

48. Letter to Marguerite de Navarre of March 6, 1522, quoted in Defaux, *Le Curieux*, p. 117.

49. After hoodwinking the young woman into marrying a Franciscan, the monks still benefit from their control of belief. When the young "married" woman sees her husband saying mass, she tells her mother what she sees, only to receive her mother's reproach, "Je vous prie, ma fille, ne mectez poinct ceste opinion dedans vostre teste, car c'est une chose totallement impossible que ceulx qui sont si sainctes gens eussent faict une telle tromperie; vous pescheriez

grandement contre Dieu d'adjouster foy à une telle opinion" (350/453). A similar attempt to mystify the laity occurs in the story of the priest whose sister, though an austere and holy virgin, became pregnant. The priest, who was his sister's lover, performed an elaborate "verification" by which she swore on the eucharist that no man had touched her any more than her brother (248/338). The force of these two examples comes from the force of the hidden, the discrepancy between what is on the surface and what is underneath. The apparent holiness of a human being makes the bursting through of sin all the more powerful and, it must be said, satisfying. At the end of the story the incestuous priest and his sister were burned together, "dont tout le peuple eut ung merveilleux esbahissement, ayant veu soubz si sainct manteau ung monstre si horrible, et soubz une vie tant louable et saincte regner ung si detestable vice" (249/339).

50. The insistence on the salvation by grace is well established in studies of Marguerite de Navarre. As Febvre summarizes her doctrine: "Justification par la foi; gratuité de la grâce divine; impuissance radicale de la créature; nullité des mérites humains; autant d'articles de la credo de Marguerite" (*Autour de l'Heptaméron*, p. 125). See also Lefranc, *Les Idées religieuses de Marguerite de Navarre*, and Cottrell, *The Grammar of Silence*. See also Roelker, "The Appeal of Calvinism."

51. Wolfgang Capito (also known as Capiton and Köpfel), contemporary and correspondent of Marguerite de Navarre, reported that her spiritual development went through two successive crises, the first when she lost confidence in the redemptive force of good works, the second when she ceased believing in exercises of mysticism (Heller, "Marguerite de Navarre and the Reformers of Meaux," pp. 301–2). Such a development would explain a resignation to grace and a doubt about the efficacy of any learning or teaching.

52. Cf. the remarks on silence made by Kahn in reference to Montaigne: "The question that Montaigne then seems to imply in the *Essais* is whether a form of writing that pretended to self-destruct, like Christ . . . would not be the most hubristic of all? A writing that pretended to silence, the most pretentious? A writing in which the writer asserted his will to nonsignification, to absolute self-referentiality (i.e. nonrefernetiality) . . . would not this be the most blasphemous of all?" (*Rhetoric, Prudence, and Skepticism in the Renaissance*, p. 150).

53. Benjamin, "The Storyteller," p. 87. Emphasis added.

Chapter III

1. Cf. Compagnon, "Le jeton résume toutes les sentences de la "Librairie" dont le sens commun serait en effet d'abstention, et Montaigne le fit frapper et circuler parmi ses amis, tel un signe monétaire dont il aurait lui-même été le référent" (*La Seconde Main*, p. 286).

2. Much excellent scholarship has been devoted to Montaigne's use of example, particularly with reference to *exemplum*. Among this work are the studies of Regosin, *The Matter of My Book*, and "Le Miroüer Vague"; Kritzman,

Destruction/découverte; Cottrell, *Sexuality/Textuality*; Blum, "La Fonction du 'déjà dit.' " Cottrell, in defining *exemplum*, points out the vague contours this concept has assumed in Renaissance scholarship: "An *exemplum* is in fact a literary genre that is based on the adage, the *sententia*, the maxim, the common place, which in the Renaissance was a subliterary genre—more a device than a genre, really—that was intended to communicate commonly held values and to transmit culture" *Sexuality/Textuality*, p. 58). In pointing to this hesitation between genre and device, Cottrell paves the way toward a renewal of the study of *exemplum* within rhetoric and outside the narrower framework of poetic (or literary) genres. In commenting on a specific instance in *Essais* 1.47, Cottrell also frees *exemplum* from the presupposition that it must be narrative in form (*Sexuality/Textuality*, p. 88). Kritzman underscores with vigor the way Montaigne subverts classical *exempla* and locates the generation of the "essai" as genre precisely in that subversion: "Le moyen traditionnel de communication, l'*exemplum* est rompu et une nouvelle forme générique, l' 'essai,' apparaît dans le travail dialectique de l'écriture" (*Destruction/découverte*, p. 31). Blum stresses the incompatibility of Montaigne's use of *exempla* or historical allegations and the apparent message (p. 42). Regosin's 1983 article ("Le Miroüer Vague") is, however, the first study to consider the Montaignian example in all its breadth, both *exemplum* and other types of example. This is particularly important insofar as Regosin overturns the conventional view that example is preponderant only in the early essays. The examples, as Regosin argues, are displaced from classical culture to nature ("Le Miroüer Vague," p. 78) but do not disappear or assume less importance.

3. All quotations of Montaigne given in English are from Donald Frame's translation, *The Complete Essays of Montaigne* (Stanford: Stanford University Press, 1958), and quotations in French are from V.-L. Saulnier's reissue of Pierre Villey's 1924 edition, *Les Essais de Michel de Montaigne* (Paris: Presses universitaires de France, 1965). Hereafter page references will be given in parentheses with the reference to the French text preceding the English.

4. "The *exempla* that are lined up like so many building blocks are meant to astonish and provoke our amazement. Indeed, Montaigne chose them precisely because they astonished *him*," writes Cottrell (*Sextuality/Textuality*, p. 37). Pertile asks the following provocative question in regard to the "material" stockpiled by Montaigne: "If in fact Montaigne's messages are as original as everybody seems to think, how could they be sustained by a type of material which draws its authority from the very fact that it is commonly accepted" ("Paper and Ink," p. 208). It seems, on the contrary, that Montaigne attempted to find material that was not commonly accepted and to point to problems in the acceptance of the examples he chose.

5. Kritzman's perception of the genesis of the "essay" in the rupture of and with *exemplum* should be reemphasized here. See also Rendall, "In Disjointed Parts/Par articles decousus."

6. A few of Montaigne's comments on his preferences in books emphasize the love of discontinuity. Plutarch and Seneca are his favorites because of their

fragmented quality, "Ils ont tous deux cette notable commodité pour mon humeur, que la science que j'y cherche, y est traictée à pieces décousues . . ." (II.10:413/300). Having raised his lack of memory to an aesthetic principle, Montaigne notes, "Ce qu'on me veut proposer, il faut que ce soit à parcelles . . ." (II.17:649/300). Reading Tacitus, he admits that he rarely spends more than an hour at a time with a book—thus reading itself for Montaigne is a practice of discontinuity and interruption—and finds that Tacitus is really not digressive enough for his taste. Montaigne describes the Latin historian as moving too rapidly ahead with his principal argument and not spending the time to narrate the bizarre and eccentric cruelties and deaths that could be found in his period (III.8:940–41).

7. Montaigne's fascination with rare and unusual examples far surpasses what we can study here. It is worth noting his own discussion on belief and disbelief of "incredible" examples in II.27: "C'est folie de rapporter le vray et le faux a nostre suffisance."

8. Cottrell shows that rarity also characterizes late examples and early ones (e.g., the goat with kidney stones, Sexuality/Textuality, p. 80).

9. In the opening passage of the essay, Montaigne challenges the rarity (and hence, value) of the philosophers' fortitude. Far from lacking fortitude, the common people have too much. They do not qualify as "exemplary" in the classical sense because they are completely and naturally indifferent to death and suffering (51–54/33–35). Montaigne suggests subversively that philosophers are examples because it is so rare to find one who endures suffering without complaint. Philosophers are thus requalified as "examples" but in a new, ironic sense based on a conception of supply and demand. Distinctions in age and also gender can be treated as class differences. Cottrell comments on the tradition of grouping women and children together in opposition to men (Sexuality/Textuality, p. 7).

10. This formula not only is similar to Genette's formula for versimilitude in Figures 2 (pp. 71–98), but the same formula used in a specialized context. The status of the father is in inverse proportion to the verisimilitude of his reaction. Because these figures behave in a way that runs counter to expectation, they become exceptions and hence "examples."

11. "History . . . appears in the essays in the fragmented form of innumerable exempla that, instead of articulating clear moral principles, form a confusing jumble of contradictory notions that ultimately tend to cancel each other out, leaving the reader at a kind of degré zéro" (Cottrell, Sexuality/Textuality, p. 65).

12. Regosin states the relationship between history and example: "By writing experience down Montaigne not only creates a past, and his own history (that is to say, his own present), he endows that experience with exemplariness and affirms a sense of temporal duration. . . . as singularity the example makes the moment primary; in its relation to the general it evokes relationships and the making of history" ("Le Miroüer Vague," p. 84). The connectedness that

is history is both source of example and its antithesis, for the example must, at least provisionally, cast history into the background.

13. Conley has treated the absence or hole around which the essay is constructed in terms of anal economics in "Cataparalysis."

14. The interplay between classical and modern or American history in "Of coaches" with reference to exemplarity is an extensive topic. Montaigne is playing with the consecration of classical *exempla* and their interaction with everyday life when he regrets that Alexander the Great was not the one who conquered the Americas and then goes on to remind his readers that the conduct of the Spanish conquerors will also become a form of (negative) exemplarity in the eyes of the Americans: "que les premiers exemples et deportmens nostres qui se sont presentez par delà eussent appelé ces peuples à l'admiration et imitation de la vertu . . ." (910).

15. "Of coaches" is Montaigne's answer to a problem described by Cottrell: "an *exemplum* . . . must be complete. Although Montaigne may feel in a general way that he is living in the final stages of a historical period that began with antiquity, he obviously cannot perceive the period as a totality . . . Only another society, outside that historical continuum (a new world, for example), would be able to perceive the history of western Europe from the Greeks and Romans to the end of the sixteenth century as a genuine *exemplum*" (*Sexuality/Textuality*, p. 62).

16. Friedrich, meaning no doubt to point out the contrast between the use of example in the *Essais* and in the compendia of oratorical raw material compiled according to Erasmus's precepts, argues that Montaigne restores the concreteness of the individual case (*Montaigne*, p. 205). This restoration is only partial. Montaigne not only remains aware of the compilation of examples by others but submits the concreteness of individual cases to the needs of his essay. This may differ from the alphabetical compilations of medieval *exempla*, but Montaigne's is not an essentially historicizing approach.

17. Cotgrave's *Dictionarie* gives the two following related and juxtaposed definitions: "Monstre: A monster; a deformed creature, a thing that's fashioned or bred contrarie to nature" and "Montre: f. A patterne, scantling, proofe, example, essay; also, a muster, view, show, or sight; the countenance, representation, or outward appearance of a thing; a demonstration; also, a watch or little clock that strikes not; also the glass box that stands on the stalls of Goldsmithes, Cutlers, & c; and generally, any thing that shewes, or points at another thing . . ." It should be recalled that the dictionary gives "Exemple, exemplaire; Monstre" as translations for "An example."

18. Especially Schon, in "Die Kompilationsliteratur," in *Vorformen des Essays in Antike und Humanismus*, pp. 63–89. Erasmus had recommended, in *De copia*, that the orator or writer lay up a store of examples (book 2, pp. 607–46).

19. Carol Clark notes Montaigne's suspicion of money and his denial of its intrinsic value in several essays (II.12;II.18;II.20): *The Web of Metaphor*, pp. 119–20.

20. For imagination and its role in Montaigne's sexuality, see Cottrell, *Sex-*

uality/Textuality, pp. 19ff. Cottrell also makes pertinent remarks on the economy of sexuality in Montaigne, e.g., pp. 146–53.

21. Cf. Wilden's comment on the absence of La Boétie and its value for Montaigne: "man's desire, as for Hegel, is defined by the Other, and . . . its object is never satisfaction or real possession, but always the metonymic *tension* of a movement towards the desire of the Other" (Par divers moyens," pp. 593–94).

22. Presumably the groom, who has "l'ame et les oreilles si battues, qu'il se trouva lié du trouble de son imagination," is fearful of a spell, as is his family. It could be that the groom is merely experiencing the preoccupation with his excessive desire (for the bride or for a vision of his own prowess), which Montaigne mentions at the beginning of the paragraph.

23. On process in Montaigne's approach to knowledge, one should note comments by several other readers. Regosin says of Montaigne's untraditional view of books: "What is in books does not constitute knowledge; rather . . . their content has been neutralized and has itself become a means to knowledge (*The Matter of My Book*, p. 92). Pertile comments on Montaigne's own use of examples: "Whereas the examples in traditional writing had only narrative functions (expounding tautologically on a preordained 'truth'), in the *Essais* they have an ideological function, in so far as they generate the need for and the practice of an undogmatic, critical analysis of reality" ("Paper and Ink," p. 208). Blum likewise refers to Montaigne's quotations and examples as a form of "seminal" material that engages the reader to figure out where such references lead ("La Fonction du 'déjà dit,' " pp. 46–47).

24. Cave puts the use of example in the *Essais* in the context of early humanist doctrines of the pregnancy of meaning in such privileged texts as the Bible and Homer and adds, "it is clear from his practice of interpretation, if not from his overt statements, that any reading is acceptable if it is profitable to the reader, that is to say, if it prompts self-awareness or helps to train the judgment" ("Problems of Reading in the *Essais*," p. 143).

25. Such an interpretation agrees with comments made by Wilden (see note above) and others concerning the role of the absent deal figure of La Boétie in Montaigne's *Essais*.

26. On "Du Jeune Caton" and Montaigne's possible acquaintance with Longinus, see Logan's insightful article, "Montaigne et Longin."

27. *The Matter of My Book*, p. 86.

28. As Blum says, "la citation, juridique ou rhétorique, instaure une relation entre deux sujets (celui qui cite; celui qui est cité à comparaître), tandis que l'allégation le fait entre un sujet et un objet" ("La Fonction du 'déjà dit,' " p. 38).

29. Although Montaigne's awareness of his bodily functions is unusually acute, that *awareness* appears as an ability to put his sensations into words. I must disagree with Friedrich's insistence on the nonmediated nature of self-analysis. In speaking of "cette immédiateté qui offre à l'analyste de soi la garantie de toucher au vif de la chose" (*Montaigne*, p. 17), Friedrich seems to

ignore his own acknowledgment of Montaigne's thorough literary formation and mentality.

30. "L'observateur [Montaigne] se regarde *de biais*, à travers le discours des autheurs, depuis cette marge nécessaire de la culture ancienne qui, paradoxalement, libère le moy de l'autorité, de l'altérité" (Rigolot, "Montaigne et la poétique de la marge," p. 140).

31. It is undoubtedly significant for Montaigne's relationship to his own writing that he began life without a "mother tongue" (*langue maternelle*) and instead spoke a language imposed by his father. Although the young Montaigne did not apparently realize this (if one can believe that he never heard anything but Latin), retrospectively he must have realized the unusual, unique, and bizarre nature of his own language. By the time he wrote the *Essais* he seems to be looking at his own first language as being somehow an external language, a language of others (in quotations), and his "self" linguistically somewhere in between.

32. On the structure of "Par divers moyens," see Cottrell, "Croisement chiasmatique dans le premier Essai de Montaigne."

33. Auerbach, *Mimesis*, p. 254.

34. See Patrick Henry, "Recognition of the Other and Avoidance of the Double."

35. "La continuité interne prend sa source dans la fidélité au modèle externe. Telle est, notamment, la fonction que le spectateur assignera aux existences exemplaires: l'exemple est la figure qui, mise à part (*ex-emplum*), mais appelant l'imitation et la généralisation, peut conforter l'individu, dans sa singularité vertueuse: faisant effort pour se maintenir en état de ressemblance continue à l'égard de ceux qui furent des miracles de constance, il s'exercera à devenir identique à soi-même" (*Montaigne en mouvement*, p. 29).

36. Despite its title, Gutwirth's study of Montaigne (*Michel de Montaigne ou le pari d'exemplarité*) does not devote too much space to the question of example. In a brief passage in which the subject appears, however, Gutwirth seems to indicate that Montaigne does present himself as a model to influence the conduct of others (pp. 157–62).

37. Wilden, "Par divers moyens," p. 581: "Montaigne's division from himself, both for him and for us, depends upon the alienation of the self which is described, accepted, and rejected in the discourse of the *Essais*."

38. Friedrich not only notes of III.2 that the claim "Je ne peints pas l'estre je peints le passage . . ." is related to division and fragmentation, but emphasizes that Montaigne's interest in Plutarch is linked to the fragmentation of history: "Les biographies de Plutarque, qui ont pour sujets les acteurs de grands événements historiques et leur théâtre, ne sont pas de l'historiographie. Les moments de l'histoire nationale ou universelle dont elles parlent y sont présentés fragmentairement, sans qu'aucune fin les oriente, qu'aucune vue d'ensemble les englobe . . ." (*Montaigne*, p. 87). Friedrich also says of the collections of *sententiae* and maxims: "Même les recueils de sentences et de maximes, si formalistes qu'ils puissent parfois paraître, fragmentent l'Homme en cas particu-

lier, en combinaisons infinies, et replacent les vieilles assertions dans le jeu perpétuellement mouvant des perspectives observées" (p. 193).

39. Cottrell, *Sexuality/Textuality*, p. 80. In this section, "Away from exemplarity," Cottrell links exemplarity with the exercise of the will: "In the A passages of the earliest essays, the rare and memorable events that he has culled from history all illustrate the power of the will to overcome or to manipulate external circumstances . . . If Montaigne's first-person narratives are unexemplary, it is basically because they do not recount a triumph of the will" (p. 79).

CHAPTER IV

1. "La manière d'écrire d'Epictète, de Montaigne, et de Salomon de Tultie est la plus d'usage, qui s'insinue le mieux, qui demeure plus dans la mémoire et qui se fait le plus citer, parce qu'elle est toute composée de pensées nées sur les entretiens ordinaires de la vie . . ." (*Pensées*, 745/18bis). Quotations from the *Pensées* are from Louis Lafuma's edition (Paris: Le Seuil ["L'Intégrale"] 1963).

2. On the self in general and the work of Pascal in particular, I wish to thank Milad Doueihi for allowing me to read his manuscript, *Deus Zelotes: Pascal's Subject*. Doueihi's argument and mine touch on numerous points, especially in the definition of the self through the other. His treatment of figure ("The Figure of the Middle") is pertinent and differs from what follows here in its approach to the temporality of figure.

3. *Discours de la méthode pour bien conduire sa raison*, p. 126. The English translation of this passage, like all subsequent ones, is from the edition by Laurence J. Lafleur, *Discourse on Method*, p. 1. Page references in the text give first the page of the French and then the page of the English edition. I have occasionally modified Lafleur's translation (and have used italics) to clarify terms important for the study of example.

4. Gilson in the notes (p. 83) to his edition and Simpson in his "Putting One's House in Order" have indicated the problems of interpreting this sentence. Gilson sees it as containing a trace of irony, while Simpson sees it as a "shaming" based on the rapid passage between ironic and serious modes that is forced on the reader. Montaigne makes a similar comment toward the beginning of *Essais* 1.14: "les hommes sont tous d'une espece, et sauf le plus et le moins, se trouvent garnis de pareils outils et instrumens pour concevoir et juger" (p. 51).

5. Although the first paragraph does not contain the first-person singular, it makes extensive use of the first-person plural, which is here conflated with the third-person plural.

6. Italicized terms emphasized by Descartes.

7. Here I am not making the discourse/history as established by Benveniste in "L'homme dans la langue" (*Problèmes de linguistique générale*, pp. 223–85). "History" here is rather what comes to the subject from a time-dominated external realm.

8. I have modified Lafleur's translation here. Descartes uses the term *histoire*, which Lafleur renders as "autobiography," and the term *fable*, which Lafleur Englishes as "story."

9. In Lafleur's translation this is rendered: "that all will take my frankness kindly" (p. 3).

10. See Nancy's comments on the problems of Descartes's own belief in frankness: "How could he have confidence in frankness who singly has just invented frankness as method . . ." ("Larvatus pro Deo," p. 34).

11. Although Nancy attends to Descartes's use of such generic categories as *fable, epic*, and *autobiography*, he seems to neglect the specific qualities of *roman* in Descartes's text and context. See Nancy, "Larvatus pro deo," and "Mundus est fabula."

12. For an extremely rich overview of the theory of romance as genre, see the editors' introduction to *Romance*, eds. Kevin Brownlee and Marina Scordillis Brownlee, pp. 1–22.

13. "La multitude des lois fournit souvent des excuses aux vices . . ." (137/12).

14. The image of the man of letters and his solitary effort at writing a persuasive and verisimilar account may be another cleavage of the subject between the discoverer and the writer (cf. in part 4: "Je ne sais si je dois vous entretenir des premières méditations que j'y ai faites; car elles sont si métaphysiques et si peu communes qu'elles ne seront pas au gré de tout le monde," 147/20). This hesitation is in keeping with the Cartesian *topos* of suspicion of texts—a variant of the long Western tradition of logocentrism—of inciting the reader to maintain a distance from all written philosophy, as Derrida points out ("Du supplément à la source," in *De la grammatologie*, pp. 379–445). Since Descartes manifests suspicion of all language, and not only written language, his philosophy is attempting to found itself in a prelinguistic apprehension of the idea, but the most basic moment, the Cogito, seems able to be conceived in an act of speech. For Port-Royal's attempt to deal with this apparent need for speech, see Marin, *La Critique du discours*, especially chap. 2, "Du mot, valeur d'échange aux corps-langages." The fear of abstraction leads back to the self of the reader through the return to "les raisonnements que chacun fait touchant les affaires qui lui importent, et dont l'événement le doit punir bientôt après s'il a mal jugé" (131/6). This suspicion of texts is in keeping with the Cartesian preoccupation with *vraisemblance* (e.g., "je ne choisissais que les plus modérées [des opinions], tant à cause que ce sont toujours les plus commodes pour la pratique, et *vraisemblablement* les meilleures, tous excès ayant coutume d'être mauvais . . ." (141/15) and "s'ils ne vont justement où ils désirent, ils arriveront au moins à la fin quelque part où *vraisemblablement* ils seront mieux que dans le milieu d'une forêt" (142/16), for the *vraisemblable* is a conventional element of rhetoric, of which Descartes, as rhetorician, makes abundant use. At the same time his protagonist's experience as reader makes him point out the danger of the adherence to the verisimilar (as opposed to the true), which the *Discourse* itself calls upon. The use of the categories *vraisemblable* and *vrai* in the

same text links Descartes's work to the problematic novels of Lafayette, as we will see later.

15. The protagonist—"I"—becomes a metonymy for the educational institution: "j'étais en l'une des plus célèbres écoles de l'Europe, où je pensais qu'il devait y avoir de savants hommes, s'il y en avait en aucun endroit de la terre. J'y avais appris tout ce que les autres y apprenaient . . . je ne voyais point qu'on m'estimait inférieur à mes condisciples . . ." (128/3). In a sense the structure of the opening of the *Discourse*, the passage in which the author presents himself as being essentially similar to his fellow men, recurs here within the "history or fable." There is an initial moment of total identification of the subject with all others of a certain category. Thereafter the whole effort of the author is toward creating difference from this original sameness.

16. When the protagonist, at the beginning of part 2, leaves behind school and traveling for the solitude of the winter quarters, the cluster of discredited figures of the "I" and others (the preceptor, the man of letters, the "I" as former student and as former traveler) is recalled just before the dense and repetitive insistence on unicity that announces the foundation of the rules of method: "les bâtiments qu'un seul architecte a entrepris . . . ," "les sciences des livres . . . s'étant composées et grossies peu à peu des opinions de plusieurs diverses personnes . . ." We are led toward the will of the "I" to be in a sense unique and self-created, to assume a role *not* dependent on example. The beginning of part 3 is directly connected to the opening of part 2 by the building simile, but in part 3 the construction is linked to the way in which the "I" is *perceived* as behaving.

17. "Pour savoir quelles étaient véritablement leurs opinions, je devais plutôt prendre garde à ce qu'ils pratiquaient qu'à ce qu'ils disaient; non seulement à cause qu'en la corruption de nos moeurs il y a peu de gens qui veuillent dire tout ce qu'ils croient, mais aussi à cause que plusieurs l'ignorent eux-mêmes" (141/15).

18. "Il est bien plus vraisemblable qu'un homme seul les ait rencontrées que tout un peuple" (136/11). On "unicity" in Descartes, see Goux, "Descartes et la perspective."

19. Again the mask (Nancy) but of a specific type, one that borrows from the reader's image as established by the text.

20. The moment of withdrawal into the heated room of the winter quarters in part 2 is the beginning of the narrative of methodical doubt and of methodical solitude, but it is also the moment of particularly dense historical reference: "J'étais alors en Allemagne, où l'occasion des guerres qui n'y sont pas encore finies m'avait appelé; et, comme je retournais du couronnement de l'empereur vers l'armée, le commencement de l'hiver m'arrêta en un quartier où, ne trouvant aucune conversation qui me divertît, et n'ayant d'ailleurs, par bonheur, aucuns soins ni passions qui me troublassent, je demeurais tout le jour enfermé seul dans un poêle . . ." (132/7). This anecdotal, physical solitude is a step on the path that leads from the initial fusion with humanity toward the utter metaphysical solitude of the Cogito. Two paragraphs before the Cogito, Des-

cartes mentions the heated room once more, long after apparently dropping the physical setting of the protagonist. The heated room is first mentioned in part 2 (132) and then next in the second paragraph from the end of part 3 (144). Descartes returns to the topic of his travels, declaring that he left "le poêle où j'avais eu toutes ces pensées" (144/18). Immediately before the paragraph of the Cogito, the protagonist explains the advantages of being settled in Holland. The operation of the Cogito takes on a negating force that it would lack if it had not been placed in opposition to this particularly strong characterization of the subject as autobiographical protagonist, as physical being. The effect of this narrative preparation of the Cogito can be seen by comparing the Cogito in the *Discourse* to the Cogito as it appears early in the *Méditations*, without the buildup.

21. The Cogito can take place only in the present. Descartes's thought runs somewhat like this: "I think, therefore I am, but I cannot affirm that I was nor that I will be. I cannot affirm the existence of other reasonable beings equal to myself except by passing through the truthful God who would not allow us to be completely deluded" (for the solitude of the Cogito, see Poulet, "La 'nausée' de Sartre et le 'Cogito' cartésien"). It seems significant that Descartes's reflections in part 4 on "des pensées que j'avais de plusieurs autres choses hors de moi" do not include the possibility of another *equal* being but instead pass from things "comme du ciel, de la terre, de la lumière," etc., to the idea of a being more perfect than the "I" (148–49/22). Descartes arrives at the thought of imperfect intelligences only later, as things dependent on God (150/23). Thus the solitude of the metaphysical subject is characterized by an absence of any *similar* subject.

22. One of the reasons for the conspicuous gap between example and authority in the *Discourse* is the problem of the "I" as narrative authority and narrative figure. Examples can be, in fact almost always are, *given* by an authoritative speaker or writer. But the authority of the speaker is distanced from the example in such a way that the example forms an ostensible common ground between the speaker and the listener. This distancing permits rhetorical flexibility, since the listener may challenge the example without engaging in a direct assault on the authority of the speaker. At the same time the speaker may attempt to obtain the compliance of the listener but will avoid directly imperative language. In the *Discourse*, imitation of the example would almost certainly require the listener to *replace* the speaker, eliminating the concept of common ground and opening an endless chain of *coups d'état* or *coups de parole*. The self-suspicion, which grows through Cartesianism in a terrain prepared by neostoicism and Montaignian self-observation (or self-creation in language) also prospers in a period of "direction of conscience." See Foucault's remarks on the "discursive fermentation" caused by the elaboration of confession in the Catholic church after the Council of Trent in *La Volonté de savoir*, pp. 25ff. St. François de Sales recommends weekly confession and daily examination of conscience.

23. This fragment is headed "Pyrr." in the Lafuma and other editions. We

accept Le Guern's reading of the manuscript as "Prin." for *Principes* (Principles) and not "Pyrr." See Le Guern, *Pascal et Descartes*, p. 48. This passage seems to set forth one of the principles of organization of the *Pensées*. The fragment numbers given hereafter in parentheses will indicate the Lafuma numbering.

24. Among the most important of these studies are Topliss, *The Rhetoric of Pascal*; Davidson, *The Origins of Certainty*; Nelson, *Pascal*; and Pugh, *The Composition of Pascal's Apologia*.

25. I am here using "metonym" in the limited sense proposed by Rice and Schofer in *Rhetorical Poetics*, pp. 24–28.

26. On *enargeia* and *evidentia* in the theory and practice of rhetoric in the Renaissance, see Cave, *The Cornucopian Text*, and Norton, *The Ideology and Language of Translation in the Renaissance*.

27. This passage from Pascal could easily have been taken from La Bruyère's *Caractères* (1688), a work that demonstrates a similar tendency toward the fragmentation of social observation, but with a different motivation from Pascal's. La Bruyère seems to offer a kind of limitless and insignificant fragmentation, but Pascal's creation of characters invites a search for the explanation of such irruptions of noncoherence.

28. Is it accidental that Pascal demonstrates the danger of the *image*, through which the imagination controls us, with an example of a *magistrat*, whose title is almost an anagram for the *image* through which he controls society? At the same time, the magistrate serves didactically to teach us, thus returning us to the etymology of *magister*, "teacher."

29. "Etant le plus souvent fausse elle [l'imagination] ne donne aucune marque de sa qualité marquant du même caractère le vrai et le faux. Je ne parle pas des fous, je parle des plus sages, et c'est parmi eux que l'imagination a le grand droit de persuader les hommes. La raison a beau crier, elle ne peut mettre le prix aux choses."

30. "D'autant plus fourbe qu'elle ne l'est pas toujours, car elle serait règle infaillible de vérité, si elle l'était infaillible du mensonge . . ."

31. This syncopated incorporation of gestures outside itself may make Pascal's text especially Jansenist, since Arnauld and Nicole's *Logique* also includes many examples from everyday situations and from familiar authors. Marin points out that the *Pensées* themselves play a role in the *Logique* as a "privileged punctuation," which distances the didactic discourse of the *Logique* from itself (*La Critique du discours*, p. 17). Such a distancing of the theoretical text from itself may be part of a broader Jansenist distrust of theory. The *Logique* and the *Grammaire* represent undoubtedly the extreme theoretical reach of Port-Royal, as against Le Maistre de Sacy's strongly anti-intellectual and antitheoretical bent. Arnauld was apparently atypical of Port-Royal in his pro-Cartesian stance (Le Guern, *Pascal et Descartes*, p. 129). Despite the prevalent conviction that Port-Royal is strongly committed to the doctrine of a transparency of the signifier (a conception corrected in part by the work of Marin), the *Pensées* are a reminder that all social phenomena, in their opacity and disorder, are potentially signifiers.

32. Commentators of the text who attempt to reconstruct Pascal's line of reasoning point repeatedly to examples in the text: "The examples Pascal gives are familiar from other fragments . . . ," Pascal "gives several examples from the Old Testament," and one fragment "groups examples of prophecies fulfilled within Old Testament times." These quotations are from Pugh, *The Composition of Pascal's Apologia*, pp. 219, 220, 240, and 252, respectively. Other commentators locate examples in similar fashion. Cf. Wetsel's discussion of Le Maistre de Sacy's *Préface à la Genèse*: "Sacy cites additional examples of how Jesus' explication of passages from the Old Testament serves to establish the authority of Moses" (*L'Ecriture et le Reste*, p. 75). Example here appears as the privileged figure of textual commentary in its segmentation and extraction of a primary text.

33. For the relationship between Pascal's argument and the biblical exegetics of Port-Royal, especially on the thought of Le Maistre de Sacy, see Wetsel, *L'Ecriture et le Reste*, chaps. 4–6.

34. This is not the place for a lengthy discussion of Pascal's doctrine of biblical figure in relation to the religious and semiotic thought of his time. For detailed considerations on these points, see Gounelle, *La Bible selon Pascal*; Lhermet, *Pascal et la Bible*; Marin, *La Critique du discours*; Miel, *Pascal and Theology*; and especially Wetsel, *L'Ecriture et le Reste*.

35. Gounelle emphasizes the sobriety of Pascal's use of figure as a hermeneutic tool in comparison with the practice of many exegetes of his time (*La Bible selon Pascal*, p. 35).

36. "Ce qui nous gâte pour comparer ce qui s'est passé autrefois dans l'église à ce qui s'y voit maintenant est que ordinairement on regarde saint Athanase, sainte Thérèse et les autres, comme couronnés de gloire et d'ans, jugés avant nous comme des dieux. A présent que le temps a éclairci les choses cela paraît ainsi, mais au temps où on le persécutait ce grand saint était un homme qui s'appelait Athanase et sainte Thérèse une fille. Elie était un homme comme nous et sujet aux mêmes passions que nous, dit saint Pierre pour désabuser les chrétiens de cette fausse idée, qui nous fait rejeter *l'exemple* des saints comme disproportionné à notre état. C'étaient des saints, disons-nous, ce n'est pas comme nous" (598).

37. Cf. the views of Le Maistre de Sacy as expounded by Wetsel, *L'Ecriture et le Reste*, pp. 54ff.

38. "On ne peut faire une bonne physionomie qu'en accordant toutes nos contrariétés et il ne suffit pas de suivre une suite de qualités accordantes sans accorder les contraires; pour entendre le sens d'un auteur il faut accorder tous les passages contraires.

"Ainsi pour entendre l'Ecriture il faut avoir un sens dans lequel tous les passages contraires s'accordent; il ne suffit pas d'en avoir un qui convienne à plusieurs passages accordants, mais d'en avoir un qui accorde les passages même contraires."

39. "On ne saurait pas même accorder les passages d'un même auteur, ni

d'un même livre, ni quelquefois d'un même chapitre, ce qui marque trop quel était le sens de l'auteur."

40. "Les Juifs avai(en)t vieilli dans ces pensées terrestres: que Dieu aimait leur père Abraham, sa chair et ce qui en sortait, que pour cela il les avait multipliés et distingués de tous les autres peuples sans souffrir qu'ils s'y mélassent, que quand ils languissaient dans l'Egypte il les en retira avec tous ses grands signes en leur faveur . . . [etc.]" (270).

41. "Les autres religions, comme les païennes, sont plus populaires, car elles sont en extérieur, mais elles ne sont pas pour les gens habiles. Une religion purement intellectuelle serait plus proportionnée aux habiles, mais elle ne servirait pas au peuple. La seule religion chrétienne est proportionnée à tous, étant mêlée d'extérieur et d'intérieur. Elle élève le peuple à l'intérieur, et abaisse les superbes à l'extérieur, et n'est pas parfaite sans les deux, car il faut que le peuple entende l'esprit de la lettre et que les habiles soumettent leur esprit à la lettre" (219).

42. "Le monde juge bien des choses, car il est dans l'ignorance naturelle qui est le vrai siège de l'homme. Les sciences ont deux extrémités qui se touchent, la première est la pure ignorance naturelle où se trouvent tous les hommes en naissant, l'autre extrémité est celle où arrivent les grandes âmes qui ayant parcouru tout ce que les hommes peuvent savoir trouvent qu'ils ne savent rien et se rencontrent en cette même ignorance d'où ils étaient partis, mais c'est une ignorance savante qui se connaît" (83).

43. An apparent reference to *Essais* 1.42. See Croquette, *Pascal et Montaigne*, p. 26.

44. Goldmann, *Le Dieu caché*. See especially chaps. 9, "Le Paradoxe et le fragment," and 13, "La Morale et l'esthétique." Pascal did not practice or advocate permanent retreat from the world, since man's actions cannot by themselves lead to salvation, nor can man realize on earth the higher ethical values, such as justice.

45. "Ainsi on se prend mal pour les blâmer; leur faute n'est pas en ce qu'ils cherchent le tumulte. S'ils ne le cherchaient que comme un divertissement, mais le mal est qu'ils le recherchent comme si la possession des choses qu'ils recherchent les devait rendre véritablement heureux, et c'est en quoi on a raison d'accuser leur recherche de vanité . . ." (136).

46. Davidson, *The Origins of Certainty*, p. 5.

47. For an example of a more simply illustrative use, see in Lafuma's edition, *Ecrits sur la grâce*, sec. 4, p. 336: "s'il est besoin d'éclaircir une chose si claire par des exemples, n'est-il pas véritable qu'il n'est pas impossible aux hommes de faire la guerre? et cependant il n'est pas toujours au pouvoir de tous les hommes de la faire." This is part of an example series illustrating the principal that if something is possible sometimes, one cannot say that it is impossible.

48. Cf. De Man's analysis of the opposite conceptualization of a substitution of selves in Rousseau's second *Discourse*, where substitution of selves is

the very meaning of love: "The portrait allows for the bizarre substitution of self for other, and of other for self, called love" (*Allegories of Reading*, p. 162).

49. The principal difference between the selves in the two writers is neatly conveyed by the difference in pronoun with which they treat the self. Readers of Descartes usually adopt the "je" or "ego" of his Cogito—the first-person subjective or nominative form—as the typical representation of selfhood, the "I." This distinction is not advanced on the basis of any difference in statistically obtainable distribution. Descartes writes of entering "en moi-même" and "pour moi." The prominence of the ego/je at the moment of the *Cogito*, however, effectively marks the priority of the grammatical subject form, or nominative, in Descartes. In Pascal, the "moi," an objective form (corresponding to the dative, accusative, and ablative of Latin declension) dominates and serves Pascal himself as the "name," so to speak, of the self. This difference in pronominal emphasis corresponds to a real difference in the way the self stands in relation to other selves, or the possibility of other selves. Descartes attempts to construct a self as free as possible from dependency on all that is not-self, foreign, doubtful. This attempt at a noncontingent self, which ultimately must limit itself by conceding an origin in a superior being, amply justifies the prominence accorded the "I" in readings of Descartes. Pascal, on the other hand, finds the self in the position of receptive or comparative object. The self would like to draw everything to itself ("pour moi," "à moi") and judges both itself and others in a constant back-and-forth movement of recognition ("comme moi," "semblables à moi").

50. This does not mean that Pascal resolutely rejects mind-body dualism, but merely that such a dualism is too simple to explain the more radical form of alienation in Pascal, for whom the self as soul or *res cogitans* is vitiated and alienated from its own thoughts and not merely from the body. See Le Guern, *Pascal et Descartes*, p. 149.

51. This seems to be one interpretation of the celebrated fragment that concludes, against Descartes, that one must not bother with the details of the "machine," a term Pascal often uses to mean the body: "Il faut dire en gros: cela se fait par figure et mouvement. Car cela est vrai, mais de dire quelles et composer la machine, cela est ridicule" (84).

52. "Pourquoi par exemple, cette étrange diversité entre les hommes qui sont tous de même nature? Comment la chose du monde la plus simple, qui est l'âme, ou la pensée, peut-elle se trouver si diversifiée? . . . et cela avec tant de différence et de mélange de ces qualités l'une avec l'autre, et de celles mêmes qui sont opposées, qu'il n'y a pas deux hommes au monde qui se ressemblent, ni même un homme qui ne soit dissemblable à lui-même d'un moment à l'autre? Que si l'âme passe des pères aux enfants, comme les philosophes le croyaient, d'où peut encore venir cette diversité?" Filleau de la Chaise, "Discours sur les Pensées de M. Pascal où l'on essaie de faire voir quel était son dessein," in Pascal *Oeuvres*, ed. L. Brunschvicg, vol. 12, p. CCXII.

53. One can argue that the example of the solitary is not impossible, since hermites and saints have achieved this solitude. But, as the example of Saint

Theresa indicates, these solitaries offer an outside and an inside, and only the invisible inside of their experience constitutes a valid example. The outside, or appearance of solitude, can only be dangerous precisely because it invites the adherence to surface values. At the same time, the cultivation of the examples of the saints as repositories of what we could call "invisible exemplarity" reinforces the anguish of an always escaping phenomenal evidence of *positive* faith, of present grace.

Chapter V

1. Letter to Lescheraine, April 16, 1678, quoted in Laugaa, *Lectures de Madame de Lafayette*, p. 16.

2. Marie Madeleine Pioche de La Vergne de Lafayette, *Romans et Nouvelles*, ed. Emile Magne (Paris: Classiques Garnier, 1970), p. 241. Page references after quotations are to the French text of this Magne-Garnier edition. English translations given here are my own.

3. Valincour, *Lettres à Madame la Marquise*, pp. 5–6.

4. Bussy-Rabutin, Letter to Madame de Sévigné, June 29, 1678 (quoted in Laugaa, *Lectures de Madame de Lafayette*, pp. 18–19).

5. Valincour, *Lettres à Madame la Marquise*, p. 100.

6. Valincour, *Lettres à Madame la Marquise*, pp. 88–89.

7. The primacy of verisimilitude is pointed out by Monsieur ★★★ when he says of pure fiction, "il est permis à l'Auteur de suivre son imagination en toutes choses, sans avoir aucun égard à la vérité: pourveû qu'il n'aille point contre le vray-semblable, il n'importe qu'il nous dise des choses qui ne sont jamais arrivées . . ." (p. 94). This pronouncement, though useful in establishing a hierarchy of values, is not in itself complete, for it neglects to account for the standard of verisimilitude itself. This standard, like the purely aesthetic *je ne sais quoi*, cannot in fact be enunciated within the classical system. It constitutes the blindspot, which is also the point of view of the reader or beholder of a work of art.

8. In describing the triumph of the novella over "fables à dix ou douze volumes," Du Plaisir condemns the latter for "leur longueur prodigieuse, ce mélange de tant d'histoires diverses, leur grand nombre d'acteurs, la trop grande antiquité de leurs sujets, l'embarras de leur construction, leur peu de vraisemblance, l'excès dans leur caractère . . ." (*Sentiments sur les lettres*, p. 44).

9. "Il me semble que c'est la différence qu'il y a entre le roman et la nouvelle, que le roman écrit ces choses comme la bienséance le veut et à la manière du poète; mais que la nouvelle doit un peu davantage tenir de l'histoire et s'attacher plutôt à donner les images des choses comme d'ordinaire nous les voyons arriver que comme notre imagination se les figure" (quoted in Deloffre, *La Nouvelle en France à l'âge classique*, p. 32). Deloffre comments: "La nouvelle, genre attaché au réel ou à l'imitation du réel, s'oppose ainsi aux imaginations des romans."

10. See Sfez, "Le roman polylexique du XVIIe siècle": "La parole sur le texte e(s)t la parole du texte," and Laugaa, *Lectures de Madame de Lafayette*.

11. These "homodiegetic" narratives are closer to the romance tradition than to the Boccaccian novella tradition, which is dominated by heterodiegetic narratives in which characters tell third-, rather than first-, person stories. The notable exception to the predominance of homodiegetic narrative in *Zayde* concerns Alamir, whose story is told by Félime.

12. Zeta and tau are thus recognizable in the *Z* and *T* written by Consalve, thus coinciding with the initials of Zayde and Théodoric, since the latter name would for the French begin with a plosive and not with a labiodental, despite the Greek origins of the name Théodoric. Thus tau rather than theta is needed in the marking on the painting.

13. The distinction between Consalve's statement of his beliefs about love and his narration of the events that occur when he has occasion to test those beliefs does not match the dichotomy between "discourse" (*discours*) and "history" (*histoire*) in the strictest application of Benveniste's doctrines about subjectivity in language (since Consalve tells his story in the first person, whereas Benveniste excludes all but the third person from strict, objective historical narration). Nonetheless, there is a perceptible difference in the degree of subjectivity in the two uses of language ("L'homme dans la langue," *Problèmes de linguistique générale*, p. 239). Consalve's general principles, while they can be cast in an impersonal grammatical form, are assertions not yet engaged in the temporal reality of events. They represent merely *his* word against those of others. The events that follow, though narrated by Consalve, are presented as factual and as offering the possibility of corroboration.

14. For another instance of the separation between name and appearance, consider Consalve's experience in the garden at Tortosa, where he hears Zayde but cannot see her. She is speaking the wrong words as well, since in the meanwhile she has miraculously learned Spanish.

15. The astrologer had found from Zayde's father that his intention was to require her to marry the prince of Fez. Believing the portrait to be of the prince, the astrologer had said, "il lui dit, sans aucun dessein de faire passer ses paroles pour une prédiction, qu'elle était destinée à celui dont elle avait vu le portrait" (p. 234). Common sense, the belief in certain traditions passed from generation to generation, leads the astrologer to know that a daughter will marry the husband chosen by her father. There is, as Albumazar says, no need to consult the stars. The knowledge of the future that he gives is entirely accessible through a familiarity with the political structure of the present.

16. Alphonse tells, "Ainsi j'aimai Bélasire et je fus assez heureux pour toucher son inclination; mais je ne le fus pas assez pour lui persuader mon amour. Elle avait une défiance naturelle de tous les hommes; quoiqu'elle m'estimât beaucoup plus que tous ceux qu'elle avait vus, et par conséquent plus que je ne méritais, elle n'ajoutait pas de foi à mes paroles. Elle eut néanmoins un procédé avec moi tout différent de celui des autres femmes et j'y trouvai quelque chose de si noble et de si sincère que j'en fus surpris. Elle ne demeura pas longtemps sans m'avouer l'inclination qu'elle avait pour moi; elle m'apprit ensuite le progrès que je faisais dans son coeur; mais, comme elle ne me cachait

point ce qui m'était avantageux, elle m'apprenait aussi ce qui ne m'était pas favorable" (p. 109).

17. Alphonse's criticisms of Bélasire's writing anticipates some of the debates about the *Princesse de Clèves*. As De Jean has shown, to a large extent the various criticisms of the style of the *Princesse de Clèves* center on Lafayette's use of ellipsis ("Lafayette's Ellipses"). Citing Valincour's grammarian from the *Lettres à Mme la Marquise*, De Jean notes, "He uses a variety of terms for this stylistic fault—ambiguity, brevity, abbreviation, laconism, and so on—but his meaning is always the same: *La Princesse de Clèves* is too elliptical" (p. 890). Alphonse's criticism of Bélasire's narrative (like Valincour, a male "critic" reading a woman's writing) is based on the fear that she has left too much out.

18. E.g., the case of a woman named Elsibery, "elle avait le plaisir d'avoir persuadé son attachement à Alamir sans le connaître pour le prince; enfin, elle était dans une joie que son coeur était à peine capable de contenir. Elle la laissa voir tout entière à Alamir, mais cette joie lui fut suspecte; il crut que le prince de Tharse y avait part, et qu'Elsibery était touchée du plaisir de l'avoir pour amant. Néanmoins il ne le lui témoigna pas et continua de la voir avec soin . . . Il était impossible que des choses aussi extraordinaires que celles qu'Alamir avait faites pour Elsibery n'apportassent une nouvelle vivacité à la passion qu'elle avait pour lui. Ce prince s'en aperçut: ce redoublement d'amour lui parut une infidélité . . ." (p. 197).

19. *Madame de Lafayette. La Princesse de Clèves*, p. 63.

20. "En effet, sa simplicité me paroist outrée," Valincour, *Lettres à Madame la Marquise*, p. 129.

21. See Weinstein, "Public Intimacy: *La Princesse de Clèves*," in *Fictions of the Self, 1550–1800*, pp. 66–83.

22. Goldin, "Maximes et fonctionnement narratif."

23. Meleuc has set forth this suggestive hypothesis about the maxims of La Rochefoucauld: "est-ce que la Maxime n'est pas, au moins très fréquemment, la négation d'un certain énoncé du lecteur (c'est-à-dire de tous les lecteurs possibles)? . . . est-ce que la Maxime ne consisterait pas en la négation d'un énoncé 'bien-formé', c'est-à-dire conforme aux règles de la langue, du lecteur par l'auteur?" ("Structure de la maxime," p. 84). Although one might well object to certain aspects of this formulation, in particular to the use of the term *reader* to designate the source of the negated utterance, Meleuc's suggestion for describing the Rochefoucauldian maxim is stimulating and persuasive. If one takes the maxim (number 44), "La force et la faiblesse de l'esprit sont mal nommées; elles ne sont en effect que la bonne ou la mauvaise disposition des organes du corps," one can, following Meleuc's suggestion, divide it into the reported utterance ("La force et la faiblesse de l'esprit"), the mark of distinction ("sont mal nommées," "ne . . . que"), and the author's utterance ("elles . . . sont en effect . . . la bonne au mauvaise disposition des organes du corps"). There is a strange resemblance between the negating structure that constitutes this type of maxim, a structure that can be described simply as "Reader's utterance" *plus*

"negations," and the structure of the hero–society relationship in the novels of Lafayette.

24. For a recent reading of this outcome in the light of religious education in the seventeenth century, see Patrick Henry, "*La Princesse de Clèves* and *L'Introduction à la vie dévote.*"

25. For more detailed consideration of painting and ontology, see my "Speaking in Pictures, Speaking of Pictures: Problems of Representation in the Seventeenth Century," in *Mimesis. From Mirror to Method.*

26. Arnauld and Nicole, *La Logique,* pp. 110ff.

27. De Jean, "Lafayette's Ellipses."

28. De Jean, "Lafayette's Ellipses," p. 899.

29. *Discours de la méthode,* part 6, 175/46.

CONCLUSION

1. Burckhardt, *The Civilization of the Renaissance in Italy.*

2. Mary McKinley deals with this point in a highly original way in her unpublished paper, "Traduire/ecrire/croire: sebond, les anciens et Dieu dans le discours des *Essais.*"

3. Castiglione's *Libro del cortegiano* is the most explicit description of the sixteenth-century consciousness of the need to create appearances and of the relationship between such artificial appearances and the theory of language.

4. See Lajarte, "Le Prologue de l'*Heptaméron,*" and Foucault, *Les Mots et les choses,* pp. 32–91.

Académie française. *Dictionnaire de l'Académie française*. Paris: Veuve de Jean Baptiste Coignard, 1694.

Agricola, Rudolf. *De inventione dialectica*. Cologne: 1523. Reprint Frankfurt am Main: Minerva Verlag, 1967.

Alan of Lille. *The Art of Preaching (Ars praedicandi)*. Translated by Gillian R. Evans. Kalamazoo, Michigan: Cistercian Publications, Inc., 1981.

Ali Bouacha, Abdelmadjid. *Le Discours universitaire. La Rhétorique et ses pouvoirs*. Berne: Peter Lang, 1984.

Angenot, Marc. "Fonctions narratives et maximes idéologiques." *Orbis Litterarum* 33 (1978): 95–110.

Anglo, Sydney. *Machiavelli: A Dissection*. London: Victor Gollancz, 1969.

apRoberts, Robert P. "Exemplum." In *Princeton Encyclopedia of Poetry and Poetics*. Princeton: Princeton University Press, 1974.

Aristotle. *The "Art" of Rhetoric*. Edited and translated by John Henry Freese. Loeb Classical Library, 1926.

———. *Poetics*. Edited and translated by Gerald F. Else. Ann Arbor: University of Michigan Press, 1967.

———. *Rhétorique*. Edited and translated by Médéric Dufour. Paris: Les Balles Lettres, 1967.

Arnauld, Antoine. *Réflexions sur l'éloquence des prédicateurs*. Paris: Delaulne, 1695.

Arnauld, Antoine, and Claude Lancelot. *Grammaire générale et raissonnée*. Paris: Republications Paulet, 1969.

Arnauld, Antoine, and Pierre Nicole. *La Logique ou l'art de penser*. Edited by P. Clair and F. Girbal. Paris: Presses universitaires de France, 1965.

Atance, Felix R. "Les Religieux de l'*Heptaméron*: Marguerite de Navarre et les novateurs." *Archiv für Reformationsgeschichte* 65 (1974): 185–210.

Auerbach, Erich. *Zur Technik der Frührenaissancenovelle in Italien und Frankreich*. Heidelberg: Winter Verlag, 1921.

———. *Mimesis. The Presentation of Reality in Western Literature*. Translated by Willard Trask. Reprint. Garden City: Doubleday Company, 1957.

Bacon, Francis. *Works*. Edited by J. Spedding et al. London: Longmans and Co., 1889.

———. *The Advancement of Learning*. Edited by G. W. Kitchin. London: J. M. Dent, 1915. Reprint. Totowa, N.J.: Rowman and Littlefield, 1978.

Baillet, Adrien. *La Vie de M. Descartes*. Paris: Antoine Lambin, 1691.

Baker, M. J. "Didacticism and the *Heptaméron*: The Misinterpretation of the Tenth Tale as an *Exemplum*." *French Review* 45, no. 3 (Special Issue, 1971): 84–90.

Baker, M. J. "The Role of the Moral Lesson in *Heptaméron* 30." *French Studies* 31, no. 1 (1977): 18–25.

Barbéris, Pierre. *Le Prince et le marchand. La Littérature, l'histoire, l'idéologie.* Paris: Fayard, 1980.

Barberi-Squarotti, Giorgio. *La forma tragica del "Principe" e altri saggi sul Machiavelli.* Florence: Olschki, 1966.

Barker, John. *Strange Contrarieties. Pascal in England during the Age of Reason.* Montreal: McGill-Queen's University Press, 1975.

Baron, Hans. *Humanistic and Political Literature in Florence and Venice at the Beginning of the Quattrocento.* Cambridge: Harvard University Press, 1955.

———. *The Crisis of the Early Florentine Renaissance. Civic Humanism and Republican Liberty in an Age of Classicism and Tyranny.* Princeton: Princeton University Press, 1966.

Barthes, Roland. "L'Ancienne Rhétorique. Aide-mémoire." *Communications* 16 (1970): 172–229.

Battaglia, Salvatore. *La coscienza letteraria del Medioevo.* Naples: Liguori, 1965.

Beaujour, Michel. *Miroirs d'encre.* Paris: Le Seuil, 1980.

Bénichou, Paul. *Morales du grand siècle.* 1948. Reprint. Paris: Gallimard ("Idées" collection), 1967.

Benjamin, Walter. "The Storyteller. Reflections on the Works of Nicolai Leskov." In *Illuminations*, introduced by Hannah Arendt, and translated by Harry Zohn, 83–109. New York: Schocken Books, 1969.

Benveniste, Emile. *Problèmes de linguistique générale.* Paris: Gallimard (Bibliothèque des sciences humaines), 1966.

Berlin, Isaiah. "The Originality of Machiavelli." In *Studies on Machiavelli*, edited by Myron Gilmore, 149–206. Florence: Sansoni, 1972.

Berlioz, Jacques. "Le Récit efficace: l'*Exemplum* au service de la prédication (XIII*e*–XV*e* siècles)." *Mélanges de l'école française de Rome* 92, no. 1 (1980): 113–46.

Blanchot, Maurice. "La Pensée tragique." In *L'Entretien infini.* Paris: Gallimard, 1969.

Blum, Claude. "La Fonction du 'déjà dit' dans les Essais: emprunter, alléguer, citer." *CAIEF* 33 (May 1981): 35–51.

Boccaccio, Giovanni. *Decamerone.* In *Tutte le opere*, edited by Vittorio Branca. Milan: Arnaldo Mondadori, 1976.

Bondanella, Peter E. "The Style and Function of Machiavelli's Character Sketches." *Forum Italicum* 4 (1970): 58–69.

———. *Machiavelli and the Art of Renaissance History.* Detroit: Wayne State University Press, 1974.

Borel, M.-J., J.-B. Grize, and D. Miéville. *Essai de logique naturelle.* Berne: Peter Lang, 1983.

Borsellino, Nino. *Lettura del Principe.* Bari: Laterza, 1976.

Bowen, Barbara. *The Age of Bluff: Paradox and Ambiguity in Rabelais and Montaigne.* Urbana, Illinois: University of Illinois Press, 1972.

Brody, Jules. "*La Princesse de Cléves* and the Myth of Courtly Love." *University of Toronto Quarterly* 38 (1969): 105–35.

———. *Lectures de Montaigne*. Lexington, Ky.: French Forum, 1982.

Brooks, Peter. *The Novel of Worldliness*. Princeton: Princeton University Press, 1969.

Brousseau-Beuerman, Christine. "La Copie de Montaigne." Ph.D. diss., Harvard University, 1985.

Brownlee, Marina S. *The Status of the Reading Subject in the Libro de Buen Amor*. North Carolina Studies in the Romance Languages and Literatures. Chapel Hill: University of North Carolina Press, 1985.

Brownlee, Kevin S. and Marina Scordilis Brownlee, eds. *Romance: Generic Transformations from Chrétien de Troyes to Cervantes*. Hanover, N.H.: University Press of New England, 1985.

Burckhardt, Jacob. *The Civilization of the Renaissance in Italy*. Translated by S.G.C. Middlemore. 1929. Reprint. New York: Harper and Row, 1958.

Burks, Don M., ed. *Rhetoric, Philosophy, and Literature: An Exploration*. West Lafayette, Indiana: Purdue University Press, 1978.

Busson, Henri. *La Pensée religieuse française de Charron à Pascal*. Paris: Vrin, 1933.

Butor, Michel. *Essais sur les Essais*. Paris: Gallimard, 1968.

Cameron, Keith. *Montaigne and His Age*. Exeter: University of Exeter, 1981.

Campbell, George. *The Philosophy of Rhetoric*. London: Thomas Tegg and Son, 1938.

Campion, Edmund J. "Erasmus's *De Copia*: Classical Learning and Epideictic Rhetoric in Montaigne's *Essais*." *Fifteenth-Century Studies* 4 (1981): 47–60.

Carlson, William R. " 'Pensées' and 'Pensées diverses.' The Art of Persuasion in Pascal and Bayle." *French Forum* 4 (1979): 137–46.

Carroll, David. "For Example: Psychoanalysis and Fiction or the Conflict of Generation(s)," *Sub-Stance* 21 (1978): 49–67.

Castelvetro, Lodovico. *Chiose intorno al secondo libro del comune di Platone* in *Opere varie critiche*. Lyons: Pietro Foppens, 1727.

Castiglione, Baldassare. *Il Libro del Cortegiano*. Edited by Bruno Maier. Turin: UTET, 1964.

Castro, Américo. "La ejemplaridad de las novelas cervantinas." In *Semblanzas y estudios espanoles*, 297–315. Princeton: no publisher, 1956.

Caton, Hiram. *The Origin of Subjectivity: An Essay on Descartes*. New Haven: Yale University Press, 1973.

Cave, Terence. *The Cornucopian Text. Problems of Writing in the French Renaissance*. Oxford: The Clarendon Press, 1979.

———. "Problems of Reading in the *Essais*." In *Montaigne, Essays in Memory of Richard Sayce*, edited by I. D. McFarlane and Ian Maclean, 133–66. Oxford: Clarendon Press, 1982.

Cazauran, Nicole. "La Trentième Nouvelle de l'*Heptaméron* ou la médiation d'un 'exemple.' " *Mélanges de littérature du moyen âge au XXe siècle offerts à Mlle Jeanne Lods*. Prais: Ecole normale supérieure de jeunes filles, 1978.

Chabod, Federico. *Machiavelli and the Renaissance*. Translated by David Moore. London: Bowes and Bowes, 1958.

Charaudeau, Patrick. *Langage et discours. Eléments de sémiolinguistique*. Paris: Hachette, 1983.

Chénon, Emile. *Histoire générale du droit français public et privé des origines à 1815*. 2 vols. Paris: Sirey, 1926.

Cholakian, Patricia F., and Rouben Charles Cholakian. *The Early French Novella*. Albany: State University of New York Press, 1972.

Cicero (attributed). *Rhetorica ad Herennium*. Edited and translated by Harry Caplan. Loeb Classical Library, 1954.

Cicero. *Orator*. Edited and translated by H. M. Hubbell. Loeb Classical Library, 1971.

Cicero. *De inventione*. Edited and translated by H. M. Hubbel. Loeb Classical Library, 1976.

——. *De oratore*. Edited and translated by E. W. Sutton and H. Rackham. Loeb Classical Library, 1976.

Clark, Carol. *The Web of Metaphor: Studies in the Imagery of Montaigne*. Lexington, Ky.: French Forum, 1978.

——. "Montaigne and Law." In *Montaigne and His Age*, edited by K. Cameron, 49–68. Exeter: University of Exeter, 1981.

Clark, Richard C. "Machiavelli: Bibliographical Spectrum," *Review of National Literatures* 1, no. 1 (Spring 1970): 93–135.

Colie, Rosalie. *Paradoxica epidemica*. Princeton: Princeton University Press, 1966.

Colombin, Marie-Pierre. "Rolandine ou la 'vérité' du romanesque dans la vingt-et-unième nouvelle de *L'Heptaméron*." In *Figures féminines et roman*, edited by Jean Bessière, 49–57. Paris: Presses universitaires de France, 1982.

Coman, Colette. "Noms propres et durée dans *La Princesse de Clèves*," *French Review* 51 (December 1977): 197–203.

Compagnon, Antoine. *La Seconde Main ou le travail de la citation*. Paris: Le Seuil, 1979.

——. *Nous, Michel de Montaigne*. Paris: Le Seuil, 1980.

Compayré, G. *Histoire critique des doctrines de l'éducation en France depuis le XVIe siècle*. Paris: Hachette, 1879.

Conche, Marcel. "Le Temps dans les 'Essais.' " *Bulletin de la Société des amis de Montaigne* 5, nos. 25–26 (January–June 1978): 11–28.

Conley, Tom. "Cataparalysis," *Diacritics* 8, no. 3 (Fall 1978): 41–59.

Corpus Iuris Civilis. Geneva: Jean Vignon, 1614.

Cotgrave, Randle, and R.S.L. *A Dictionarie of the French and English Tongues . . . Whereunto is also annexed a most copious Dictionarie, of the English set before the French*. London: Adam Islip, 1632.

Cottino-Jones, Marga. "Fabula vs. Figura: Another Interpretation of the Griselda Story." *Italica* 50: 38–52.

Cottrell, Robert D. *Sexuality/Textuality: A Study of the Fabric of Montaigne's Essais.* Columbus: Ohio State University Press, 1981.

———. "Croisement chiasmatique dans le premier Essai de Montaigne." *BSAM* 6, nos. 11–12 (July–December 1982): 65–71.

———. *The Grammar of Silence. A Reading of Marguerite de Navarre's Poetry.* Washington, D.C.: The Catholic University of America Press, 1986.

Coulet, Henri. *Le Roman jusqu'à la Révolution.* 2d ed. Paris: A. Colin, 1967.

Crane, Thomas F. *The Exempla or Illustrative Stories from the Sermones Vulgares of Jacques de Vitry.* London: David Nutt for the Folk-Lore Society, 1890.

Croce, Benedetto. "L'Efficacia dell'esempio." In *Etica e politica*, 148–52. Bari: Laterza, 1945.

Croquette, Bernard. *Pascal et Montaigne. Etude des réminiscences des Essais dans l'oeuvre de Pascal.* Geneva: Droz, 1974.

Culler, Jonathan. "Prolegomena to a Theory of Reading." In *The Reader in the Text*, edited by S. Suleiman and I. Crosman, 46–66. Princeton: Princeton University Press, 1980.

Curtius, Ernst Robert. *European Literature and the Latin Middle Ages.* Translated by Willard R. Trask. New York: Harper and Row, 1963.

Danto, Arthur C. *Analytical Philosophy of History.* Cambridge: Cambridge University Press, 1965.

David, Jean-Michel. "Présentation." *Mélanges de l'école française de Rome* 92, no. 1 (1980): 9–14.

———, ed. "Rhétorique et histoire. L'Exemplum et le modèle de comportement dans le discours antique et médiéval." *Mélanges de l'école française de Rome* 92, no. 1 (1980): 9–179.

Davidson, Hugh M. *Audience, Words, and Art.* Columbus: Ohio State University Press, 1965.

———. "Le Pluralisme méthodologique chez Pascal." In *Méthodes chez Pascal. Actes du Colloque tenu à Clermont-Ferrand, 10–13 juin, 1976*, 19–26. Paris: Presses universitaires de France, 1976.

———. *The Origins of Certainty.* Chicago: University of Chicago Press, 1979.

Davidson, Hugh M., and Pierre H. Dubé. *A Concordance to Pascal's Pensées.* Ithaca: Cornell University Press, 1976.

Davis, Betty J. *The Storytellers in Marguerite de Navarre's Heptaméron.* Lexington, Ky.: French Forum, 1978.

Davis, Natalie Zemon. *Society and Culture in Early Modern France.* Stanford: Stanford University Press, 1975.

———. *The Return of Martin Guerre.* Cambridge, Mass.: Harvard University Press, 1983.

———. *Fiction in the Archives. Pardon Tales and Their Tellers in Sixteenth-Century France.* Stanford: Stanford University Press, 1987.

de Beaumanoir, Philippe (Philippe de Rémi). *Les Coutumes du Beauvoisis.* 2 vols. Edited by Beugnot. Paris: Jules Renouard, 1982.

Defaux, Gérard. *Le Curieux, le glorieux, et la sagesse du monde dans la première moitié du XVIe siècle (L'Exemple de Panurge, Ulysse, Démosthène, Empédocle).* Lexington, Ky.: French Forum, 1982.

———. "Un cannibale en haut de chausses: Montaigne, la différence et la logique de l'identité." *MLN* 97 (1982): 919–57.

———. *Montaigne: Essays in Reading. Yale French Studies* 64 (1983).

De Jean, Joan. "Lafayette's Ellipses: The Privileges of Anonymity." *PMLA* 99, no. 5 (October 1984): 884–902.

Delègue, Yves. "L'*Heptaméron* est-il un anti-Boccace?" *Travaux de linguistique et de littérature* 4 (1966): 23–37.

Deloffre, Frédéric. *La Nouvelle en France à l'âge classique.* Paris: Didier, 1967.

De Man, Paul. *Allegories of Reading. Figural Language in Rousseau, Nietzsche, Rilke, and Proust.* New Haven: Yale University Press, 1979.

———. "Pascal's Allegory of Persuasion." In *Allegory and Representation*, edited by Stephen J. Greenblatt, 1–25. Baltimore: Johns Hopkins University Press, 1981.

Deprun, Jean. "La Parabole de la seconde *Provinciale.*" In *Méthodes chez Pascal. Actes du Colloque tenu à Clermont-Ferrand, 10–13 juin, 1976,* 241–52. Paris: Presses universitaires de France, 1976.

Derrida, Jacques. "Cogito et histoire de la folie." In *L'Ecriture et la différence,* 51–97. Paris: Le Seuil, 1967.

———. "Du supplément à la source: la théorie de l'écriture." In *De la grammatologie,* 379–445. Paris: Minuit, 1967.

———. *Marges de la philosophie.* Paris: Minuit, 1972.

———. *La Vérité en peinture.* Paris: Flammarion, 1978.

Descartes, René. *Oeuvres.* Edited by Charles Adam and Paul Tannery. Paris: Léopold Cerf, 1891–1912.

———. *Discours de la méthode.* Edited by Etienne Gilson. Paris: J. Vrin, 1930.

———. *Discourse on Method.* Translated by Laurence J. Lafleur. 1950. Reprint. Indianapolis: Bobbs-Merrill, 1980.

———. *Correspondance.* Edited by Charles Adam and G. Milhaud. Paris: Presses universitaires de France, 1951.

———. *Oeuvres et lettres.* Edited by André Bridoux. Paris: Gallimard ("Pléiade" Collection), 1953.

de Vinsauf, Geoffroi. *Poetria Nova.* Translated by Margaret F. Nims. Toronto: Pontifical Institute of Medieval Studies, 1967.

Dickson, Colin. "L'Humour dans 'Sur des vers de Virgile.'" *Bulletin de la Société des amis de Montaigne* 7–8 (July–December 1981): 39–52.

Dionysius the Areopagite [Pseudo-Dionysius]. *The Divine Names.* 1920. Translated by C. E. Rolt. 2d ed. London: Macmillan, 1940.

Doubrovsky, Serge. *Parcours critique.* Paris: Galilée, 1980.

Droz, Eugénie. "La Reine Marguerite de Navarre et la vie littéraire à la cour de Nérac, 1579–1582." Bordeaux: Taffard, 1964.

Dubuis, R. *Les Cent Nouvelles et la tradition de la nouvelle en France au moyen âge.* Grenoble: Presses universitaires de Grenoble, 1973.

Du Cange, Charles de Fresne, sieur. *Glossarium mediae et infimae latinitatis.* Edited by D. P. Charpentier et al. Niort: Favre, 1883.

Ducrot, Oswald. *Dire et ne pas dire.* Paris: Hermann, 1972.

Ducrot, Oswald, et al. *Les Mots du discours.* Paris: Minuit, 1980.

Du Plaisir. *Sentiments sur les lettres et sur l'histoire avec des scrupules sur le style.* Edited by Philippe Hourcade. Geneva: Droz, 1975.

Dupleix, Scipion. *Corps de philosophie, contenant la logique, la physique, la métaphysique et l'éthique.* Geneva: Balthasar l'abbé, 1623.

Dupriez, Bernard. *Gradus. Les Procédés littéraires.* Paris: Union générale d'editions ("10/18" Collection), 1984.

Du Vair, Guillaume. *De l'éloquence françoise.* Edited by R. Radouant. Paris: E. Cornély et Cie, 1911.

Duval, Edwin M. "Lessons of the New World: Design and Meaning in Montaigne's 'Des cannibales' (I,31) and 'Des coches' (III:6)." *Yale French Studies* 64 (1983): 95–112.

———. "Rhetorical Composition and 'Open Form' in Montaigne's Early *Essais.*" *Bibliothèque d'Humanisme et Renaissance* 43 (1981): 269–87.

Du Verger de Hauranne, Jean, Abbé de St Cyran. *Lettres chrétiennes et spirituelles.* Paris: Rolet Le Duc, 1645.

Duvernoy, Jean-François. *Pour mieux connaître le pensée de Machiavel.* Paris: Bordes, 1974.

Ehrlich, Hélène Hedy. "La Fable dans les Essais de Montaigne: Sa valeur formelle et épistémologique: Le Signifié et le signifiant." *Bulletin de la Société des amis de Montaigne* 14–15 (1975): 65–74.

Eliade, Mircea. *Le Mythe de l'éternel retour. Archétypes et répétition.* Paris: Gallimard, 1949.

Erasmus, Desiderius. *Collected Works.* Edited by James K. McConica et al. Toronto: University of Toronto Press, 1974–1979.

———. *Opera omnia.* Amsterdam: North-Holland Publishing Co., 1969–1982.

Febvre, Lucien. *Autour de l'Heptaméron.* Paris: Gallimard, 1944.

Ferrier, Janet. *Forerunners of the French Novel: An Essay on the Development of the Novella in the Late Middle Ages.* Manchester: Manchester University Press, 1954.

Filleau de la Chaise. "Discours sur les Pensées de M. Pascal où l'on essaie de faire voir quel était son dessein." In Pascal. *Oeuvres.* Vol. 12, edited by Léon Brunschvicg, pp. CXCIX–CCXXXVIII. Paris: Hachette ("Les Grands Ecrivains de la France"), 1904–1921.

Fontanier, Pierre. *Les Figures du discours.* Paris: Flammarion, 1977.

Forestier, Georges "Mme de Chartres, personnage-clé de *La Princesse de Clèves.*" *Les Lettres Romanes* 34 (1980): 67–76.

Foucault, Michel. *Les Mots et les choses. Une archéologie des sciences humaines.* Paris: Gallimard, 1966.

———. *L'Archéologie du savoir.* Paris: Gallimard, 1969.

———. *L'Ordre du discours.* Paris: Gallimard, 1971.

———. *La Volonté de savoir.* Paris: Gallimard, 1976.

———. *Discipline and Punish. The Birth of the Prison.* Translated by Alan Sheridan. New York: Random House, Vintage Books, 1979.

France, Peter. *Rhetoric and Truth in France.* Oxford: Clarendon Press, 1972.

Frame, Donald M., and Mary B. McKinley. *Columbia Montaigne Conference Papers.* Lexington, Ky.: French Forum, 1981.

Francillon, Roger. *L'Oeuvre romanesque de Madame de Lafayette.* Paris: Corti, 1973.

François, Alexis. "De l'*Heptaméron* à la *La Princesse de Clèves.*" *Revue d'histoire littéraire de la France* 49 (1949): 305–21.

Franklin, Julian H. *Jean Bodin and the Sixteenth-Century Revolution in the Methodology of Law and History.* New York: Columbia University Press, 1963.

Friedrich, Hugo. *Montaigne.* Translated into French by Robert Rovini. Paris: Gallimard, 1968.

Froment, Théodore. *L'Eloquence judiciaire en France avant le dix-septiéme siècle.* Paris: E. Thorin, 1874.

Fromilhague, René. "Montaigne et la nouvelle rhétorique." In *Critique et création littéraires au XVIIe siècle*, pp. 55–67. Paris: Editions du CNRS, 1977.

Fumaroli, Marc. "Pascal et la tradition rhétorique gallicane." In *Méthodes chez Pascal. Actes du Colloque tenu à Clermont-Ferrand, 10–13 juin, 1976*, 359–70. Paris: Presses universitaires de France, 1976.

———. *L'Age de l'éloquence. Rhétorique et "res literaria" de la Renaissance au seuil de l'époque classique.* Geneva: Droz, 1980.

Furetière, Antoine. *Dictionnaire universel.* 2d ed. 2 vols. Revised by Basnage de Bauval. The Hague and Rotterdam: A. and R. Leers, 1702.

Garver, Eugene. "Machiavelli's *The Prince*: A Neglected Rhetorical Classic." *Philosophy and Rhetoric* 13 (Spring 1980): 99–120.

Gassendi, Pierre. *Institutio Logica.* Edited and translated by Howard Jones. Assen: Van Gorcum, 1981.

Gélas, Bruno. "La Fiction manipulatrice." In *L'Argumentation, linguistique et sémiologie.* Lyons: Presses universitaires de Lyon, 1981.

Gelernt, Jules. *World of Many Loves: The Heptaméron of Marguerite de Navarre.* Chapel Hill: University of North Carolina Pres, 1966.

Gelley, Alexander. "Frame, Instance, Dialogue: Narrative Structures in the *Wanderjahre.*" In *J. W. v. Goethe*, edited by U. Boebel and W. T. Zyla, 61–78. Lubbock, Texas: Texas Tech Press, 1984.

Gellius, Aulus. *Attic Nights.* Edited and translated by John C. Rolfe. Loeb Classical Library, 1927–1928.

Genette, Gérard. *Figures.* Paris: Le Seuil, 1966–1972.

Gentillet, Innocent. *Anti-Machiavel.* Edited by C. Edward Rathé. Geneva: Droz, 1968.

Geremek, Bronislaw. "L'*Exemplum* et la circulation de la culture au moyen âge." *Mélanges de l'école française de Rome* 92, no. 1 (1980): 153–79.

Gilbert, Allan H. *Machiavelli's Prince and its Forerunners. The Prince as a Typical Book de Regimine Principum.* Durham, N.C.: Duke University Press, 1938.

Gilbert, Felix. "The Humanist Concept of the Prince and 'The Prince' of Machiavelli." *Journal of Modern History* 11 (1939): 449–93.

———. *Machiavelli and Guicciardini: Politics and History in Sixteenth-Century Florence.* Princeton: Princeton University Press, 1965.

———. "The Composition and Structure of Machiavelli's *Discorsi*." In *History: Choice and Commitment.* Cambridge, Mass.: Harvard University Press, 1977.

Gilmore, Myron P. *Humanists and Jurists.* Cambridge, Mass.: Harvard University Press, 1963.

Gilmore, Myron P., ed. *Studies on Machiavelli.* Florence: Sansoni, 1972.

Girard, René. *Deceit, Desire, and the Novel.* Translated by Y. Freccero. Baltimore: Johns Hopkins University Press, 1965.

———. *La Violence et le sacré.* Paris: Grasset, 1972.

Glauser, Alfred. *Montaigne paradoxal.* Paris: Nizet, 1972.

Glidden, Hope. *The Storyteller as Humanist: The "Serées" of Guillaume Bouchet.* Lexington, Ky.: French Forum, 1981.

Godefroy, Fréderic. *Dictionnaire de l'ancienne langue française et de tous ses dialectes du IXe au XVe siècle.* Paris: F. Vieweg, 1881–1902.

Godenne, René. *Histoire de la nouvelle française aux 17e et 18e siècles.* Geneva: Droz, 1970.

Goldin, Jeanne. "Maximes et fonctionnement narratif dans *La Princesse de Clèves*." *Papers on French Seventeenth-Century Literature* 10, no. 2 (1978–1979): 155–76.

Gouchier, Henri. *Cartèsianisme et augustinisme au XVIIe siècle.* Paris: J. Vrin, 1978.

Gounelle, André. *La Bible selon Pascal.* Paris: Presses universitaires de France, 1970.

Goux, Jean-Joseph. "Descartes et la perspective." In *L'Esprit créateur* 25, no. 1 (Spring 1985): 10–20.

Goyet, Thérèse, ed. *Méthodes chez Pascal. Actes du Colloque tenu à Clermont-Ferrand, 10–13 juin, 1976.* Paris: Presses universitaires de France, 1976.

Grammont, Scipion de. *La Rationnelle ou l'art des conséquences pour bien inférer et conclure.* Paris: Fleury Bourriquant, 1614.

Grassi, Ernesto. *Rhetoric as Philosophy. The Humanist Tradition.* University Park: Pennsylvania State University Press, 1980.

Gray, Floyd. *Le Style de Montaigne.* Paris: Nizet, 1958.

Greene, Thomas M. *The Light in Troy. Imitation and Discovery in Renaissance Poetry.* New Haven: Yale University Press, 1982.

Greene, Thomas M. *The Vulnerable Text. Essays on Renaissance Literature*. New York: Columbia University Press, 1986.

Grene, Marjorie. *Descartes*. Minneapolis: University of Minnesota Press, 1985.

Guillemin, Bernard. *Machiavel. L'Anthropologie politique*. Geneva: Droz, 1977.

Gutwirth, Marcel. *Michel de Montaigne ou le pari d'exemplarité*. Montréal: Les Presses de l'Université de Montréal, 1977.

Joukovsky, Françoise. *Montaigne et le problème du temps*. Paris: Nizet, 1972.

Hallie, Philip P. *The Scar of Montaigne. An Essay in Personal Philosophy*. Middletown, Conn.: Wesleyan University Press, 1966.

Hallyn, Fernand. "Port-Royal versus Tesauro: signe, figure, sujet." *Baroque* 9–10 (1980): 76–86.

Hardee, A. Maynor. "Sur l'art narratif dans les anecdotes de Montaigne." *Bulletin de la Société des amis de Montaigne* 6, nos. 7–8 (July–December 1981): 53–65.

Harth, Erica. *Ideology and Culture in Seventeenth-Century France*. Ithaca: Cornell University Press, 1983.

Heinz, R. "Auctoritas." *Hermes* (Berlin) 60 (1925): 348–66.

Heller, Henry. "Marguerite de Navarre and the Reformers of Meaux." *Bibliothèque d'Humanisme et Renaissance* 33 (1971): 271–310.

Henry, Albert. *Métonymie et métaphore*. Paris: Klincksieck, 1971.

Henry, Patrick. "Recognition of the Other and Avoidance of the Double: The Self and the Other in the *Essais* of Montaigne." *Stanford French Review* 6, nos. 2–3 (1982): 175–87.

———. "*La Princesse de Clèves* and *L'Introduction à la vie dévote*." In *French Studies in Honor of Phillip A. Wadsworth*, edited by D. W. Tappan and Wm. A. Mould, 79–100. Birmingham, Ala.: Summa Publications, 1985.

Hipp, Marie-Thérèse. *Mythes et réalitiés*. Paris: Klincksieck, 1976.

Houston, John Porter. *The Traditions of French Prose Style. A Rhetorical Study*. Baton Rouge: Louisiana State University Press, 1981.

Howell, Wilbur Samuel. *Logic and Rhetoric in England, 1500–1700*. New York: Russell and Russell, 1961.

———. *Poetics, Rhetoric, and Logic. Studies in the Basic Disciplines of Criticism*. Ithaca: Cornell University Press, 1975.

Ingarden, Roman. *Time and Modes of Being*. Translated by Helen R. Michejda. Springfield, Ill.: Charles C. Thomas, 1964.

Iser, Wolfgang. *The Implied Reader*. Baltimore: Johns Hopkins University Press, 1974.

Isidore of Seville. *Etymologiarum sive originum Libri XX*. Edited by W. M. Lindsay. Oxford: Clarendon Press, 1911.

Jakobson, Roman. *Essais de linguistique générale: Les Fondations du langage*. Translated by Nicholas Ruwet. Paris: Minuit, 1963.

Jauss, Hans Robert. "Theory of Genres and Medieval Literature." In *Toward an Aesthetic of Reception*, translated by Timothy Bahti, 76–109. Minneapolis: University of Minnesota Press, 1982.

Jolles, A. *Formes simples*. Translated into French by Antoine Marie Buguet. Paris: Editions du Seuil, 1972.

Jordan, Constance. "Montaigne's 'Chasse de cognoissance': Language and Play in the *Essais*." *Romanic Review* 71 (1979): 265–80.

Jourda, Pierre. *Marguerite d'Angoulême, duchesse d'Alençon. reine de Navarre (1492–1549). Etude biographique et littéraire*. Paris: Champion, 1930.

———. *Répertoire analytique et chronologique de la correspondance de Marguerite de Navarre*. Paris: Champion, 1930.

Judovitz, Dalia. *Subjectivity and Representation in Descartes: The Origins of Modernity*. Cambridge: Cambridge University Press, 1988.

Kahn, Victoria. *Rhetoric, Prudence, and Skepticism in the Renaissance*. Ithaca: Cornell University Press, 1985.

Kelley, Donald R. *Foundations of Modern Historical Scholarship*. New York: Columbia University Press, 1970.

———. *The Beginning of Ideology. Consciousness and Society in the French Reformation*. Cambridge: Cambridge University Press, 1981.

Kennedy, G. *The Art of Persuasion in Greece*. Princeton: Princeton University Press, 1963.

———. *The Art of Rhetoric in the Roman World*. Princeton: Princeton University Press, 1972.

———. *Classical Rhetoric and its Christian and Secular Tradition from Ancient to Modern Times*. Chapel Hill: University of North Carolina Press, 1980.

Kennedy, William J. *Rhetorical Norms in Renaissance Literature*. New Haven: Yale University Press, 1978.

Kerbrat-Orecchioni, Catherine. *L'Enonciation. De la subjectivité dans le language*. Paris: A. Colin, 1980.

Kessler, Eckhard. *Das Problem des fruehen Humanismus: Seine philosophische Bedeutung bei Coluccio Salutati*. Munich: Fink, 1968.

Kibédi-Varga, Aron. *Rhétorique et littérature, études de structures classiques*. Paris: Didier, 1970.

———. "L'Invention de la fable." *Poétique* 25 (1976): 107–15.

Kiefer, Frederick. "The Conflation of Fortune and Occasio in Renaissance Thought and Iconography." *Journal of Medieval and Renaissance Studies* 9, no. 1 (Spring 1979): 1–27.

Klapper, Joseph. *Exempla aus Handschriften des Mittelalters*. Heidelberg: C. Winter, 1911.

Koehler, Erich. *Madame de Lafayettes La Princesse de Clèves*. Studien zur Form des Klassichen Romans. Hamburg: Kommissionsverlag: Cram, De Gruyter and Co., 1959.

Kofman, Sarah. "Nietzsche et la métaphore." *Poétique* 5 (1971): 77–98.

Koppisch, Michael S. "The Dynamics of Jealousy in the Works of Madame de Lafayette." *MLN* 94 (1979): 757–73.

Kornhardt, Hildegard. *Exemplum. Eine bedeutungsgeschichtliche Studie*. Borna-Leipzig: Robert Noske, 1936.

Körting, Gustav. *Lateinisch-Romanisches Wörterbuch*. Paderborn: Ferdinand Schöningh, 1901.

Kraft, Joseph. "Truth and Poetry in Machiavelli." *Journal of Modern History* 23 (June 1951): 109–21.

Krailsheimer, A. J. *Studies in Self-Interest from Descartes to La Bruyère*. Oxford: Clarendon Press, 1962.

———. *Rabelais and the Franciscans*. Oxford: Clarendon Press, 1963.

———. "The *Heptaméron* Reconsidered." In *The French Renaissance and its Heritage. Essays Presented to Alan M. Boase*, edited by D. R. Haggis et al., 75–92. London: Methuen, 1968.

Krauss, Werner. "Novela-Novella-Roman." *Gesammelte Aufsaetze zur Literatur und Sprachwissenschaft*, 50–67. Frankfurt: Vittorio Klostermann, 1949.

Krieger, L. "The Idea of Authority in the West." *American Historical Review* 82, no. 2 (April 1977): 249–70.

Kristeva, J., et al. *Langue, discours, société. Pour Emile Benveniste*. Paris: Le Seuil, 1975.

Kritzman, Lawrence D. *Destruction/découverte: Le Fonctionnement de la rhétorique dans les Essais de Montaigne*. Lexington, Ky.: French Forum, 1980.

———. "Pedagogical Graffiti and the Rhetoric of Conceit." *Journal of Medieval and Renaissance Studies* 15 (1985): 69–83.

———, ed. *Fragments: Incompletion and Discontinuity*. New York: New York Literary Forum, 1981.

Kuizenga, Donna. *Narrative Strategies in La Princesse de Clèves*. Lexington, Ky.: French Forum, 1976.

Kusch, Manfred. "Narrative Techniques and Cognitive Modes in *La Princesse de Clèves*." *Symposium* 30, no. 4 (Winter 1976): 308–24.

La Capra, Dominick. *Rethinking Intellectual History: Texts, Contexts, Language*. Ithaca: Cornell University Press, 1983.

La Charité, Raymond C. *The Concept of Judgment in Montaigne*. The Hague: M. Nijhoff, 1968.

———, ed. *O, Un Amy! Essays on Montaigne in Honor of Donald M. Frame*. Lexington, Ky.: French Forum, 1972.

Lafayette, Madame de. *Mémoires de Mme de Lafayette*. Edited by Eugène Asse. Paris: Librairie des bibliophiles, 1890.

———. *Correspondance*. Edited by André Beaunier. Paris: Gallimard, 1942.

———. *La Princesse de Clèves*. Edited by Emile Magne. Geneva: Droz, 1950.

———. *Vie de la princesse d'Angleterre*. Edited by Marie-Thérèse Hipp. Geneva: Droz, 1967.

———. *Romans et nouvelles*. Edited by Emile Magne. Paris: Classiques Garnier, 1970.

———. *Zaïde, histoire espagnole*. Edited by Janine Anseaume Kreiter. Paris: Nizet, 1982.

Lafond, Jean. *La Rochefoucauld: Augustinisme et littérature*. Paris: Klincksieck, 1977.

Lajarte, Phillippe de. "*Heptaméron* et la naissance du récit moderne: Essai de lecture épistémologique d'un discours narratif." *Littérature* 17 (1975): 31–42.

———. "Le Prologue de l'*Heptaméron* et le processus de production de l'oeuvre." In *La Nouvelle française à la Renaissance*, edited by Lionello Sozzi, 397–423. Geneva: Slatkine, 1981.

Lampe, G.W.H. *A Patristic Greek Lexicon*. Oxford: Clarendon Press, 1961.

Lanham, Richard A. *A Handlist of Rhetorical Terms*. Berkeley: University of California Press, 1969.

———. *The Motives of Eloquence. Literary Rhetoric in the Renaissance*. New Haven: Yale University Press, 1976.

Laudy, Bernard. "La Vision tragique de Madame de La Fayette, ou un jansénisme athée." *Revue de l'Institut de sociologie de l'Université libre de Bruxelles* 3 (1969): 449–62.

Laugaa, Maurice. *Lectures de Madame de Lafayette*. Paris: A. Colin, 1971.

Lausberg, Heinrich. *Handbuch der literarischen Rhetorik*. Munich: M. Hueber, 1960.

Lebègue, Raymond. "La femme qui mutile son visage (*Heptaméron* X)." *Comptes rendus de l'Académie des inscriptions et belles lettres* (April–December 1959): 176–84.

Lefort, Claude. *Le Travail de l'oeuvre: Machiavel*. Paris: Gallimard, 1972.

Lefranc, Abel. *Les Idées religieuses de Marguerite de Navarre d'après son oeuvre poétique*. Paris: Fischbacher, 1898.

———. *Grands écrivains français de la renaissance*. Paris: Champion, 1914.

Le Guern, Michel. *L'Image dans l'oeuvre de Pascal*. Paris: Colin, 1969.

———. *Pascal et Descartes*. Paris: Nizet, 1971.

———. "Pascal et la métaphore." *Vie et langage* 22 (1973): 62–69.

———. *Sémantique de la métaphore et de la métonymie*. Paris: Larousse, 1973.

———. "Pascal et la métonymie." In *Méthodes chez Pascal. Actes du Colloque tenu à Clermont-Ferrand, 10–13 juin, 1976*, 383–88. Paris: Presses universitaires de France, 1976.

Lennon, Thomas M. "Jansenism and the *Crise pyrrhonienne*." *Journal of the History of Ideas* 38 (1977): 297–306.

Lever, Maurice. *Le Roman français au XVIIe siècle*. Paris: Presses universitaires de France, 1981.

Lewis, Philip E. *La Rochefoucauld: The Art of Abstraction*. Ithaca: Cornell University Press, 1977.

Lhermet, J. *Pascal et la Bible*. Paris: Vrin, 1931.

Lilly, Graham C. *An Introduction to the Law of Evidence*. St. Paul, Minnesota: West Publishing Company, 1978.

Logan, John L. "Montaigne et Longin: une nouvelle hypothèse." *Revue d'histoire littéraire de la France* 83, no. 3 (May–June 1983): 355–70.

Lorian, Alexander. *Tendances stylistiques dans la prose narrative française du XVIe siècle*. Paris: Klincksieck, 1973.

Lotringer, Sylvère. "La Structuration romanesque." *Critique* 277 (June 1970): 498–529.

Lotringer, Sylvère. "Le Roman impossible." *Poétique* 3 (1970): 297–321.

Lukács, Georg. *The Theory of the Novel.* Translated by Anna Bostock. Cambridge, Mass.: MIT Press, 1971.

Lyons, John D. "Speaking in Pictures, Speaking of Pictures: Problems of Representation in the Seventeenth Century." In *Mimesis. From Mirror to Method*, 166–87. Hanover, N.H.: University Press of New England, 1982.

McCanles, Michael. "Machiavelli's *Principe* and the Textualization of History." *MLN* 97, no. 1 (January 1982): 1–18.

———. *The Discourse of Il Principe.* Malibu: Undena Publications (Humana Civilitas, no. 8), 1983.

McGowan, Margaret. *Montaigne's Deceits: The Art of Persuasion in the Essays.* Philadelphia: Temple University Press, 1974.

McKinley, Mary B. *Words in a Corner. Studies in Montaigne's Latin Quotations.* Lexington, Ky.: French Forum, 1981.

Macherey, Pierre. *Pour une théorie de la production littéraire.* 1966. Reprint. Paris: Maspero, 1971.

Machiavelli, Niccolò. *The Prince.* Translated by Luigi Ricci. *The Discourses.* Translated by Christian E. Detmold. New York: Modern Library, 1940.

———. *The Prince and Other Works.* Edited and translated by Allan H. Gilbert. Chicago: Packard, 1941.

———. *Opere.* Edited by Ezio Raimondi. Milan: Mursia, 1969.

———. *The Prince.* Edited and translated by James B. Atkinson. Indianapolis: Bobbs-Merrill, 1976.

Maingueneau, Dominique. *Initiation aux méthodes de l'analyse du discours.* Paris: Hachette, 1976.

Malandain, Pierre. "Ecriture de l'histoire dans 'la Princesse de Clèves,' " *Littérature* 36 (December 1979): 19–36.

———. *Madame de Lafayette. La Princesse de Clèves.* Paris: Presses universitaires de France, 1985.

Mansfield, Harvey C. *Machiavelli's New Modes and Orders. A Study of the Discourses on Livy.* Ithaca: Cornell University Press, 1979.

———. "Machiavelli's Political Science." *American Political Science Review* 75, no. 2 (June 1981): 293–305.

Marguerite de Navarre. *L'Heptaméron.* Edited by Michel François. Paris: Classiques Garnier, 1967.

———. *Nouvelles.* Edited by Yves Le Hir. Paris: Presses universitaires de France, 1967.

———. *La Coche.* Edited by Robert Marichal. Geneva: Droz, 1971.

———. *Le Miroir de l'âme pécheresse.* Edited by Joseph L. Allaire. Munich, Fink, 1972.

———. *Les Prisons.* Edited by Simone Glasson. Geneva: Droz, 1978.

Marin, Louis. "Réflexions sur la notion de modèle chez Pascal." *Revue de métaphysique et morale* 72 (1967): 89–108.

————. *La Critique du discours*. Paris: Minuit, 1975.

————. "On the interpretation of ordinary language. A Parable of Pascal." In *Textual Strategies*, edited by Josué V. Harrari, 239–59. Ithaca: Cornell University Press, 1979.

Marion, Jean Luc. *Sur l'ontologie grise de Descartes. Science cartésienne et savoir aristotélicien dans les Regulae*. Paris: J. Vrin, 1975.

Maritain, Jacques. *The Dream of Descartes*. New York: Philosophical Library, 1944.

Markie, Peter J. *Descartes's Gambit*. Ithaca: Cornell University Press, 1986.

Martin, Daniel. "Pour une lecture mnémonique des 'Essais'; une image et un lieu." *Bulletin de la Société des amis de Montaigne* 5 (July–December 1979): 31–32, 51–58.

Mattingly, Garrett. "Machiavelli's *Prince*: Political Science or Political Satire?" *American Scholar* 27 (1958): 482–91.

Mazzeo, J. A. *Renaissance and Seventeenth-Century Studies*. New York: Columbia University Press, 1964.

————. "The Poetry of Power: Machiavelli's Literary Vision." *Review of National Literatures* 1, no. 1 (1970): 38–62.

Meleuc, Serge. "Structure de la maxime." *Languages* 13 (March 1969): 69–98.

Melzer, Sara E. " 'Invraisemblance' in Pascal's *Pensées*. The Anti-rhetoric." *Romanic Review* 73 (1982): 33–44.

————. "Pascal's *Pensées*: Economy and the Interpretation of Fragments." *Stanford French Review* 6 (Fall–Winter 1982): 207–19.

Merrell, Floyd. "Understanding Fictions." In *Kodikas/Code* 2, no. 3 (1980): 235–48.

Mesnard, Jean. "Jansénisme et littérature." In *Le Statut de la littérature. Mélanges offerts à Paul Bénichou*, edited by Marc Fumaroli, 117–35. Geneva: Droz, 1982.

Meurillon, Christian. "Un concept problématique dans les *Pensées*: 'le moi.' " In *Méthodes chez Pascal. Actes du Colloque tenu à Clermont-Ferrand, 10–13 juin, 1976*, 269–80. Paris: Presses universitaires de France, 1976.

Meyer-Lübke, W. *Romanisches etymologisches Wörterbuch*. Heidelberg: Carl Winter, 1911.

Michel, Alain. "Saint Augustin et la rhétorique pascalienne. La Raison et la beauté dans *l'Apologie de la religion chrétienne*." *XVIIe siècle* 34 (1982): 133–48.

Miel, Jan. *Pascal and Theology*. Baltimore: Johns Hopkins University Press, 1969.

————. "Les méthodes de Pascal et l'*épistémè* classique." In *Méthodes chez Pascal. Actes du Colloque tenu à Clermont-Ferrand, 10–13 juin, 1976*, 27–36. Paris: Presses universitaires de France, 1976.

Miller, John William. *The Philosophy of History with Reflections and Aphorisms*. New York: W. W. Norton, 1981.

Miller, Joseph M., et al. eds. *Readings in Medieval Rhetoric*. Bloomington: Indiana University Press, 1973.

Miller, Nancy K. "Emphasis Added: Plots and Plausibilities in Women's Fiction." *PMLA* 96 (January 1981): 36–48.

Mink, Louis O. "History and Fiction as Modes of Comprehension." *New Literary History* 2 (1971): 541–58.

Molho, R. *L'Ordre et les ténèbres ou la naissance d'un mythe du XVIIe siècle chez Sainte-Beuve*. Paris: A. Colin, 1972.

Montaigne, Michel de. *Essais*. Edited by Pierre Villey. 1924. Reprint. Paris: Presses universitaires de France, 1965.

———. *The Complete Essays of Montaigne*. Translated by Donald Frame. Stanford: Stanford University Press, 1958.

Montgomery, Robert L. *The Reader's Eye: Studies in Didactic Literary Theory from Dante to Tasso*. Berkeley: University of California Press, 1979.

Moore, Ann M. "Temporal Structure and Reader Response in *La Princesse de Clèves*." *French Review* 56, no. 4 (March 1983): 563–71.

Mouligneau, Geneviève. *Madame de Lafayette, romancière?* Bruxelles: Université de Bruxelles, 1980.

Munteano, Basil. *Constantes dialectiques en littérature et en histoire. Problèmes, recherches, perspectives*. Paris: Didier, 1967.

Murphy, James J. *Rhetoric in the Middle Ages*. Berkeley: University of California Press, 1974.

Murray, Michael. *Modern Philosophy of History: Its Origin and Destination*. The Hague: Martinus Nijhoff, 1970.

Najemy, John M. "Machiavelli and the Medici: The Lessons of Florentine History." *Renaissance Quarterly* 35, no. 4 (Winter 1982): 551–76.

Nancy, Jean-Luc. "Larvatus pro Deo," *Glyph 2* (1977): 14–36.

———. "Mundus est fabula." *MLN* 93 (1978): 635–53.

Natanson, Maurice. "The Arts of Indirection." In *Rhetoric, Philosophy, and Literature: An Exploration*, 35–47. West Lafayette, Indiana: Purdue University Press, 1978.

Negri, Antonio. *Descartes politico o della ragionevole ideologia*. Milan: Feltrinelli, 1970.

Nelson, Robert J. *Pascal. Adversary and Advocate*. Cambridge, Mass.: Harvard University Press, 1981.

Nicole, Pierre. "De la connoissance de soi-même." In *Essais de morale* 3:1–132. Paris: G. Desprez, 1723.

Norman, Buford. "Thought and Language in Pascal." *Yale French Studies* 49 (1973): 110–19.

———. "Logic and Anti-Rhetoric in Pascal's *Pensées*." *French Forum* 2 (January 1977): 22–33.

———. "Nicole's *Essais de morale*. Logic and Persuasion." In *The French Essay*, 9–17. Columbia: University of South Carolina Press, 1982.

Norton, Glyn. *Montaigne and the Introspective Mind*. The Hague: Mouton, 1975.

———. "Narrative Function in the *Heptaméron* Frame-Story." In *La Nou-*

velle française à la Renaissance, edited by Lionello Sozzi, 435–47. Geneva: Slatkine, 1981.

———. *The Ideology and Language of Translation in the Renaissance*. Geneva: Droz, 1984.

Obertello, Luca. *John Locke e Port-Royal. Il problema della probabilità*. Trieste: Publicazioni dell'Instituto di Filosophia, 1964.

Oesterley, Hermann, ed. *Gesta Romanorum*. Berlin: Weidmann, 1872.

Ollier, Marie-Louise. "Proverbe et sentence: le discours d'autorité chez Chrétien de Troyes." *Revue des sciences humaines* 41 (1976): 327–57.

Olschski, Leonardo. *Machiavelli the Scientist*. Berkeley: Gilman Press, 1945.

O'Malley, John W. *Praise and Blame in Renaissance Rome: Rhetoric, Doctrine and Reform in the Sacred Orators of the Papal Court, c. 1450–1421*. Durham, N.C.: Duke University Press, 1979.

O'Neill, John. *Essaying Montaigne: A Study of the Renaissance Institution of Writing and Reading*. London: Routledge and Kegan Paul, 1982.

Ong, Walter J. *Ramus: Method and the Decay of Dialogue*. 1958. Reprint. Cambridge, Mass.: Harvard University Press, 1983.

Orcibal, Jean. *Origines du Jansénisme*. Paris: J. Vrin, 1947–1962.

Ortega y Gasset, José. *History as a System and Other Essays toward a Philosophy of History*. Edited with an afterword ("The Ahistoric and the Historic") by J. W. Miller. 1941. Reprint. New York: W. W. Norton, 1961.

Oxford Latin Dictionary. Oxford: Clarendon Press, 1911.

Pabst, Walter. *Novellentheorie und Novellendichtung*. Heidelberg: Carl Winter, 1967.

Paris, Gaston. "La Nouvelle française aux XVe et XVIe siècles." In *Mélanges de littérature française du moyen âge*, edited by Mario Roques. Paris: Champion, 1912.

Pascal, Blaise. *Oeuvres*. Edited by Léon Brunschvicg and Pierre Boutroux. Paris: Hachette ("Les Grands Ecrivains de la France"), 1904–1925.

———. *Pensées sur la religion et sur quelques autres sujets*. Edited by Louis Lafuma. Paris: Editions du Luxembourg, 1951.

———. *Oeuvres complètes*. Edited by Louis Lafuma. Paris: Le Seuil ("L'Intègrale"), 1963.

Perelman, Chaïm, and Lucie Olbrechts-Tyteca. *Rhétorique et philosophie*. Paris: Presses universitaires de France, 1952.

Perelman, Chaim, and Lucie Olbrechts-Tyteca. *Rhétorique et philosophie*. Paris: Presses universitaires de France, 1952.

———. *The New Rhetoric: A Treatise on Argumentation*. Translated by John Wilkinson and Purcell Weaver. Notre Dame, Ind.: University of Notre Dame Press, 1969.

Pérouse, Gabriel-A. *Les Nouvelles françaises du XVIe siècle: Images de la vie du temps*. Geneva: Droz, 1977.

Pertile, Lino. "Paper and Ink: The Structure of Unpredictability." In *O un amy! Essays on Montaigne in Honor of Donald M. Frame*, edited by Raymond La Charité, 190–218. Lexington, Ky.: French Forum, 1981.

Phillips, Margaret Mann. *The "Adages" of Erasmus: A Study with Translations.* Cambridge: Cambridge University Press, 1964.

Phillips, Mark. "Machiavelli, Guicciardini, and the Tradition of Vernacular Historiography." *American Historical Review* 84 (1979): 86–105.

Pingaud, Bernard. *Madame de Lafayette, par elle-même.* Paris: Le Seuil ("Ecrivains de toujours"), 1978.

Pirie, W. T., and W. M. Lindsay, eds. *Glossaria Latina.* Hildesheim: Georg Olms, 1965.

Pitkin, Hanna Fenichel. *Fortune is a Woman. Gender and Politics in the Thought of Niccolò Machiavelli.* Berkeley: University of California Press, 1984.

Pizzorusso, Arnaldo. *La poetica del romanzo in Francia (1660–1685).* Caltanisetta: Salvatore Sciascia, 1962.

Poirion, Daniel. "L'histoire antique devant l'humanisme à la fin du Moyen Age." In *Actes du IXe Congrès de l'Association Guillaume Budé,* 512–19. Paris: "Les Belles Lettres," 1975.

Polydore Virgil. *De rerum inventoribus.* Translated by John [Thomas] Langley, and edited by W. A. Hammond. New York: Agathynian Club, 1868.

Pouilloux, Jean-Yves. *Lire les Essais de Montaigne.* Paris: Maspero, 1969.

Poulet, G. "La 'nausée' de Sartre et le 'Cogito' cartésien." *Studi Francesi* 15 (1961): 452–62.

Preminger, Alex, et al. *The Princeton Encyclopedia of Poetry and Poetics.* Princeton: Princeton University Press, 1974.

Prezzolini, Giuseppe. *The Legacy of Italy.* New York: Vanni, 1948.

Pugh, Anthony R. *The Composition of Pascal's Apologia.* University of Toronto Romance Series 49. Toronto: Toronto University Press, 1984.

Quintilian. *Institutio oratoria.* Edited and translated by H. E. Butler. Loeb Classical Library, 1920–1922.

Rabinowitz, Peter. "Truth in Fiction: A Reexamination of Audiences." *Critical Inquiry* 4 (1977): 121–42.

Ramus, Petrus. *Dialectique.* Edited by Michel Dassonville. Geneva: Droz, 1964.

———. *The Logike of the Moste Excellent Philosopher P. Ramus Martyr.* Translated by Roland MacIlmaine, and edited by Catherine M. Dunn. Northridge, California: San Fernando Valley State College Renaissance Editions, no. 3, 1969.

Regalado, Nancy Freeman. " 'Des contraires choses': La fonction poétique de la citation et des *exempla* dans le 'Roman de la Rose' de Jean de Meun." *Littérature* 41 (February 1981): 62–81.

Regosin, Richard. *The Matter of My Book. Montaigne's Essais as the Book of the Self.* Berkeley: University of California Press, 1977.

———. "Le Miroüer Vague: Reflections of the Example in Montaigne's *Essais.*" *Oeuvres & Critiques* 8, nos. 1–2 (1983): 73–86.

Reisler, Marsha. "Persuasion through Antithesis: An Analysis of the Dominant Rhetorical Structure of Pascal's *Lettres Provinciales.*" *Romanic Review* 69: 172–85.

Rendall, Steven. "In Disjointed Parts/Par articles decousus." In *Fragments: Incompletion and Discontinuity*, edited by Lawrence D. Kritzman, 71–83. New York: New York Literary Forum, 1981.

Respaut, Michèle. "Un texte qui se dérobe: narrateur, lecteur et personnages dans *La Princesse de Clèves*." *L'Esprit créateur* 19, no. 1 (Spring 1979): 64–73.

Rice, Donald, and Peter Schofer. *Rhetorical Poetics. Theory and Practice of Figural and Symbolic Readings in Modern French Literature*. Madison: University of Wisconsin Press, 1983.

Richards, I. A. *The Philosophy of Rhetoric*. New York: Oxford University Press, 1936.

Richelet, Pierre. *Dictionnaire français*. Revised edition. Amsterdam: Jean Elzevir, 1706.

Richetti, John J. *Philosophical Writing. Locke, Berkeley, Hume*. Cambridge, Mass.: Harvard University Press, 1983.

Rigolot, François. "Le Langage des *Essais*: Références ou mimologiques?" *CAIEF* 33 (May 1981): 19–34.

———. *Le Texte de la Renaissance: Des rhétoriqueurs à Montaigne*. Geneva: Droz, 1982.

———. "Montaigne's Maxims: From the Discourse of Other to the Expression of Self." *L'Esprit créateur* 22, no. 3 (Fall 1982): 8–18.

———. "Montaigne et la poétique de la marge." In *Actes du Colloque international Montaigne*, edited by M. Tétel, 140–74. Paris: Nizet, 1983.

Roelker, Nancy. "The Appeal of Calvinism to French Noblewomen in the Sixteenth Century." *The Journal of Interdisciplinary History* 2 (1972): 391–418.

Romanowski, Sylvie. *L'Illusion chez Descartes: La Structure du discours cartésien*. Paris: Klincksieck, 1974.

Rossi, Mario M. *A Plea for Man*. Edinburgh: The University Press, 1956.

Sanders, Sylvia G. "Montaigne et les idées politiques de Machiavel." *Bulletin de la Société des amis de Montaigne*, nos. 18–19: 85–98.

Sasso, Gennaro. *Niccolò Machiavelli. La storia del suo pensiero politico*. Naples: Istituto italiano per gli studi storici, 1958.

Schenck, Mary Jane Stearns. "Narrative Structure in the Exemplum, Fabliau, and the Nouvelle." *Romantic Review* 72, no. 4 (1981): 367–82.

Schenda, R. "Stand und Aufgaben der Exemplaforschung." *Fabula* 10 (1969): 69–85.

Schiffman, Zachary Sayre. "Montaigne and the Problem of Machiavellism." *Journal of Medieval and Renaissance Studies* 12, no. 2 (Fall 1982): 237–58.

Schon, Peter. *Vorformen des Essays in Antike und Humanismus*. Wiesbaden; Franz Steiner Verlag (Mainzer Romanistische Arbeiten), 1954.

Scott, J. W. "The Digressions in *La Princesse de Clèves*." *French Studies* 11 (1957): 315–22.

Screech, M. A. *Montaigne and Melancholy*. Selinsgrove: Susquehanna University Press, 1983.

Sebba, Gregor. "Descartes and Pascal: A Retrospect." *MLN* 87, no. 6 (1971): 96–120.

Sellier, Philippe. "Rhétorique et *Apologie*: Dieu parle bien de Dieu." In *Méthodes chez Pascal. Actes du Colloque tenu à Clermont-Ferrand, 10–13 juin, 1976*, 373–81. Paris: Presses universitaires de France, 1976.

Sellier, Philippe. *Pascal et Saint Augustin*. Paris: A. Colin, 1970.

Sellstrom, A. D. "Rhetoric and the Poetics of French Classicism." *French Review* 34 (1960): 428–29.

Sfez, Fabien. "Le Roman polylexique du XVIIe siècle." *Litérature* 13 (February 1974): 19–57.

Shell, Marc. *Money, Language, and Thought: Literary and Philosophical Economies from the Medieval to the Modern Era*. Berkeley: University of California Press, 1982.

———. *The Economy of Literature*. Baltimore: Johns Hopkins University Press, 1978.

Sidney, Sir Philip. *An Apology for Poetry*. Edited by Geoffrey Shepherd. Manchester: Manchester University Press, 1973.

Siegel, Jerrold E. *Rhetoric and Philosophy in Renaissance Humanism*. Princeton: Princeton University Press, 1968.

Simone, Franco, ed. *Culture et politique en France à l'époque de l'humanisme et de la Renaissance*. Turin: Accademia delle Scienze, 1974.

Simonin-Grumbach, Jenny. "Pour une typologie des discours." In *Langue, discours, société*, edited by J. Kristeva, J.-C. Milner, N. Ruwet, 85–121. Paris: Le Seuil, 1975.

Simpson, David. "Putting One's House in Order. The Career of the Self in Descartes' Method." *New Literary History* 9, no. 1 (Autumn 1977): 83–101.

Singleton, Charles. "The Perspective of Art." *Kenyon Review* 15, no. 2 (Spring 1953): 169–89.

Smalley, B. *The Study of the Bible in the Middle Ages*. Oxford: The Clarendon Press, 1941.

Smith, Hilary D. *Preaching in the Spanish Golden Age*. Oxford: Oxford University Press, 1978.

Snyders, Georges. *La Pédagogie en France aux XVIIe et XVIIIe siècles*. Paris: Presses universitaires de France, 1965.

Sommers, Paula. "Feminine Authority in the *Heptaméron*: A Reading of Oysille." *Modern Language Studies* 13, no. 2 (Spring 1983): 52–59.

Souter, Alexander. *A Glossary of Later Latin to 600 A.D.* Oxford: Clarendon Press, 1949.

Sozzi, Lionello, ed. *La Nouvelle française à la Renaissance*. Geneva: Slatkine, 1981.

Starobinski, Jean. *Montaigne en mouvement*. Paris: Gallimard, 1982.

Stierle, Karlheinz. "L'histoire comme exemple, l'exemple comme histoire." *Poétique* 10 (1972): 176–98.

Stone, Donald, Jr. "Narrative Techniques in *L'Heptaméron*." *Studi Francesi* 2 (1967): 473–76.

———. *From Tales to Truths. Essays on French Fiction in the Sixteenth Century*. Analecta Romanica 34. Frankfurt am Main: Klostermann, 1972.

Strauss, Leo. *Thoughts on Machiavelli*. Chicago: University of Chicago Press, 1958.

———. "Machiavelli and Classical Literature." *Review of National Literature* 1, no. 1 (1970): 7–25.

Struever, Nancy. *The Language of History in the Renaissance*. Princeton: Princeton University Press, 1970.

———. "Machiavelli, Montaigne, and the Problem of External Address in Renaissance Ethics." In press.

———. "Pasquier's *Recherches de la France*; The Exemplarity of his Medieval Sources." In press.

Suleiman, Susan. "Le Récit exemplaire." *Poétique* 32 (1977): 468–89.

———. *Authoritarian Fictions. The Ideological Novel as a Literary Genre*. New York: Columbia University Press, 1983.

Suleiman, Susan, and Inge Crosman, eds. *The Reader in the Text*. Princeton: Princeton University Press, 1980.

Tarlton, Charles D. "The Symbolism of Redemption and the Exorcism of Fortune in Machiavelli's *Prince*." *Review of Politics* 30 (1968): 332–48.

Terrasse, Jean. *Rhétorique de l'essai littéraire*. Montreal: Les Presses de l'Université du Québec, 1977.

Tetel, Marcel. "Ambiguité chez Boccace et Marguerite de Navarre." In *Il Boccaccio nella cultura francese*, edited by Carlo Pellegrini, 557–65. Florence: Olschki, 1971.

———. "Marguerite de Navarre et Montaigne: Relativisme et paradoxe." *Kentucky Romance Quarterly* 19, supplement 1 (1972): 125–35.

———. *Marguerite de Navarre's Heptaméron: Themes, Language, and Structure*. Durham, N.C.: Duke University Press, 1973.

———. "*L'Heptaméron*: Première nouvelle et fonction des devisants." In *La Nouvelle française à la Renaissance*, edited by Lionello Sozzi, 449–58. Geneva: Slatkine, 1981.

———. ed. *Actes du Colloque international Montaigne*. Paris: Nizet, 1983.

Thweatt, Vivien. *La Rochefoucauld and the Seventeenth-Century Conception of the Self*. Geneva: Droz, 1980.

Tiefenbrun, Susan. *A Structural Stylistic Analysis of La Princesse de Clèves*. The Hague, Mouton: 1972.

Tobler, Adolf, and Erhard Lommatzsch. *Altfranzösisches Wörterbuch*. Berlin: Weidmann, 1925–.

Toccanne, Bernard. "Flottements méthodologiques chez Pascal." In *Méthodes chez Pascal. Actes du Colloque tenu à Clermont-Ferrand, 10–13 juin, 1976*, 45–50. Paris: Presses universitaires de France, 1976.

———. *L'Idée de la nature en France dans la seconde moitié du XVIIe siècle*. Paris: Klincksieck, 1978.

Todorov, Tzvetan. *Théories du symbole*. Paris: Le Seuil, 1977.

———. *Les Genres du discours*. Paris: Le Seuil, 1978.

Toffanin, Giuseppe. *Machiavelli e il "Tacitismo."* Naples: Guida, 1972.

Topliss, Patricia. *The Rhetoric of Pascal*. Leicester: Leicester University Press, 1966.

Tournon, André. *Montaigne, La Glose et l'essai*. Lyons: Presses universitaires de Lyon, 1983.

Tubach, F. C. "Exampla in the Decline." *Traditio* 18 (1962): 407–17.

———. "Strukturanalytische Probleme: das mittelalterliche Exemplum." *Hessische Blätter für Volkskunde* 59 (1968): 25–29.

———. *Index exemplorum*. Helsinki: Suomalainen Tiedeakatemia, 1979.

Turbayne, Colin M. *The Myth of Metaphor*. Columbia: University of South Carolina Press, 1970.

Uhlir, A. "Montaigne et Pascal." *Revue d'histoire littéraire de la France* 14 (1907): 442–57.

Ullman, Walter. *The Medieval Idea of Law as Represented by Lucas de Penna. A Study in Fourteenth-Century Legal Scholarship*. London: Methuen, 1946.

Valerius Maximus. *Dictorum factorumque memorabilium exempla*. Paris: Robert Estienne, 1544.

Valesio, Paolo. *Novantiqua. Rhetorics as a Contemporary Theory*. Bloomington: Indiana University Press, 1980.

Valincour, Jean-Baptiste-Henry du Trousset de. *Lettres à Madame la Marquise *** sur le sujet de la Princesse de Clèves*. Tours: Université de Tours, 1972.

Van Delft, Louis. *Le Moraliste classique. Essai de définition et de typologie*. Geneva: Droz, 1982.

Villey, Pierre. *Les Sources et l'évolution des Essais de Montaigne*. Paris: Hachette, 1908.

Vitale-Brovarone, Alessandro. "Persuasione e narrazione: l'*Exemplum* tra due retoriche (VI–XII secoli)." *Mélanges de l'école française de Rome—Moyen âge–Temps modernes* 92, part 1 (1980): 83–112.

Vives, Juan Luis. *Obras completas*. 2 vols. Translated into Spanish by Lorenzo Riber. Madrid: Aguilar, 1947.

Wallace, John M. "Examples Are Best Precepts: Readers and Meanings in Seventeenth-Century Poetry." *Critical Inquiry* 1 (1974): 273–90.

Warminski, Andrzej. "Reading for Example: 'Sense-Certainty' in Hegel's *Phenomenology of Spirit*." *Diacritics* 11, no. 2 (Summer 1981): 83–94.

Wartburg, Walther von. *Französisches etymologisches Wörterbuch*. Leipzig and Berlin: B. G. Teubner, 1928–.

Watt, E. D. *Authority*. New York: St. Martin's Press, 1982.

Weaver, F. Ellen. *The Evolution of the Reform of Port-Royal. From the Rule of Citeaux to Jansenism*. Paris: Editions Beauchesne, 1978.

Weber, Joseph. "Person as Figure of Ambiguity and Resolution in Pascal." *PMLA* 84 (1969): 312–20.

Weinberg, Bernard. *History of Literary Criticism in the Italian Renaissance*. Chicago: University of Chicago Press, 1961.

Weinberg, Kurt. "The Lady and the Unicorn, or M. de Nemours à Coulommiers. Enigma, Device, Blazon and Emblem in *La Princesse de Clèves*." *Euphorion* 71, no. 4 (1977): 306–35.

Weinstein, Arnold. *Fictions of the Self*. Princeton: Princeton University Press, 1981.

Welter, J.-T. *L'Exemplum dans la littérature religieuse et didactique du moyen âge*. Paris: Occitania, 1927.

Wetsel, David. *L'Ecriture et le Reste. The "Pensées" of Pascal in the Exegetical Tradition of Port-Royal*. Columbus: Ohio State University Press, 1981.

White, Hayden. *Tropics of Discourse. Essays in Cultural Criticism*. Baltimore: Johns Hopkins University Press, 1978.

Whitfield, J. H. "Machiavelli's Use of Livy." In *Livy*, edited by T. A. Dorey, 73–96. London: Routledge and Kegan Paul, 1971.

Wigmore, John Henry. *The Principles of Judicial Proof or the Process of Proof*. 2d ed. Boston: Little, Brown, and Company, 1931.

Wilden, Anthony. "Par divers moyens on arrive à pareille fin: A Reading of Montaigne." *MLN* 83 (1968): 577–97.

Winandy, André. "Piety and Humanistic Symbolism in the Works of Marguerite d'Angoulême, Queen of Navarre." *Yale French Studies* 47 (1972): 145–69.

Winterowd, W. Ross. *Rhetoric: A Synthesis*. New York: Holt, Rinehart, and Winston, 1968.

Wood, Michael. "Montaigne and the Mirror of Example." *Philosophy and Literature* 13, no. 1 (April 1989): 1–15.

Woshinsky, Barbara R. *La Princesse de Clèves: The Tension of Elegance*. The Hague: Mouton, 1973.

———. "Biblical Discourse. Reading the Unreadable." *L'Esprit créateur* 21, no. 2 (Summer 1981): 13–24.

Zimmermann, Jacquelyn. "L'emploi des citations chez Montaigne." *Bulletin de la Société des amis de Montaigne* 5, no. 21 (January–March 1977): 63–68.

Zorzetti, Nevio. "L''Esemplarità' come problema di 'psicologia storica': un bilancio provvisorio." *Mélanges de l'école française de Rome* 92, no. 1 (1980): 147–52.

315